INTRODUCTION TO PRACTICAL LINEAR PROGRAMMING

INTRODUCTION TO PRACTICAL LINEAR PROGRAMMING

DAVID J. PANNELL
The University of Western Australia

A Wiley-Interscience Publication
JOHN WILEY & SONS, INC.
New York / Chichester / Brisbane / Toronto / Singapore / Weinheim

Library of Congress Cataloging in Publication Data:
Pannell, David J., 1960–
    Introduction to practical linear programming / David J. Pannell.
      p.   cm.
    ''A Wiley-Interscience publication.''
    Includes index.
    ISBN 0-471-51789-5 (cloth : alk. paper)
    1. Linear programming. I. Title.
T57.74.P37   1996
658.4'033—dc20   96-6185

To my father, John

CONTENTS

PREFACE

Although there are many books on linear programming (LP), I have long felt the need for a text with a different emphasis. New LP packages for microcomputers are extremely easy to use, making LP much more accessible and increasing its use by nonspecialists. Hirshfeld (1990) has observed that desktop computing is bringing a new class of analysts to the LP community. These people are familiar with LP but they do not wish to become experts. New users include business managers, consultants, farmers, social scientists, government planners, and applied economists. In order to make use of the computer packages these users do not need to understand the mathematics used to solve an LP model: the simplex algorithm (or one of its relatives). They only need to know how to prepare input, how to interpret output, and how to deal with a number of problems that can arise. There has been, until now, no book that provides for all these needs in an easily understandable, nonmathematical way. The aim of this book is to fill the need for a text that stresses practical aspects of applying LP models in the real world without focusing on the underlying mathematical procedures.

This is not the first practically oriented text for LP, but I believe it is the first to include no coverage at all of the simplex algorithm. In its place are several sections that are far more important to LP practitioners but normally given scant attention, even in applied texts. These include detailed coverage of interpretation of LP output, the problems that can beset LP models (no feasible solution, unboundedness, degeneracy, and multiple optimal solutions), techniques for testing the sensitivity of model solutions to changes, and methods for debugging LP models. All these are explained in simple terms, with no reference to the simplex algorithm. The book covers in detail the skill of model construction, with particular attention paid to negative coefficients, an area of some difficulty for many students of the technique. There is also a discussion and some practical advice on how best to have an impact when developing and using an LP model in a real-world setting.

I have three target audiences: students undertaking applied courses in linear programming; individuals who have previously undertaken a mathematically oriented LP course who now wish to make practical use of the technique; and individuals who wish to teach themselves about LP. Throughout the book, explanations are kept simple and, where possible, given in several ways: diagrammatically, intuitively, algebraically, and by reference to mental devices. There are many examples given, as well as exercise problems with solutions at the back of the book. A degree of jargon is unavoidable but is carefully explained on first mention and included in a glossary.

The book proceeds through an introduction to LP concepts (Chapters 1 and 2), a guide to LP model construction and output interpretation (Chapters 3 to 9 and 13), and a range of topics related to real-world LP applications (Chapters 10 to 12 and 14). Here are the chapter contents in a little more detail: Chapter 1 describes the basic structure of an LP problem, gives examples of LP applications, and briefly describes the steps in applying LP in the real world. In Chapter 2, graphical representation of simple models is used to instill an understanding of key concepts. Chapter 3 is a step-by-step presentation of the concepts necessary to build simple LP matrices. Chapter 4 covers the main output produced with every LP solution. Chapter 5 presents a number of examples to reinforce Chapters 3 and 4. Chapter 6 returns to matrix construction and deals with some of the more complex matrix structures involving negative coefficients and transfer rows. Chapter 7 presents specialized matrix structures for representing nonlinear relationships, multiperiod models, and multiregion models. Chapter 8 contains further examples to reinforce Chapters 6 and 7. Chapter 9 explains a useful feature of LP: the ability to obtain range analysis, which indicates the stability of the optimal solution. Chapter 10 covers the difficulties and complications that can arise when solving an LP model or interpreting its solution. Chapter 11 deals with the difficult task of ensuring that a model is free of errors. Chapter 12 stresses the importance of testing the sensitivity of a model to changes and suggests several approaches for doing this. In Chapter 13 I outline some methods for explicitly representing risk and uncertainty in an LP model. The book finishes in Chapter 14 with a discussion of practical issues not otherwise mentioned and a review of the strengths and weakness of LP.

It is intended that the book be self-contained and suitable for self-instruction, working progressively through from Chapter 1. For a briefer coverage of the material, a course could be based on Chapters 1 to 7 and 10 to 12. The essential chapters for a newcomer to LP are Chapters 1 to 7. These contain the information most likely to be covered directly in formal courses on LP. Chapters 9 provides a deeper coverage of output interpretation, which may be skipped or covered briefly in a short course. Chapters 10 to 12 are essential for any course with a practical orientation. Chapters 13 is somewhat specialized and perhaps more difficult than earlier chapters. Chapter 14 is relatively short and could reasonably be omitted from the formal presentations of a short course.

Even experienced LP users involved in implementing an LP model for a real-world problem will benefit from the information in the later chapters of the book; much of it is hard learned from practical experience. They will also find some ideas of value on matrix construction and output interpretation.

A number of people have contributed in one way or another during the writing of this book. I am especially grateful to Vanessa Stewart, Ian Moncrieff, and Andrew Bathgate for their detailed criticisms and corrections to various drafts; to Amir Abadi, David Falconer, Nicole Free, Peter James, Ross Kingwell, Beryl Luke, Barbara Luyben, Lisa Mahoney, Carmel McGinley, David Morrison, Eddy Pol, and Doug Sawkins for their various contributions; to the Department of Agricultural Economics at the University of Saskatchewan for hosting me during the study leave that I used to complete the book; to Elvis Costello and Andy Partridge for providing the music that fueled me through many late nights; and to my wife Pauline and daughters Hannah and Rosie for their patience and for bearing a share of the sacrifices this effort required.

DAVID J. PANNELL

CHAPTER 1

INTRODUCTION

Several years ago, when introductory quantitative courses were designed, it may have seemed far-fetched that a manager with a powerful desktop computer would actually formulate and solve real linear programming models based on the training obtained in an introductory course. This fantasy, however, has become reality. Consequently, some syllabi for introductory quantitative courses may need revising.

—(Rubin and Wagner, 1990, p. 157)

Linear programming (LP) can ease the task of solving a particular type of planning problem. Solving a planning problem with LP requires building a "model"; that is, a mathematical representation of the problem. This book is concerned with practical aspects of building LP models, solving them on computer, and interpreting LP solutions.

LP is not to be confused with computer programming; the term *programming* in LP is used in the general sense of devising a plan or strategy. LP is a mathematical technique and consequently does not necessarily involve computers. In practice, however, the many calculations required to solve even small LP models are usually conducted on a computer (using an LP *program* in the computer sense. In future the term computer *package* will be used to avoid confusion).

The mathematical technique for solving LP problems was developed by George Dantzig in 1947 to solve planning problems in the U.S. Air Force (Dorfman et al., 1958). LP is now used in many fields, including economics, engineering, mathematics, agriculture, business, transport, and manufacturing.

1.1 STRUCTURE OF A LINEAR PROGRAMMING PROBLEM

To analyze a problem using LP, it must have or must be moulded into a particular structure. The often unstructured mass of information that makes up the problem must be broken into the following components: an objective, activities or decision variables, and constraints.

An Objective

LP is designed to find the best or "optimal" solution to a problem. Depending on the problem, the optimal solution might be that which

- maximizes profit,
- minimizes cost,
- minimizes labor usage,
- maximizes chances of economic survival,
- minimizes distance traveled,
- minimizes pollution, or
- minimizes variability of income.

These are all potential objectives of an LP model. In LP the objective is always to minimize or maximize something. The optimal solution is the solution that minimizes or maximizes the objective. You, as the modeler, must decide what is to be optimized. Examples in this book include a range of objectives, but the most common are to maximize profit or minimize cost.

Although most LP models only include a single objective, various techniques have been developed for using LP to analyze problems in which there is a trade-off between objectives (e.g., between benefit and risk) or between multiple objectives. Methods of modeling the trade-off between benefit and risk are presented in Chapter 13. For information on methods for dealing with multiple objectives, see Hipel (1992), Romero and Rehman (1984; 1989), or Hwang and Masud (1979).

Sometimes the objective of a modeling project is not to maximize or minimize something but to find *any* solution that satisfies a particular set of requirements or constraints. In a problem with many constraints this can be extremely difficult to achieve by trial and error, but LP makes easy work of it.

Activities or Decision Variables

When devising a plan or strategy, the planner is typically faced with deciding what to do, how to do it, and how much of it to do. Each of the available alternatives, when deciding what to do and how to do it, is called an *activity*, a *decision variable*, or sometimes just a *variable*. For example, if a car manufacturer wants to use LP to decide how many of six alternative types of vehicle should be produced, each of these types would be an activity in the LP model. If a particular type can be manufactured in different ways (e.g., with different levels of automation/manual labor), each of the alternative manufacturing methods could be an activity.

Consider another example: a political party wants to use LP to select how to allocate its election budget between competing uses in order to maximize its chances of election. It has to allocate funds to television advertising, radio advertising, newspaper advertising, magazine advertising, rallies and meetings, and it has to decide how to allocate spending between different regions and different interest groups. Each alternative use of funds in each region would be an LP activity.

As a third example, consider a farmer trying to decide which combination of feeds to give a herd of cattle in order to provide adequate nutrients at the lowest cost. The alternative feeds would be activities in an LP model.

The common thread through these examples is that the activities are the variables for which the decision maker wants to select the levels. The car manufacturer wants to select the number of each type of vehicle, the political party wants to select the number of dollars spent on each possible use in each region, and the farmer wants to know how much of each feed to provide.

Constraints

An LP problem includes a number of restrictions (called *constraints* or sometimes *restraints*) on which combinations of activities can be selected. The constraints included in an LP model ensure that the solution is realistic, logical, and achievable.

Each constraint specifies a minimum, maximum, or exact level of some factor in the solution. The range of constraints that can be represented in an LP model is very wide and may include

- limits on the availability of resources such as land, labor, or finance,
- biological relationships (e.g., between fertilizer application rate and crop yield),
- technical constraints representing, for example, machinery work rates,
- logical constraints such as specifying that the amount of produce sold must not exceed the amount produced, and
- preference constraints representing the decision maker's own likes and dislikes or "gut feelings."

The solution selected by a model has to satisfy *all* the constraints specified. Any solution that satisfies all the constraints is called "feasible." There may be many feasible solutions to any problem, but LP identifies the single feasible solution that is also optimal; that is, that maximizes or minimizes the objective.

No solution that breaks or violates even one of the constraints will ever be selected by an LP model, no matter how much more profitable it is than the optimal feasible solution. However, as part of the description of the optimal solution, LP does indicate the value of relaxing each constraint, and thus you can see how much better the solution could become if an existing constraint were allowed to be violated. This will be explained in Chapter 4 on interpreting output.

1.2 EXAMPLES OF APPLICATIONS

Although the particular structure required for an LP model may seem restrictive, it is relevant to an enormous range of problems. LP has been used to solve problems of resource allocation, blending, distribution, marketing, depot location, scheduling, assignment, investment, and pricing. Here are some examples of actual applications:

- Allocating classes to classrooms in an educational institution (Gosselin and Truchon, 1986).
- Selecting the combination of crop and livestock enterprises that will maximize profits on a farm (Morrison et al., 1986).
- Choosing efficient water treatment methods to meet pollution standards in a river (Loucks et al., 1967).
- Selecting salary levels for staff (Fabozzi and Daddio, 1977).
- Formulating least-cost mixtures of various components such as livestock feeds (Glen, 1980).
- Planning advertising strategies (Thomas, 1971).
- Energy planning (Meier and Mubayi, 1983).
- Forest management and planning (Kent et al., 1991).
- Financial planning (Vandeputte and Baker, 1970; Spath et al., 1975).
- Scheduling of petroleum refining operations (Manne, 1956).
- Military defense planning (Beare, 1987).

Examples and exercises in this book are from a diverse range of fields, including some of those just mentioned.

1.3 ASSUMPTIONS OF LINEAR PROGRAMMING

Underlying all applications of LP are a number of assumptions: (a) divisibility, (b) linearity, (c) additivity, and (d) non-negativity of variables. These assumptions restrict the types of problems for which LP can be used. In most cases, however, there are ways of overcoming or, at least, minimizing the degree of the restriction.

Divisibility

Activities can be set at any fractional level. You may not actually be able to produce 127.38 cars, but an LP model could indicate that you should. In an example like this, the divisibility of decision variables is not a serious problem. You can easily round off the answer to the nearest whole number. However, there are decision problems for which the nondivisibility of inputs or outputs is important. For example one decision variable may be to build a new factory. There are ways to partially cope with simple indivisible variables in LP (see Chapter 7), but if there are many integer variables, it may be necessary to use the related technique of ''integer programming.'' Since many LP packages do not include the option of integer programming, it is not described in detail here. However, if the facility is available, the addition of integer variables to the sorts of models presented in this book should be straightforward.

Linearity

Relationships within the model must be straight lines. Although many LP texts present this as a simple statement of fact and suggest that ''nonlinear programming'' be used for problems that are not linear, it is possible to closely approximate many nonlinear problems using LP. In some circumstances this may even be preferable to using nonlinear programming (see Chapter 7).

Additivity

In an LP model, the effects of any two variables on the objective value or the level of resource use can be added together to obtain the combined effect. You may read in other texts that this means that the profitability of a mixture of activities is the weighted average of the individual activities; there can be no positive synergism or negative interference between activities selected in a mixture. Again, this is true of simple LP models, but with the techniques in Chapter 6, it is quite easy to represent positive or negative interactions between activities.

Non-Negative Variables

Variables cannot take negative values. In practice, this assumption causes very little trouble. In most applications of LP you do not need to be able to select negative values of a variable. For example, you do not want to be told by the model that your vehicle assembly line should be producing -200 sedans. On the other hand you may want to know whether following a particular strategy will result in your company finishing in credit or in debt. In a sense, being in debt is the negative of being in credit. Thus, the model will use two variables: one to represent debt and one for credit. In other words, the issue is not that it is impossible to represent a negative level of something in LP, but that no individual activity in the model can take negative values. The credit and debt example is covered in detail in Chapter 6.

Data Certainty

Another assumption sometimes mistakenly listed as being made in LP models is that data and relationships are known with certainty. Many useful LP models are based on this simplifying assumption, and it is made for many of the examples in this book. Nevertheless, it is quite possible to explicitly model uncertainty in an LP model, and even to represent a decision maker's attitude to different levels of uncertainty (Chapter 13).

1.4   STAGES IN APPLYING LINEAR PROGRAMMING

The following sections describe the seven stages of applying LP to a real problem.

Defining the Problem

Often the hardest part of an LP analysis is to precisely identify the relevant components of the problem: the objective to be solved, the alternative activities, and the constraints on the selection of activities. Initially it is probably unnecessary to worry about how to incorporate the information into an LP model. Instead, you should concentrate on formulating a clear definition of the problem in words and on collecting quantitative information about the problem.

In the examples given in this book, the important elements of the problem have already been specified and quantified. Although experience in developing problem definitions can only be gained in the real world, you will find advice on this issue throughout the book, especially regarding the importance of good communication.

Building a Matrix

After defining the problem but before entering it on a computer, the second stage of applying LP is to organize the problem into a "matrix," meaning a block or table of numbers. An LP matrix has a very specific structure. Columns of the matrix represent the alternative activities of the problem, while rows represent constraints. There is one special row that contains the "objective function," that is, the effect of each activity on the objective. In a cost-minimizing model, this row contains the costs for each activity; in a profit-maximizing problem, it contains the profit from each activity; and in a model designed to minimize staff turnover, it includes the effect of each activity on staff turnover. There is also a special column that contains "constraint limits" or "right-hand side" terms; that is, the value for each constraint that must not be exceeded, must be at least met or exactly met. Coefficients (numbers) in the matrix represent the amount each activity draws on or contributes to each constraint. Chapter 3 explains LP matrix structure in detail.

Matrix construction is a crucial stage in the practical application of LP. In this text much more emphasis and space is given to matrix construction than is usual in LP texts.

Solving the Problem

Solving even a small LP problem involves many calculations, so the potential for human error is considerable. However, given the large number of very easy to use LP computer packages that have recently become available, there is no need to spend hours in tedious calculations. These packages are making LP widely available to general users for the first time.

Interpreting Output

Besides the optimal levels of activities and the optimal objective function value, the output from an LP package provides a range of other valuable information about the problem. For example, all packages provide "shadow costs" of activities. Shadow costs indicate how much more favorable an activity would have to be before it would be selected in the optimal solution. A good understanding of this and other output components can make the LP model even more productive.

Verifying/Validating the Model

It is very unusual to construct an LP matrix that solves perfectly at the first attempt. This is because it is very easy to make a typing mistake, to forget to enter a coefficient, to leave out a necessary constraint, or to enter a constraint that does not behave as intended. These errors or "bugs" can cause the model to not solve at all, to solve but give a nonsensical result, or to solve and give an apparently reasonable result that is actually incorrect. The last of these errors is particularly difficult to cope with, but without giving it explicit attention it is very likely to occur, especially in large models. Advice on "debugging" models is given in Chapter 11.

Testing the Stability of Results

Experienced users of LP know that it is often not the single optimal solution that provides the most useful information. Rather it can be the results of looking at changes in the optimal set of activities resulting from changes in coefficients of the matrix. This is because the coefficients of an LP model are never known with certainty. The process of testing the impacts of changes to the model is called *sensitivity analysis*. Such testing should be part of any serious LP application. Chapter 12 contains advice on how to carry out such analyses.

Acting on the Results

There are no rules that can tell you the extent to which the results from an LP model should be implemented. This is very much a matter for individual decision makers. However, it is probably true to say that in many cases the greatest value of an LP model is not the prescription for action it provides, but the way it affects the thinking of decision makers. They may not follow the optimal LP solution to the letter, but they may still feel that the LP model was very useful. This is why testing the stability of results is such an important phase of the process. It is the phase that can have greatest impact on decision makers' understanding of the problem. In other words, one should not view an LP model as a substitute for the decision maker's judgment, but as a valuable input to that judgment.

1.5 KEY POINTS

- An LP problem has three components: an objective (something to be minimized or maximized), activities (alternative ways of achieving the objective), and constraints (limits on the allowable levels of factors in the solution).
- There are several stages in the application of LP to a problem: problem definition, matrix construction, model solution, interpretation of output, debugging the model, testing the stability of results, and implementation of results.

CHAPTER 2

GRAPHICAL SOLUTION OF LINEAR PROGRAMMING

It is quite feasible to build and use linear programming (LP) models without having a deep understanding of the "simplex method," the mathematical technique used to solve an LP problem. Although the simplex method is not covered in this book, this chapter covers a graphical solution method. This method is too limited to be used for practical purposes but it can be helpful in developing a general understanding of LP, especially with regard to interpretation of output. The reason why this graphical approach is not very useful for solving realistic problems is that it can only handle problems with two (or, at very most, three) activities. All real-world problems have many more than two activities and for practical purposes must be solved by computer.

2.1 A MAXIMIZATION EXAMPLE

Let us start with an example in which the objective is to maximize profits.

Example 2.1: Shoe Making

A shoemaker specializing in quality handmade shoes wants to allocate time between production of men's and women's shoes. Each pair of women's shoes takes four hours to produce, whereas a men's pair requires only three hours. The shoemaker is prepared to work no more than 40 hours per week. The shoes are made with a very high-quality leather, but this is available only in limited quantities of no more than 3 square meters (m^2) per week. The amount of leather used in producing a pair of shoes is 0.2 m^2 for women's shoes and 0.3

m^2 for men's. Men's shoes can be sold for a profit of $34 per pair, while women's shoes return $36 per pair. How many pairs of men's shoes and how many pairs of women's shoes should be produced each week if the shoemaker wishes to make the highest possible profit? ∎

Before graphing this problem we must summarize it mathematically. Here, the decision variables or activities are the numbers of men's and women's shoes. The variable W is the number of pairs of women's shoes produced in a week, and M is the weekly production of pairs of men's shoes. The objective is to maximize weekly profit (P). It is necessary to specify separately the contributions of each decision variable to total weekly profit. Total profit attributable to women's shoes is $36 times the number of pairs of women's shoes produced: $36 \times W$. The contribution of men's shoes to weekly profit is $34 per pair, so the total is $34 \times M$. Mathematically, the objective is to maximize P, where

$$P = 36W + 34M$$

This equation is referred to as the objective function. The objective function calculates the level of the factor that is to be minimized or maximized. For any levels of W and M, this equation calculates the corresponding value of P.

There are two constraints facing the shoemaker: the amount of time each pair of shoes takes to produce and the amount of leather each pair requires. If there are W pairs of women's shoes produced in a week, women's shoes require a total of $4 \times W$ hours per week. For example, if the shoemaker makes five pairs of women's shoes, each requiring four hours of labor, the total time spent making women's shoes is $4 \times 5 = 20$ hours. Two pairs of women's shoes require a total of $4 \times 2 = 8$ hours. In general, W shoes require a total of $4 \times W$ hours.

Similarly, women's shoes use up 0.2 m^2 of leather, so the total leather requirement of women's shoes is $0.2 \times W$ m^2. Men's shoes, on the other hand, have total requirements for $3 \times M$ hours of labor and $0.3 \times M$ m^2 of leather per week.

Remember that the total time worked on both types of shoe per week cannot exceed 40 hours. Mathematically, this can be represented as

$$4W + 3M \leq 40$$

In a similar way, the total usage of leather for women's shoes plus the total usage of leather for men's shoes cannot exceed 3 m^2 per week, so

$$0.2W + 0.3M \leq 3$$

These constraints are called *inequalities*, because they can be true even if the left-hand sides are not equal to the right-hand sides. Finally, there is a set of constraints that applies to all LP problems: the variables cannot take negative values:

$$W \geq 0; \quad M \geq 0$$

This requirement may seem obvious, as you clearly cannot produce a negative number of shoes, but it is essential to bear in mind because in some problems it is not self-evident.

In summary, Example 2.1 can be stated as

maximize

$$P = 36W + 34M$$

subject to

$$4W + 3M \leq 40$$

$$0.2W + 0.3M \leq 3$$

$$W \geq 0; \quad M \geq 0$$

This system of stating an LP problem algebraically is very common and is used in most other LP texts. However, it will not be emphasized in this book. It is used here because graphing a problem requires that it be described algebraically.

Finding an LP solution graphically consists of two stages: finding the set of feasible solutions, and identifying the best of them. A feasible solution is one that satisfies all the constraints of the problem.

Start by graphing the non-negativity constraints that limit the solution to positive values of W and M. These constraints require that the optimal combination of men's and women's shoes must be one of the shaded points in Figure 2.1. The shaded region includes the W and M axes.

Now consider the time constraint. First graph the combinations of women's and men's shoes that would require a combined total of exactly 40 hours of labor. These are the points for which the constraint is satisfied as an *equality* rather than as the *inequality* originally specified. The equality is

$$4W + 3M = 40$$

which is the equation for a straight line. We will graph this line without limiting the graph to whole numbers of shoes. This is most easily done by finding the points at which the line intersects the axes and joining them with a straight line.

To find the intersection with the W axis, set M equal to zero and solve for W:

$$4W = 40$$

FIGURE 2.1

so

$$W = 10$$

Similarly, to find where the line intersects the M axis, set W equal to zero:

$$3M = 40$$

so

$$M = 13.33$$

Figure 2.2 shows the line segment that connects these two points. It also shows that above the line

$$4W + 3M > 40$$

while below the line

$$4W + 3M < 40$$

It is easy to verify that this is true. Pick any point that is not on the line, determine the values of W and M, and then calculate $4W + 3M$. The origin (where $W = 0$ and $M = 0$) is often convenient for this purpose (as long as it is not on the line):

$$(4 \times 0) + (3 \times 0) = 0$$

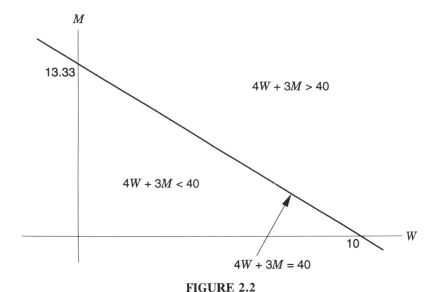

FIGURE 2.2

The result is less than 40, so *all* points on the same side of the constraint as the origin have labor requirements less than 40, while all points on the other side of the line require more than 40 hours of labor. The reason for doing this is to identify the set of points that satisfy the labor constraint

$$4W + 3M \leq 40$$

The feasible points for this constraint include the line and all points below it or to the left. The set of potential solutions that satisfy this time constraint as well as the non-negativity constraints is shown as the shaded region in Figure 2.3.

In a graph of a linear equation (such as $4W + 3M = 40$) it is always true that for all points on one side of the line, the left-hand side of the equation is less than the right-hand side, and that the reverse is true on the other side of the line. This means that it is only necessary to test one point to determine which is the less-than side and which is the greater-than side. We can graph the leather constraint in a similar way, giving Figure 2.4.

Now we are interested in the feasible set of points: points where all constraints are satisfied. Some points that satisfy the time constraint do not satisfy the leather constraint, and some that satisfy the leather constraint require too much time. The feasible region for all constraints is the shaded region in Figure 2.5. It includes the shaded area and the lines that border it.

The feasible region has the following corner points: $(W, M) = (0, 0)$, (10, 0), (0, 10), (5, 6.67). (The values of W and M at the last of these points are found by calculating where the two constraints intersect.)

Now identify which of the points in this feasible region is best; which gives the highest value for profit (P):

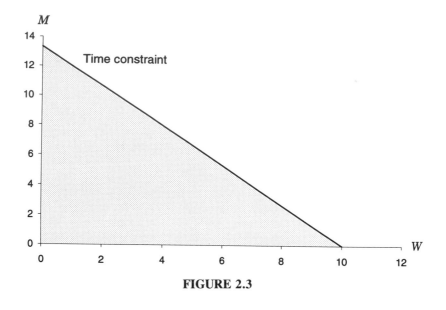

FIGURE 2.3

$$P = 36W + 34M$$

If P is set at a particular value, we can graph all combinations of W and M that result in that level of profit. Start by examining a profit level of \$200 per week. Figure 2.6 shows the feasible region together with the line

$$36W + 34M = 200$$

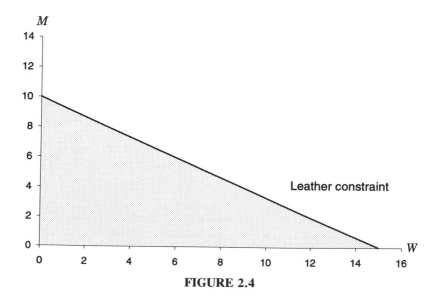

FIGURE 2.4

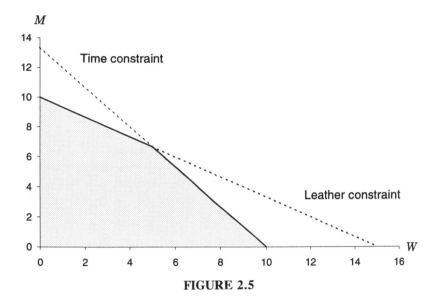

FIGURE 2.5

Any point on the dashed line corresponds to a weekly profit of $200 and any shaded point is a feasible solution. The section of the dashed line that passes through the feasible region identifies combinations of W and M that are feasible and result in $200 weekly profit. Clearly it is feasible for the shoemaker to make $200 per week, and it can be done in a number of ways.

However $200 is not the highest profit that can be made. Figure 2.7 shows

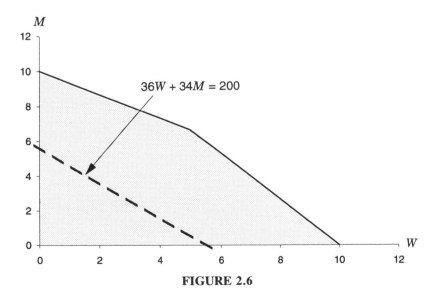

FIGURE 2.6

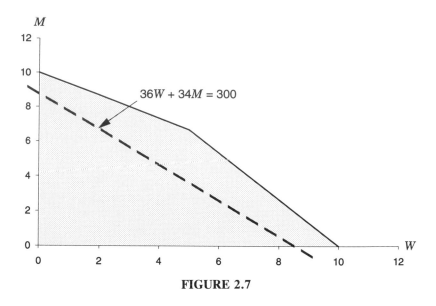

FIGURE 2.7

the line

$$36W + 34M = 300$$

which reveals that there are a number of feasible solutions giving \$300 per week profit. Notice that the new objective function is parallel to the old one, but has been moved upward and to the right.

By repeatedly adjusting the profit value and redrawing the objective function we can identify the highest profit value for which there is at least one feasible solution (Figure 2.8). The slope of the line depends only on the coefficients of W and M (36 and 34, in this case). For this reason, when drawing objective function lines for different values of total profit, the slope is always the same. As you increase the profit value, the objective function moves in parallel upward and to the right.

The optimal solution is at one of the corners to the feasible region. The shoemaker should produce 5 pairs of women's shoes and 6.67 pairs of men's shoes per week. (You can interpret the fractional part of the men's shoes as having a pair of shoes partly finished). The highest weekly profit that can be made is \$406.67, which can be calculated as

$$(\$36 \times 5) + (\$34 \times 6.6667) = \$406.67$$

It is clear from this graphical approach that the optimal solution will always be on the boundary of the feasible region. The profit achievable at any point within the shaded region can always be bettered by drawing a higher line that just touches the boundary (i.e., a line that is a "tangent" to the boundary).

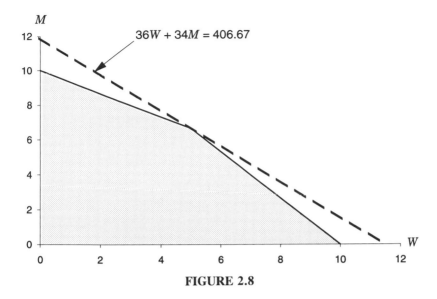

FIGURE 2.8

Most commonly the optimal solution will be a single corner point. The only exception to this will be where the objective function is exactly parallel to one of the constraints that forms part of the boundary of the feasible region. In this case all points along this segment of the boundary will be equally good.

Another principle is that the optimal solution depends on the slope of the objective function. This slope is determined by the ratio of objective function coefficients (i.e., profits in this case) of the two activities. If the activities' profits were both halved or both doubled, the optimal solution would not change.

On the other hand, if we halved returns from women's shoes only, the optimal solution would change. Figure 2.9 shows the optimal solution for this scenario. Reducing the price of women's shoes reduces the slope of the objective function line. As a result, adjusting the profit figure and redrawing the objective function identifies a different optimal solution. The highest attainable profit would now be reduced to $340 per week, and to achieve that the shoemaker would have to produce 10 pairs of men's shoes and no women's shoes.

If the shoemaker were to persist in producing 5 pairs of women's shoes and 6.67 men's, profits would be reduced by an even greater amount. The new profit would be

$$(\$18 \times 5) + (\$34 \times 6.67) = \$316.67$$

Another point to note is that the feasible region is "convex." This means that a line joining any two points in the set would never pass outside the set. At each corner the angle at which constraints meet is less than 180 degrees when viewed from within the set. The feasible set of an LP problem must be convex. It would be impossible, for example, to correctly solve an LP model

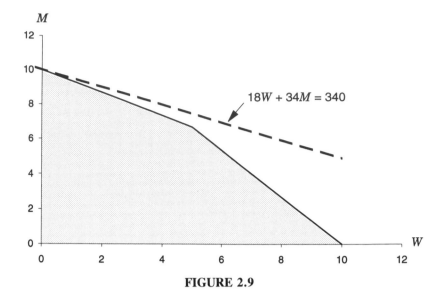

FIGURE 2.9

with the feasible set shown in Figure 2.10. The line joining points *A* and *B* passes outside the feasible set. This can occur because one of the angles of the border of the feasible region is greater than 180 degrees (when viewed from inside the region). The significance of this restriction on LP problems is that it allows very efficient computational methods for solving LP problems. You need to be aware of the restriction so that you can recognize problems that are not suitable for solution by LP.

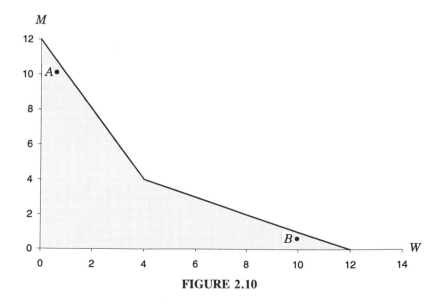

FIGURE 2.10

TABLE 2.1 Objective Function Values at Extreme Points for Example 2.1

Extreme Point (L, M)	Profit ($/week)
(0, 0)	0
(10, 0)	360
(0, 10)	340
(5, 6.67)	406.67

The fact that the optimal solution always includes a corner (a so-called *extreme point*) greatly reduces the number of combinations of possible solutions that needs to be considered. In a small problem, a quick way to find the optimum without using a computer is to calculate the objective function value (i.e., the profit in this example) at each extreme point. Table 2.1 shows profit calculated at each extreme point for the shoemaker example. It confirms that the profit-maximizing strategy is to produce 5 women's pairs and 6.67 men's pairs per week.

Having set up the problem, it is easy to include additional constraints. For example, suppose that the shoemaker prefers making women's shoes and would not be prepared to produce more than eight pairs of men's shoes per week, even if it meant sacrificing some profit. This new constraint can be stated as

$$1M \leq 8$$

or for convenience

$$M \leq 8$$

Note that the W variable does not appear in the constraint. This can be interpreted as W having a zero coefficient. If desired the constraint could be written

$$0W + 1M \leq 8$$

Adding this constraint to the existing problem reduces the feasible area (see Figure 2.11). However, assuming the price of women's shoes stays at $36, the optimal solution does not change; the highest objective function still passes through the point $(W, M) = (5, 6.67)$. This illustrates that if an optimal solution is still feasible after the addition of a new constraint, then it is also still optimal (as long as the objective function coefficients have not changed). There is no way that removing part of a feasible set can change the optimal solution unless the original optimal solution is one of the points removed.

To illustrate further, suppose the shoemaker becomes even more negative about producing men's shoes and decides to set a maximum level of five pairs

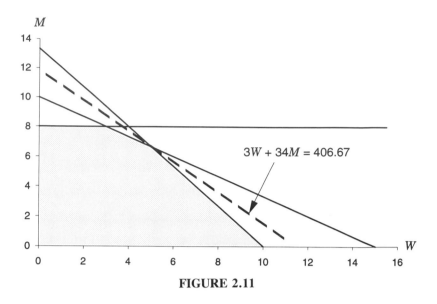

FIGURE 2.11

per week. The set of feasible solutions now no longer includes the previous optimum (see Figure 2.12). The new optimal solution is to produce 5 pairs of men's shoes and 6.25 of women's, giving weekly profits of ($36 × 6.25) + ($34 × 5) = $395. Without this constraint on men's shoes, the maximum profit was $406.67 per week, so meeting the shoemaker's preference for making women's shoes requires a sacrifice of $11.67 profit per week.

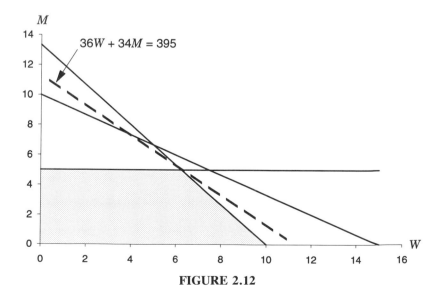

FIGURE 2.12

2.2 A MINIMIZATION EXAMPLE

Now consider a second example: one in which the objective is to minimize cost rather than maximize profits.

Example 2.2: Feeding Pigs

A farmer wishes to minimize the daily cost of feeding 50 pigs. There are two feeds available: lupins at $0.20 per kilogram (kg) and wheat at $0.15/kg. Each pig must receive at least 70 megajoules (MJ) of energy and 1000 grams of protein each day. The available wheat grain contains 11 percent protein and 13 MJ/kg energy, while lupins contain 28 percent protein and 14 MJ/kg energy. Find the cheapest combination of these feeds that meets the pigs' nutritional requirements. ∎

In this problem there are two activities: feeding a kilogram of wheat (W) and a kilogram of lupins (L). There are also two constraints: a minimum level of protein and a minimum level of energy.

Each kilogram of wheat provides 110 g of protein, while a kilogram of lupins provides 280 g. The total minimum requirement for protein is 50 pigs × 1000 g/pig = 50,000 g. Thus the protein constraint is

$$110W + 280L \geq 50,000$$

which states that the total amount of protein provided by wheat plus the amount provided by lupins must be at least 50,000.

Wheat and lupins, respectively, provide 13 and 14 MJ/kg of energy, and the total minimum requirement is 50 pigs × 70 MJ/pig = 3500 MJ. The energy constraint is

$$13W + 14L \geq 3500$$

which represents the requirement that total energy provided by wheat and lupins must be at least 3500.

Remembering the additional constraints that $W \geq 0$ and $L \geq 0$, the feasible region is shown in Figure 2.13.

In this example, the objective is to minimize costs (C), which consist of $0.15 per kilogram of wheat and $0.20/kg of lupins.

$$C = 0.15W + 0.20L$$

The method of solving a minimization problem is similar to that for a maximization problem. Figure 2.14 shows the process of trying out various cost

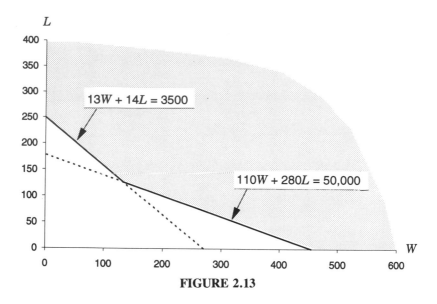

FIGURE 2.13

levels to find the lowest cost solution that is feasible. The cheapest ration in this example is to feed 133.33 kg of wheat and 126.2 kg of lupins at a cost of

$$(\$0.15 \times 133.33) + (\$0.20 \times 126.2) = \$45.24$$

There are many other feasible solutions but they all cost more than this one, and the objective is to minimize cost. There are potential solutions costing less than \$45.24; the lowest dashed line in Figure 2.14 shows the set of wheat and

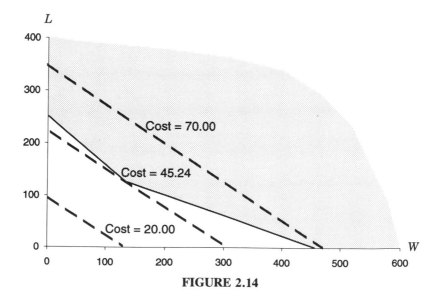

FIGURE 2.14

TABLE 2.2 Objective Function Values at Extreme Points for Example 2.2

Extreme Point (W, L)	Cost ($)
(454.5, 0)	68.18
(0, 250)	50.00
(133.3, 126.2)	45.24

lupin levels costing $20.00. However, none of these solutions provides adequate levels of the nutrients; they are cheap but not feasible.

A minimization problem like this is similar to a maximization problem in that the optimal solution will always be at a corner (or possibly will span two corners) of the feasible set. This allows us to use the same simple approach of calculating the objective function value at each of the corner points in order to identify the optimal solution. Table 2.2 shows the results of these calculations for Example 2.2, confirming that 133.33 kg of wheat and 126.2 kg of lupins is the cheapest possible ration.

2.3 LIMITATIONS OF THE GRAPHICAL APPROACH

To conclude this chapter it should be noted that while the graphical approach is useful in coming to understand LP, it is not useful for solving practical problems. The graphical approach can only be used for problems with two (or, at most, three) decision variables, whereas all realistic problems have tens, hundreds, or even thousands of variables, so the only practical way to solve them is on a computer. In the next chapter we move on to look at building an LP matrix for solution by computer.

2.4 KEY POINTS

- Solving an LP problem graphically involves two stages: (a) graphing the feasible region and (b) identifying the feasible point that is optimal.
- The feasible region is always convex.
- The optimal solution is always at a corner (an extreme point) of the feasible region.
- The graphical approach can only be applied easily to problems with two variables.

Exercises

At this stage we have barely touched on the process of converting an LP problem from a description in words into a mathematical statement of the variables, constraints, and objective function. That is the main topic of Chapters 3, 6, and 7. For this reason, in the following exercises the problems have already been converted into algebraic form. This allows you to concentrate on graphical solutions, the main topic of this chapter. The cost of this convenience is that there is no clear link between these exercises and the real world.

In each of the following exercises you should:

- plot all constraints and identify the feasible region by shading.
- calculate the values of X and Y at each corner of the feasible region.
- draw one or more objective functions to identify the optimal point of the feasible region.
- calculate the value of the objective function at each corner of the feasible region to confirm that the point you selected graphically is, in fact, optimal.

2.1 Maximize

$$P = 5X + 4Y$$

Subject to

$$3X + 4Y \leq 7$$

$$5X + 2Y \leq 5$$

$$X \geq 0; \quad Y \geq 0$$

2.2 Minimize

$$P = 22X + 18Y$$

Subject to

$$X + Y \geq 20$$

$$5X + 2Y \geq 50$$

$$X + 3Y \geq 15$$

$$X \geq 0; \quad Y \geq 0$$

2.3 Calculate the objective function value at the following nonextreme points for the problem in Exercise 2.2: $(X, Y) = (25, 0), (15, 5), (10, 10), (12, 12)$. Compare the values at these points with those at the extreme points.

2.4 Maximize

$$P = X + Y$$

Subject to

$$3X + 2Y \leq 10$$
$$3X + 4Y \leq 20$$
$$X \leq 3$$
$$X \geq 0; \quad Y \geq 0$$

2.5 Minimize

$$P = 5X + 6Y$$

Subject to

$$X + Y \geq 20$$
$$8X + Y \geq 40$$
$$Y \geq 8$$
$$X \geq 0; \quad Y \geq 0$$

2.6 Suppose the objective function in Exercise 2.5 changes to
Minimize

$$P = 7X + 6Y$$

Regraph the objective function to test whether the optimal solution changes.

2.7 Suppose the objective function in Exercise 2.5 changes further to
Minimize

$$P = 25X + 6Y$$

Regraph the objective function to test whether the optimal solution changes.

2.8 Maximize

$$P = 50X + 10Y$$

Subject to

$$5X + 4Y \leq 600$$
$$2X + 3Y \leq 300$$
$$X \leq 100$$
$$Y \leq 100$$
$$X \geq 0; \quad Y \geq 0$$

CHAPTER 3

INTRODUCTION TO MATRIX CONSTRUCTION

Before a linear programming problem can be solved on a computer, it must be represented in a matrix. As noted in Chapter 1, the word *matrix* simply means a block of numbers, but a linear programming (LP) matrix has a particular structure. After reading this chapter you should be able to construct a matrix for a relatively simple problem such as those in Chapter 2. Construction of matrices for more complex models is dealt with in Chapters 6, 7, 8, and 13.

We start with a simple model definition. A matrix for this model is presented and its structure described in detail. Following this, the objective function is examined in more depth. Subsequent sections cover the various types of constraints that can be represented in an LP model (i.e., maximum, minimum, and exact constraints). As each new constraint type is described, the problem definition is modified to include an example. Following this, we see how to set the level of an activity to a desired value. Then there is a discussion of the importance of being consistent with units of measurement and, finally, a general strategy for matrix building is suggested. In Chapter 5 this strategy is illustrated with examples from several disciplines.

3.1 STRUCTURE OF A LINEAR PROGRAMMING MATRIX

Example 3.1: Paper Milling

The manager of a paper mill wants to plan daily production. Two types of paper are produced: computer paper and writing paper. The mill employs 126 workers. Each tonne of computer paper produced requires 4 days of labor, whereas production of writing paper is more labor intensive, requiring 6 days of labor per tonne. Each tonne of paper (of either type) requires two tonnes of wood chips and there are 56 tonnes of wood chips available each day. The mill is situated on a river that provides water for the production process. In order to make the paper white, the mill uses chlorine-based bleaches. This process causes contamination of the water that is discharged back into the river with traces of the extremely toxic chemical, dioxin. To avoid pollution of the river the government has imposed strict environmental regulations on the mill; no more than 24 kg of chlorine residues per day may be discharged. Each tonne of writing paper produced results in the discharge of 1.5 kg of chlorine. Computer paper does not have to be so white and so is much cleaner to produce, with only $\frac{2}{7}$ kg of chlorine residue per tonne. Net profits after deducting all input and payroll costs are $600 per tonne for computer paper and $1000 per tonne for writing paper. Construct a matrix to select the levels of writing paper and computer paper that maximize profits for the mill subject to the constraints of mill capacity, wood chip availability, and chlorine pollution limits. ∎

An appropriate matrix for this problem is represented in Table 3.1. There are two activities in the model, one representing production of a tonne of computer paper and the other a tonne of writing paper. Each activity is represented by a column in the matrix labeled either *Computer* or *Writing*. There are three constraints represented by appropriately labeled rows, for maximum levels of labor, wood chips, and chlorine discharge.

Theoretically it would be acceptable to represent activities in rows and constraints in columns, but it is a universally accepted convention not to do this, and among practitioners of LP the term *columns* is often used synonymously with *activities* and *rows* is taken to mean *constraints*. There is an extra row of figures in the matrix for the *Objective*. In some texts this is shown at the bottom of the matrix, but here it will always be at the top.

There are two other columns, labeled *Type* and *Limit*. The *Limit* is the value that must be at least met, not exceeded, or exactly met if the constraint is to be satisfied. The *Type* indicates whether, for this constraint, the limit must be at least met ($\geq$), not exceeded ($\leq$), or exactly met ($=$). These constraint types are described in more detail in Sections 3.3 to 3.5.

It is most common for the *Type* and *Limit* columns to be drawn on the right-hand side of the matrix. In fact constraint limits are often referred to as *right-hand-side terms*.

TABLE 3.1 Matrix for Example 3.1

	Computer (tonnes)	Writing (tonnes)	Type	Limit
Objective ($)	600	1000	max	
Labor (days)	4	6	$\leq$	126
Wood chips (tonnes)	2	2	$\leq$	56
Chlorine (kg)	0.2857	1.5	$\leq$	24

When building an LP model, it is very important to be clear about the units of measurement used. Every row, including the objective function row, has a unit of measurement. In Table 3.1, the objective function represents profit and is measured in dollars. Of the constraints, labor is measured in days, wood chips are in tonnes, and chlorine is in kilograms of chlorine residue. The activity columns also have units of measurement (tonnes for both types of paper), but the *Limit* column does not, because each coefficient in this column uses the same unit of measurement as its corresponding constraint.

The coefficients in the matrix depend on the problem definition and on which units of measurement are used. The derivation of matrix coefficients are explained in the following sections, starting with the objective function row.

We now summarize the main points of this section.

- Each activity is represented by a column of coefficients.
- There is an extra column of coefficients for constraint limits and a column indicating whether the constraint limit is a minimum, maximum, or exact value.
- Each constraint is represented by a row of coefficients.
- There is an extra row of coefficients for objective function values.
- Each activity column has a specific unit of measurement that applies to all coefficients in the column.
- The constraint limit column does not have a common unit of measurement for all its coefficients. Each coefficient is measured in the units of its constraint.
- Each row, including the objective function, has a specific unit of measurement.

3.2 SPECIFYING THE OBJECTIVE FUNCTION

The coefficients of the objective function represent the extent to which each activity helps or hinders in meeting the objective. The objective for our simple example is to maximize net profit (in dollars). We have arbitrarily decided that computer paper and writing paper are both to be measured in tonnes, so the objective function coefficient for each is the net profit in dollars per tonne. Example 3.1 specifies that computer paper and writing paper give net profits of $600/tonne and $1000/tonne, respectively. These are the objective function coefficients in Table 3.1.

It would be possible to use different units of measurement for the activities. For example, we might decide to measure computer paper and writing paper in kilograms instead of tonnes. In that case, the objective function coefficients would be the profits in $/kg instead of $/tonne; that is, $0.60 and $1.00 instead of $600 and $1000. Changing the units in this way does not affect the nature of the planning problem, only the numbers used to represent the activities.

The unit for each coefficient of the objective function is thus **unit of the row** per **unit of the column,** or in Table 3.1, **dollars** per **tonne.** (Incidentally this is also true for the constraints, as shown in the following sections).

The entry in the *Type* column of the objective row indicates the problem aim: whether the objective function is to be maximized or minimized. However, this representation is specific to this book. When the problem is to be solved on a computer, the aim is specified differently by different computer packages.

3.3 SETTING THE MAXIMUM LEVEL OF A FACTOR

The term *factor* in the title of this section refers to a resource, an input or an output that is the subject of a constraint. Each constraint of the matrix specifies that the solution must contain either a minimum, maximum, or exact level of some factor. In Table 3.1 the factors are labor, wood chips, and chlorine, each of which must not exceed a particular maximum level. Note that items that are represented in constraints do not necessarily have to be decision variables in the model and often are not. In Table 3.1, the levels of labor, wood chips, and chlorine are not decision variables; their levels follow automatically from the levels of computer paper and writing paper selected.

Let us now examine how to represent in a matrix the maximum level of a factor. Consider the labor constraint in Table 3.1. The problem definition specifies that there are 126 employees working in the mill, so whichever combination of computer paper and writing paper is produced, the total workforce cannot exceed 126 workdays per day (assuming that there are no absences). The number 126 is the constraint limit for labor and is placed in the *Limit* column. The constraint limit must be specified using the unit of measurement selected for this constraint: "days" of labor. The constraint limit is 126 days.

Similarly, the maximum allowable levels of wood chips and chlorine are 56 tonnes and 24 kg, and these also go into the *Limit* column.

The *Type* column specifies the direction of the constraint. The total levels of labor and wood chips required by the selected activities have to be "less than or equal to" the available levels of 126 workdays and 56 tonnes, just as chlorine emissions must be less than or equal to the allowable level (24 kg). Therefore, the constraint type for each is $\leq$.

It is possible to specify that the level of a factor must exactly equal some value, but that would not be appropriate for any of the constraints of this model. There is no reason why all the available workforce or wood chips should be used up if it turns out that it is more profitable to leave some workers idle or some wood chips unused. Furthermore, there is certainly no reason why the level of chlorine emissions should be restricted to exactly the maximum allowable level. The river environment would benefit from lower chlorine levels, so if the mill can profitably discharge lower levels, it should be allowed to.

Note also that the constraint types are less than or equal to ($\leq$) not strictly less than ($<$). It is impossible in linear programming to specify that a factor must be strictly less than but not equal to some value, because it is not possible to make activities "lumpy." That is, it is not possible to specify that activities can only be selected at integer levels (0, 1, 2, 3, . . .) and not 1.75, 0.012, or any other real number. (Integer programming is a related technique that can represent lumpy variables. Methods for dealing with simple integer variables using LP are presented in Chapter 7.) In LP all activities are infinitely divisible, which means that if you wanted to specify that chlorine must be strictly less than 24 kg, there would be nothing preventing the selection of 23.999, 23.99999999, or any other number less than, but very close to, 24. A number could be selected so close to 24 as to be indistinguishable from it. Similarly the constraint type ≥ represents a "greater than or equal to," not a strictly "greater-than" constraint.

Having clarified this, it is a nuisance always to write greater than or equal to and less than or equal to, so in the remainder of this book greater than and less than will often be used instead.

Consider now those numbers in Table 3.1 that are in activity columns and constraint rows. An important part of the skill of building LP models is in knowing which values to put in the matrix. We discuss the topic in some detail here, and again in Chapters 6 and 7. Each coefficient in this part of the matrix represents the effect of selecting one unit of the corresponding activity on the level of the factor represented in the constraint. That is, each coefficient represents the effect of an activity on a constraint.

These numbers are necessary to determine how many units of the activity can be selected without violating the constraint. For example, they allow us to calculate which combinations of computer paper and writing paper are possible without requiring more wood chips than are actually available. There are several approaches available for deciding what value a particular coefficient should take. Three different approaches are presented below. You might find different approaches to be useful for formulating different types of constraints. Understanding these three approaches may also help you understand how a constraint operates.

Setting the Value of a Coefficient: Method 1

First consider the computer paper activity and the labor constraint. Ask the question, "How much of the available labor (in days) is required for each unit of computer paper (in tonnes)?" The answer, 4, was given in the problem definition. The appropriate units of measurement to use are those you have decided to use for that particular activity and that particular constraint, that is tonnes for the activity and days for labor. Thus, the coefficient is 4 days labor per tonne of computer paper. This value is placed in the appropriate cell of the matrix: [*Labor, Computer*]. (In future, particular cells of the matrix will be referred to in this format using square brackets: [Row name, Column name].) Note that the units for constraint coefficients follow the same pattern as do objective function coefficients: **unit of the row** per **unit of the column.**

Similarly, for writing paper the appropriate question for cell [*Labor, Writing*] is, "How many days of labor are required for each tonne of writing paper?" The answer, 6, is placed in cell [*Labor, Writing*] in the matrix. Again the unit is **unit of the row** per **unit of the column:** 6 days per tonne.

As noted earlier, these coefficients are used during the solution of the problem (by computer) to determine whether particular levels of computer paper and writing paper satisfy the labor constraint. For example, suppose one strategy under consideration is to produce 20 tonnes of computer paper and 10 tonnes of writing paper each day. The computer needs to test this strategy to ensure that it does not require more labor than is available. The total level of a constrained factor is the sum of its levels for all activities. The level of a factor for an individual activity is the number of units of the activity times its coefficient in the constraint row. Thus the level of labor required to adopt the strategy just described is $(20 \times 4) + (10 \times 6) = 140$, but there are only 126 workers, not 140. The constraint is "violated," so this strategy could not be adopted. Alternatively test the strategy of producing 20 tonnes of computer paper and 7 tonnes of writing paper per day. Total labor requirements would be $(20 \times 4) + (7 \times 6) = 122$, which is less than the total available workforce. This strategy would be feasible to adopt, at least with regard to the labor constraint. It would now be necessary to check that the wood chip and chlorine constraints were not violated, and then to see whether any of the other strategies that satisfy all three constraints is more profitable.

Coefficients in the wood chip and chlorine rows are similarly derived. Simply ask, "How much of the available resource is used up by each unit of this activity?" The specific questions for the *Computer* activity are (a) "How many tonnes of wood chips are required by each tonne of computer paper?" and (b) "How many kilograms of the allowable output of chlorine residue are produced by each tonne of computer paper?" The problem definition shows that the answers to these questions are (a) 2 tonnes of wood chips per tonne of computer paper and (b) 0.2857 (i.e., $\frac{2}{7}$) kg of chlorine per tonne of computer paper. These are the coefficients shown in Table 3.1.

Setting the Value of a Coefficient: Method 2

Sometimes you may have trouble deriving coefficients in the way described before because of the way the problem is defined, in which case a second approach may be appropriate. This second approach is useful when it is obvious what level of an activity would, by itself, just satisfy the constraint. For example, the problem definition may not have given the wood-chip requirements of a tonne of computer paper, but may instead have specified that if all available wood chips are used for computer paper, 28 tonnes per day can be produced. In this case we can make use of the following relationship to identify the coefficient [*Woodchips, Computer*]:

$$a \times X = L$$

where X = the level of the activity that just satisfies the constraint, a = the coefficient in the constraint, and L = the constraint limit.

The value of X used must be based on an assumption that no other activity is selected; all the available resource must be allocated to this activity. The relationship can be rearranged to give

$$a = L/X$$

The coefficient [*Woodchips, Computer*] would thus be:

56 tonnes wood chips/28 tonnes paper

= 2 tonnes woodchips per tonne paper

This is the same as would be derived by the previous method, by asking, "How many tonnes of wood chips are required for each tonne of computer paper?" From the problem definition, the answer is 2. Note that this second approach is not appropriate for Example 3.1 because of the way the information is presented. However, in other examples, as in the real world, the information will sometimes be presented in a way that requires this second approach.

As an aside, if the constraint coefficient (a) and the constraint limit (L) are known, then the formula just given can be useful for calculating the activity level which, for that activity alone, would just satisfy the constraint:

$$X = L/a$$

So if we want to know what is the greatest amount of computer paper that can be produced with the available labor, we divide

126 days/4 days per tonne = 31.5 tonnes

This is based on an assumption that only computer paper is to be produced and that other constraints (wood chips and chlorine) are not binding. On the other hand, if the total available workforce was devoted to production of writing paper, maximum output would be

126 days/6 days per tonne = 21 tonnes

Again we are assuming that only writing paper is produced and that the mill would not run out of wood chips or produce too much chlorine. These other constraints would have to be examined as well to ensure that they were not violated.

Setting the Value of a Coefficient: Method 3

The third approach to deriving matrix coefficients is to consider each constraint as an algebraic inequality. Some people find this to be the easiest approach in all circumstances, but even those who do not may have to use it sometimes.

In the algebraic approach activities are variables in the inequality and their coefficients are the parameters. We have already seen in Chapter 2 that constraints can be represented in this way. The labor constraint of Example 3.1 would be represented as

$$4C + 6W \leq 126$$

where C represents the number of tonnes of computer paper produced and W represents the number of tonnes of writing paper. This inequality represents the fact that total labor requirements for production of computer paper plus total labor requirements for production of writing paper must not exceed the total amount of labor that is available.

We can express the whole problem algebraically, as in Chapter 2:

Maximize

$$600C + 1000W$$

Subject to

$$4C + 6W \leq 126$$
$$2C + 2W \leq 56$$
$$0.2857C + 1.5W \leq 24$$
$$C \geq 0; \quad W \geq 0$$

This is by far the most common way of presenting LP constraints in textbooks. However, it is still necessary to use one of the two approaches outlined earlier to identify the parameters of the inequality (the matrix coefficients 4, 6, 2, etc.). Just knowing that a constraint is an algebraic inequality does not necessarily make the choice of matrix coefficients obvious.

All the constraints in Table 3.1 are of the same type: less than. Thus we have now covered enough material to understand all the constraints in this simple model. However, recall that in Chapter 2, it was stated that every LP problem has some extra constraints that limit the decision variables to be greater than or equal to zero. These are shown in the algebraic summary of the problem just presented, but they do not have to be included explicitly in the matrix as well. This is because they apply to every variable in every LP problem, so computer packages know to make allowance for them. All LP computer packages will automatically only select non-negative values of the variables. When interpreting the matrix, always keep in mind that negative activity levels are not allowed. At times this will influence the structure of your matrix.

This does not mean, however, that you cannot use negative coefficients within the matrix. To the contrary, negative coefficients are very important and are the main topic of Chapter 6. The non-negativity constraints apply to the levels of activities, not the coefficients of the matrix.

These three ways of thinking about matrix coefficients are not mutually exclusive. Often it can be very valuable to test your idea of what the coefficient should be by considering it in each of the three ways. What is difficult to think about in one way can sometimes become much clearer when viewed from a different angle.

BOX 3.1 Three Approaches to Setting Matrix Coefficient Values

(a) Ask "What is the effect of this activity on this constraint?" or "How many units of the constraint are there in one unit of the activity?"

(b) Calculate the constraint limit divided by the level of the activity that would just satisfy the constraint.

(c) Think of the constraint as an algebraic inequality. The matrix coefficient is the parameter of the relevant variable in the inequality.

Optimal Solution for Example 3.1

Using the approach described in Chapter 2, the constraints from Example 3.1 can be graphed as shown in Figure 3.1. The combinations of both variables that satisfy all three constraints are shown by the shaded region. The combination of computer paper and writing paper that gives the highest level of profit *and* satisifes all three constraints is the point where the dashed line just touches the shaded region: 10.5 tonnes of computer paper and 14.0 tonnes of writing paper per day.

After entering the matrix into a computer package, it gives a printout something like Table 3.2. The various components of this output table are described

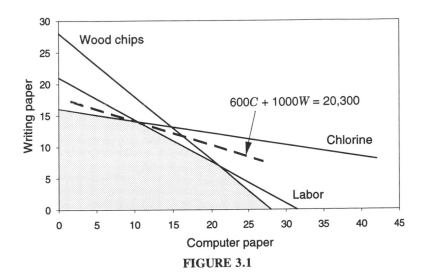

FIGURE 3.1

TABLE 3.2 Optimal Solution for Example 3.1

Objective function value: 20,300.000000
Problem direction: max

Activity		Level	Shadow cost
1 Computer	A	10.5000	0.0000
2 Writing	A	14.0000	0.0000

Constraint		Slack	Shadow Price
1 Labor	L	0.0000	143.3333
2 Wood chips	L	7.0000	0.0000
3 Chlorine	L	0.0000	93.3333

in detail in Chapter 4. For now note that the maximum level of profit ($20,300) is shown at the top of the table; the optimal levels of computer paper and writing paper are shown as 10.5 and 14.0; the Slack column indicates that with these levels of computer paper and writing paper, the level of usage of wood chips is 7 tonnes less than the specified limit of 56 tonnes; the Shadow price column indicates that if an extra unit of labor could be obtained, it would increase profits by $143.33. Similarly, if the constraint on chlorine emissions could be relaxed by one unit, profits would increase by $93.33. The Shadow cost column only contains useful information for activities that are at zero level, and there are none of these in this example. Shadow costs are covered fully in the next chapter.

Rounding Off Coefficients

The coefficient for [*Chlorine, Computer*] illustrates that coefficients of the matrix must be specified as fixed, decimal numbers. It is not possible to specify that the coefficient is a ratio (e.g., $\frac{2}{7}$ as in this case) or that it is the result of a formula (e.g., $1 - 4 \times \frac{2}{11}$). You must first convert the ratio or formula into a decimal number and enter that into the matrix. This may require rounding the numeral off to a reasonable number of decimal places. In this example, $\frac{2}{7}$ results in a recurring decimal number that has been rounded off to four decimal places.

3.4 SETTING THE MINIMUM LEVEL OF A FACTOR

Greater-than constraints are conceptually very similar to less-than constraints. This section describes the inclusion of a greater-than constraint in the simple model already presented.

Suppose that the paper mill has a contract to provide 5 tonnes of computer paper per day to a large retailer. It is possible to produce more than 5 tonnes of computer paper and to sell the excess to other buyers, but the contract means

TABLE 3.3 Matrix for Example 3.1 with Extra Contract Constraint

	Computer (tonnes)	Writing (tonnes)	Type	Limit
Objective ($)	600	1000	max	
Labor (days)	4	6	≤	126
Wood chips (tonnes)	2	2	≤	56
Chlorine (kg)	0.2857	1.5	≤	24
Contract (tonnes)	1		≥	5

that it is not possible to produce less than 5 tonnes. A new matrix including this extra constraint is shown in Table 3.3.

There is a new constraint labeled *Contract* at the bottom of the matrix. The measurement unit for the constraint is tonnes of computer paper. The constraint type is ≥, and the constraint limit is five. The coefficient in the *Computer* column is one. Together these mean that the number of tonnes of computer paper must be greater than or equal to five. The derivation of the *Computer* coefficient (one) is similar to the process described earlier for less-than constraints. Ask, "What is the effect of this activity on this constraint?" or "How many units of the constraint are there in one unit of the activity?" As noted before, the units for the constraint are tonnes of computer paper. These are the same as the units for the activity, so the question is equivalent to "How many tonnes of computer paper are there in a tonne of computer paper?" The obvious answer is one.

Another way of asking the same question, which is relevant to greater-than constraints, is "How much does each unit of this activity contribute toward meeting the minimum requirement for this constraint?" In this case, each tonne of computer paper contributes one unit toward the minimum requirement of five tonnes.

The unit of measurement for the writing paper activity is "tonnes of writing paper." Thus in deriving the matrix coefficient for [*Contract*, *Writing*], ask "How many tonnes of computer paper are there in a tonne of writing paper?" or "How much does each unit of writing paper contribute toward meeting the minimum requirement for computer paper?" Clearly, the answer is zero. In Table 3.3, the [*Contract*, *Writing*] coefficient is blank. It is very common for zeros to simply be left out of the matrix, so interpret a blank as a zero. The reason for leaving zeros blank is that in large LP models, it is common for more than 90 percent of the matrix coefficients to be zero, and it would be very tedious to have to write them all in.

Let us look at the other two methods of deriving matrix coefficients. In this example we can use the second approach: dividing the constraint limit by the activity level that will just satisfy the constraint. If computer paper were the only activity selected in the solution, what level of computer paper would just satisfy the contract constraint? Five tonnes. Using the formula given earlier,

$$a = L/X = 5/5 = 1$$

This corresponds to the coefficient already derived using the first approach.

This approach does not really make sense with the [*Contract, Writing*] coefficient since there is no level of writing paper that would just satisfy the constraint. However, it is usually easy to tell whether a particular coefficient should be zero—it is when the constraint has no *direct* effect on the activity. The contract in this example places a minimum level on the level of computer paper but places no restrictions on writing paper (except indirectly by affecting the other constraints). In situations like this the coefficient is always zero.

For this particular constraint, the easiest way of deriving the coefficients is probably to state it as an algebraic inequality. The algebraic inequality that represents the contract constraint is

$$C \geq 5$$

This inequality is the same as

$$(1 \times C) + (0 \times W) \geq 5$$

You can see from this the connection to the other two approaches. The parameters derived previously appear as parameters in this inequality.

Figure 3.2 shows a graphical representation of the problem with the contract constraint included. The feasible region (shaded) has been reduced by the inclusion of the new constraint. Apart from showing that we could no longer

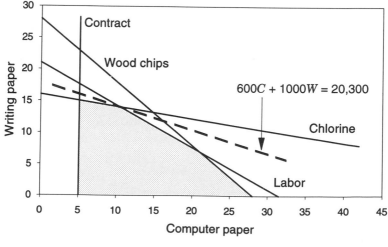

FIGURE 3.2

select less than five tonnes of computer paper, the figure also gives some other information about the new problem. It shows that the inclusion of the new constraint does not change the optimal solution, which is still to produce 10.5 tonnes of computer paper and 14 tonnes of writing paper. This is so because the highest feasible objective function is the same as it was in Figure 3.1. The newly added contract constraint requires the solution to include at least 5 tonnes of computer paper, but since it already includes 10.5 tonnes, there is no need to change.

As noted in Chapter 2, the addition of a new constraint can never change the optimal solution if the original optimal solution does not violate the new constraint. This is because an additional constraint can only reduce the number of feasible solutions or, at best, leave them unchanged. If a particular solution is the best from a set of possibilities, removing inferior options from the set will not change the relative ranking of the remaining options.

If the original optimal solution violates the new constraint, the new optimal solution will have a less favorable objective function value than before the constraint was added. On the other hand, removing a constraint from the problem can result in a better solution becoming available or it may leave the optimal solution unchanged but it cannot make the optimal solution worse.

Another thing apparent from Figure 3.2 is that by increasing the minimum level of computer paper, the maximum feasible level of writing paper has been reduced. Previously it was possible to produce up to 16 tonnes of writing paper without violating any constraint, although in order to satisfy the chlorine constraint, the level of computer paper would have to be reduced to zero. If there must be at least 5 tonnes of computer paper, some of the allowable chlorine emissions will be due to computer paper production, reducing the maximum amount of chlorine that can be released during production of writing paper. The maximum feasible level of writing paper is now 15 tonnes per day. If the actual level of computer paper is greater than 5 tonnes per day, the maximum level of writing paper is reduced even further.

3.5 SETTING THE EXACT LEVEL OF A FACTOR

The third and final type of constraint is the equals constraint. This specifies that the solution must include an exact level of some factor. For example, suppose that the mill receives an offer to purchase 15 tonnes per day of computer paper for $800 per tonne (i.e., $200 above the usual price) on condition that the purchaser have exclusive rights to the mill's output of computer paper. If the mill accepts the offer, it is limited to producing exactly 15 tonnes per day of computer paper since, under the terms of the contract, any production beyond that cannot be sold. Assume the mill accepts the new offer. The new matrix is shown in Table 3.4.

TABLE 3.4   Matrix for Example 3.1 with Revised Contract Constraint

	Computer (tonnes)	Writing (tonnes)	Type	Limit
Objective ($)	800	1000	max	
Labor (days)	4	6	≤	126
Wood chips (tonnes)	2	2	≤	56
Chlorine (kg)	0.2857	1.5	≤	24
Contract (tonnes)	1		=	15

The contract constraint is a little different now. It represents the following equality:

$$C = 15$$

which is the same as

$$(1 \times C) + (0 \times W) = 15$$

Thus the only changes from the previous contract constraint are that the objective function value for *Computer* is now 800, the constraint type is now $=$ rather than $\geq$, and the constraint limit is increased to 15. The measurement unit for the constraint is still tonnes of computer paper, while the derivation of the coefficients 1 and 0 is exactly the same as described in Section 3.4. However, the set of feasible solutions would be greatly reduced, as shown in Figure 3.3.

The feasible region now consists of the thick segment of the contract con-

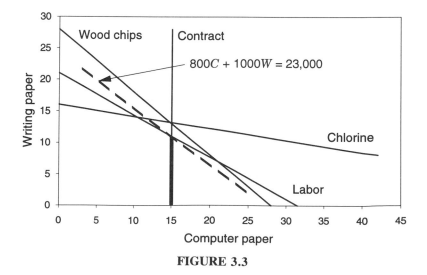

FIGURE 3.3

straint bounded from below by the *Computer paper* axis and from above by the *Labor* constraint. Although there is now no choice about the level of computer paper, the mill still has a choice about the level of writing paper. However the level of writing paper produced must be consistent with the other contraints (*Labor*, *Chlorine*, and *Wood chips*), which are still in operation. On the feasible line segment, all four constraints are satisfied: the level of *Labor* required is less than or equal to 126 workers per day, the amount of wood chips used is less than 56 tonnes per day, the level of chlorine released is less than 24 kg per day, and the level of computer paper produced exactly equals 15 tonnes per day.

The dashed line in Figure 3.3 shows the highest valued objective function given the new higher price for computer paper. The new optimal solution is the point where the objective function intersects with the feasible line segment: 15 tonnes of computer paper and 11 tones of writing paper.

Consider what would happen if the labor constraint were also converted from a less-than constraint to an equals constraint. This corresponds to a decision to have no unused labor capacity. In this case, the feasible region would be reduced to a single point at the intersection of the labor and contract constraints. That is, if we specified that the mill must produce exactly 15 tonnes of computer paper and must fully employ all 126 workers, there is only one combination of computer paper and writing paper that will provide this: 15 tonnes of computer paper and 11 tonnes of writing paper, which happens to be the optimal solution in Figure 3.3.

We noted that the question ''What is the effect of this activity on this constraint?'' has slightly different connotations for less-than and greater-than constraints. For less-than constraints, the question really means ''How much of the available resource is used up by each unit of this activity?'' whereas for greater-than constraints the question is ''How much does each unit of this activity contribute toward meeting the minimum requirement for this constraint?'' An equals constraint can have a similar impact on the model as either a less-than or a greater-than constraint, depending on the circumstances, so either of these versions of the question may be appropriate.

To illustrate, in Figure 3.3, the equals constraint causes a lower level of production of computer paper than would otherwise be the case, given the new higher price for computer paper. If this high price could be maintained, the optimal output levels but for the contract constraint would be 21 tonnes of computer paper and 7 tonnes of writing paper. The contract constraint acts in the way that a less-than constraint would act. If the mill management agreed to increase the contract so that exactly 25 tonnes of computer paper were produced, the contract would be acting like a greater-than constraint. Thus the appropriate question can be either ''How much of the resource (which must be completely consumed) is used up by each unit of this activity?'' or ''How much does each unit of this activity contribute toward meeting the exact requirement for this constraint?''

BOX 3.2   The First Approach to Setting Matrix Coefficient Values: Variations of the Question

General

(a) "What is the effect of this activity on this constraint?"

(b) "How many units of this constraint are there in one unit of this activity?"

For Less-than Constraints

(c) "How much of the available resource is used up by each unit of this activity?"

For Greater-than Constraints

(d) "How much does each unit of this activity contribute toward meeting the minimum requirement for this constraint?"

For Equals Constraints

(e) "How much of the resource (which must be completely consumed) is used up by each unit of this activity?"

(f) "How much does each unit of this activity contribute toward meeting the exact requirement for this constraint?"

3.6   SETTING THE LEVEL OF AN ACTIVITY

The constraints in the original Example 3.1 affected the allowable levels of both activities in the model. However, as we have seen, it is possible to specify constraints that act only on a subset of the activities. The contract constraints in Tables 3.3 and 3.4 directly affect the level of computer paper, but leave writing paper to be determined by the objective function and the other constraints.

The structure of the *Contract* row can be applied whenever there is a need to set the minimum, maximum, or exact level of an activity. The units of the row are the same as for the column, a one is entered in the column to be constrained, the limit is entered, and the appropriate constraint type specified. All other coefficients in the row are zeros.

Bounds

Some LP packages include the facility to specify "bounds" on each activity. These bounds can set a minimum, maximum, or exact level for each activity in exactly the same way that a constraint on the individual activity does.

The advantage of bounds is that they are more efficient than standard constraints; they take less time to solve and they result in a smaller LP matrix by replacing constraints on individual activities. These advantages are possible because bounds represent a very specialized and narrow type of constraint for which it is possible to avoid some of the steps and checks required for standard constraints.

Bounds are especially useful where there are many constraints on individual variables. They are only able to act on individual activities; it is not possible to specify in a bound that activity 1 plus activity 2 must be less than some value. For that, you must use a standard constraint. The advantage of the approach shown in Tables 3.3 and 3.4 is that it is usable in *all* LP packages.

3.7 THE IMPORTANCE OF UNITS OF MEASUREMENT

Units of measurement for activities and constraints have been mentioned repeatedly in the text so far. Units are one of the factors considered when matrix coefficients are being derived. There has been no discussion of the selection of "good" units because in general, one unit of measurement is as good as another; it does not matter whether wood chips are measured in kilograms, tonnes, pounds, or truck loads. What is important, however, is that once a unit is adopted, it is applied correctly and consistently. This section reiterates and expands on these points.

Table 3.5 shows the units of each coefficient in Table 3.4. First look at the *Computer* and *Writing* columns. For any cell, the unit of the coefficient is **row units** per **column unit.** Within one row the constraint unit appears in the numerator of each cell unit. For example, each coefficient in the labor row is in days; in the *Computer* column it is the number of days of labor per tonne

TABLE 3.5   Units of Measurement for Each Coefficient in Table 3.3

	Computer (tonnes CP)	Writing (tonnes WP)	Type	Limit
Objective ($)	$\dfrac{\$}{\text{tonne CP}}$	$\dfrac{\$}{\text{tonne WP}}$	max	
Labor (days)	$\dfrac{\text{days}}{\text{tonne CP}}$	$\dfrac{\text{days}}{\text{tonne WP}}$	$\leq$	days
Wood chips (tonnes)	$\dfrac{\text{tonnes WC}}{\text{tonne CP}}$	$\dfrac{\text{tonnes WC}}{\text{tonne WP}}$	$\leq$	tonnes WC
Chlorine (kg)	$\dfrac{\text{kg}}{\text{tonne CP}}$	$\dfrac{\text{kg}}{\text{tonne WP}}$	$\leq$	kg
Contract (tonnes)	$\dfrac{\text{tonnes CP}}{\text{tonne CP}}$	$\dfrac{\text{tonnes CP}}{\text{tonne WP}}$	$=$	tonnes CP

Abbreviations: CP = computer paper; WP = writing paper; WC = wood chips.

of computer paper, and in the *Writing* column it is days of labor per tonne of writing paper.

By contrast, within one column the numerator of the units varies between cells. Moving down a column, the coefficients represent a number of dollars, a number of days of labor, a number of tonnes of wood chips, and so on. The common factor is that the denominator of each cell unit stays constant within a column. For example, all coefficients within the *Computer* column are expressed per tonne of computer paper.

In the *Limit* column, the units are the same as for the rows; they are not divided by any column unit.

Changing Units

Although it does not matter which units are used, this does not mean that units have no effect on the matrix. Suppose that in the original Example 3.1 (without a contract constraint) we change the units of the wood chips row from tonnes to kilograms. The new matrix is shown in Table 3.6. The new wood-chip coefficients can be derived using the same approach as previously. How many kilograms of the available wood chips are used up in the production of a tonne of computer paper? (2000). How many for a tonne of writing paper? (2000). What is the maximum availability of wood chips in kilograms? (56,000). Alternatively the new coefficients can be derived easily and quickly from Table 3.1. Tonnes can be converted to kilograms by multiplying by 1000. The figures in the *Wood chips* row of Table 3.6 are just those of Table 3.1 multiplied by 1000.

What if, in addition to measuring wood chips in kilograms, we measure computer paper (but not writing paper) in kilograms? Asking the question "How many units of a factor are required for one unit of computer paper?" now yields answers 1000 times smaller than it did before because one unit of computer paper is now 1000 times smaller (1 tonne = 1000 kg). We divide the coefficients in the Computer paper column of Table 3.6 by 1000 to give Table 3.7.

Notice that when we decreased the unit of measurement for the row by 1000 the coefficients in the row were multiplied by 1000, but a 1000-fold decrease in column units led to the columns' coefficients decreasing by a factor of 1000.

TABLE 3.6 Matrix for Example 3.1 with Wood-Chips Row Measured in Kilograms

	Computer (tonnes)	Writing (tonnes)	Type	Limit
Objective ($)	600	1000	max	
Labor (days)	4	6	≤	126
Wood chips (kg)	2000	2000	≤	56,000
Chlorine (kg)	0.2857	1.5	≤	24

TABLE 3.7 Matrix for Example 3.1 with Wood-Chips Row and Computer-Paper Column Measured in Kilograms

	Computer (kg)	Writing (tonnes)	Type	Limit
Objective ($)	0.6	1000	max	
Labor (days)	0.004	6	≤	126
Wood chips (kg)	2	2000	≤	56,000
Chlorine (kg)	0.0002857	1.5	≤	24

The reason is that row units appear in the numerator of the cell units, whereas column units are in the denominator (see Table 3.5):

$$\text{Cell unit} = \text{row unit/column unit}$$

Decreasing the row unit decreases the cell unit and increases the coefficient. (If I ask how many pounds does an elephant weigh, the answer is a larger number than if I ask how many tons.) Conversely, decreasing the column unit increases the cell unit and decreases the coefficient.

In the preceding discussion, we have argued that changing units does not affect a problem's solution and can be achieved by multiplying or dividing all the entries in a row or column by an appropriate figure. This implies that multiplying a row or column does not affect the solution. As long as all the entries in the row or column are multiplied, any number at all can be used to "scale" the entries. There are, however, two points to stress about scaling.

First, the effects of scaling rows and columns are cumulative. If the entries of a row are scaled by one factor and the entries of a column by another, the coefficient of the cell where this row and column intersect must be scaled by both. This is illustrated in Table 3.7 where the coefficients of the wood-chips row have been multiplied by 1000, and those of the computer paper column by 0.001 (relative to Table 3.1). The [*Woodchips, Computer*] cell is thus back to its original value of 2. However, now the units of the cell are kilograms of wood chips per kilogram of computer paper instead of tonnes of wood chips per tonne of computer paper.

Second, although scaling does not affect the solution, it does affect the interpretation of the solution. If the solution to a problem includes 15 tonnes of writing paper and then the units for writing paper are changed to kilograms, the solution will include 15,000 kg of writing paper. The computer printout of the solution will show the number 15,000 instead of 15.

This sets a practical limitation on how the matrix can be scaled; unless you are not interested in the output for a particular row or column, it should only be scaled so that it is measured in interpretable units. You could scale the writing paper column so that its units were 72.3 kg, but the answer would then be to make 207.4689 units of writing paper. You would have to multiply this by 72.3 to find that it corresponded to 15,000 kg. Choice of units and interpretation of output is discussed again later in the book.

3.8 A SUGGESTED STRATEGY FOR MATRIX BUILDING

Matrix building is something of an art and, as such, all individuals have their own approach. Nevertheless, there are some guidelines that can be helpful, particularly for beginners. The box below shows one approach that may be helpful. Even if you do not follow this approach exactly, a key requirement is to be systematic.

BOX 3.3   A Suggested Strategy for Matrix Building

(a) Read through the problem definition carefully (assuming that you have a written problem definition).

(b) Identify the objective and choose suitable units for measuring it (e.g., $)

(c) Identify the variables in the problem that are under the decision maker's control and for which you wish to determine the optimal levels. These are the activities. Choose for each a meaningful, unique name and a suitable unit of measurement.

(d) Identify the various constraints (limitations and restrictions) on the activities. For each constraint write down in words the nature of the constraint: What is it constraining and to what level? Initially do not worry about how to represent the constraints in the matrix. Choose a name and unit for each constraint, as well as the constraint type. To avoid confusion, it is wise not to name a row the same as any column.

(e) On paper or in a computer package, put the activity and constraint names, units, and constraint types into a matrix like those shown in this chapter. Initially leave blanks for the coefficients and constraint limits.

(f) For each row, work through each coefficient and the constraint limit, deriving the appropriate value from the problem definition.

In Chapter 5, this matrix-building strategy is illustrated in detail for examples of several types.

3.9 KEY POINTS

- Each constraint is represented by a row of coefficients.
- There are three types of constraint: (a) less than or equal to, (b) greater than or equal to, and (c) equal to.

- There is an extra row of coefficients for objective function values.
- Each activity is represented by a column of coefficients.
- There is an extra column of coefficients for constraint limits and one indicating the type of constraint.
- Each activity column has a specific unit of measurement that applied to all coefficients in the column. However, the constraint-limit column does not have a unit of measurement that applies to all of its coefficients.
- Each row, including the objective function, has a specific unit of measurement.
- Coefficients of the matrix must be specified as fixed, decimal numbers.
- The unit of measurement for a matrix coefficient is **unit of the row** per **unit of the column.**
- There are several mental approaches to deciding on the value of a particular coefficient of the matrix: (a) ask "What is the effect of this activity on this constraint?" or "How many units of the constraint are there in one unit of the activity?" (see Box 3.2 for further variations on this approach); (b) calculate the constraint limit divided by the level of the activity that would just satisfy the constraint; (c) think of the constraint as an algebraic inequality. The matrix coefficient is the parameter of the relevant variable in the inequality.
- In general, one unit of measurement is as good as another. However, it is important that once a unit is adopted, it is applied correctly and consistently.
- Changing units does not affect a problem's solution and can be achieved by multiplying or dividing all the entries in a row or column by an appropriate figure. Such a change does affect the interpretation of numbers in the solution.

CHAPTER 4

INTERPRETING MAIN OUTPUT

One of the advantages of linear programming (LP) over less sophisticated planning techniques is the range and detail of information obtained automatically with each solution. This chapter explains the meaning and usefulness of the main elements of the output: the objective function value, activity levels, activity shadow costs, constraint slacks, and constraint shadow prices. There is also a section describing the effect of changing units of measurement on interpretation of output.

Example 3.1 is the basis for the discussion in the first part of this chapter. Recall that the problem is to determine the optimal production levels of computer paper and writing paper for a paper mill. The constraints were the availability of labor and wood chips and a need to comply with environmental regulations about the release of chlorine into the river. If necessary, refer again to the problem definition and the matrix in Table 3.1. Output from this model is shown in Table 4.1.

4.1 OBJECTIVE FUNCTION VALUE

The objective function value in the output gives the optimal (maximum or minimum) value of the objective. In Example 3.1 the objective is profit maximization, so the objective-function value in Table 4.1 is simply the maximum possible profit achievable without violating any of the constraints of the problem. The units of measurement for the objective function are the same as were used in the original matrix, in this case, dollars.

TABLE 4.1 Optimal Solution for Example 3.1

Objective function value: 20,300.000000
Problem direction: max

Activity		Level	Shadow Cost
1 Computer	A	10.5000	0.0000
2 Writing	A	14.0000	0.0000
Constraint		Slack	Shadow Price
1 Labor	L	0.0000	143.3333
2 Wood chips	L	7.0000	0.0000
3 Chlorine	L	0.0000	93.3333

4.2. ACTIVITY LEVELS

The level of each activity is the number of units selected in the optimal solution. The levels are expressed in the same units as were used when the matrix was constructed. In the matrix for Example 3.1 (Table 3.1) we expressed computer paper and writing paper in tonnes, so these are the units used in the solution in Table 4.1. The optimal strategy is to produce 10.5 tonnes of computer paper and 14 tonnes of writing paper. This corresponds to the point in Figure 3.1 at which the objective function line is tangent to the feasible region.

4.3 ACTIVITY SHADOW COSTS

Shadow costs indicate how far each activity is from entering the optimal solution. That is, they indicate by how much the objective function value of each activity would have to improve before the activity would be selected as part of the optimal solution. In Table 4.1 both activities are selected at positive levels so the objective value of each would not have to improve for the activity to be selected in the optimal solution. For this reason the shadow costs are zero in each case. An activity can only have a positive* shadow cost if it is not selected in the optimal solution: that is, if its level in the solution is zero. Notice that in the optimal solution either the activity level or the shadow cost is always zero. If the activity level is greater than zero, the shadow cost must be zero and if the shdow cost is not zero, the activity level must be zero. It is possible, however, for both the activity level and the activity shadow cost to be zero. This possibility is explained in detail in Chapter 10.

*In some LP computer packages, shadow costs are printed in the optimal-solution output as negative numbers. In this book we will assume that shadow costs are shown as positive numbers, but the same logic applies to packages that show them as negatives.

To further illustrate shadow costs, consider Example 4.1.

Example 4.1: Paper Milling with Lower Pollution

Suppose that in the paper milling problem described in Example 3.1 a new bleaching technology is introduced that reduces the level of pollution in writing paper production. The new process results in only 1 unit of chlorine output per tonne of writing paper. Apart from this change the problem is identical to Example 3.1. ∎

The matrix for the problem is shown in Table 4.2. The matrix is exactly the same as that for Example 3.1 (in Table 3.1) except that the [*Chlorine, Writing*] coefficient is now different. To determine the new value of the coefficient ask "How many units of chlorine residues are there per tonne of writing paper?" or "How much of the available capacity to release chlorine is used by each unit of writing paper?" Given the problem description, the answer is now 1.00 instead of 1.50.

Figure 4.1 shows that with this new technology, the chlorine constraint has been lifted sufficiently for it not to limit the feasible region. It is now optimal to switch production over to writing paper only (see the point where the objective function line is tangent to the new feasible region). It was only the pollution constraint that was preventing the mill from producing more of the highly profitable writing paper before.

Table 4.3 shows the solution to this modified problem. The optimal levels of computer paper and writing paper are zero and 21 tonnes, respectively. Because computer paper is not selected, it has a positive shadow cost of $66.67. This indicates that given the constraints of this problem, the profitability of computer paper would have to increase by at least $66.67 (i.e., up from $600 to at least $666.67 per tonne) before computer paper would form part of the optimal solution.

It is not clear from the output in Table 4.3 exactly how the solution would change if the price of computer paper increased by this amount. In general, although the shadow cost gives a reliable indication of how large an improvement is necessary for a nonoptimal activity to enter the optimal solution, it does not indicate what the optimal level of the activity would be if it did enter

TABLE 4.2 Matrix for Example 4.1

	Computer (tonnes)	Writing (tonnes)	Type	Limit
Objective ($)	600.00	1000.00	max	
Labor (days)	4.00	6.00	≤	126.00
Wood chips (tonnes)	2.00	2.00	≤	56.00
Chlorine (kg)	0.2857	1.00	≤	24.00

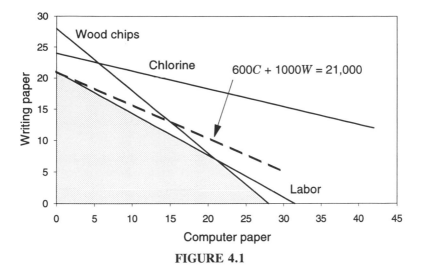

FIGURE 4.1

the solution. Nor does it indicate how the optimal levels of other activities currently in the solution would be affected. The optimal levels of some variables may be increased while others are decreased, possibly even to zero. To determine exactly what changes would occur it is necessary to alter the model and re-solve it.

For example, suppose the mill found a new buyer willing to pay more for computer paper, such that profitability became $670 per tonne. The new solution shown in Table 4.4 includes 21 tonnes of computer paper and 7 tonnes of writing paper. These levels could not be predicted from the output in Table 4.3. We could predict that the level of computer paper would increase if its profit exceeded $666.67, but not by how much unless we graphed the problem (as in Figure 4.1).

An alternative interpretation of shadow costs is that they represent the wors-

TABLE 4.3 Optimal Solution for Example 4.1

Objective function value: 21,000.000000
Problem direction: max

Activity		Level	Shadow Cost
1 Computer	Z	0.0000	66.6667
2 Writing	A	21.0000	0.0000

Constraint		Slack	Shadow Price
1 Labor	L	0.0000	166.6667
2 Wood chips	L	14.0000	0.0000
3 Chlorine	L	3.0000	0.0000

TABLE 4.4 Optimal Solution for Example 4.1 with Objective-Function Value for Computer Paper Increased to 670

Objective function value: 21,070.000000
Problem direction: max.

Activity		Level	Shadow Cost
1 Computer	A	21.0000	0.0000
2 Writing	A	7.0000	0.0000

Constraint		Slack	Shadow Price
1 Labor	L	0.0000	165.0000
2 Wood chips	L	0.0000	5.0000
3 Chlorine	L	11.0000	0.0000

ening of the objective function that would occur if a zero-leveled activity was forced into the solution. If a constraint was added to Example 4.1 specifying that the solution had to include at least one tonne of computer paper, the profitability of the optimal solution would fall by $66.67. A similar constraint, if added to the matrix for Example 3.1, would have no impact on the optimal solution, because computer paper is already included in the optimal solution at a level greater than one (see Table 4.1). That is why the shadow cost for computer paper was zero in Table 4.1.

Opportunity Costs

Whichever interpretation you use, shadow costs are calculated subject to all the constraints of the problem still being met. If you just added a tonne of computer paper to the solution in Table 4.3, profits from computer paper would rise by $600 (its objective function value). However, in conflict with this gain in production is a sacrifice of income from writing paper, because the labor constraint forces you to reduce its production. Thus, the gain of $600 can only be achieved through suffering a loss of $666.67 due to this lower production of writing paper, giving a net loss of $66.67, the shadow cost of computer paper in Table 4.3.

The origin of the figure of $666.67 can be understood by viewing Figure 4.1 and Table 4.2. Figure 4.1 shows that labor is the one constraint that is fully exhausted, so that any increase in computer paper would be directly reducing labor availability for the production of writing paper. Table 4.2 shows that labor usage per tonne of computer paper is only two-thirds of the usage for writing paper, so a one-tonne increase of computer paper would require only two-thirds of a tonne reduction in output of writing paper. That reduction would come at the direct financial cost of $1000 per tonne (the objective function value of writing paper), so the value of the reduction is $\frac{2}{3} \times \$1000$ = \$666.67.

The \$666.67 loss of income from writing paper is, in effect, a cost that should be attributed to the extra computer paper produced. It is not a direct financial cost, but it is a cost due to a lost opportunity to make income from writing paper. For this reason it is often called an *opportunity cost.* The opportunity cost of an activity is the returns from other potential activities that must be foregone in order to undertake the activity in question. In solving an LP problem, the computer package automatically takes into account the opportunity costs of all activities, as well as their direct financial costs and returns.

Reasons for Caution when Interpreting Shadow Costs

There is a need for care when interpreting shadow costs. The reasons for this are (a) shadow costs apply only to small changes in the strategy or plan, (b) they only apply if a single change is made at a time, and (c) the solution may be "degenerate."

First consider the "small changes" issue. If we are interpreting the shadow cost as "the worsening of the objective function that would occur if a zero-leveled activity were forced into the solution," we need to check how far the activity can be forced into the solution without changing the rate at which the objective function is declining. In Example 4.1 it is not possible to go on increasing the level of computer paper production indefinitely, suffering a \$66.67 loss per tonne. Beyond a certain level of computer paper, the shadow cost may increase as additional resources become limiting. If this occurs, further increases in production of computer paper would reduce profits by more than \$66.67 per tonne. This would occur if the solution was constrained to include more than 21 tonnes of computer paper. Beyond this level, wood chips would become the most limiting factor and a further one-tonne increase in computer paper would require a one-tonne decrease in writing paper (instead of just two-thirds of a tonne). The opportunity cost of computer paper would then be \$1000 per tonne. Given receipts of \$600 per tonne, the net reduction in overall profit would be \$400 for each extra tonne of computer paper produced. Thus the shadow cost of \$66.67 per tonne would no longer be relevant.

Beyond some level of computer paper, it will not be possible to increase the production at any cost. In our small example, this would be the case if we tried to increase the production of computer paper beyond 28 tonnes. Figure 4.1 shows this to be the highest feasible level. Beyond this level sufficient wood chips are no longer available to meet production requirements.

We have several times referred to constraining the model to include one unit of the activity in question. However, it should be apparent that it will not always be possible to increase the level of the activity by a full unit without changing the shadow cost in the process. For example if we had used units of 100 tonnes instead of one tonne to measure paper production, forcing the model to select one unit of computer paper would be impossible. The shadow cost of computer paper would only be relevant within the range zero to 0.21 unit of computer paper (0.21 unit = 0.21 × 100 tonnes = 21 tonnes).

Strictly speaking, shadow costs only apply to "marginal" increases in the activity. They indicate the rate of worsening of the objective function per unit of the activity, but there is no guarantee that they apply to a full unit of the activity. In some cases, marginal might mean very small indeed.

For small increases in the activity, the shadow cost gives the worsening of the objective function *per unit of the activity* that is forced into the solution. If 0.0001 unit of the activity is forced into the solution, the worsening of the objective function is 0.0001 times the shadow cost.

Now consider the second issue, that shadow costs apply only if one change is made at a time. If another matrix coefficient or objective function coefficient is changed, a given shadow cost is likely to change. For example, if the [*Objective, Writing*] coefficient in Table 4.2 is increased to 1050, the shadow cost of computer paper in the optimal solution increases from $66.67 to $100. This higher shadow cost indicates that with an increase in the profitability of writing paper, the profitability of computer paper needs to increase by even more than it did for any computer paper to become optimal. Alternatively, if one tonne of computer paper is forced into the solution, the opportunity cost is still two-thirds of a tonne of writing paper, but the value of this is greater than it was previously.

As a second example, consider an increase in the [*Labor, Computer*] coefficient in Table 4.2 from 4.0 to 4.5. That is, the labor requirement of each tonne of computer paper is 4.5 worker days instead of 4.0. This small change has a relatively large impact on the shadow cost of computer paper: up from $66.67 to $150.00. If computer paper were to be produced in these circumstances, each tonne of computer paper produced would reduce overall profits by $150. On the other hand, if the price of computer paper were to increase by more than $150 per tonne, it would be worth producing. These examples indicate that shadow costs are not necessarily stable if another part of the matrix is changed.

The third reason for caution when interpreting shadow costs is that the solution may be "degenerate," which means that a solution has more than one valid set of shadow costs. This is explained fully in Chapter 10, and is mentioned here for completeness.

Despite these complications, shadow costs can still be useful indicators of the robustness of a solution. Large shadow costs generally mean that a solution is stable, that large changes would be required for the solution to change. Conversely, small shadow costs indicate that the solution is less robust.

An LP model of a real-world problem is usually intended to provide the decision maker with information and advice. This decision maker will have (or can be given) an idea of the variability of each activity's objective function value (e.g., input costs or output prices). If there is reason to believe that variations may be larger than the indicated shadow costs, further model runs to investigate alternative solutions should probably be conducted (see Chapter 12 on sensitivity analysis).

BOX 4.1   Alternative Interpretations of Shadow Costs

(a) Shadow costs indicate by how much the objective function value of an activity would have to improve before the activity would be selected as part of the optimal solution.

(b) Shadow costs represent the rate of worsening of the objective function that would occur if an activity was forced into the solution. This interpretation may only be valid for small levels of the activity.

Different Interpretation for Maximization and Minimization Problems

The preceding discussion relates to maximization problems like Examples 3.1 and 4.1. In problems where the objective is to minimize something (e.g., costs or distance traveled), the interpretation of shadow costs is a little different. For both maximization and minimization problems, the shadow cost gives the *improvement* in objective function required for an activity to be selected. In a maximization problem an improvement means a larger or more positive objective value, while in a minimization problem an improvement means a smaller or more negative value. This is discussed further in the examples given in Chapter 5.

Finally, it should be noted that shadow costs go by a variety of names. In different texts and different computer packages they may be referred to as marginal costs, reduced costs, opportunity costs, implicit costs, dual values, dual costs, or even (to really confuse matters) shadow prices.

4.4   CONSTRAINT SLACKS

Most productive processes use a range of resource types; LP models of these processes would include at least one constraint for each resource. There is no reason to expect that for any particular problem, the optimal solution will involve using up all available stocks of all resources. It may be that the most profitable strategy leaves some unused resources: some idle workers, some underutilized machinery or some unexploited borrowing capacity. If the optimal solution does not use up all resources, the solution will include *slack* for the unused resources.

In setting up the matrix we allow for the possibility of slack resources by specifying that resources use must be *less than or equal* to resource availability rather than strictly *equal to* resource availability. This is because use of less-than constraints means that our choices are not unnecessarily restricted. For example, Figure 3.3 provides a graphical illustration of how equals constraints can dramatically reduce the range of feasible solutions available.

In Table 4.3 there are two constraints with slack in the optimal solution: *Wood chips* and *Chlorine*. The slack value for the *Wood chips* constraint indicates that 14 of the available 56 tonnes of wood chips per day are not required. We can easily check that this makes sense. Remember that each tonne of writing paper uses 2 tonnes of wood chips. The solution in Table 4.3 contains 21 tonnes of writing paper and no computer paper, so total wood chip use is 42 tonnes per day, leaving 14 unused.

This slack can be seen in Figure 4.2. The optimal solution at point A includes 21 tonnes of writing paper and zero tonnes of computer paper. The fact that the *Wood chips* constraint does not pass through point A indicates that the constraint is not "binding," that is, it does not affect the solution, as there are more wood chips available than are needed. Remember that the line marking the boundary of the woodchips constraint indicates all combinations of writing paper and computer paper for which all the available wood chips are used up. On the side of the line containing the point (0, 0), the amount of wood chips required is less than the available amount, while on the other side, requirements exceed the available level.

The distance between point A and the *Wood chips* constraint indicates how much slack there is. The vertical distance, AC, is 7 tonnes of writing paper. This means that if all the slack wood chips were used to produce writing paper, there would be enough for 7 tonnes of it. (Of course, the slack wood chips cannot actually be used to make 7 extra tonnes of writing paper because there are not enough workers available.) Remember that each tonne of writing paper requires two tonnes of wood chips, so there must be 14 tonnes of wood chips. This is consistent with the solution in Table 4.3.

If instead all the slack wood chips were used to make computer paper, there would be sufficient for 7 tonnes of it (the horizontal distance AD is 7 tonnes of computer paper). Again this is consistent with there being 14 tonnes of slack wood chips, as each tonne of computer paper requires 2 tonnes of wood chips.

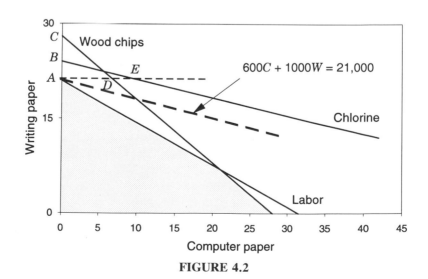

FIGURE 4.2

If a resource constraint has zero slack, it means that all available stocks of this resource are used up in the process of implementing the optimal solution. As noted earlier, constraints with zero slacks are often described as being "binding," meaning that they are actively constraining the model to the current optimal solution. If a resource constraint is binding, increasing the availability of the resource will probably make it possible to select an improved optimal solution. For exceptions to this generalization see the section in Chapter 10 on degeneracy.

Of course, constraints other than those representing resources can also have slack. In Table 4.3, the chlorine constraint, representing a legal upper limit, has slack. In fact Figure 4.2 shows that in this problem, the *Chlorine* constraint must always have slack. This is because the wood chip and labor constraints limit the levels of paper production to such low levels that emitted chlorine levels are environmentally safe, even without legal intervention. The amount of slack is enough to allow production of *AB* units of writing paper or *AE* units of computer paper. The chlorine constraint states that there must not be more than 24 kg of chlorine residues released per day, but the highest level of chlorine residues that is consistent with the other two constraints is 21 kg at point *A*, the current optimal solution. This is less than the maximum level by 3 kg, which is the slack shown in Table 4.3.

The level of slack on a constraint depends on what the selected activity levels are. In Figure 4.2 it is obvious that the amount of slack on the *Chlorine* constraint is going to depend on whether the optimal solution is at point *A* or one of the other two extreme points. The slack value that is printed by the LP computer package is the slack *at the current optimal solution*. The only way to make it print the slack values at some other solution is to manipulate it (with constraints or changes in the objective function) so that the solution of interest becomes the *optimal* solution.

The previous discussion on slack relates to less-than constraints. It should be noted that slack values mean different things for less-than and greater-than constraints. For a less-than constraint the slack is the amount by which the limit value has been undershot. In a resource constraint the slack is the amount by which total resource use is less than total availability of the resource. On the other hand, for a greater-than constraint the slack represents the amount by which the limit has been exceeded. This difference is easy to remember. By definition the limit in a less-than constraint cannot be exceeded, so any slack must represent a shortfall. Conversely, the limit of a greater-than constraint cannot be undershot, so a slack value implies that the limit has been exceeded. In either case, a positive slack means that the constraint is not binding.

To illustrate a greater-than constraint with slack, consider the matrix in Table 4.5 (which was originally shown in Table 3.3). This is similar to the original matrix for the paper mill problem (Example 3.1) except that it also includes a *Contract* constraint limiting production of computer paper to at least 5 tonnes per day. The problem is graphed in Figure 4.3 with the optimal solution indicated by the point of tangency of the dashed objective function line with the

TABLE 4.5   Matrix for Example 3.1 with Extra Contract Constraint for 5 Tonnes of Computer Paper

	Computer (tonnes)	Writing (tonnes)	Type	Limit
Objective ($)	600	1000	max	
Labor (days)	4	6	≤	126
Wood chips (tonnes)	2	2	≤	56
Chlorine (kg)	0.2857	1.5	≤	24
Contract (tonnes)	1		≥	5

shaded feasible region. The computer output for this optimal solution is given in Table 4.6.

The constraint sets the minimum level of computer paper at 5.0 tonnes, but the actual level is 10.5, so the slack is $10.5 - 5.0 = 5.5$. Thus the optimal solution in Table 4.6 includes a slack of 5.5 on the *Contract* constraint, which means that the optimal solution includes 5.5 tonnes of computer paper in excess of what would be required to just satisfy the *Contract* constraint.

This slack can be seen in Figure 4.3. The optimal solution of 10.5 tonnes of computer paper and 14 tonnes of writing paper is the point where the dashed objective function line is tangent to the shaded feasible region. The optimal level of computer paper is to the right of the line indicating the border of the contract constraint. The border represents the minimum allowable level of computer paper. The difference between the actual level of computer paper and the minimum level according to the contract constraint is 5.5 tonnes. This is the level of slack for the constraint.

The distance between the point representing the optimal solution and any

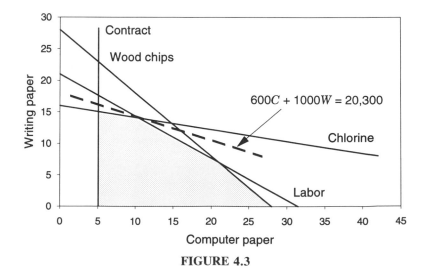

FIGURE 4.3

TABLE 4.6 Optimal Solution for Matrix in Table 4.5

Objective function value: 20,300.000000
Problem direction: max

Activity		Level	Shadow Cost
1 Computer	A	10.5000	0.0000
2 Writing	A	14.0000	0.0000

Constraint		Slack	Shadow Price
1 Labor	L	0.0000	143.3333
2 Wood chips	L	7.0000	0.0000
3 Chlorine	L	0.0000	93.3333
4 Contract	G	5.5000	0.0000

particular constraint line reflects the level of slack. In the optimal solution illustrated in Figure 4.3, all the available workers are used and the maximum allowable level of chlorine residues is produced. Thus there is no slack on either of these constraints (see the zero slacks in Table 4.6) and the optimal solution sits on the border of each constraint. By contrast the borders of the *Contract* and *Wood chip* constraints do not intersect with the optimal solution. Table 4.6 shows that these are the constraints with positive slack.

Note that any constraint with positive slack is not influencing the optimal solution. If either or both of the wood chip and contract constraints were removed from the model in Figure 4.3, the optimal solution would be unchanged. The feasible region would be increased by deleting the constraint, but the point where the highest objective function line intersected with the new feasible region would be unchanged.

Consider what the feasible region would be if both the *Contract* and *Wood chip* constraints were deleted. From this, it should be clear that the optimal solution would not change. Remember that the optimal solution is the point at which the highest possible objective function line is tangent to the feasible region and that as the objective function is moved outward its slope is unchanged.

There has been no mention of ''equals'' constraints in the preceding discussion of slack. The situation for equals constraints is different again from that for less-than and greater-than constraints because, by definition, equals constraints must be exactly met. Consequently any equals constraint in a valid solution can never have any slack; the output for any optimal solution will always show that each equals constraint has a slack of zero.

Some LP computer packages allow you to print out the best solution found so far if the package is unable to find a valid optimal solution. In these circumstances there could be slack on an equals constraint. If there is, it means that the constraint is not satisfied in the corresponding solution. Of course, this means that an optimal feasible solution was not found. You should not attempt to draw any management conclusions from these outputs of nonoptimal solutions. They are provided merely to assist in debugging.

On the other hand, if a computer package claims to have found an optimal solution but the solution includes an equals constraint with nonzero slack, it means that an undetected error has occurred in the program. This is not unheard of. There are some rather famous cases of supposedly reliable commercial LP packages on large mainframe computers giving incorrect results. This is not very likely with a commercially available package, but you should not dismiss altogether the possibility of there being bugs in the program if it is giving nonsensical results, but be cautious about jumping to conclusions. Experience shows that the majority of the "bugs" identified by users are from user error, not hardware or software problems. Chapter 11 deals in detail with the issue of preventing, diagnosing, and correcting bugs.

Finally, note that the intepretation of constraint slack is not affected by whether the objective is to maximize or minimize something.

BOX 4.2   Interpretations of Constraint Slack

Less-than Constraint Slack

The amount by which the constraint limit exceeds the actual level of the constrained factor in the optimal solution. For resource constraints this indicates that unused part of the resource.

Greater-than Constraint Slack

The amount by which the constraint limit has been exceeded by the level of the constrained factor in the optimal solution.

Equals Constraint Slack

By definition, equals constraints must be exactly met. Consequently any equals constraint in a valid solution can never have any slack.

4.5 CONSTRAINT SHADOW PRICES

Shadow prices (which are referred to in some other texts as marginal values or dual prices) indicate the effect on the objective function of a small change in a constraint limit. A shadow price can be interpreted either as the rate of improvement in the objective function if a constraint limit is relaxed slightly, or as the rate of the worsening of the objective function if a constraint limit is tightened slightly. Whichever of these interpretations you use, the shadow price gives the effect of a change in the constraint limit on the objective function after all necessary changes and all desirable changes to the solution have been made.

As with constraint slacks, interpretation of shadow prices is different for greater-than and less-than constraints, and equals constraints are something of a special case. Interpretation is also different depending on whether the problem is a maximization or a minimization. In a maximization problem, an improvement in the objective function is obviously an increase, while in a minimization problem, an improvement is a decrease. The interpretation of shadow prices is illustrated below for each of these different circumstances.

First consider aspects of shadow prices that do not depend on the constraint type or the direction of optimization (maximization or minimization). The first point to note is that the relationship between constraint slacks and shadow prices is similar to that between activity levels and shadow costs. At least one must be zero, so that if one is not zero the other *must* be zero. This is illustrated in Table 4.6, where there are zero levels of slack for *Labor* and *Chlorine*. These constraints have shadow prices of $143.33 and $93.33, respectively. On the other hand, the *Wood chips* and *Contract* constraints have nonzero slacks and so each has a zero shadow price.

The reason for this pattern is quite logical. If a less-than constraint has a positive* slack, it means that the maximum level has not been reached. In this case, if the maximum level for the constraint is changed a little, it makes no difference to the fact that the maximum level has been undershot; if the change in constraint limit is not too great, it will still be undershot. Consequently, the change can have no effect on the optimal solution. Thus the shadow price, which indicates the effect on the optimal objective function value of a small change in the constraint limit, must be zero.

Similarly, a positive slack on a greater-than constraint signifies that the minimum level has been exceeded, so very small variations in the minimum level again have no effect on the solution, resulting in a zero shadow price. If there is some slack for a constraint, small changes in the constraint limit affect nothing except the level of slack.

On the other hand, if either type of constraint has a zero slack, it indicates that the constraint is "binding" in the optimal solution. It is directly affecting the choice of activities and the value of the objective function. In this case, any change in the constraint limit will change the optimal solution and the objective function value. The amount of change in the objective function per unit change in the constraint limit is reported in the shadow price.

To illustrate, the *Contract* constraint in Table 4.6 has a zero shadow price and a slack of 5.5 tonnes. As Figure 4.3 shows, the limit of the constraint would have to increase by 5.5 before it could cause any change in the optimal solution, which is currently at the point (*Computer*, *Writing*) = (10.5, 14.0). Smaller changes in the limit of the *Contract* constraint would move the contract constraint in Figure 4.3, but it would remain to the left of the current optimal

---

*As with shadow costs, some LP computer packages show constraint slacks as negative numbers.

solution. Although the feasible region would be affected, the optimal solution, as indicated by the point where the objective function line is tangent to the feasible region, would not change. Hence the shadow price is zero.

By contrast, the *Labor* constraint in Figure 4.3 *is* binding. This means, first, that it has zero slack and, second, that any change in the availability of workers would have a direct impact on the optimal solution. This is why the *Labor* constraint has a shadow price other than zero. The effect on the objective function of a change in the constraint limit for labor is $143.33 per unit change in the availability of labor (see Table 4.6).

Shadow Prices Are for Marginal Changes

Shadow prices are similar to shadow costs in that they represent the results of *marginal* (i.e., very small or incremental) changes. Although we referred earlier to changing the constraint limit by one unit, it may not be possible to change the constraint limit by a full unit without another constraint having an effect on the solution. If the constraint is made less binding, a constraint that previously was not binding may become binding. If the constraint is made more binding, another constraint that previously was binding may become slack. If either of these cases occurs when the constraint limit is changed by one unit, the shadow price does not apply to a change of a full unit.

This is illustrated in Figure 4.4. Suppose the initial model includes three less-than constraints: 1, 2*b*, and 3. Given the slope of the objective function in this hypothetical model, the optimal solution is at point *B*. Now suppose constraint 2*b* is replaced in the model by 2*c*. Constraint 2*c* is similar to 2*b* except that the constraint limit has been increased (relaxed) by one unit. Fol-

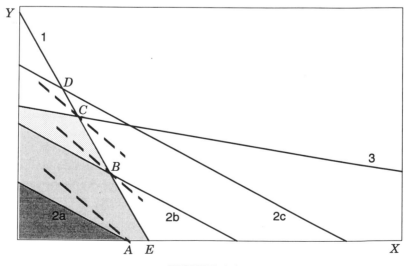

FIGURE 4.4

lowing this relaxation, constraint 3 becomes limiting and the new optimal solution is at point C. There is now slack on constraint $2c$ since the combination of feasible regions for the other two constraints (1 and 3) does not include point D, which is the point that would have been optimal if not for the existence of constraint 3.

The difference in objective function values between points B and D would equal the shadow price on constraint $2b$. This is so because the movement of constraint 2 from $2b$ to $2c$ is the result of changing the constraint limit by a full unit. However, the influence of constraint 3 means that it is not possible to move to point D, so the result of the one-unit change in the constraint limit will be less than would be expected from the shadow price.

Suppose instead that constraint 2 is tightened, reducing the constraint limit by one unit. The new constraint would be $2a$ and the new optimal solution in this case is at point A. Notice that in this case there is now slack on both constraints 1 and 3. The implicit constraint that no activity can take a negative value means that it is not possible to move along constraint 1 to the point where it intersects with constraint $2a$. If this *was* possible, the difference in objective function value between that point and point b would again have equaled the shadow price of constraint 2. However, with the intervention of the X axis, the actual reduction in objective function value would be greater than indicated by the shadow price.

Overall, shadow prices apply to changes in constraint limits that are not so great as to cause any change in the "optimal basis." The optimal basis is a set that includes all activities that are part of the optimal solution and all constraints that are slack. From this you can see that the original shadow price for point B would be valid only for changes in the constraint limit of constraint 2 that were not so great as to make the optimal solution lie outside the range C to E. Between C and E the optimal basis includes activity X, activity Y, and constraint 3. Loosening constraint 2 beyond point C would cause constraint 2 to be slack so it would become part of the basis. Constraint 3 would become binding and so would leave the basis. On the other hand, tightening constraint 2 beyond point E would cause constraint 1 to become slack and enter the basis. Whenever any activity or constraint enters or leaves the optimal basis, the set of shadow prices changes.

It is often possible to change a constraint limit by many units without changing the optimal basis. In such a case, the shadow price for the constraint applies to each unit change in the constraint limit. For example, provided the optimal basis does not change, the effect of a five-unit change in a constraint limit is five times the shadow price of the constraint. Similarly, the effect of a 2.75 unit change in a constraint limit is 2.75 times the shadow price. It is possible to tell the range of constraint limit values within which the shadow price is unchanged using "range analysis" output. This is covered in Chapter 9.

The other comments made earlier about interpretation of activity shadow costs also apply to the interpretation of shadow prices. Shadow prices are calculated subject to the other constraints of the problem still being met. They only apply if there are not other simultaneous changes to the model structure or parameters. If a coefficient, constraint limit, or objective function value changes, the shadow price of any given constraint can change.

Maximization Problem

Now consider the interpretation of the different types of constraints in a maximization problem. Recall that, in general, shadow prices give the *improvement* in the objective function if a constraint limit is *relaxed* by one unit. For a less-than constraint the shadow price indicates the *increase* in the objective-function value that would occur if the constraint limit were *increased* by one unit. This is consistent with the general rule cited earlier: for a maximization problem an "improvement" is an increase in the objective function, and for a less-than constraint, "relaxing" the constraint means increasing the constraint limit. An increase in the latter constraint limit increases the number of potential solutions that satisfy the constraint, so the constraint is said to be relaxed or less strict than it was before the increase.

The same shadow price also represents the *worsening* of the objective function if a constraint limit is *tightened* by one unit. For a less-than constraint in a maximization problem, this is the *reduction* of the objective function value if the constraint limit is *decreased* by one unit.

To illustrate, the *Labor* constraint in Table 4.6 has zero slack, indicating that all the available workers are used up. The shadow price for labor is $143.33, which means that if an extra worker were available, daily profits would be increased by $143.33. Alternatively if a worker did not show up (due to illness, for example), profits would be reduced by $143.33 for that day.

It is important to recognize that the shadow cost is calculated on the assumption that the relaxation of the constraint limit could be obtained at no cost or that the tightening of the constraint has no direct offsetting benefits. For example, the cost of hiring the extra worker for a day is not included, and it is assumed that the pay of an absent worker is not withheld. Thus the shadow price does not indicate the change in *net* returns resulting from a change in the constraint limit. What it does give, however, is an indication of the maximum amount worth paying for an extra unit of the resource or to prevent the loss of a unit of a resource. In the labor example, an extra day of work increases returns by $143.33, so if extra workers can be hired for any amount less than $143.33 per day, net profits will be increased. However, if a worker costs more than $143.33 per day, it is not worth hiring anyone.

It is also important to understand that shadow prices calculated by the LP package account for all changes in the optimal solution that would result from the changed constraint limit. These include all desirable changes and all necessary changes. In Example 3.1, an increase in labor availability would make possible the desirable change of an increase in production of computer paper. However, the *Chlorine* constraint would mean that such an increase could only be achieved if the level of writing paper was reduced somewhat to offset the resulting increase in chlorine output. The shadow price of $143.33 for *Labor*

TABLE 4.7 Matrix for Example 3.1 with Contract Constraint for 15 Tonnes of Computer Paper

	Computer (tonnes)	Writing (tonnes)	Type	Limit
Objective ($)	600	1000	max	
Labor (days)	4	6	≤	126
Wood chips (tonnes)	2	2	≤	56
Chlorine (kg)	0.2857	1.5	≤	24
Contract (tonnes)	1		≥	15

includes both the positive and negative aspects of changing the constraint limit in question.

The sign of a greater-than constraint's shadow price is different from that for a less-than constraint's because they act in opposite direction. Unlike a less-than constraint, to *relax* a greater-than constraint means to *reduce* its constraint limit, and to *tighten* a greater-than constraint means to *increase* its constraint limit. Thus the absolute value of the shadow price for a greater-than constraint shows how much the objective function improves after a reduction in the constraint limit, or reduces following an increase in the constraint limit. This is illustrated in the following example.

Suppose that the paper mill enters into a new contract that requires it to provide at least 15 tonnes of computer paper. This is clearly going to change the solution because previously the optimal level of computer paper was only 10.5 tonnes. With this change, the contract constraint becomes binding. The revised matrix is shown in Table 4.7, while Table 4.8 shows the optimal solution for this matrix.

The shadow price for the contract constraint is −$66.67, which means that if the contract constraint limit is increased by one tonne, the objective function will worsen by $66.67. Alternatively, if the constraint limit is reduced by one tonne, the objective function will improve by $66.67.

The negative* value of the shadow price for a greater-than constraint indicates that an increase in the constraint limit of a greater-than constraint has the opposite effect of an increase in the limit of a less-than constraint. Thus, increasing the constraint limit of a less-than constraint loosens the constraint and may allow a higher objective function value, while increasing the constraint limit for a greater-than constraint reduces the size of the feasible set. This cannot improve the objective function value and may make it worse.

Understanding the difference between shadow prices for less-than and greater-than constraints is useful for determining what effect an equals constraint has on the solution. As noted previously, an equals constraint must have no slack. There are three possibilities for its shadow price. If it is acting as a less-than

---

*In this book, shadow prices for less-than constraints are positive, while shadow prices for greater-than constraints are negative. In some computer packages this convention is reversed.

TABLE 4.8   Optimal Solution for Matrix in Table 4.7

Objective function value: 20,000.000000
Problem direction: max

Activity		Level	Shadow Cost
1 Computer	A	15.0000	0.0000
2 Writing	A	11.0000	0.0000

Constraint		Slack	Shadow Price
1 Labor	L	0.0000	166.6667
2 Wood chips	L	4.0000	0.0000
3 Chlorine	L	3.2143	0.0000
4 Contract	G	0.0000	−66.6667

constraint, keeping activity levels below their otherwise optimal levels, the equals constraint will have a positive shadow price just like a less-than constraint. If the equals constraint is acting as a greater-than, increasing activity levels, it will have a negative shadow price like a greater-than constraint. In rare circumstances, it is possible for an equals constraint to have a zero shadow price. One requirement for this is that the optimal solution would be unchanged even if the equals constraint was removed. Even in this circumstance, however, the shadow price will usually not be zero.

When an equals constraint has a zero shadow price, it does not mean that changes in the limit of the equals constraint would have no effect on the solution. If the constraint limit is increased or decreased, the constraint is likely to start affecting the solution.

When an equals constraint does have a zero shadow price, we get the relatively unusual result of zero slack and zero shadow price. (Remember that equals constraints always have zero slack.) It is also possible for less-than and greater-than constraints to have both zero slacks and zero shadow prices (see Chapter 10). However, it is not possible in LP for any type of constraint to have nonzero values simultaneously for both slack and shadow price.

Suppose that the *Contract* constraint of Table 4.7 is an equals constraint instead of greater-than. How is the optimal solution affected? Not at all, because even when the constraint is specified as a greater-than, there is no slack in the optimal solution. The optimal solution for this scenario is the same as Table 4.8 except that *Contract* is an equals constraint.

Suppose also that the objective function coefficient for computer paper is increased from $600/tonne to $800/tonne. Table 4.9 shows the revised matrix. The feasible region and optimal solution for this model were shown graphically in Figure 3.3. The complete optimal solution is shown in Table 4.10.

Because the *Contract* constraint is now an equals it has zero slack. The shadow price in this example is positive $133.33 (rather than −66.6667, as in Table 4.8). This indicates that the constraint is now behaving like a less-than

TABLE 4.9 Matrix for Example 3.1 with Equals Contract Constraint and Higher Profit for Computer Paper

	Computer (tonnes)	Writing (tonnes)	Type	Limit
Objective ($)	800	1000	max	
Labor (days)	4	6	≤	126
Wood chips (tonnes)	2	2	≤	56
Chlorine (kg)	0.2857	1.5	≤	24
Contract (tonnes)	1		=	15

constraint; increases in the constraint limit would improve the objective function.

If the model did not include the contract constraint and the objective-function value for computer paper was 600, the optimal level of computer paper would be less than 15. Consequently, an equals constraint for the contract would behave like a greater-than constraint and would therefore have a negative shadow price, just like all binding greater-than constraints (Table 4.8). However, if the objective function value for computer paper was increased to 800, the preferred level of computer paper would be greater than 15 tonnes. Hence a constraint limiting computer paper to exactly 15 tonnes would behave as a less-than constraint and have a positive shadow price (Table 4.10).

Minimization Problem

So far this discussion of shadow prices has focused on their interpretation for a maximization problem. In a minimization problem a shadow price still represents "the improvement in the objective function if a constraint limit is relaxed by one unit." However, in a minimization problem an improvement

TABLE 4.10 Optimal Solution Matrix in Table 4.9

Objective function value: 23,000.000000
Problem direction: max

Activity		Level	Shadow Cost
1 Computer	A	15.0000	0.0000
2 Writing	A	11.0000	0.0000

Constraint		Slack	Shadow Price
1 Labor	L	0.0000	166.6667
2 Wood chips	L	4.0000	0.0000
3 Chlorine	L	3.2143	0.0000
4 Contract	E	0.0000	133.3333

is a *decrease* in the objective function value. Similarly, the interpretation of a shadow price as "the worsening of the objective function if a constraint limit is tightened by one unit" is still valid, but now a worsening of the objective function is an increase.

In practice the main use of shadow price is to estimate the value of obtaining extra units of a resource. Further examples of shadow-price interpretation are presented in Chapter 5 when we look at output for a number of examples. For further practical advice on interpretation of shadow prices, see Greenberg (1993a, 1993b).

BOX 4.3   Interpretations of Shadow Prices

In General

The rate of change in the objective function if a constraint limit is changed. A shadow price gives the change in the objective function per unit change in the constraint limit after all necessary changes and all desirable changes to the activity levels have been made. It may only apply to marginal or incremental changes in the constraint limit.

Maximization Problems

(a) Less-than constraints have *positive* shadow prices that represent the rate of *increase* in the objective function value per unit *increase* in the constraint limit, or the rate of *decrease* in the objective function value per unit *decrease* in the constraint limit.

(b) Greater-than constraints have *negative* shadow prices that represent the rate of *increase* in the objective function value per unit *decrease* in the constraint limit, or the rate of *decrease* in the objective function value per unit *increase* in the constraint limit.

(c) Equals constraints: either (a) or (b), depending on whether the equals constraint is acting as a greater-than or as a less-than constraint.

Minimization Problems

(a) Less-than constraints have *positive* shadow prices that represent the rate of *decrease* in the objective function value per unit *increase* in the constraint limit, or the rate of *increase* in the objective function value per unit *decrease* in the constraint limit.

(b) Greater-than constraints have *negative* shadow prices that represent the rate of *decrease* in the objective function value per unit *decrease* in the constraint limit, or the rate of *increase* in the objective function value per unit *increase* in the constraint limit.

(c) Equals constraints: either (a) or (b), depending on whether the equals constraint is acting as a greater-than or as a less-than constraint.

4.6 THE EFFECT OF DIFFERENT UNITS

Section 3.7 explained that the units used in matrix construction affect the interpretation of output. This section expands on this point. The reason for looking at units of measurement in so much detail is to stress how important it is to be very clear about which units are used for each activity and each constraint. Most of the errors made by people learning to use LP are from carelessness with units. The following discussion may help clarify the relationship between a matrix and the optimal solution output.

In Table 3.1 the *Wood chips* constraint is measured in tonnes:

$$(2 \times C) + (2 \times W) \leq 56$$

In Table 3.6, exactly the same constraint is measured in kilograms and represented as

$$(2000 \times C) + (2000 \times W) \leq 56,000$$

This is the only difference between the two matrices. In particular, note that computer paper (C) and writing paper (W) are measured in tonnes in each matrix.

The optimal solution for the original problem with wood chips measured in tonnes was shown in Table 4.1. The optimal solution with wood chips measured in kilograms is shown in Table 4.11. Clearly, these two outputs represent the same solution. The only difference between them is in the interpretation of the numbers.

The difference between the two outputs is that the slack for the wood chips constraint in Table 4.11 is 7000 compared with 7 in Table 4.1. In Table 4.11, because the constraint is now measured in kilograms, the slack represents the difference *in kilograms* between the constraint limit and the actual level of use

TABLE 4.11 Optimal Solution for Example 3.1 with Wood Chips Measured in Kilograms

Objective function value: 20,300.000000
Problem direction: max

Activity		Level	Shadow Cost
1 Computer	A	10.5000	0.0000
2 Writing	A	14.0000	0.0000

Constraint		Slack	Shadow Price
1 Labor	L	0.0000	143.3333
2 Wood chips	L	7000.0000	0.0000
3 Chlorine	L	0.0000	93.3333

TABLE 4.12   Optimal Solution for Example 3.1 with Labor Measured in Days

Objective function value: 20,300.000000
Problem direction: max

Activity		Level	Shadow Cost
1 Computer	A	10.5000	0.0000
2 Writing	A	14.0000	0.0000

Constraint		Slack	Shadow Price
1 Labor	L	0.0000	17.9166
2 Wood chips	L	7.0000	0.0000
3 Chlorine	L	0.0000	93.3333

of wood chips. In Table 4.1 the slack represents the difference *in tonnes*. Clearly the 7000 kg of slack in Table 4.11 is equivalent to the 7 tonnes of slack in Table 4.1.

The shadow price of the *Wood chips* constraints is zero in both cases. However, if a constraint with a nonzero shadow price is scaled (i.e., if its unit of measurement is changed), the shadow price *is* affected. To illustrate, suppose that labor is to be measured in hours instead of days, there being eight working hours in a day. The coefficients of the *Labor* constraint would be multiplied by eight. Table 4.12 shows the output for this revised model. The shadow price has been reduced by a factor of 8. The shadow price still indicates the value of obtaining an extra unit of labor, but now an extra unit is only an extra hour instead of an extra day, so the shadow price is reduced accordingly.

Notice that the effect on the shadow price of changing the unit of measurement for a constraint is the opposite to its effect on constraint slacks. Using a smaller unit of measurement increases the slack but reduces the shadow price. Also notice that changing the unit for a constraint only affects the output for that constraint. All other activities and constraints are unaffected.

Changing activity units also affects the output for activities. The generalizations noted earlier also apply to activities: the effect of a unit change is the opposite for activity levels and shadow costs, and it only affects the output for the particular activity for which the unit has been changed.

Consider again the matrix in Table 4.2 and its associated output in Table 4.3. Suppose that the computer paper and writing paper activities are both to be measured in kilograms instead of tonnes. The output is shown in Table 4.13. The level of writing paper has been multiplied by 1000 compared to Table 4.3, because the levels now indicate the number of kilograms of each type of paper instead of the number of tonnes.

On the other hand, decreasing the unit of measurement from tonnes to kilograms reduces the shadow cost of an activity. In the case of a profit maximization problem, the shadow cost indicates how much the profit per unit would need to increase before the activity would be selected. If you are using a smaller unit of measurement, you need a smaller profit increase per unit. For

TABLE 4.13 Optimal Solution for Example 4.1 with Computer Paper and Writing Paper Measured in Kilograms

Objective function value: 21,000.000000
Problem direction: max

Activity		Level	Shadow Cost
1 Computer	Z	0.0000	0.0667
2 Writing	A	21000.0000	0.0000

Constraint		Slack	Shadow Price
1 Labor	L	0.0000	166.6667
2 Wood chips	L	14.0000	0.0000
3 Chlorine	L	3.0000	0.0000

example $1 per kg is equivalent to $1000 per tonne. Similarly, the $66.67 per tonne shadow cost in Table 4.3 is equivalent to the $0.0667/kg shadow cost in Table 4.13.

BOX 4.4 Effects on Output of Changing Units of Measurement

Activities

A larger unit of measurement (e.g., tonnes instead of kilograms, miles instead of feet) will:

(a) Decrease the numeric magnitude of the activity level.
(b) Increase the numeric magnitude of the shadow cost.

Constraints

A larger unit of measurement (e.g., tonnes of kilograms, miles instead of feet) will:

(a) Decrease the numeric magnitude of the constraint slack.
(b) Increase the numeric magnitude of the shadow price.

In all cases the magnitude of the effect on output values is the same as the magnitude of the change in units of measurement. For example, if the units of an activity are multiplied by a number X (i.e., the coefficients in the relevant column of the matrix are multiplied by X), the optimal level of the activity is multiplied by X and its shadow cost by $1/X$. If the units of a constraint are multiplied by a number Y (i.e., the coefficients in the relevant row of the matrix are multiplied by $1/Y$), its slack is multiplied by $1/Y$ and its shadow price by Y.

4.7 KEY POINTS

- There are two main sections to the output from an LP package: activity output and constraint output.
- The "level" of an activity indicates the amount of the activity in the optimal solution.
- The "shadow cost" of an activity indicates how far it is from entering the optimal solution.
- Alternatively, a shadow cost indicates the worsening of the objective function that would occur if an activity was forced into the solution.
- Care is needed when interpreting shadow costs because (a) shadow costs apply only to small ("marginal") changes in the strategy or plan, (b) they only apply if a single change is made at a time, and (c) the solution may be degenerate.
- The slack of a constraint is the difference between the constraint's limit and its actual level in the solution.
- The "shadow price" of a constraint indicates the change in objective function value per unit change in the constraint limit. This is particularly useful for indicating the gross value of extra units of a resource.
- Like shadow costs, shadow prices also (a) only apply to small ("marginal") changes in the strategy or plan, and (b) generally only apply if a single change is made at a time.
- If the units of an activity are multiplied by a number X (i.e., the coefficients in the relevant column of the matrix are multiplied by X), the optimal level of the activity is multiplied by X and its shadow cost by $1/X$.
- If the units of a constraint are multiplied by a number Y (i.e., the coefficients in the relevant row of the matrix are multiplied by $1/Y$), the slack of the constraint is multiplied by $1/Y$ and its shadow price by Y.

CHAPTER 5

EXAMPLES AND EXERCISES

Example 5.1: Crop Selection

A farmer has 10 hectares (ha) in which to grow potatoes and/or tomatoes in the combination that will yield greatest profits. A contract has been signed by the farmer in which a purchaser guarantees to buy the produce from 2 ha of tomatoes. After meeting other commitments, the farmer has enough labor available to spend 12 hours a week on the area. Each hectare of potatoes requires 2 hours of labor per week, while tomatoes require only 0.5 hour per week/ha. Potatoes give gross returns (before deducting costs) of $400/ha, while tomatoes give $300/ha. Fertilizer costs $100/tonne and must be applied at the following rates: 1 tonne/ha for potatoes and 0.5 tonne/ha for tomatoes. The farmer requires that there must be no land left unused. ■

The first step is to be sure you understand all aspects of the problem definition. Secondly, identify the objective. The problem definition states that the farmer wants to grow the combination that will "yield greatest profits," so the objective is to maximize profits. Coefficients in the *Objective* row will be profits from each activity. Costs and returns are given in dollars, so this is a suitable unit to use for the objective row.

Now in step (c) identify the activities. Activities are the variables for which you want to select optimal levels. They should be under the decision maker's control (exceptions to this are given in later chapters). The two most obvious candidates in the problem definition are the area of potatoes and the area of tomatoes. But we also want to know the optimal level of fertilizer and the optimal level of profit. Should these be variables too? They do not need to be, because the level of profit will be counted by the objective function row and, because of the way the problem is defined, the level of fertilizer follows automatically from the areas of potatoes and tomatoes. Fertilizer itself is not a decision variable. So there are two activities that we will name *Potatoes* and *Tomatoes*. We want to know the optimal area for each, so use hectares as the units.

Step (d) is to identify constraints. One obvious constraint on how many hectares of potatoes and/or tomatoes can be grown is the availability of land. Let us call this constraint *Land* and measure it in hectares. The farmer requires that there be no unused land, so the *Land* constraint must be an equals, signifying that the use of land must exactly equal its availability. In words, the *Land* constraint specifies that the area of tomatoes plus the area of potatoes must equal 10 ha.

Because of the forward sale contract, the solution must be constrained to include at least 2 ha of tomatoes. Call this constraint *Contract*. As the constraint is expressed in hectares, these will be suitable units for the matrix. The contract is not for exclusive rights to this farmer's tomatoes, so the constraint type is greater-than. The *Contract* constraint means that the area of tomatoes must be greater than or equal to 2 ha.

The availability of labor is another constraint on what can be selected. A suitable name is *Labor* and we will measure it in hours per week. It would be possible to use less than 12 hours a week but not more, so the constraint is a less-than. (The problem definition does not allow for the possibility of hiring extra workers, so assume that it is not available.) In words, the *Labor* constraint specifies that the total labor requirement of the plan must be less than or equal to 12 hours per week.

Concluding step (d), the final candidate for a constraint is fertilizer. However, the problem definition does not specify that there is a limit on the availability of fertilizer, so it seems reasonable to assume that there is enough fertilizer available to cover the area, regardless of the areas of potatoes and tomatoes. If fertilizer does not limit any activity, it does not need to be a constraint, but if it is not a constraint and not an activity, how does it influence the solution to the problem? The answer is that it affects the profitability and thus the objective function coefficient of each activity. The cost of fertilizer will be accounted for when we calculate the values of the objective function coefficients.

Step (e) in the suggested strategy is to organize the row and column names, units, and constraint types into a matrix ready for coefficients to be included. Such a matrix is shown in Table 5.1.

Finally, step (f) is to quantify matrix coefficients.

Objective

For each activity, determine net profit per unit of the activity by subtracting the cost of fertilizer from the gross returns. For potatoes the gross returns are

TABLE 5.1   Empty Matrix for Example 5.1

	Potatoes (ha)	Tomatoes (ha)	Type	Limit
Objective ($)			max	
Land (ha)			=	
Contract (ha)			≥	
Labor (h/week)			≤	

$400 per hectare and the cost of fertilizer is 1 (tonne per ha) times $100 (per tonne). Thus the objective function coefficient is $400 − (1 × $100) = $300. For tomatoes the value is $300 − (0.5 × $100) = $250.

Land

Each hectare of potatoes or tomatoes uses one hectare of land, so the land coefficient for each activity is 1. The constraint limit on land is 10 ha since exactly 10 ha must be used. After entering these values into the matrix, check that the constraint in the matrix accurately represents the verbal statement of the constraint given earlier: "the area of tomatoes plus the area of potatoes must equal the available area of 10 ha." It is perhaps easiest to check that the constraint in the matrix does represent this by writing it in algebraic form:

$$(1 \times P) + (1 \times T) = 10$$

where P represents the number of hectares of potatoes and T is the area in hectares of tomatoes. One times the number of units (hectares) of potatoes (P) is the area of potatoes and ($1 \times T$) is the area of tomatoes, so the left-hand side of this equation gives the "the area of tomatoes plus the area of potatoes." The right-hand side of the equation specifies that the left-hand side "must equal the available area of 10 ha," so the constraint as a whole does represent the correct thing.

Contract

Each hectare of tomatoes contributes one unit toward meeting the contract, so the contract coefficient for tomatoes is 1. Potatoes contribute nothing toward the contract, and so have a zero coefficient. The limit is the minimum area of tomatoes allowed under the contract: 2 ha. The constraint in the matrix requires that

$$(0 \times P) + (1 \times T) \geq 2$$

or

$$T \geq 2$$

which is consistent with our verbal definition that the area of tomatoes must be greater than or equal to 2 ha.

Labor

From the problem definition, potatoes and tomatoes require 2 and 0.5 hours of labor per week, respectively, so these are the *Labor* coefficients. The constraint limit on labor availability is specified as 12 hours per week. The algebraic version of the constraint is

$$(2 \times P) + (0.5 \times T) \leq 12$$

The verbal definition specified that "total labor requirement of the plan must be less than or equal to 12 hours per week." Since the left-hand side of the constraint gives the total labor requirement of the plan, the algebraic and verbal versions of the constraint are consistent.

The matrix with all these coefficients included is shown in Table 5.2.

In this example, checking the verbal constraint against the numerical version has been relatively easy and you may have felt that it was too obvious to be worth doing. However, when building larger matrices it is necessary to be very careful that you are representing what you intend to.

Optimal Solution

The optimal solution for Example 5.1 is shown in Table 5.3. In all these examples, the interpretation of the activity levels in the optimal solution is straightforward. In Example 5.1, the optimal area of potatoes is 4.6667 ha, while tomatoes should be grown on 5.333 ha. Given these optimal levels, the maximum achievable level of profit for this farmer from these 10 hectares is $2733.33. The optimal activity levels can be seen from the graph of this problem in Figure 5.1. The point where the dashed objective function line is tangent to the shaded feasible region corresponds with the optimal solution in Table 5.3.

In this example, both activities are "active," meaning that they are both included in the optimal solution at nonzero levels. Therefore they both have shadow costs of zero. How much would their profitabilities need to improve

TABLE 5.2   Completed Matrix for Example 5.1

	Potatoes (ha)	Tomatoes (ha)	Type	Limit
Objective ($)	300	250	max	
Land (ha)	1	1	=	10
Contract (ha)		1	≥	2
Labor (h/week)	2	0.5	≤	12

TABLE 5.3   Optimal Solution for Example 5.1

Objective function value: 2733.333333
Problem direction: max

Activity		Level	Shadow Cost
1 Potatoes	A	4.6667	0.0000
2 Tomatoes	A	5.3333	0.0000

Constraint		Slack	Shadow Price
1 Land	E	0.0000	233.3333
2 Contract	G	3.3333	0.0000
3 Labor	L	0.0000	33.3333

before they would be included in the optimal solution? Zero, as they are already included.

Only one of the constraints has any slack. Figure 5.1 shows that the constraints for land and labor are binding but that there are more tomatoes produced than would be needed to satisfy the contract constraint. The contract requires a minimum of 2 ha of tomatoes, but the actual solution contains 5.3333 ha, so the slack for the constraint is 3.3333. Because it is a greater-than constraint, the existence of slack indicates that the constraint limit has been exceeded.

If the constraint limit for land could be increased by one unit through the acquisition of more land, profit could be increased by \$233.33 for each extra hectare. This is the message of the shadow price of land. The cost of acquiring the extra land is not included in this figure, so it provides a useful indication of how much it might be worth paying for extra land. Similarly, extra workers

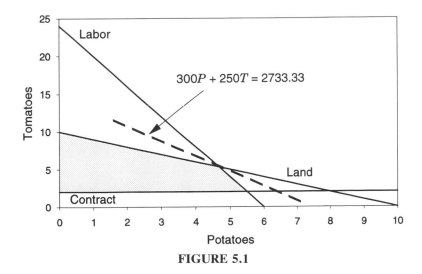

FIGURE 5.1

would increase gross returns at the rate of $33.33 per hour worked. If hired workers are available for less than this amount, they would be worth hiring.

Example 5.2: Musical Instrument Manufacture

A musical instrument maker wishes to plan production of violins and cellos for the coming year. Wood for the instruments has to be of the highest quality. For most parts of the instruments, adequate wood is available. However, the instrument maker is only able to obtain 4800 cubic centimeters (cm) of rosewood of sufficient quality for the fingerboards. Allowing for faults in the wood, wastage and offcuts, each violin fingerboard requires an average of 200 cubic cm of rosewood, while each cello fingerboard requires 1600 cubic cm. The other constraint on production is the instrument maker's available time in the year: 48 weeks. Production of a violin takes four weeks, while the much larger cello requires eight weeks per instrument. The instruments are very much in demand so profit per instrument is high at $2000 per violin and $8000 per cello. Construct a matrix to find how many violins and how many cellos should be produced to maximize profits given the limited availability of rosewood and time.   ∎

First, read the problem definition through carefully. Second, identify the objective. From the problem definition it is clear that the objective is to maximize profits. Coefficients in the *Objective* row will be profits from each activity. Costs and returns are given in dollars.

Now identify the activities. Activities are the variables for which the instrument maker wants to select optimal levels. The obvious candidates in the problem definition are the number of violins and the number of cellos. We also want to know the required levels of rosewood and labor and the optimal level of profit. Should these be decision variables too? They do not need to be because the level of profit will be counted by the objective row and the required levels of rosewood and labor follow automatically once the numbers of violins and cellos are selected. So there are two activities that we will name *Violins* and *Cellos*. We want to know the optimal numbers for each so use "numbers of instruments" for the unit of measurement.

The next step is to identify constraints. One constraint on the number of violins and cellos that can be produced is the availability of rosewood. Let us call this constraint *Rosewood* and measure it in cubic centimeters. In words, the rosewood constraint specifies that the total use of rosewood cannot exceed 4800 cubic cm (cm^3).

The availability of labor is also a constraint. A suitable name is *Labor*, and we will measure it in weeks per year. Note that the unit of measurement of labor is different here than in Example 5.1. In that example, because of the way the problem was presented it was most convenient to use hours per week as the unit. Here, weeks per year of labor is the most convenient unit. It would

TABLE 5.4 Empty Matrix for Example 5.2

	Violins (number)	Cellos (number)	Type	Limit
Objective ($)			max	
Rosewood (cm³)			≤	
Labor (weeks)			≤	

be possible to use less than 48 weeks of labor but not more (if the instrument maker is to have a four week holiday), so the constraint is a less-than. (There is no possibility of hiring extra workers with the necessary skills). In words, the *Labor* constraint specifies that total labor requirement of the plan must be less than or equal to 48 weeks of labor.

The next step is to organize the row and column names, units, and constraint types into a matrix ready for coefficients to be included. See the empty matrix in Table 5.4.

The final step is to quantify matrix coefficients.

Objective

For each activity, determine net profit per unit of the activity. In this example net profit per instrument is obvious since it is given in the problem definition: $2000 for violins and $8000 for cellos.

Labor

From the problem definition, violins and cellos require 4 and 8 weeks of labor, respectively, so these are the *Labor* coefficients. The constraint limit on labor availability is 48 weeks. The algebraic version of the constraint is

$$(4 \times V) + (8 \times C) \le 48$$

where V represents the number of violins produced in the year and C represents the annual number of cellos produced. The verbal definition specified that "total labor requirement of the plan must be less than or equal to 48 weeks of labor." Four times the number of violins plus eight times the number of cellos corresponds to the total labor requirement, so the algebraic and verbal versions of the constraint are consistent.

Rosewood

The rosewood constraint is measured in cubic centimeters. Each violin requires 200 cm³ of rosewood, while each cello requires 1600 cm³. These are the coefficients of the matrix. The constraint limit is 4800 cm³. The algebraic

TABLE 5.5   Completed Matrix for Example 5.2

	Violins (number)	Cellos (number)	Type	Limit
Objective ($)	2,000	8,000	max	
Rosewood (cm^3)	200	1,600	$\leq$	4,800
Labor (weeks)	4	8	$\leq$	48

version of the constraint is

$$(200 \times V) + (1600 \times C) \leq 4800$$

This is consistent with the verbal definition that "the total use of rosewood cannot exceed 4800 cm^3."

The matrix with all these coefficients included is shown in Table 5.5.

Optimal Solution

The optimal solution for Example 5.2 is shown in Table 5.6 and illustrated in Figure 5.2. The optimal strategy is to produce 8 violins and 2 cellos. This strategy gives the instrument maker an annual profit of $32,000. Again, both levels are greater than zero, so shadow costs are zero.

In this example, there is no slack on either of the constraints. The optimal solution is bound by the available levels of rosewood and labor.

If more of these resources could be obtained, the gross effect on profit would be $3.33 for each extra cubic centimeter of suitable rosewood and $333.33 for each extra week of labor. If extra rosewood can be purchased for less than $3.33, the instrument maker should purchase it. It will enable an increase in profit without the need to work harder. The benefit would arise because it would become possible to substitute some relatively profitable cello production for violin production.

TABLE 5.6   Optimal Solution for Example 5.2

Objective function value: 32,000.000000
Problem direction: max

Activity		Level	Shadow Cost
1 Violins	A	8.0000	0.0000
2 Cellos	A	2.0000	0.0000

Constraint		Slack	Shadow Price
1 Rosewood	L	0.0000	3.3333
2 Labor	L	0.0000	333.3333

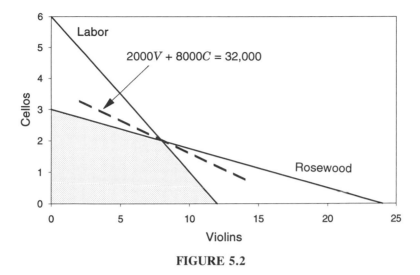

FIGURE 5.2

Example 5.3: Breakfast Cereal Manufacture

A breakfast cereal manufacturer produces two types of cereal: Frostoes and Cornbits. Each is made from different combinations of three ingredients. Frostoes are 40% sugar, 55% corn, and 5% bran, while Cornbits are 10% sugar, 80% corn, and 10% bran. Available stocks of sugar, corn, and bran are 200 kg, 400 kg, and 300 kg, respectively. Net profits differ for the two cereals: $0.40/kg for Frostoes and $0.55/kg for Cornbits. Given that the manufacturer wants to maximize profits, construct a linear programming (LP) matrix to find how many kilograms of Frostoes and Cornbits should be produced from the available ingredients. ■

After reading the problem definition through carefully, identify the objective. From the problem definition it is stated that the objective is to maximize profits. Coefficients in the *Objective* row will be profits in dollars from each activity.

Now identify the activities, the variables for which you want to select optimal levels. The obvious candidates in the problem definition are the quantities of Frostoes and Cornbits. We also want to know the quantities of sugar, corn, and bran that are used and the optimal level of profit. However, these do not need to be activities. The level of profit will be counted by the objective row, and the required levels of sugar, corn, and bran follow automatically once production levels of each breakfast cereal have been selected. So there are two activities named *Frostoes* and *Cornbits* for which we will use kilograms as the unit of measurement.

The next step is to identify the constraints. In this example, production is limited only by the availabilities of each of the ingredients (sugar, corn, and bran), so the availability of each of the ingredients imposes a constraint. Name

TABLE 5.7 Empty Matrix for Example 5.3

	Frostoes (kg)	Cornbits (kg)	Type	Limit
Objective ($)			max	
Sugar (kg)			≤	
Corn (kg)			≤	
Bran (kg)			≤	

the constraints *Sugar*, *Corn*, and *Bran* and use kg as the measurement unit for each. In words, the constraints specify that the total level of sugar used cannot exceed 200 kg, use of corn cannot exceed 400 kg, and use of bran must be less than or equal to 300 kg.

Now organize the row and column names, units, and constraint types into a matrix ready for coefficients to be included. See the empty matrix in Table 5.7.

Now quantify matrix coefficients.

Objective

For each activity, determine net profit per unit of the activity. In this example net profit per kilogram of each cereal is given in the problem definition: $0.40 for *Frostoes* and $0.55 for *Cornbits*.

Sugar

How much of the available stock of sugar does each unit of cereal use up? From the problem definition, each kilogram of *Frostoes* requires 0.4 kg of sugar while a kilogram *Cornbits* requires 0.1 kg of sugar. The constraint limit on sugar availability is specified as 200 kg. The algebraic version of the constraint is

$$(0.4 \times F) + (0.1 \times C) \leq 200$$

where F represents the number of kilograms of *Frostoes* produced, and C represents the number of kilograms of *Cornbits*. The verbal definition specified that "total use of sugar cannot exceed 200 kg." The number of kilograms of *Frostoes* times 0.4 plus the number of kilograms of *Cornbits* times 0.1 equals the total use of sugar, so the algebraic and verbal versions of the constraint are consistent.

Corn and Bran

The corn and bran constraints are very similar to the sugar constraint. The coefficients for each are the number of kilograms of each ingredient required

TABLE 5.8 Completed Matrix for Example 5.3

	Frostoes (kg)	Cornbits (kg)	Type	Limit
Objective ($)	0.4	0.55	max	
Sugar (kg)	0.4	0.1	≤	200
Corn (kg)	0.55	0.8	≤	400
Bran (kg)	0.05	0.1	≤	300

for each kilogram of cereal and the constraint limits are the maximum availabilities of each ingredient. The algebraic version of the corn constraint is

$$(0.55 \times F) + (0.8 \times C) \leq 400$$

This is consistent with the verbal definition that "use of corn cannot exceed 400 kg." For the bran constraint the algebraic version is

$$(0.05 \times F) + (0.1 \times C) \leq 300$$

which is consistent with the verbal definition that "use of bran must be less than or equal to 300 kg."

The matrix with all these coefficients included in shown in Table 5.8.

Optimal Solution

The optimal solution for Example 5.3 is shown in Table 5.9 and illustrated in Figure 5.3. The optimal levels of cereal production are 452.8 kg of Frostoes and 188.7 kg of Cornbits, resulting in maximum profits of $284.91. Because both cereals are active, they both have shadow costs of zero.

Figure 5.3 shows that the optimal point is at the intersection of the sugar and corn constraints. This means that all of the available stocks of sugar and

TABLE 5.9 Optimal Solution for Example 5.3

Objective function value: 284.905660
Problem direction: max

Activity		Level	Shadow Cost
1 Frostoes	A	452.8302	0.0000
2 Cornbits	A	188.6792	0.0000

Constraint		Slack	Shadow Price
1 Sugar	L	0.0000	0.0660
2 Corn	L	0.0000	0.6792
3 Bran	L	258.4906	0.0000

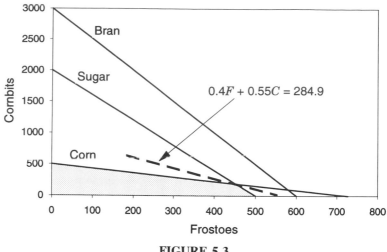

FIGURE 5.3

corn are used up, resulting in zero slacks in Table 5.9. On the other hand, the bran constraint is satisfied in the solution, but not in a way that uses it all. The optimal point in Figure 5.3 is not on the bran constraint, resulting in the slack level of bran of 258.5 kg (see Table 5.9).

The shadow prices of the constraints indicate that if extra corn could be obtained, it would be worth up to $0.68/kg, and extra sugar would be worth buying at any price up to $0.066/kg. Because there is slack bran already, obtaining more bran would be of no value, hence the zero shadow price.

Suppose that the attitude of consumers changes. They become more concerned about overconsumption of sugar, a change that favors Cornbits at the expense of Frostoes. (Frostoes get their name from a coating of white sugar crystals.) As a result, consumers are only willing to pay the company $0.35/kg for Frostoes, but will now pay $0.60/kg for Cornbits. The new optimal solution is shown in Table 5.10.

TABLE 5.10   Optimal Solution for Example 5.3 with Changed Prices

Objective function value: 300.000000
Problem direction: max

Activity		Level	Shadow Cost
1 Frostoes	A	0.0000	0.0625
2 Cornbits	A	500.0000	0.0000

Constraint		Slack	Shadow Price
1 Sugar	L	150.0000	0.0000
2 Corn	L	0.0000	0.7500
3 Bran	L	250.0000	0.0000

The new prices result in a complete shift away from producing Frostoes. The new optimal level of Cornbits is 500 kg. The shadow cost for Frostoes shows that their price is $0.0625/kg too low to be worth producing. Another way of looking at this is that if the company ignored the change in prices and continued to produce Frostoes, it would be foregoing potential profits of $0.0625 for each kilogram of Frostoes produced.

The new optimal strategy is constrained only by the level of corn. Extra corn would be worth up to $0.75/kg. There are 150 kg of unused sugar and 250 kg of unused bran.

Example 5.4: Feed Formulation

A pig farmer wishes to minimize the daily cost of feeding 50 pigs. There are two feeds available: wheat, which costs $130 per tonne, and lupins, which cost $150 per tonne. Each pig must receive at least 72.5 megajoules (MJ) of digestible energy and 1000 grams (g) of crude protein per day. A chemical analysis conducted for the farmer has shown that the available wheat grain contains 11.0% crude protein and 14.6 MJ digestible energy per kilogram (kg), while the lupins contain 28% crude protein and 14.2 MJ digestible energy per kilogram. In addition to the constraints on minimum nutrient levels, there is also a constraint on the concentration of nutrients in the feed. This is achieved by placing a maximum constraint on the total weight of feed: the feed for the 50 pigs must not weigh more than 350 kg. ∎

After reading the problem definition through carefully, identify the objective. This is the first example in this chapter in which the objective is to minimize something. From the problem definition it is stated that the objective is to minimize daily feed costs. Coefficients in the *Objective* row will be costs in dollars from each activity.

Now identify the activities, the variables for which you want to select optimal levels. The items for which we want to select levels are the two feed components: wheat and lupins. We also want to know the amounts of crude protein, digestible energy, and total feed weight for the selected mix of feeds and the minimum level of costs, but the levels of these factors follow automatically from the selected amounts of each feed. The two activities of the model will be named *Wheat* and *Lupins* and we will use kilograms as the unit of measurement.

The next step is to identify constraints. In this example the constraints are the minimum levels of each of the nutrients (energy and protein) and the maximum feed weight. Name the constraints *Energy*, *Protein*, and *Mass*. The units of measurement are MJ for *Energy*, g for *Protein*, and kg for *Mass*. In words, the constraints specify that the total level of energy must be at least 72.5 MJ per pig, the total level of protein must be at least 1000 g per pig, and the total mass of feed must not exceed 7 kg per pig.

TABLE 5.11   Empty Matrix for Example 5.4

	Wheat (kg)	Lupins (kg)	Type	Limit
Objective ($)			min	
Energy (MJ)			≥	
Protein (g)			≥	
Mass (kg)			≤	

Now organize the row and column names, units, and constraint types into a matrix ready for coefficients to be included (see Table 5.11).

Finally, quantify the coefficients of the matrix.

Objective

For each activity, determine the cost per unit of the activity. In this example the cost of each feed is given in the problem definition in $ per tonne: $130 for *Wheat* and $150 for *Lupins*. Since there are 1000 kg in a tonne, these costs correspond to $0.13 and $0.15/kg, respectively. We have to express costs on a per kg basis because the feeds are measured in kilogram. These per kg costs are entered in the objective row of the matrix in Table 5.12.

Energy

For each activity ask "How much does each unit of this activity contribute toward meeting the minimum requirement for this constraint?" From the problem definition, each kilogram of wheat provides 14.6 MJ of energy, while a kilogram of lupins provides 14.2 MJ. The total requirement for energy is calculated by multiplying the requirement per pig times the number of pigs: $72.5 \times 50 = 3625$. The algebraic version of the constraint is

$$(14.6 \times W) + (14.2 \times L) \geq 3625$$

where W represents the number of kilograms of wheat fed, and L represents the number of kilograms of lupins fed. The verbal definition specified that "the total level of energy must be at least 72.5 MJ per pig." The left-hand side of

TABLE 5.12   Completed Matrix for Example 5.4

	Wheat (kg)	Lupins (kg)	Type	Limit
Objective ($)	0.13	0.15	min	
Energy (MJ)	14.6	14.2	≥	3,625
Protein (g)	110	280	≥	50,000
Mass (kg)	1	1	≤	350

the preceding inequality gives the total level of energy provided, and the right-hand side corresponds to 72.5 MJ/pig for 50 pigs, so the algebraic statement is consistent with the verbal statement of the constraint.

Protein and Mass

The *Protein* constraint is very similar to the *Energy* constraint. The coefficients for it are the number of grams of each protein contained in each kilogram of feed. The constraint limit is the minimum protein requirement per pig times 50 (the number of pigs). The algebraic version of the *Protein* constraint is

$$(110 \times W) + (280 + L) \geq 50,000$$

This is consistent with the verbal definition that "the total level of protein must be at least 1000 g per pig."

For the *Mass* constraint the algebraic version is

$$(1 \times W) + (1 \times L) \leq 350$$

which is consistent with the verbal definition that "the total mass of feed must not exceed 7 kg/pig." The matrix with all these coefficients included in shown in Table 5.12.

Notice that although this was a problem with an objective to minimize something, the procedure for building the matrix and the rationale for selecting particular coefficients followed the same principles as for the previous maximization problems.

Optimal Solution

The optimal solution for Example 5.4 is shown in Table 5.13 and Figure 5.4. The lowest feasible cost of providing the required nutrients is $35.37, when

TABLE 5.13   Optimal Solution for Example 5.4

Objective function value: 35.367181
Problem direction: min

Activity		Level	Shadow Cost
1 Wheat	Z	120.7443	0.0000
2 Lupins	A	131.1362	0.0000
Constraint		Slack	Shadow Price
1 Energy	G	0.0000	−0.0079
2 Protein	G	0.0000	−0.0001
3 Mass	L	98.1196	0.0000

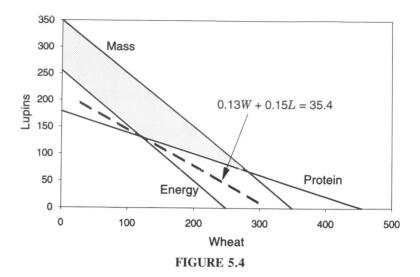

FIGURE 5.4

the ration includes 120.7 kg of wheat and 131.1 kg of lupins. Both the greater-than constraints, *Energy* and *Protein*, are binding, with zero slacks and nonzero shadow prices. As in Example 3.1 (a maximization problem), the shadow price of a binding, greater-than constraint is negative (see Table 4.8).

The minimum level of energy in this problem is 3625 MJ. The shadow price indicates that, at the margin, each megajoule increase in this minimum level would worsen the objective function (increase the total feed cost) by \$0.0079. Alternatively, a decrease in the constraint limit makes the constraint less strict and would allow a \$0.0079 reduction in the feed cost. Variations in the requirement for protein would have an impact of \$0.0001 per gram.

Suppose that there is an extreme shortage of lupin grain on the market so that the cost of lupins increases from \$0.15 to \$0.35/kg. The new optimal solution in this circumstance is shown in Table 5.14. The least costly ration is

TABLE 5.14   Optimal Solution for Example 5.4 with Higher Lupin Price

Objective function value: 60.382353
Problem direction: min

Activity		Level	Shadow Cost
1 Wheat	Z	282.3529	0.0000
2 Lupins	A	67.6471	0.0000

Constraint		Slack	Shadow Price
1 Energy	G	1,457.9412	0.0000
2 Protein	G	0.0000	−0.0013
3 Mass	L	0.0000	0.0124

now much more expensive: up from \$35.37 to \$60.38. The less-than constraint *Mass* is now limiting and, just like the less-than constraints in a mazimization problem, it has a positive shadow price. As before, the fact that greater-than and less-than constraints have shadow prices with opposite signs indicates that an increase in the constraint limit is bad in one case and good in the other.

We noted previously that the interpretation of shadow prices is different for minimization and maximization problems. A less-than constraint has a positive shadow price in each case, but in a maximization problem, it implies that an increase in the constraint limit would allow an increase in the objective function. For a minimization problem it implies that a higher constraint limit would allow a lower objective function value. Similarly, the interpretation of shadow prices of greater-than constraints needs to be adjusted depending on the direction of optimization.

Example 5.5: Labor Scheduling

The customs service of a country conducts inspections of all imported goods passing through a particular airport. Inspectors work one 6-hour shift per day. The number of inspectors required at any one time varies during the course of a day according to the rate at which goods arrive at the airport. The requirement for inspectors is known in advance to follow the following pattern: 8 A.M.–10 A.M., 9; 10 A.M.–12 noon, 7; 12 noon–2 P.M., 14; 2 P.M.–4 P.M., 8; 4 P.M.–6 P.M., 12; 6 P.M.–8 P.M., 4. Outside these hours, no inspectors are required. Potential starting times for shifts are 8 A.M., 10 A.M., 12 noon, and 2 P.M.

The managers of the custom service do not wish to employ more inspectors than necessary to meeting this pattern of requirements. Construct an LP matrix to determine the pattern in which inspectors should be scheduled to commence their 6-hour shifts during the day. ∎

After reading the problem definition through carefully, identify the objective. It is stated that the managers do not want to employ any excess of inspectors, so the objective is to minimize the number of inspectors. Coefficients in the *Objective* row will be the number of inspectors associated with each of the activities.

Now identify the activities, the variables for which you want to select optimal levels. For this example the aim is to determine how many inspectors are needed and when they should be scheduled to start. Thus the decision variables are the number of inspectors commencing at each possible time. The possible starting times are 8 A.M., 10 A.M., 12 noon, and 2 P.M. An activity is required for each of these starting times, representing one inspector commencing at that time. We will name the activities according to the starting time of the shift. The units for the activities will be number of inspectors.

Now what are the constraints? There must be a sufficient number of inspectors to meet the demand for inspections at all times of the day. Each of the

TABLE 5.15 Empty Matrix for Example 5.5

	8 A.M. (No.)	10 A.M. (No.)	12 noon (No.)	2 P.M. (No.)	Type	Limit
Objective (No.)					min	
8–10 (No.)					≥	
10–12 (No.)					≥	
12–2 (No.)					≥	
2–4 (No.)					≥	
4–6 (No.)					≥	
6–8 (No.)					≥	

Note: No. = number of inspectors.

time periods for which a given number of inspectors is required is a constraint affecting the total requirement for inspectors. It may be that the optimal schedule includes excess numbers of inspectors at particular times, so the constraint types are greater-thans rather than equals in each case. The objective to minimizing the number of inspectors ensures that there will only be an excess if it cannot be avoided. Overall there are six constraints named *8–10*, *10–12*, *12–2*, *2–4*, and *6–8*. The units for the constraints will again be number of inspectors.

Now organize the row and column names, units, and constraint types into a matrix ready for coefficients to be included (see Table 5.15).

Finally, quantify the coefficients of the matrix.

Objective

The objective is to minimize the number of inspectors, and each activity represents the use of one inspector. Therefore the objective function coefficient of each activity is one. The units for each objective function coefficient are inspectors per inspector (so it is obvious that the value of each coefficient is one).

Constraints

For each activity ask "How much does each unit of this activity contribute toward meeting the minimum requirement for this constraint?" Each inspector scheduled to start at 8 A.M. will provide one inspector worth of inspection in three of the time periods: *8–10*, *10–12*, and *12–2*. Thus within the *8 A.M.* column there is a one in each of these three constraints and zeros in the other time periods for which an 8 A.M. start would provide no inspector. An inspector scheduled to start at 10 A.M. does not make any contribution at *8–10*, *4–6*, or *6–8*, but is active during *10–12*, *12–2* and *2–4*. Similarly, the *10 A.M.* activity has ones in the constraints for which an inspector is active.

For each coefficient within the body of the matrix, the unit of measurement is inspectors per inspector. This might seem to imply that *every* coefficient of the matrix should take the value 1, just as was the case in the objective function. However, the units are actually slightly different for each row and column. For example, the unit of measurement for the *8–10* constraint is actually "inspectors working between 8 A.M. and 10 A.M.," while for the *8 A.M.* activity, the unit is "inspectors working between 8 A.M. and 2 P.M." Consequently, the unit of the cell [*8–10, 8 A.M.*] is "inspectors working between 8 A.M. and 10 A.M." per "inspector working between 8 A.M. and 2 P.M." Such a coefficient will clearly have a value of one since there is one inspector working between 8 A.M. and 10 A.M. for each inspector working between 8 A.M. and 2 P.M. On the other hand, the unit for cell [*8–10, 10 A.M.*] is "inspectors working between 8 A.M. and 10 A.M." per "inspector working between 10 A.M. and 4 P.M." The value of this cell is zero since there are no "inspectors working between 8 A.M. and 10 A.M." for each "inspector working between 10 A.M. and 4 P.M." The key difference between the constraints and the objective function of this problem is that the units for the objective function are the total number of inspectors in all periods, not in any particular period.

The completed matrix is shown in Table 5.16. Let us look at one of the constraints as an algebraic inequality. The *10–12* constraint is

$$(1 \times A) + (1 \times B) + (0 \times C) + (0 \times D) \geq 7$$

or

$$A + B \geq 7$$

where A, B, C, D represent the four activities of the model: *8 A.M.*, *10 A.M.*, *12 noon*, and *2 P.M.* $A + B$ gives the total number of inspectors who are working between 10 A.M. and 12 noon. Any workers who start work at 8 A.M. or 10 A.M. will be working at this time, but a starting time of 12 noon or later contributes nothing toward meeting the requirement for seven inspectors during this time period. The coefficients of 1 in front of A and B are the coefficients of this constraint in the matrix shown in Table 5.16.

TABLE 5.16   Completed Matrix for Example 5.5

	8 A.M. (No.)	10 A.M. (No.)	12 noon (No.)	2 P.M. (No.)	Type	Limit
Objective (No.)	1	1	1	1	min	
8–10 (No.)	1				≥	9
10–12 (No.)	1	1			≥	7
12–2 (No.)	1	1	1		≥	14
2–4 (No.)		1	1	1	≥	8
4–6 (No.)			1	1	≥	12
6–8 (No.)				1	≥	4

Note: No. = number of inspectors.

Optimal Solution

The optimal solution for Example 5.5 is shown in Table 5.17. It is not possible to draw a single graph to represent all of this problem due to the number of activities. The value of the objective function in the optimal solution gives the smallest number of inspectors that can be employed to meet all the required inspection capacity (21). These are allocated according to the activity levels indicated in the optimal solution: 9 start at 8 A.M., 5 at 12 noon, and 7 at 2 P.M. No allocation with fewer than 21 inspectors meets the constraints of the problem.

The interpretation of the shadow cost for the *10 A.M.* activity is not straight-forward. According to one of our previous explanations, the shadow price gives the amount by which the objective function value for an activity would need to improve for the activity to become part of the optimal solution. According to Table 5.17, if the objective function value for the *10 A.M.* activity were *reduced* by at least one unit (this is a minimization problem, so an improvement is a reduction), the optimal solution would include some positive level of the activity, meaning that some inspectors would be scheduled to start at 10 A.M.

However, this interpretation does not make sense for this model. The *10 A.M.* activity represents one inspector being scheduled to start at 10 A.M. The activity is measured in units of one inspector and the objective function is specified using the same units. Because of the way the model is specified, the objective function value for the *10 A.M.* activity must always be one. It is not possible to schedule an inspector at 10 A.M. for any "cost" (in terms of the objective function) of less than one inspector. It certainly would not make sense to reduce the objective function value to zero (which would be necessary to make the activity enter the optimal solution), as this would imply that any

TABLE 5.17   Optimal Solution for Example 5.5

Objective function value: 21.000000
Problem direction: min

Activity		Level	Shadow Cost
1 8 A.M.	A	9.0000	0.0000
2 10 A.M.	Z	0.0000	1.0000
3 12 noon	A	5.0000	0.0000
4 2 P.M.	A	7.0000	0.0000

Constraint		Slack	Shadow Price
1 8–10	G	0.0000	−1.0000
2 10–12	G	2.0000	0.0000
3 12–2	GM	0.0000	0.0000
4 2–4	G	4.0000	0.0000
5 4–6	G	0.0000	−1.0000
6 6–8	G	3.0000	0.0000

inspector starting at 10 A.M. could somehow be ignored when counting the total number of inspectors.

Fortunately, the other approach to interpreting shadow costs does make more sense for this example. This interpretation is that a shadow cost gives the worsening of the objective function that would occur for each unit increase in the level of the activity. In the case of the *10 A.M.* activity, if an inspector started at 10 A.M., the total number of inspectors would be increased by one. This implies that starting an inspector at 10 A.M. does not allow any compensating decrease in the number of inspectors starting at other times. The pattern of demand for inspections is such that an inspector starting at 10 A.M. would be completely redundant, idle for their entire shift, given the availability of inspectors already scheduled.

The most efficient scheduling of inspectors does not necessarily imply that all inspectors have to be busy at all times. The constraint slacks in Table 5.17 show that there will be two idle inspectors between 10 A.M. and 12 noon, four between 2 P.M. and 4 P.M., and three between 6 P.M. and 8 P.M. In fact, it is impossible to devise a schedule for this problem in which there are no idle inspectors at any time. We could attempt to do this by specifying that all constraints of the model are equals constraints instead of greater-than constraints, but the model would not solve.

Both the *8–10* and *4–6* constraints have zero slacks and shadow prices of -1. This means that if the requirement for inspectors in either of these periods were to be increased by one, it would not be possible to meet that requirement without scheduling an extra inspector.

The *12–2* constraint also has a slack of zero, indicating that it is exactly met, but it has a shadow price of zero; changing the requirement for inspectors between 12 noon and 2 P.M. would not affect the total requirement for inspectors. The change could be accommodated by rearranging the schedule. In particular, there is scope to reduce the number of inspectors starting at 2 P.M. to offset an increase in starters at 12 noon.

Exercises

In Exercises 5.1 to 5.6 you are asked to create a linear programming matrix to solve a particular problem. In Exercises 5.7 to 5.12 you are asked to interpret optimal solutions from Exercises 5.1 to 5.6.

5.1   A car manufacturer has an assembly line that can be used to assemble two different types of cars: a sedan and a wagon. If the assembly line is dedicated to production of one or the other type of car, the potential throughput of cars is a maximum of 90 sedans or 120 wagons per day. A mix of sedans and wagons is allowable. Assume that it takes no time to convert the production line from one type of car to the other. There is currently a shortage of tires, so that not more than 110 vehicles of either type can be assembled per day. The manufacturer also has to meet contracts to supply 33 sedans and 20 wagons per day. Production above these levels is at the discretion of the manufacturer. If profit per car is $1800 per sedan and $1500 per wagon, set up an LP matrix to select the profit maximizing combination of cars.

5.2   A company uses both radio and television advertisements to promote its product. A radio advertisement costs $100 and, on average, generates sales of 20 additional units of the product. A television advertisement costs $700 and generates extra sales of 150 units. The only radio station in town has a policy of not allowing an advertisement to be played more than once a day. There is a contract with the only television station in town to run at least two advertisements per month. The budget for advertising in September is $4200. Formulate an LP matrix to maximize the number of extra sales generated through advertising in September.

5.3   Construct an LP matrix to solve the following problem. A farmer wants to plan farm activities for the coming year so as to maximize profits. The following resources are available:

- 50 hours of labor per week
- 3000 hectares of usable land
- access to finance totaling $30,000 (all expenses during the year must be paid from this source)

To avoid running down soil fertility the farmer has decided that no more than two-thirds of the land should be planted with cereals (wheat, barley, or oats). Because of crop disease considerations, not more than 1500 hectares of wheat nor more than 1500 hectares of the legume crop, lupins, can be sown. The farmer insists on having at least 500 ewes.

A hectare of wheat requires $40 of finance for chemicals, fuel, and so on, and produces $160 worth of wheat grain. A hectare of barley costs $35 and grosses $140. A hectare of oats costs $35 and grosses $135. A hectare of lupins costs $42 and grosses $160.

An hour of average weekly labor is required for every 50 hectares of wheat, oats, and barley and every 40 hectares of lupins.

The costs and gross returns of sheep are shown in Table 5.18.

Sheep require pasture for feed. Each hectare of pasture can carry 2.5 ewes or four wethers (castrated rams). An hour of average weekly work is required for every 200 ewes or 500 wethers.

TABLE 5.18   Sheep Costs and Returns

	Costs	Returns
Merino ewes	$3	$24
Cross-bred ewes	$3	$21
Wethers	$2	$14

5.4   With one week to go, a student wishes to minimize the number of hours spent studying for three exams: one each for mathematics, history, and literature. Suppose that with no further study, the student would score 40 for mathematics, 30 for history, and 45 for literature. Each hour of study would improve these marks by 1 mark, 2 marks, and 0.5 mark, respectively. To pass a particular course the student must score at least 70 in mathematics and 50 each in history and literature. In addition, the total combined score of the three units must be at least 185. Set up an LP matrix to minimize study effort.

5.5   Suppose the work-scheduling problem described in Example 5.5 is altered slightly. There are exactly three part-time inspectors who only work a 4-hour shift. The organization is contractually committed to include these three inspectors in their daily schedule, and they do not wish to employ more than three part-time workers. Adjust the matrix in order to determine how the part-timers should be included.

5.6   Over the summer months a dairy farmer plans to milk 100 cows yielding an average of 15 liters of milk per cow per day. The farmer wants to work out the least expensive feeding strategy that will achieve this level of production.

     Each cow has the following daily maintenance requirement: 71.8 MJ metabolizable energy, 320 g of digestible crude protein, and 28 g of phosphate. Each cow has the capacity to eat up to 14 kg of food per day plus a further 0.2 kg for each liter of milk it produces. Once maintenance requirements are met, the following nutrients are required for each liter of milk produced: 5.04 MJ of metabolizable energy, 49 g of digestible crude protein, and 1.7 g of phosphate.

     The farmer has enough hay on hand to feed up to 250 kg per day, but is not able to buy any extra hay. The cost and nutrient content of alternative feeds is summarized in Table 5.19. Values are for a kilogram of the feed.

     Formulate an LP matrix to calculate the least cost feed ration for the entire 100 cow herd.

The following exercises are questions of interpretation of the optimal solutions of the models from Exercises 5.1 to 5.6. The matrices from which these so-

TABLE 5.19   Costs and Nutrient Contents of Feeds (per kg)

	Costs (c)	Energy (MJ)	Protein (g)	Phosphate (g)
Lupins	14.0	11.9	219.0	2.88
Oats	12.5	10.3	54.0	3.06
Hay	8.0	7.8	85.5	2.16
Wheat	15.5	11.5	58.5	2.61
Rock phosphate	13.0	—	—	150.0

lutions are derived are shown in the "Solutions to Exercises" appendix at the back of the book.

5.7 Based on the optimal solution in Table 5.20:

(a) Suppose we added a constraint to the model specifying that the number of sedans plus the number of wagons must be greater than or equal to 20. What effect would this have on the optimal solution?

(b) Suppose that it became possible to speed up the throughput of cars by 1 wagon and/or 1.33 sedans per day. What would be the impact on profit?

(c) Suppose that extra stocks of tires could be obtained. What should the manufacturer be prepared to pay for them?

(d) Which of the two existing contracts to provide cars should the manufacturer attempt to renegotiate?

(e) How much profit do they stand to gain if they are successful in these negotiations?

(f) Why do the shadow prices of *Thru-put* and *Min sedan* have opposite signs?

5.8 Based on the optimal solution in Table 5.21:

(a) How many extra sales should the company expect as a result of its total advertising campaign?

(b) Explain the shadow cost of radio advertising.

(c) At the margin, how many extra sales does each dollar of advertising expenditure generate?

(d) Suppose the radio station offered cheaper rates to encourage advertising. By how much would they need to reduce their fees before it would be worthwhile for the company to include any radio advertising?

TABLE 5.20 Optimal Solution for Exercise 5.1

Objective function value: 173,400.000000
Problem direction: max

Activity		Level	Shadow Cost
1 Sedans	A	33.0000	0.0000
2 Wagons	A	76.0000	0.0000

Constraint		Slack	Shadow Price
1 Thru-put	L	0.0000	1500.0000
2 Tires	L	1.0000	0.0000
3 Min sedan	G	0.0000	−200.0000
4 Min wagon	G	56.0000	0.0000

TABLE 5.21   Optimal Solution for Exercise 5.2

Objective function value: 900.000000
Problem direction: max

Activity		Level	Shadow Cost
1 Radio	Z	0.0000	1.4286
2 TV	A	6.0000	0.0000

Constraint		Slack	Shadow Price
1 Budget	L	0.0000	0.2143
2 Radio max	L	30.0000	0.0000
3 TV contract	G	4.0000	0.0000

5.9   Based on the optimal solution in Table 5.22:

(a) Suppose the farmer had been planning to grow barley. How much profit would be sacrificed for each hectare increase in the area of barley that was grown (at the margin)?

(b) By how much would the profitability of oats need to improve before they would be worth growing?

TABLE 5.22   Optimal Solution for Exercise 5.3

Objective function value: 173,076.923080
Problem direction: max

Activity		Level	Shadow Cost
1 Wheat	A	230.7692	0.0000
2 Barley	Z	0.0000	4.6154
3 Oats	Z	0.0000	9.6154
4 Lupins	Z	0.0000	6.1538
5 M ewes	A	6,923.0769	0.0000
6 X ewes	Z	0.0000	3.0000
7 Wethers	Z	0.0000	1.3846

Constraint		Slack	Shadow Price
1 Labor	L	10.7692	0.0000
2 Land	L	0.0000	36.9231
3 Finance	L	0.0000	2.0769
4 Cereal max	L	1,769.2308	0.0000
5 Wheat max	L	1,269.2308	0.0000
6 Lupin max	L	1,500.0000	0.0000
7 Ewe min	G	6,423.0769	0.0000

(c) If the returns from wethers fall by $2, should the farmer choose to include wethers in the flock?

(d) How many hours of work are actually required by the optimal strategy? (Remember the farmer was willing to work up to 50 hours per week.)

(e) The farmer has an option to lease a small amount of additional land for $30 per hectare. Would this be worth doing?

(f) Explain the level of slack on the *Ewe min* constraint.

5.10 Based on the optimal solution in Table 5.23:

(a) How many hours must the student study to achieve the required minimum scores?

(b) If the student chose to spend 31 hours studying mathematics, by how much would the total hours of study have to be increased relative to the minimum level in the optimal solution?

(c) Explain the shadow price of the *Litr min* constraint.

(d) What do the levels of slack on the *Math max*, *Hist max*, and *Litr max* constraints tell us?

(e) If the minimum combined score for the three units was increased by one, how much extra study would be required?

(f) Look at the matrix for Exercise 5.4 (in the solutions section at the back of the book) and see if you can work out why history is the only subject for which the student does more than the minimum level of study.

TABLE 5.23   Optimal Solution for Exercise 5.4

Objective function value: 57.500000
Problem direction: min

Activity		Level	Shadow Cost
1 Maths	A	30.0000	0.0000
2 History	A	17.5000	0.0000
3 Literature	A	10.0000	0.0000

Constraint		Slack	Shadow Price
1 Math min	G	0.0000	−0.5000
2 Hist min	G	15.0000	0.0000
3 Litr min	G	0.0000	−1.5000
4 Total min	G	0.0000	−0.5000
5 Math max	L	30.0000	0.0000
6 Hist max	L	35.0000	0.0000
7 Litr max	L	50.0000	0.0000

5.11 Based on the optimal solution in Table 5.24:

(a) How should the three part-time inspectors be scheduled.

(b) By how much does the availability of three part-time inspectors reduce the total requirement for inspectors? (Part-time inspectors count as two-thirds of an inspector when calculating the total number of inspectors.)

(c) The activity *10 A.M. PT* represents starting a part-time inspector at 10 A.M. Such an inspector counts as only two-thirds of an inspector, so why is the shadow cost of the activity equal to 1, rather than $\frac{2}{3}$?

(d) *PT eq* is an equals constraint specifying the level of part-time inspectors. Is it acting as a greater-than or as a less-than constraint? In other words, is it constraining the model to selecting more or less part time inspectors than would be the case if the constraint were removed from the model?

(e) In which periods are there idle inspectors?

(f) Interpret the shadow price of -1 for the *8 A.M.–10 A.M.* constraint.

TABLE 5.24   Optimal Solution for Exercise 5.5

Objective function value: 20.000000
Problem direction: min

Activity		Level	Shadow Cost
1 8 A.M.	A	9.0000	0.0000
2 10 A.M.	Z	0.0000	1.0000
3 12 noon	A	5.0000	0.0000
4 2 P.M.	A	4.0000	0.0000
5 8 A.M. PT	ZM	0.0000	0.0000
6 10 A.M. PT	Z	0.0000	1.0000
7 12 noon PT	Z	0.0000	1.0000
8 2 P.M. PT	ZM	0.0000	0.0000
9 4 P.M. PT	A	3.0000	0.0000

Constraint		Slack	Shadow Price
1 8 A.M.–10 A.M.	G	0.0000	−1.0000
2 10 A.M.–12 noon	G	2.0000	0.0000
3 12 noon–12 P.M.	G	0.0000	0.0000
4 2 P.M.–4 P.M.	G	1.0000	0.0000
5 4 P.M.–6 P.M.	G	0.0000	−1.0000
6 6 P.M.–8 P.M.	G	3.0000	0.0000
7 PT eq	E	0.0000	0.3333

TABLE 5.25   Optimal Solution for Exercise 5.6

Objective function value: 171.956579
Problem direction: min

Activity		Level	Shadow Cost
1 Lupins	A	1,074.7899	0.0000
2 Oats	Z	.0000	0.0033
3 Hay	A	250.0000	0.0000
4 Wheat	Z	0.0000	0.0199
5 Rock phos	A	11.4307	0.0000

Constraint		Slack	Shadow Price
1 MEnergy	G	0.0000	−0.0116
2 CProtein	G	151,253.992	0.0000
3 Phosphate	G	0.0000	−0.0009
4 Hay max	L	0.0000	0.0120
5 Intake	L	363.7794	0.0000

5.12   Based on the optimal solution in Table 5.25:

(a) What is the cost of the least expensive feasible ration?

(b) How much rock phosphate is in the optimal ration?

(c) Suppose the price of wheat rose by $0.02 per kilogram. Would wheat enter the optimal solution?

(d) Suppose the price of wheat fell by $0.02 per kilogram. Would wheat enter the optimal solution?

(e) If the farmer decided to increase the minimum energy content of the ration, at what rate would increases in the minimum energy content affect the cost of the ration?

(f) If the farmer decided to increase the minimum protein content of the ration, at what rate would increases in the minimum protein content affect the cost of the ration?

(g) If extra hay became available for $0.09 per kilogram, would it be worth buying?

CHAPTER 6

NEGATIVE COEFFICIENTS AND NEGATIVE FACTOR LEVELS

Matrices presented so far have included only positive coefficients but from here on most will include some negative numbers. Negative coefficients give linear programming (LP) extra power and flexibility in two ways. First, they allow the representation of linkages between activities. For example, they make it possible to specify that the level of one activity must not exceed that of another. If only positive coefficients are used, you must specify the constraint limit in advance. By using negative coefficients it is possible to make a constraint limit dependent on the levels of one or more other activities: levels that are not known in advance.

Second, by using "transfer rows," negative coefficients make it possible to represent problems using matrix structures that are more efficient and/or easier to relate to the original problem definition. We consider the use of negative coefficients for these purposes in some detail in Sections 6.1 and 6.2.

Although no activity in an LP model can take on a negative level in the optimal solution, it is sometimes necessary to represent variables that are, in some sense, negative. An example is the representation of both credit and debt in the same model. Section 6.3 shows how this can be accomplished.

6.1 LINKING ACTIVITIES

We start with a simple model in which there are no direct linkages between activities. Later we modify the model to include various types of linkage.

101

Example 6.1: Ration Formulation

We are building a model to select the least expensive ration for the egg-laying hens of a poultry enterprise. A potential ingredient of the ration is lime, a useful source of calcium, which is needed by hens to make egg shells. One constraint of the problem is that lime must not exceed 5 percent of a one-tonne ration. Another ingredient is lupins. The cost of lupins is $0.12 per kilogram, while lime costs $0.03 per kilogram. There are also other potential feeds and other constraints, but we will focus on these two feeds. Assume that the farmer wishes to produce exactly one tonne of the ration and that the objective is to minimize its cost.   ■

This problem might be represented in a matrix as shown in Table 6.1. The activities *Lupins* and *Lime* and the constraints *Lime max* and *Mass* all use the units kilograms (kg). The *Other feeds* column and *Other rows* constraint indicate that this is only part of a larger matrix. This model is similar to the kinds of matrix covered in Chapter 3. We have specified in advance the upper limit for lime. The right-hand side term for *Lime max* is 50, representing the maximum allowable number of kilograms of lime in the 1000-kg ration.

Now suppose that the upper limit for lime must be dependent on the level of lupins in the diet. There are at least four forms that the dependency might take. It may be necessary to specify that the level of lime must not exceed

(a) A proportion (e.g., 10 percent) of the level of lupins.
(b) Five percent of the diet or a proportion of the level of lupins, whichever is smaller.
(c) Five percent of the diet, unless it also includes lupins, in which case the limit is increased by a proportion of the level of lupins.
(d) Five percent of the diet or a proportion of the level of lupins, whichever is greater.

Figure 6.1 represents the original *Lime max* constraint. The shaded area represents the feasible set of outcomes for levels of lime and lupins. The feasible area includes the constraint (i.e., the line at 50 kg of lime is part of the feasible area). The maximum level of lime is independent of the level of lupins.

TABLE 6.1   Lime Limited to 5 Percent of the 1000-kg Diet

	Lupins (kg)	Lime (kg)	Other Feeds (kg)	Type	Limit
Objective (c)	12	3	*	min	
Lime max (kg)		1		≤	50
Mass (kg)	1	1	1	=	1,000
Other rows	*	*	*	*	*

FIGURE 6.1

The four types of linkages between lupins and the maximum level of lime are shown in Figures 6.2 to 6.5. Relationships of type (a), (b), and (c) (Figures 6.2, 6.3, and 6.4) can be easily incorporated in an LP matrix. Type (d) (Figure 6.5) can also be included in the analysis although it may require two solutions of the model to identify the optimal solution.

Let us first consider a relationship of type (a) (Figure 6.2). Suppose that the level of lime must not exceed 10 percent of the level of lupins. A suitable matrix structure is shown in Table 6.2. The coefficient for [*Lime max*, *Lupins*] is -0.10.

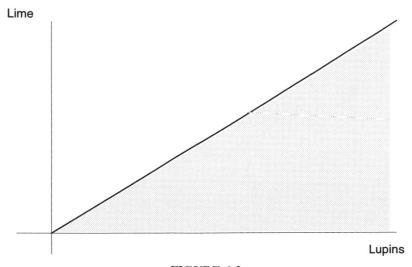

FIGURE 6.2

TABLE 6.2   Lime Limited to 10 Percent of the Level of Lupins

	Lupins (kg)	Lime (kg)	Other Feeds (kg)	Type	Limit
Objective (c)	12	3	*	min	
Lime max (kg)	−0.1	1		≤	0
Mass (kg)	1	1	1	=	1,000
Other rows	*	*	*	*	*

There are at least three possible approaches to the interpretation of a negative coefficient such as this. First, one can look at a negative coefficient as if it were a positive coefficient in the *Limit* column. The difference between a negative coefficient in the matrix and a normal, positive coefficient in the *Limit* column is that the positive *Limit* coefficient is, within one solution, fixed and unchanging. On the other hand, the limit of the *Lime max* constraint in Table 6.2 depends on the level of lupins. If the solution contained exactly 1 kg of lupins, the limit on lime would be 0.1 kg. If it contained 50 kg of lupins, the limit would be 5.0 kg (= 50 kg × 0.1). In other words, the limit of *Lime max* is increased by 0.1 for every unit of lupins in the ration.

The second way of thinking about the difference between positive and negative coefficients is to look at negative coefficients as generating a resource and positive coefficients as using it up. In Table 6.2 lupins generate a resource that might be called "capacity to feed lime." Each kilogram of lupins generates 0.1 kg of capacity, and each kilogram of lime uses up 1 kg of that capacity (the coefficient in [*Lime max, Lime*] is 1). The constraint, which is a less-than, can thus be interpreted as follows: the amount of lime feeding capacity used must be less than or equal to the amount of capacity generated. The amount used is the sum of positive coefficients in the constraint times the levels of their respective activities in the optimal solution. Similarly, the amount generated is the sum of negative coefficients multiplied by their activity levels. This interpretation of negative coefficients only applies to less-than constraints. Greater-than constraints are discussed later in this chapter.

The third interpretation of the *Lime max* constraint is to look at it as an algebraic inequality:

$$(-0.1 \times Lupins) + (1.0 \times Lime) \leq 0$$

That is, −0.1 times the number of kilograms of lupins in the ration, plus 1.0 times the number of kilograms of lime in the ration must be less than or equal to zero. This inequality can be rearranged by adding (0.1 × *Lupins*) to each side, giving

$$(1.0 \times Lime) \leq (0.1 \times Lupins)$$

Different people have different preferences among these alternative interpretations. It is often helpful to use more than one of these approaches to check your interpretation of a constraint.

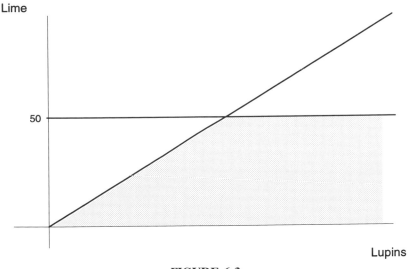

FIGURE 6.3

So far we have dealt only with type (a) (Figure 6.2) from our original list. Let us move on to type (b), as shown in Figure 6.3. How would we construct a matrix if we wanted the constraint limit on *Lime max* to be 5 percent of the ration or 10 percent of the level of lupins, whichever is the smaller? Table 6.3 shows one possibility.

This time there are two different *Lime max* constraints numbered 1 and 2. *Lime max1* is exactly the same as the *Lime max* constraint in Table 6.1, while *Lime max2* is the same as *Lime max* in Table 6.2. In this model, both are applied. The level of lime has to be less than 50 kg and at the same time it has to be less than 10 percent of the level of lupins. Which constraint is limiting depends on the level of lupins. If it is less than 500 kg, then *Lime max2* limits the level of lime, since the limit on *Lime max2* will effectively be less than 50 kg. In this case there is some slack in the solution for *Lime max1*. On the other hand, if there are more than 500 kg of lupins, *Lime max1* becomes limiting and *Lime max2* is slack. If there are exactly 500 kg of lupins in the ration, there is no slack in either constraint.

TABLE 6.3 Lime Limited to 5 Percent of the Diet or 10 Percent of the Level of Lupins, whichever Is Smaller

	Lupins (kg)	Lime (kg)	Other Feeds (kg)	Type	Limit
Objective (c)	12	3	*	min	
Lime max1 (kg)		1		≤	50
Lime max2 (kg)	−0.1	1		≤	0
Mass (kg)	1	1	1	=	1,000
Other rows	*	*	*	*	*

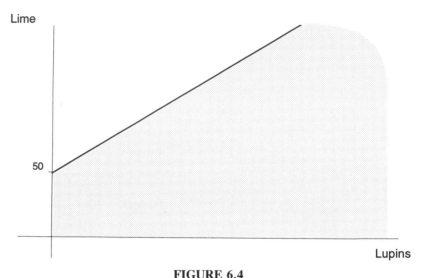

FIGURE 6.4

In constraint type (c) the limit on lime is 50 kg plus 10 percent of the level of lupins. The constraint is shown in Figure 6.4 and a suitable matrix is shown in Table 6.4.

Using the first interpretation, one can look at the negative coefficient as increasing the constraint limit. This time, however, it is increasing it above a starting point of 50 rather than zero as in Table 6.2. If the level of *Lupins* was 10 kg, the constraint limit would be increased by 1 unit ($= 10 \times 0.1$). This extra unit would be added to the initial 50 to give a new upper limit of 51 kg of lime in the ration.

Alternatively, the *Lime max* constraint can be thought of as representing a pool of "capacity to feed lime." *Lupins* can generate capacity into the pool (just as it did in Table 6.2) but this time the pool has an initial value of 50 rather than zero. Each kilogram of lupins generates 0.1 kg of capacity to feed lime, so 10 kg of lupins would generate 1 extra kilogram of lime capacity, giving a new total of 51 kg.

Finally the *Lime max* constraint may be looked on as an algebraic inequality:

$$(-0.1 \times \textit{Lupins}) + (1.0 \times \textit{Lime}) \leq 50$$

TABLE 6.4 Lime Limited to 5 Percent of the Diet Plus 10 Percent of the Level of Lupins

	Lupins (kg)	Lime (kg)	Other Feeds (kg)	Type	Limit
Objective (c)	12	3	*	min	
Lime max (kg)	−0.1	1		≤	50
Mass (kg)	1	1	1	=	1,000
Other rows	*	*	*	*	*

By rearranging this, adding (0.1 × *Lupins*) to each side, we can see that the level of lime must be less than 50 plus an extra allowance for each kilogram of lupins:

$$(1.0 \times Lime) \le 50 + (0.1 \times Lupins)$$

In the final constraint type (d), the limit on lime is 50 kg or 10 percent of the level of lupins, whichever is greater (Figure 6.5). In this case, it may not be possible to solve the problem in a single computer run. However, the following procedure will reveal the optimal solution.

First, solve the problem with either one of the two constraints included, that is, either Tables 6.1 or 6.2. Note the levels of lime and lupins in the resulting optimal solution and check whether the level of lime is being constrained to a lower level than it should be. For example, if you included the fixed-limit constraint of Table 6.1, check whether the level of lupins is greater than 500. If it is and the level of lime is 50, the fixed *Lime max* constraint is limiting lime too much. Remove the current *Lime max* constraint and include the other type, as shown in Table 6.2.

On the other hand, if you included the flexible-limit constraint of Table 6.2, check to see whether (a) the level of lupins is less than 500 and (b) there is no slack on the *Lime max* constraint. If both these conditions hold, you need to switch to the fixed-limit *Lime max* constraint.

It is rather inconvenient to have to do this, but if you are using LP it cannot be avoided. You may need to resort to this approach whenever you have a maximization model with a constraint limit that is specified as "whichever is the greater" of two or more less-than constraints (as in the preceding example) or a minimization problem with a constraint limit specified as "whichever is the smaller" of two or more greater-than constraints. Technically, the reason

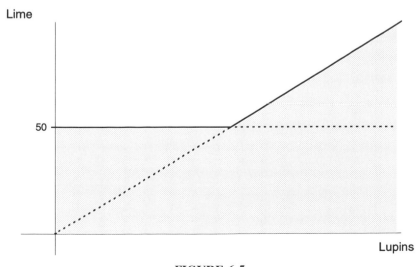

FIGURE 6.5

is that in LP the feasible set of activities must be "convex." This is explained in Section 7.1. Fortunately, the situation depicted in Figure 6.5 is relatively infrequent in real-world optimization problems.

BOX 6.1   Interpretations of Negative Matrix Coefficients

(a) An increase in the constraint limit for each unit of the activity.

(b) For less than constraints, a negative coefficient generates a resource or a capacity into some pool for use by other activities with positive coefficients.

(c) For greater than constraints, a negative coefficient increases the size of the hole that must be filled by other activities with positive coefficients.

(d) A negative parameter in an algebraic inequality or equality.

6.2   TRANSFER ROWS

Transfer rows use negative coefficients much as do the constraints that link the activities described in the previous section. The difference is that in Section 6.1, the problem definition indicated that activities should be linked; it would have been impossible to represent the desired relationships without the use of negative coefficients. Transfer rows, however, are often used by choice rather than by necessity. They can be used to improve the readability of the matrix or its output or to reduce the size of the matrix.

Example 6.2: Iron and Steel Processing

A steel factory manufactures partly processed iron ingots into various steel products. Iron ingots are available from three sources: the company's own iron plant, another local source, or from overseas. The prices for these three sources are $1000/tonne for company iron, $1200/tonne for other local iron, and $1500/tonne for imported iron. Company iron and other local iron are available in limited quantities of 3000 and 10,000 tonnes per day. The supply of imported iron is large enough not to constrain the factory.

The output of the factory is in three forms: thin sheets, thick sheets, and tubes. The amount of iron used in manufacturing these outputs is, respectively, 1.20, 1.21, and 1.25 tonnes of iron per tonne of steel. Each output has a different sale price and a different level of other fixed costs (all costs except for purchase of iron). Sale prices per tonne are $3200 for thin sheets, $3000 for thick sheets, and $3750 for tubes. Fixed costs are, respectively, $1000, $1000, and $2000 per tonne of thin, thick, and tube steel.

The steel factory has a maximum output of 15,000 tonnes per day.

Construct an LP matrix to select the pattern of purchases and outputs that will maximize profits of the steel manufacturer. ■

A complication in this problem is that the input, iron ingots, has a different cost depending on the source. As a result, each output will have a different level of profitability depending on the source of iron used in its manufacture. For example, a tonne of thin sheets sells for $3200 for fixed costs of $1000, but the cost of the iron component will be (1.2 × $1000), (1.2 × $1200), or (1.2 × $1500) depending on whether it is from company, local, or import sources. Thus the profitability of the tonne of thin sheets of steel could be $1000, $760, or $400.

There are two substantially different ways of representing this problem. One uses only positive coefficients and the other incorporates negative coefficients. A matrix with only positive coefficients is shown in Table 6.5. Because the profitability of each steel is dependent on the source of iron, three activities are needed for each type of steel. The three activities represent the same output but differnt sources of input.

Because of the many possible combinations of inputs and outputs, the matrix in Table 6.5 has to include many activities to allow for all possibilities. The objective coefficient for each of these activities is the net profit: returns minus fixed costs minus iron costs. These values must be calculated in advance.

An alternative representation of the same problem is shown in Table 6.6. The two matrices are equivalent in that they identify the same optimal solution, but there are also some striking differences between their structures.

For example, both include an *Own max* constraint to limit the availability of iron from the company's own sources, a *Local max* constraint to limit the availability of iron from local sources, and an *Output max* constraint to limit total output. Table 6.6 includes the extra constraint *Iron tr* (for iron transfer) that we will come back to shortly.

The major differences occur in the activities. Table 6.5 has nine activities, whereas Table 6.6 has six. In Table 6.5, each activity represents the purchase of some iron *and* production of a tonne of steel, while in Table 6.6, the first three activities represent purchase of a tonne of iron and the second three represent production of a tonne of steel. In other words, the activities of Table 6.6 are in two groups representing *sources* and *uses* of iron. The *sources* group represents all the different ways in which iron can be provided to the production process (*Own iron*, *Local iron*, and *Import iron*), while the *uses* group includes all the outputs manufactured from the iron (*Thin steel*, *Thick steel*, and *Tube steel*).

The *Iron tr* row imposes the constraint that the total uses of iron must not exceed the total sources of iron. It is a less-than constraint that places a limit on the use of iron, not on the sources.

There is no need for such a constraint in the other matrix (Table 6.5) because each activity incorporates both a source and a use of iron. For example, the

TABLE 6.5 Matrix for Example 6.2; No Negative Coefficients

	Thin—Own (t)	Thin—Local (t)	Thin—Import (t)	Thick—Own (t)	Thick—Local (t)	Thick—Import (t)	Tube—Own (t)	Tube—Local (t)	Tube—Import (t)	Type	Limit
Objective ($)	1,000	760	400	790	548	185	500	250	-125	max	
Own max (t)	1.2			1.21			1.25			≤	3,000
Local max (t)		1.2			1.21			1.25		≤	10,000
Output max (t)	1	1	1	1	1	1	1	1	1	≤	15,000

TABLE 6.6 Matrix for Example 6.2; Includes Negative Coefficients

	Own Iron (t)	Local Iron (t)	Import Iron (t)	Thin Steel (t)	Thick Steel (t)	Tube Steel (t)	Type	Limit
Objective ($)	-1,000	-1,200	-1,500	2,200	2,000	1,750	max	0
Iron tr (t)	-1	-1	-1	1.2	1.21	1.25	≤	
Own max (t)	1						≤	3,000
Local max (t)		1					≤	10,000
Output max (t)				1	1	1	≤	15,000

Thin–local activity represents the purchase of 1.20 tonnes of iron from the local market and production of one tonne of thin sheets of steel. The *Tube–import* activity represents the importation of 1.25 tonnes of iron and production of one tonne of tube steel. Purchase of sufficient iron is guaranteed since it is directly linked to the activities for production of steel.

When choosing the coefficients for the *Iron tr* row, only two of the three approaches suggested in Chapter 3 are appropriate. As this is a less-than constraint, one approach is to ask "How much of the available resource is used up by each unit of this activity?" The available resource in this example is iron. The three potential uses of iron require different amounts of iron. *Thin steel*, *Thick steel*, and *Tube steel* use, respectively, 1.20, 1.21, and 1.25 tonnes of iron. These numbers are the answers to the question just asked, and they become coefficients of the matrix.

The *sources* activities are somewhat different. "How much of the available resource is used up by each unit of this activity?" The activities in question (*Own iron*, *Local iron*, and *Import iron*) do not use up *any* of the resource. In fact, to the contrary, they increase the availability of iron for use in steel production. In a mathematical sense, this is the opposite of using up iron, so the coefficients have negative signs in the matrix. The coefficient of -1 for [*Own iron, Iron tr*] means that *Own iron generates* one tonne of iron into the *Iron tr* row.

The second approach to determining coefficients is to calculate the constraint limit divided by the level of the activity that just satisfies the constraint. This approach is inappropriate in this case since the constraint limit is zero. Even if we consider the constraint limit to be the amount of iron generated by the *sources* activities, we will not know how much has been generated until the model is solved, making this approach impossible to use to determine matrix coefficients.

The third approach is to consider the constraint as an algebraic inequality. The constraint is

$$uses \leq sources$$

or

$$(1.20 \times S_1) + (1.21 \times S_2) + (1.25 \times S_3)$$

$$\leq (1 \times I_1) + (1 \times I_2) + (1 \times I_3)$$

where S_1, S_2, and S_3 are the steel production activities and I_1, I_2, and I_3 represent purchase of iron from the different sources. The preceding inequality is equivalent to

$$(-1 \times I_1) + (-1 \times I_2) + (-1 \times I_3) + (1.20 \times S_1)$$

$$+ (1.21 \times S_2) + (1.25 \times S_3) \leq 0$$

This inequality is represented in the matrix by the *Iron tr* constraint, so the coefficients of this inequality are the coefficients of the *Iron tr* constraint. Constraints of the matrix must be specified in this way, with a fixed right-hand-side term independent of all activity levels.

This algebraic approach is one of the ways of making sense of negative coefficients mentioned earlier in this chapter. It is consistent with two other approaches: (a) to think of a negative coefficient in the matrix as a positive coefficient in the constraint limit, and (b) for a less-than constraint, to think of the constraint as a pool of a resource into which negative coefficients generate resource and from which positive coefficients use up the resource. Each of the *iron* activities has a −1 in the *Iron tr* row, and so each unit selected increases the constraint limit by one unit. Alternatively, each unit generates iron into a pool that can then be drawn on by the *steel* activities. Or you can think of the less-than constraint as representing a stock-pile that can be added to or drawn on by the various activities.

Note that it is generally best not to specify a transfer row as an equals constraint. It will almost always be possible to specify a less-than or greater-than constraint to achieve the same thing, and this will reduce the risk of overconstraining the model. At worst, overuse of equals constraints will result in a model with no feasible solution. In less extreme cases, the model will be more difficult (and slower) to solve than necessary. Do not use equals constraints unless it really is necessary for the constraint to have no slack.

Reasons For and Against Transfer Rows

One reason for adopting a transfer-row approach is that it can reduce the number of columns required. In general, the number of activities required for the approach in Table 6.5 is the number of sources times the number of uses. However, the transfer-row approach requires only one activity for each source and one for each use. The saving in columns can be substantial. For example, a factor with 5 sources and 10 uses would require 50 activities (10 × 5) in one approach and only 15 (10 + 5) in the other. The cost of having an extra constraint is small relative to this saving.

Another benefit of using transfer rows is that they make it simpler to interpret coefficients of the matrix and to incorporate any changes. In Table 6.6 it is easy to see the cost for each source of iron, the returns for each type of steel, and the iron requirement for each type of steel. These values appear directly as coefficients of the matrix. However, in Table 6.5, none of these magnitudes is readily apparent from looking at the matrix. The model coefficients have been calculated from these parameters, but in the process the original values of the parameters are obscured.

In the transfer row approach, the original parameters appear (more or less) directly as model coefficients, and they only appear once. For these reasons, it is relatively easy to make changes to their values. For example, if the price of *Thin steel* were to increase, the change could be incorporated in Table 6.6

by altering the [*Thin steel*, *Objective*] coefficient. However, to include the same change in Table 6.5 would require changes to three coefficients ([*Objective*, *Thin–own*], [*Objective*, *Thin–local*], and [*Objective*, *Thin–import*]), and in each case the new coefficient would have to be recalculated.

A negative impact of transfer rows is that they can sometimes lead to "degeneracy" in the optimal solution, resulting in the loss of some shadow cost information. This is explained fully in Chapter 10. Another slight negative is that each transfer row increases the number of constraints by one.

BOX 6.2   Reasons For and Against Use of Transfer Rows

For:

(a) Reduce the number of columns required. If there is an intermediate product with various *sources* and *uses*, transfer rows reduce the required number of activities from *sources* × *uses* to *sources* + *uses*.

(b) Allow the coefficients of the matrix to be easily interpreted without knowing the background assumptions of the model.

(c) Make it easier to change the assumptions of the model.

Against:

(a) Sometimes cause degeneracy in the optimal solution.

(b) Increase the number of rows required by one.

Reversing the Direction of Transfer Rows

We can reverse the direction of the *Iron tr* constraint without changing its influence on the problem. That is, instead of specifying that uses of iron must be less than or equal to sources of iron, we could specify that sources of iron must be greater than or equal to uses:

$$sources \geq uses$$

or

$$(1 \times I_1) + (1 \times I_2) + (1 \times I_3)$$
$$\geq (1.20 \times S_1) + (1.21 \times S_2) + (1.25 \times S_3)$$

which is equivalent to

$$(1 \times I_1) + (1 \times I_2) + (1 \times I_3) + (-1.20 \times S_1)$$
$$+ (-1.21 \times S_2) + (-1.25 \times S_3) \geq 0$$

This inequality is the same as the previous version except that (a) the coefficients have the opposite sign and (b) the direction of the inequality has been reversed; it is now a greater-than rather than a less-than constraint. In general, it is fine to reverse the signs of all coefficients of a row as long as you also reverse the direction of the constraint.

The matrix with this reversed constraint is shown in Table 6.7. This way of specifying transfer rows has the property that negative coefficients correspond to using up a resource while positive coefficients mean that some resource is being generated. In our example in Table 6.7, the iron activities generate iron available for use, so they have positive coefficients in the greater-than *Iron tr* constraint. The steel activities use up iron, so they have negative coefficients. Some model designers find these signs more intuitive and so routinely specify transfer rows as greater-than constraints. Others prefer to think of resource constraints as limiting the level of the resource, implying a less-than constraint. In this book transfer rows are generally specified as less-thans.

When transfer rows are specified as greater-than constraints, a useful interpretation of negative coefficients is that they increase the depth of a hole that must be filled by other activities with positive coefficients. In our example in Table 6.7, for example, the steel activities use up iron, so they have negative coefficients that create a hole. This hole must then be filled by generating iron with positive coefficients, which are provided by the iron activities.

Negative Objective Function Coefficients

The transfer row is not the only row in the preceding tables that contains negative coefficients. There are also negative coefficients in the objective function rows of Tables 6.5, 6.6, and 6.7. These negatives indicate that the activity in question would make the objective function smaller rather than larger; they would reduce, rather than increase, profit.

In Table 6.5, net profit for the *Tube-import* activity is

$$\$3750 - \$2000 - (1.25 \times \$1500) = -\$125$$

TABLE 6.7   Matrix for Example 6.2; *Iron tr* Specified as a Greater-than Constraint

	Own Iron (t)	Local Iron (t)	Import Iron (t)	Thin Steel (t)	Thick Steel (t)	Tube Steel (t)	Type	Limit
Objective ($)	−1,000	−1,200	−1,500	2,200	2,000	1,750	max	
Iron tr (t)	1	1	1	−1.2	−1.21	−1.25	≥	0
Own max (t)	1						≤	3,000
Local max (t)		1					≤	10,000
Output max (t)				1	1	1	≤	15,000

In other words, the costs of obtaining iron from the import market outweigh the returns from using it for production of tube steel. The *Tube-import* activity would therefore never be included in the optimal solution.

In Table 6.6 each of the activities for purchase of iron has a negative coefficient, indicating that the direct impacts of these activities on profit are to reduce it. However, unlike the *Tube-import* activity, at least one of these activities *will* be selected in the optimal solution because steel cannot be produced if iron is not purchased. We can see from the objective function coefficients of Table 6.5 that all but one combination of iron purchase/steel production is profitable, so any of these combinations could potentially be selected in the output for Table 6.6.

Optimal Solution

Table 6.8 shows the solution for the matrix in Table 6.5 that has only positive coefficients. The interpretation of this output is straightforward and in line with Chapter 4. The maximum profits achievable are $10,500,000, by producing 15,000 tonnes of thin steel. Of this thin steel, 2500 tonnes is manufactured from the company's own iron, 8333 tonnes is from local iron, and 4167 tonnes is from imported iron. To work out how much of each source of iron is used, it is necessary to multiply the number of tonnes of steel by the iron requirements of a tonne of steel. For thin steel, the problem definition says that this require-

TABLE 6.8   Optimal Solution for Example 6.2 for Version of Matrix Shown in Table 6.5

Objective function value: 10,500,000.000000
Problem direction: max

Activity		Level	Shadow Cost
1 Thin—own	A	2,500.0000	0.0000
2 Thin—local	A	8,333.3333	0.0000
3 Thin—import	A	4,166.6667	0.0000
4 Thick—own	Z	0.0000	215.0000
5 Thick—local	Z	0.0000	215.0000
6 Thick—import	Z	0.0000	215.0000
7 Tube—own	Z	0.0000	525.0000
8 Tube—local	Z	0.0000	525.0000
9 Tube—import	Z	0.0000	525.0000

Constraint		Slack	Shadow Price
1 Own max	L	0.0000	500.0000
2 Local max	L	0.0000	300.0000
3 Output max	L	0.0000	400.0000

ment is 1.2 tonnes of iron per tonne of steel. You can also see that this is the case by looking at the matrix; the coefficients for [*Own max, Thin–own*] and [*Local max, Thin–local*] are 1.2. Thus the steel production levels in Table 6.8 imply that the factory uses 3000 (= 2500 × 1.2) tonnes of its own iron, 10,000 (= 8333.33 × 1.2) tonnes of local iron and 5000 (= 4166.67 × 1.2) tonnes of imported iron.

The shadow costs of activities for production of thick steel are all $215 per tonne. Interpretations of this figure are (a) that the profitability of these activities would have to increase by $215 before any of them would be included in the optimal solution, or (b) if thick steel was produced, profits would be reduced by $215 (relative to the current optimal solution) for each tonne of thick steel produced. The fact that all three activities for thick steel production have the same shadow cost means that, technically, iron from the three possible sources is equivalent. The difference in profitability of *Thin–own* and *Thick–own* reflects the greater iron content of thick steel and the lower net returns of thick steel. Exactly the same can be said of the difference between *Thin–local*, and *Thick–local* and the difference between *Thin–import* and *Thick–import*. Because the differences in iron requirement and returns are the same in each case, the difference in profitability is also the same, leading to the same shadow cost for each thick steel activity.

The shadow costs of tube steel are greater than for thick steel ($525 per tonne), but they can be interpreted in the same way.

All constraints of the model are exactly met; there is no spare iron from the company's own sources nor from other local sources and the maximum output constraint is binding, so all slack values in the solution are zero.

The shadow prices of the constraints are all binding and they are all less-than constraints. The shadow price for *Own max* is $500 per tonne of iron, which is the increase in profits that would be possible if an extra tonne of iron could be obtained from the company's own smelter. Note that if an extra tonne of their own iron were used, the use of imported iron would have to be reduced by one unit in order for the *Output max* constraint to still be satisfied. The LP package assumes that all constraints will continue to be satisfied, so when calculating the shadow price of *Own max* it factors in the reduction in the level of *Thin–import* that would accompany an increase in *Thin–own*. Thus the shadow price of *Thin–own* is the net increase in returns after all other necessary adjustments are made to the solution, not the total returns from the amount of steel that would be produced from the extra tonne. Shadow prices are always like this. They factor in all necessary changes and all desirable changes to the solution as a result of changing the limit for the constraint in question.

In this example it is easy to see how the shadow price of $500 is calculated. The desirable change that one extra unit of *Own max* allows is selection of some extra *Thin–own*. Each tonne of *Thin–own* requires 1.2 tonnes of *Own max* ([*Own max, Thin–own*] = 1.2), so one extra unit of *Own max* would allow $\frac{1}{1.2} = \frac{5}{6}$ units of *Thin–own*. Given that total output is limited by *Output max*, this extra *Thin–own* would require a reduction in *Thin–import* by the same amount. We know that it is *Thin–import* that would be reduced because it has a lower net profit than *Thin–local*. We also know that it would be worth giving up $\frac{5}{6}$ units of *Thin–import* in order to achieve an equivalent increase in *Thin–own* because *Thin–own* has a much greater profit per unit.

Thus the impact of increasing the limit of *Own max* by one unit would be an increase in *Thin–own* by $\frac{5}{6}$ units and a reduction in *Thin–import* by $\frac{5}{6}$ units. The effect on profits would be the difference in profitability of these two activities times $\frac{5}{6}$

$$(1000 - 400) \times \tfrac{5}{6} = 500$$

which is the shadow price of *Own max*.

To reiterate, the shadow price gives the effect of a change in the constraint limit on the objective function after all necessary changes and all desirable changes to the solution have been made.

The shadow price for *Local max* is calculated much like *Own max*. The desirable change is an increase in *Thin–local*, and the necessary change is an equivalent reduction in *Thin–import*.

The shadow price of *Output max* is a little different. An extra unit of *Output max* would make it possible to produce more output, but the *Own max* and *Local max* constraints mean that this output could only be from imported iron. The best of the import activities is *Thin–import*. An extra unit of this iron would increase profits by $400. There would be no need for any other changes to the solution, so $400 is the shadow price of the constraint.

Now let us move to the other version of the matrix. This gives us the same information but in a somewhat different way. Some of the information in Table 6.8 is implicit in Table 6.9 and some of the information in Table 6.9 is implicit in Table 6.8. For a start, Table 6.9 (which is from the matrix in Table 6.6) gives us directly the levels of *Own iron*, *Local iron*, and *Imported iron* used; in the other version we had to calculate these levels from the levels of *Thin–own*, *Thick–own*, and *Import–own*. Although Table 6.9 also gives us directly the total amount of each type of steel produced, it does not give us the amount of each type of steel produced from each type of iron, which we could easily see in Table 6.8. Whichever version we use, it is possible to calculate all the relevant information, given our knowledge of the problem definition. However, Table 6.9 probably presents the solution in a form that is more convenient. This is often true of models in which a transfer row is used. Because the matrix is disaggregated into its components (i.e., there are separate activities for each source of iron and each type of steel), the solution contains information about each individual component, rather than about compound activities like *Thin–own*.

You can use this knowledge to your advantage. When building a real-world

TABLE 6.9 Optimal Solution for Example 6.2 for Version of Matrix Shown in Table 6.6

Objective function value: 10,500,000.000000
Problem direction: max

Activity		Level	Shadow Cost
1 Own iron	A	3,000.0000	0.0000
2 Local iron	A	10,000.0000	0.0000
3 Import iron	A	5,000.0000	0.0000
4 Thin steel	A	15,000.0000	0.0000
5 Thick steel	Z	0.0000	215.0000
6 Tube steel	Z	0.0000	525.0000

Constraint		Slack	Shadow Price
1 Iron tr	L	0.0000	1,500.0000
2 Own max	L	0.0000	500.0000
3 Local max	L	0.0000	300.0000
4 Output max	L	0.0000	400.0000

model, it is often desirable for the solution to directly show the level of a particular input or output. Usually you can use a transfer row to adjust the model so that it gives an equivalent solution that shows the desired information.

Of course, the slacks and shadow prices of *Own max*, *Local max*, and *Output max* in Table 6.9 are the same as in Table 6.8. However, there is now an extra constraint, *Iron tr*, with no slack and a shadow price of $1500. What does this mean?

Shadow Prices of Transfer Rows

First, note that a transfer row constrains the activities that use up the factor (i.e., activities with positive coefficients in a less-than transfer row or negative coefficients in a greater-than transfer row). A transfer row does not place any constraint on the levels of activities that generate the factor—if it is desirable to select more of one of these activities, a transfer row will not prevent it from happening.

Second, remember that the shadow price gives the effect of a change in the constraint limit on the objective function after all necessary changes and all desirable changes to the solution have been made. There are two possible types of desirable change that may result from a loosening of the constraint limit of a transfer row (i.e., an increase in the limit of a less-than transfer row, or a reduction in the constraint limit of a greater-than transfer row). One is that it might be desirable to produce more of an output that uses up the factor. If this is the best use of the extra factor, the shadow price represents the net benefit of this extra production, not including the cost of the extra factor. That is, it is implicit in the shadow price that the extra factor is provided at no cost.

The other type of desirable change that may occur if the constraint limit is loosened is a reduction in expenditure on purchase of the factor, with no change in the total level of use of the factor. If this is the best thing to do as a result of loosening the constraint, the shadow price represents the net savings from not having to purchase so much of the factor.

It is essential to understand how the matrix is structured in order to validly interpret a particular shadow price. In particular, note that it is only the factor constrained by the row that is assumed to come at no cost when calculating the shadow price. If extra availability of the factor would result in extra purchase of some other factor elsewhere in the model, this other factor is not assumed to be costless. Also if the costs of some other factors are already built into an activity that consumes the factor, these costs are also included in calculating the shadow price of the constraint.

Now consider our example. An increase of one unit in the limit of *Iron tr* would not allow any extra steel to be produced because the *Output max* constraint still limits output to 15,000 tonnes. It would, however, allow a reduction in the level of purchase of the most expensive iron, *Import iron*. One unit of *Import iron* costs $1500, so this is the shadow price of *Iron tr*. Note that the shadow price is based on the constraint limit being increased without any associated cost. In this example, it is as if the company were *given* an extra tonne of iron.

Notice the difference in interpretation between the shadow prices of *Local max* and *Iron tr*. *Local max* is a constraint on the amount of iron that can be purchased from local sources. It affects the level of *Local iron*; if the constraint limit of *Local max* is increased by one unit, an extra unit of *Local iron* can be selected. This extra unit would include a cost of $1200, and would allow a reduction of one unit of *Import iron*, a saving of $1500. Notice that the cost of the extra unit of *Local iron* is accounted for. This is because the *Local max* constraint does not limit the amount of iron that can be used, but instead limits the amount of iron that can be purchased. If you loosen the constraint, to get any benefit you still have to purchase the iron. On the other hand, the *Iron tr* row sets the maximum level of iron available for use. If you increase the constraint limit on *Iron tr*, extra iron is immediately available for use, without having to select a purchasing activity like *Local iron*. Thus the cost of any extra iron is accounted for in the shadow price for *Local max*, but not in the shadow price for *Iron tr*.

BOX 6.3   Interpreting Shadow Prices of Transfer Rows

The shadow price gives the effect of a constraint limit change on the objective function after all desirable or necessary changes to the solution have been made. There are two possible types of desirable change that may result from a loosening of the constraint limit of a transfer row:

(a) Produce more of an output that uses up the factor. In this case, the shadow price represents the net benefit of this extra production, not including the cost of the extra factor.

(b) Reduce expenditure on purchase of the factor, with no change in the total level of use of the factor. In this case, the shadow price represents the net savings from reducing expenditure on the factor.

Only the factor constrained by a row is assumed to come at no cost when calculating its shadow price. If extra availability of the factor would result in extra purchase of another factor elsewhere in the model, or if the costs of other factors are included in an activity that uses the factor, these costs are not ignored in calculating the shadow price of the constraint.

6.3 NEGATIVE FACTOR LEVELS

We have seen that no single activity in an LP model can take on a negative value in the optimal solution. However, this does not mean that it is impossible to represent a negative level of some factor. For example, debt is, in a sense, a negative credit; a cost is like a negative return. We have already seen that there is no problem representing costs in a model. In this section we examine various ways of using transfer rows to represent costs and returns. The techniques demonstrated will apply in any model where a factor may assume either positive or negative values.

Example 6.2 dealt with a steel factory transforming iron ingots into various steel products. Have another look at the problem definition and the matrix in Table 6.6.

Now we will change the matrix so that there is an activity that represents the total cost of iron purchases. Of course, expenditure on iron was represented in Table 6.6 by including the cost per tonne of iron in the objective function of the three iron purchase activities. The aim of this exercise is to represent the same problem in a different way. The reasons one might wish to do this are discussed later.

Table 6.10 shows a matrix that includes a separate activity that counts the total costs of iron purchases, *Iron cost*. The cost coefficients have been moved from the *Objective* row to a new *Iron $ tr* row and changed from negative to

TABLE 6.10 Matrix for Example 6.2; Includes Transfer Row for Iron Costs

	Own Iron (t)	Local Iron (t)	Import Iron (t)	Thin Steel (t)	Thick Steel (t)	Tube Steel (t)	Iron Cost ($)	Type	Limit
Objective ($)				2,200	2,000	1,750	−1	max	
Iron tr (t)	−1	−1	−1	1.2	1.21	1.25		≤	0
Own max (t)	1							≤	3,000
Local max (t)		1						≤	10,000
Output max (t)				1	1	1		≤	15,000
Iron $ tr ($)	1,000	1,200	1,500				−1	≤	0

positive coefficients. The *Iron cost* activity represents one dollar of expenditure on iron, so the total number of units of *Iron cost* will give the total expenditure on iron. *Iron cost* has a coefficient of −1 in the *Objective* row. This is why the iron purchasing activities no longer need to have cost coefficients in the objective function. The costs are transmitted to the objective function by the *Iron cost* activity.

Now because the *Iron cost* activity has a negative *Objective* coefficient, the model, which wants to maximize profit, will prefer not to select it in the optimal solution unless it has to. So what will force its selection so that the cost of iron is correctly captured? Two constraints will combine to ensure this. First, the iron transfer row, as we have already seen, ensures that no steel can be produced unless some iron is purchased. The model wishes to produce steel, since it generates positive income, but the constraint limit of *Iron tr* is zero, meaning that steel production is limited to zero unless some iron is generated into the row by the iron purchasing activities.

But selection of any iron purchasing activity has unavoidable consequences in the *Iron $ tr* row. Remember that each unit of an activity has an impact on all rows for which the activity has a nonzero coefficient. In this case, each tonne of iron purchased increases the positive value of the left-hand side of the *Iron $ tr* row. However, the constraint says that the sum of factors on the left-hand side must be less than or equal to zero. Thus any positive value placed in the row by purchasing iron must be at least offset by negative coefficients from some other activity or activities. The only negative coefficient in the row is −1 in the *Iron cost* column. Thus *Iron cost* will be forced into the solution, because making steel requires the purchase of iron, and the purchase of iron requires *Iron cost*. For example, each unit of *Thin steel* in the solution requires 1.20 units of iron, while each unit of iron requires 1000, 1200, or 1500 units of *Iron cost* (depending on the source of iron). Conveniently, the level of *Iron cost* in the optimal solution will indicate the total level of expenditure on iron.

It is also possible to move the returns coefficients out of the objective function and into their own transfer row, linked to the objective function by another activity. This is illustrated in Table 6.11. The new row (*Steel $ tr*) and column

TABLE 6.11 Matrix for Example 6.2; Includes Transfer Rows for Costs and Returns

	Own Iron (t)	Local Iron (t)	Import Iron (t)	Thin Steel (t)	Thick Steel (t)	Tube Steel (t)	Iron Cost ($)	Steel Rets ($)	Type	Limit
Objective ($)							−1	1	max	
Iron tr (t)	−1	−1	−1	1.2	1.21	1.25			≤	0
Own max (t)	1								≤	3,000
Local max (t)		1							≤	10,000
Output max (t)				1	1	1			≤	15,000
Iron $ tr ($)	1,000	1,200	1,500				−1		≤	0
Steel $ tr ($)				−2,200	−2,000	−1,750		1	≤	0

122

(*Steel rets*) are similar to those for iron except that the signs of coefficients are reversed. Because *Steel rets* has a positive objective function coefficient, the model will try to include it in the solution, but because of the *Steel $ tr* row, it can only be included if one or more of the steel-making activities is included. These activities generate the capacity to select *Steel rets* into the *Steel $ tr* row, and *Steel rets* uses up this capacity. Again the level of *Steel rets* in the optimal solution indicates the total level of returns. Of course, the selection of steel activities uses up some iron, which must then be supplied by selection of iron activities. The cost of this then flows through to the objective function via *Iron $ tr* and *Iron cost* as before.

We noted before that you can restructure the matrix in order to have different information shown in the solution. The matrix in Table 6.11 is a good example of this. It includes two extra transfer rows: one for iron costs and one for steel returns. There is an extra activity for each, transferring the costs and returns into the objective function. In the solution in Table 6.12, the level of *Iron cost* gives the total expenditure on iron, while *Steel rets* gives the total receipts from sales of steel. This is information that would have to be calculated indirectly from the solutions for the other versions of this model. The difference between the levels of *Steel rets* and *Iron cost* gives the objective function value.

The shadow prices for *Iron $ tr* and *Steel $ tr* are $1.00 in each case. In the case of *Iron $ tr*, an increase in the constraint limit by one unit would allow

TABLE 6.12 Optimal Solution for Example 6.2 for Version of Matrix Shown in Table 6.11

Objective function value: 10,500,000.000000
Problem direction: max

Activity		Level	Shadow Cost
1 Own iron	A	3,000.0000	0.0000
2 Local iron	A	10,000.0000	0.0000
3 Import iron	A	5,000.0000	0.0000
4 Thin steel	A	15,000.0000	0.0000
5 Thick steel	Z	0.0000	215.0000
6 Tube steel	Z	0.0000	525.0000
7 Iron cost	A	22,500,000.0000	0.0000
8 Steel rets	A	33,000,000.0000	0.0000

Constraint		Slack	Shadow Price
1 Iron tr	L	0.0000	1,500.0000
2 Own max	L	0.0000	500.0000
3 Local max	L	0.0000	300.0000
4 Output max	L	0.0000	400.0000
5 Iron $ tr	L	0.0000	1.0000
6 Steel $ tr	L	0.0000	1.0000

one less unit of *Iron cost* to be selected, reducing the negative impact on the objective function by one unit. For *Steel $ tr* an increase in the constraint limit would allow an extra unit of *Steel rets*, increasing the objective function by one unit. However, it is obvious that an extra dollar of returns or one less dollar of costs is worth a dollar. The information in these shadow prices is therefore not of any practical value. It is generated as a side effect when the model is restructured in order to generate the total levels of costs and returns.

Now consider Table 6.13, which is yet another matrix for the same problem. This time the costs and returns have been combined into a single constraint (*$ tr*), much as they were in the objective function row in Table 6.6. The resulting total level of returns or costs must be communicated to the objective function. However, we do not necessarily know in advance whether the net result will be a profit or a loss. Consequently we need two activities to connect the transfer row to the objective function.

If the net result is a profit, there will be more negative numbers generated into the *$ tr* row (by steel activities) than positive numbers (by iron activities), allowing the selection of *Profit* once for each dollar of profit. On the other hand, if positive numbers outweigh the negative, it will not be possible to select any of the *Profit* activity and, to offset the positive values, it will be necessary to select a unit of *Loss* for each dollar of loss.

Note that in this simple model, instead of selecting a loss-making strategy it would be preferable to select not to produce anything at all, resulting in zero gain and zero loss. However, in more realistic situations there are circumstances where a loss needs to be represented (e.g., an investment may suffer losses in the short term but larger gains in the long term).

This way of representing the financial costs and returns of the model does not indicate their individual total levels, just the net value when costs are subtracted from returns. Its advantage over including all returns and costs in the objective function (as in Table 6.6) is that it allows easier adjustment to parameters that affect *all* returns and costs, such as interest rates. This is especially useful in multiperiod models where the levels of costs and returns in a period affect the amount of interest paid or received in the next period. This is illustrated in the next chapter.

The version of the matrix in Table 6.13 differs from Table 6.11 in that there is only one transfer row that contains both costs and returns instead of separate rows for costs and returns. Thus the level of cash in the *$ tr* row is the net profit or loss for the company. It includes the same coefficients as were in the objective function in Table 6.6. If we do not know in advance whether the optimal solution will have a net profit, we need to have two activities to transfer the profit or loss into the objective function. This is because it is impossible for an activity to take on a negative value. The result will either be a positive level of profit (in which case the profit activity will be selected and the loss activity will not) or a positive level of loss (so that the loss activity is selected but the profit activity is not). In the optimal solution (Table 6.14), the *Profit* activity is selected at 10,500,000, but the *Loss* activity is not selected.

TABLE 6.13 Matrix for Example 6.2; Includes a Single Transfer Row for Costs and Returns

	Own Iron (t)	Local Iron (t)	Import Iron (t)	Thin Steel (t)	Thick Steel (t)	Tube Steel (t)	Loss ($)	Profit ($)	Type	Limit
Objective ($)							-1	1	max	0
Iron tr (t)	-1	-1	-1	1.2	1.21	1.25			$\leq$	0
Own max (t)	1								$\leq$	3,000
Local max (t)		1							$\leq$	10,000
Output max (t)				1	1	1			$\leq$	15,000
$ tr ($)	1,000	1,200	1,500	-2,200	-2,000	-1,750	-1	1	$\leq$	0

TABLE 6.14   Optimal Solution for Example 6.2 for Version of Matrix Shown in Table 6.13

Objective function value: 10,500,000.000000
Problem direction: max

Activity		Level	Shadow Cost
1 Own iron	A	3,000.0000	0.0000
2 Local iron	A	10,000.0000	0.0000
3 Import iron	A	5,000.0000	0.0000
4 Thin steel	A	15,000.0000	0.0000
5 Thick steel	Z	0.0000	215.0000
6 Tube steel	Z	0.0000	525.0000
7 Loss	ZM	0.0000	0.0000
8 Profit	A	10,500,000.0000	0.0000

Constraint		Slack	Shadow Price
1 Iron tr	L	0.0000	1,500.0000
2 Own max	L	0.0000	500.0000
3 Local max	L	0.0000	300.0000
4 Output max	L	0.0000	400.0000
5 $ tr	L	0.0000	1.0000

6.4   KEY POINTS

- Negative coefficients make it possible to link the level of one activity to another.
- There are several possible interpretations of a negative coefficient:

  a positive contributor to the constraint limit.

  for less-than constraints, a negative coefficient generates a resource or a capacity into a pool for use by activities with positive coefficients.

  for greater-than constraints, a negative coefficient increases the size of a hole that must be filled by activities with positive coefficients.

  a negative parameter in an algebraic inequality or equality.

- Use of transfer rows sometimes allows a smaller matrix to be constructed, especially in multiperiod problems.
- The direction of a transfer row constraint can be reversed by multiplying all its coefficients by -1.
- A matrix can be reconstructed in order to show different information in the solution.
- Although the level of an activity in an LP solution must be greater than or equal to zero, it is possible to represent negative magnitudes, such as costs or debts.

The main points relating to interpretation of LP solutions were presented in Chapter 4. The following points that arose in the present chapter are additional or are worth reemphasizing.

- Usually transfer rows that represent real, concrete resources do have a meaningful shadow price, but those included for structural or logical reasons often do not.
- The units of measurement for shadow costs and shadow prices are the same as for the objective function.
- For some problems not all the interpretations of shadow costs presented in Chapter 4 are appropriate. In some cases it is meaningful to talk about reductions in constraint limits, but not increases. The reverse case may also apply in some circumstances.
- Shadow prices account for all necessary changes and all desirable changes to the solution as a result of changing the constraint limit in question.
- There are two possible types of desirable change that may result from a loosening of the constraint limit of a transfer row: (a) produce more of an output that uses up the factor, or (b) reduce expenditure on purchase of the factor, with no change in the total level of use of the factor. In case (a), the shadow price represents the net benefit of the extra production, not including the cost of the extra factor. In case (b), the shadow price represents the net savings from reducing expenditure on the factor.
- Only the factor constrained by a row has no cost when calculating its shadow price. If extra availability of the factor would result in extra purchase of another factor elsewhre in the model, or if the costs of other factors are included in an activity that uses the factor, these costs are not ignored in calculating the shadow price of the constraint.

CHAPTER 7

SPECIAL TECHNIQUES

A commonly cited assumption of linear programming (LP) is that the constraints and the objective function must be linear. In Section 7.1 it is shown that, despite its name, linear programming can be used to closely approximate nonlinear relationships in many realistic situations. Sections 7.2 and 7.3 show how to construct models for problems that extend over several time periods or several regions. For example, a problem may involve planning over a period of several years and/or coordination of activities in several regions, including transport between them if needed. Although it is not possible in LP to specify that variables can take only integer values, Section 7.4 shows how such a situation can be handled if the user is willing to generate more than one model solution. Section 7.5 shows a simple way of excluding an activity or group of activities from a particular solution. Finally, Section 7.6 describes the *dual*, an alternative way of formulating any LP model.

7.1 REPRESENTING CURVES

Many texts stress that LP can only represent linear relationships, and advise that to represent nonlinear relationships you should use nonlinear programming (NLP). This is good advice if you are familiar with NLP and have access to a good NLP computer package. However, in cases where these conditions do not apply, LP can be used to closely approximate nonlinear relationships.

Example 7.1: Production-Line Output

A factory manager wishes to select the optimal number of staff to allocate to a particular production line for television sets. Increasing the number of staff will increase the throughput of the production line. However, as more staff are added, the rate of increase of throughput decreases due to factors such as crowding and the physical limitations of the production line.

The profit per television set is $120 minus labor costs. Labor costs $50 per day. The relationship between labor input and television output per day is as follows:

Labor	Television Sets
0	0
10	60
20	80
30	85
40	87

Construct an LP matrix to find the profit-maximizing level of labor.   ■

A key aspect of the problem is the way the impact of extra labor decreases as the level of labor increases. The first 10 workers employed increase production from zero to 60 television sets. The second 10 only raise it by a further 20 sets, and so on. An economist would say that in this example, labor has diminishing marginal productivity. The relationship between labor and output is illustrated in Figure 7.1. In reality there would probably be a smoother relationship than shown in the figure, but a limitation of LP is that it can only approximate a curve using a discrete number of straight line segments. Figure 7.1 shows the line segments used in this example.

We examine three different ways of representing this problem in an LP matrix, starting with what is probably the most intuitively obvious approach and finishing with the most efficient.

Table 7.1 shows the first matrix for Example 7.1. There are activities for hiring labor, for using different quantities of labor, and for selling television sets. It is not possible to have a single activity for using labor because in LP the marginal impact of an activity is the same regardless of its level. In the example, the marginal impact of labor declines as more workers are used. This is captured in the model by using several activities, each representing a different level of labor use.

The constraints of the model are a labor transfer row linking hired labor to use of labor, a television transfer row linking production to sales of television sets, and several constraints limiting the selection of the various labor-use activities.

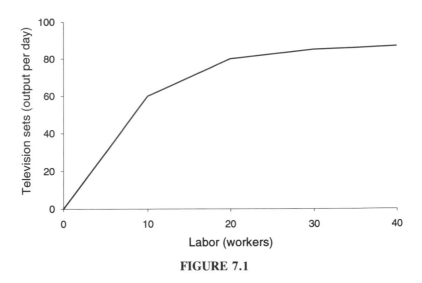

FIGURE 7.1

The objective function coefficients of the model are −50 for *Hire labor*, representing the cost per day of labor, and 120 for *Sell TVs*, representing the proceeds from selling a television set. The labor-use activities have objective function coefficients of zero. However, each is linked to particular levels of *Hire labor* and *Sell TVs*, so their indirect impacts on profit are captured.

Let us examine how the constraints of the model operate. All constraints are specified as less-thans. The unit of measurement for the four *LabXX max* constraints (and the labor activities) is given in the matrix as (−), indicating that there is no meaningful unit of measurement. The *Labor 10* activity uses 10 units of labor from the *Labor tr* row and generates 60 television sets into the *TV tr* row. This requires the selection of 10 units of *Hire labor* and allows the selection of 60 units of *Sell TVs*. Note the usage of the terms *requires* and *allows*. Because the objective function value for *Hire labor* is negative, the computer package will select as little of it as possible: no more than is required

TABLE 7.1 First Version of Matrix for Example 7.1

	Hire Labor (No.)	Labor 10 (−)	Labor 20 (−)	Labor 30 (−)	Labor 40 (−)	Sell TVs (TVs)	Type	Limit
Objective ($)	−50					120	max	
Labor tr (No.)	−1	10	10	10	10		≤	0
TV tr (TVs)		−60	−20	−5	−2	1	≤	0
Lab10 max (−)		1					≤	1
Lab20 max (−)		−1	1				≤	0
Lab30 max (−)			−1	1			≤	0
Lab40 max (−)				−1	1		≤	0

to allow the selection of other profitable activities. On the other hand, *Sell TVs* has a positive objective function coefficient, and so the solution will include as much of it as possible without violating the *TV tr* constraint.

In addition, the level of *Labor 10* is limited to one unit by the *Lab10 max* constraint. Without this constraint, it would be possible to select, say, two units of *Labor 10*, resulting in production of 120 television sets. However, the problem definition specifies that if 20 workers are employed, the output should be 80 television sets per day. We can ensure that hiring an extra 10 workers results in only an extra 20 television sets per day (to bring total production to 80 per day) by requiring extra labor to be used by the *Labor 20* activity, which generates only 20 television sets into the *Labor tr* row. The *Lab10 max* row ensures that only one unit of *Labor 10* can be selected (using 10 laborers), while the *Lab20 max* row allows one unit of *Labor 20* for each unit of *Labor 10* that is selected. The constraint specifies that

$$(-1 \times \textit{Labor 10}) + (1 \times \textit{Labor 20}) \leq 0$$

or, rearranging this,

$$(1 \times \textit{Labor 20}) \leq (1 \times \textit{Labor 10})$$

Since the level of *Labor 10* is limited to one unit, the level of *Labor 20* will be constrained to that level as well. Similarly, the selection of *Labor 20* allows one unit of *Labor 30* (via the *Lab30 max* constraint), and so on. As more workers are used, the incremental effect on television output decreases until addition of the fourth lot of 10 workers results in production of only two more television sets.

The model is an approximation of a smoother curvilinear relationship between labor use and output. For the first 10 units of labor, the output per worker is a constant 6 television sets. The next 10 workers contribute 2 sets each, the third 10 generate 0.5 set, each, and the fourth 10 give 0.2 each. In reality the output per worker may fall with each extra worker. It would be possible to represent this in Table 7.1, but it would require an activity and a constraint for each unit of labor. Some degree of aggregation is normally fine. You as the modeler must make a judgment about how much the model can be simplified without substantially reducing its usefulness.

Even if we use activities that represent multiples of 10 workers, it would be possible to select some number of workers that is not a multiple of 10. For example, if the solution included one unit of *Labor 10* and 0.5 unit of *Labor 20*, this would imply that 15 workers were used. Labor drawn from the *Labor tr* row would be 10 units by the *Labor 10* activity and 5 units (0.5 × 10) by the *Labor 20* activity, giving 15 in total. The resulting level of output of television sets would be

$$(1 \times 60) + (0.5 \times 20) = 70$$

TABLE 7.2 Second Version of Matrix for Example 7.1

	Hire Labor (No.)	Labor 10 (−)	Labor 20 (−)	Labor 30 (−)	Labor 40 (−)	Sell TVs (TVs)	Type	Limit
Objective ($)	−50					120	max	
Labor tr (No.)	−1	10	10	10	10		≤	0
TV tr (TVs)		−60	−20	−5	−2	1	≤	0
Lab10 max (−)		1					≤	1
Lab20 max (−)			1				≤	1
Lab30 max (−)				1			≤	1
Lab40 max (−)					1		≤	1

This corresponds to a point halfway along the second line segment in Figure 7.1.

The output from this model is examined later in this chapter. For now, consider an alternative representation of the same example. Table 7.2 shows a matrix that is similar in structure to Table 7.1. The differences are that the negative coefficients of the *Labor max* rows in Table 7.1 have been moved into the constraint limit column on Table 7.2. This means that it would be feasible to select a unit of *Labor 30* without having to select a unit of *Labor 20*, whereas in Table 7.1 this was prevented by the *Lab30 max* constraint.

You might be concerned that this change allows the model to select the twenty-first worker before it has selected the first. However, the model does not do this because although such behavior would be feasible, it could never be optimal. The objective, remember, is to maximize profits, so the model would never select the *Labor 30* unit in preference to the more productive activities, *Labor 20* and *Labor 10*. *Labor 30* generates only 0.5 television set per worker, whereas it is possible to generate 2 or 6 television sets per worker by selecting *Labor 20* or *Labor 10*. Higher labor levels will never be selected unless the capacity to select lower labor levels has been exhausted. To further emphasize the point, no solution would include units of *Labor 10* and *Labor 30* but not of *Labor 20*, because the workers used by the *Labor 30* activity could be more productively used by the *Labor 20* activity.

The structure of Table 7.2 relies on our understanding of the way the model will behave when solved. This is taken a step further in Table 7.3, which shows a third representation of the same model. This time the set of constraints that applied to each labor-use activity has been compressed into a single constraint.

In previous versions, the selection of an activity for higher labor use was in addition to the lower levels of use. If the optimal solution was to use 20 workers, the optimal activity levels in the solution would be 1 for *Labor 10* and 1 for *Labor 20*. The impact of the higher labor use was in addition to the impact of the lower labor level.

TABLE 7.3   Third Version of Matrix for Example 7.1

	Hire Labor (No.)	Labor 10 (−)	Labor 20 (−)	Labor 30 (−)	Labor 40 (−)	Sell TVs (TVs)	Type	Limit
Objective ($)	−50					120	max	
Labor tr (No.)	−1	10	20	30	40		≤	0
TV tr (TVs)		−60	−80	−85	−87	1	≤	0
Labor unit (−)		1	1	1	1		≤	1

In Table 7.3 each level of labor use is an alternative. If the optimal level is 20, the model solution would include *Labor 20* instead of *Labor 10*, not in addition to it. This is achieved by having a single *Labor unit* constraint and limiting the level of all labor use activities to a total of 1.

$$(1 \times Labor\ 10) + (1 \times Labor\ 20)$$
$$+ (1 \times Labor\ 30) + (1 \times Labor\ 40) \leq 1$$

As a consequence, the coefficients of the *TV tr* row have been changed so that they now represent the full impact of the relevant level of labor use, not just the incremental difference between this level of labor and the next lower level.

In considering whether to increase labor use from 10 to 20, the model now must give up a unit of *Labor 10* in order to gain a unit of *Labor 20*. Thus the *increases* in labor use and television production are the same as represented in the *Labor 20* activity in Tables 7.1 and 7.2.

As before, the unit of measurement for the four labor-use activities and for the *Labor unit* constraint is given in the matrix as (−), indicating that there is no meaningful unit of measurement. The unit of *Labor unit* is not "number of workers" because the number of workers corresponding to a coefficient of 1 in the row is different for each column. If anything, the unit for *Labor unit* is "units of any labor-use activity." In this context, each labor-use column effectively has the unit of measurement "one unit of a labor-use activity." The *Labor unit* constraint limits the total number of labor-use activities to one.

We might be concerned that the optimal solution could contain, say, 0.5 of a unit of the *Labor 10* activity and 0.5 of the *Labor 30* activity instead of a single unit of *Labor 20*. The labor use of the combination would be equal to 20, but the level of output of television sets would differ from that specified in the problem definition for 20 workers. Again, however, this would be feasible but it would never be optimal. Compare the output of the preceding combination of activities with that of *Labor 20*. Total output of the combination would be

$$(0.5 \times 60) + (0.5 \times 85) = 72.5$$

whereas a single unit of *Labor 20* generates 80 television sets. The only time the optimal solution will include a combination of activities from an approximated curve is when the optimal solution lies between two adjacent corner points.

The net result of these matrix differences is a model that behaves in an identical fashion to those in Tables 7.1 and 7.2, but requiring many fewer rows, thus solving more quickly. The savings in rows for a large model can be very substantial. This is important because most computer packages used to solve large LP models employ the "revised simplex" method as the mathematical technique for solving them. The time required to solve a model using this technique is much more sensitive to the number of rows in a model than to the number of columns.

The idea for the very efficient method of representing curves in Table 7.3 is usually attributed to Duloy and Norton (1975). However, the approach was used previously by Vandeputte and Baker (1970) to represent a progressive income tax scale.

Optimal Solutions

Table 7.4 shows the solution for the matrix in Table 7.1. It shows that the optimal level of labor to hire is 30 workers per day (the level of *Hire labor*), which produces 85 television sets (the level of *Sell TVs*). The model includes four activities to represent the relationship between labor and output: *Labor 10*, *Labor 20*, *Labor 30*, and *Labor 40*. The first three of these are selected at a level of one, while *Labor 40* is not selected. Let us relate this to the original matrix in Table 7.1. The selection of one unit of *Labor 10* uses 10 units of

TABLE 7.4 Optimal Solution for Example 7.1 for Version of Matrix Shown in Table 7.1

Objective function value: 8700.000000
Problem direction: max

Activity		Level	Shadow Cost
1 Hire labor	A	30.0000	0.0000
2 Labor 10	A	1.0000	0.0000
3 Labor 20	A	1.0000	0.0000
4 Labor 30	A	1.0000	0.0000
5 Labor 40	Z	0.0000	260.0000
6 Sell TVs	A	85.0000	0.0000

Constraint		Slack	Shadow Price
1 Labor tr	L	0.0000	50.0000
2 TV tr	L	0.0000	120.0000
3 Lab10 max	L	0.0000	8,700.0000
4 Lab20 max	L	0.0000	2,000.0000
5 Lab30 max	L	0.0000	100.0000
6 Lab40 max	L	1.0000	0.0000

labor (see the *Labor tr* row) and generates 60 television sets. The level of *Labor 10* is limited to a maximum of one unit by the *Lab10 max* constraint, and that unit generates the capacity to select a unit of *Labor 20* because of the -1 coefficient in *Lab20 max*.

Labor 20 uses another 10 units of labor (to take the total to 20) and generates another 20 television sets, while *Labor 30* uses another 10 units of labor (to take the total to 30) and generates another 5 television sets. You can see from this why the solution in Table 7.4 includes one unit of each of the three units *Labor 10*, *Labor 20*, and *Labor 30*. Each of these activities uses up 10 units of labor, so to use up 30 units the model has to select all three. Because it is only possible to select one unit of each of them, the declining productivity of each increase in labor usage is captured. If the desired number of workers is 20, the most productive way of employing them is by selecting two units of *Labor 10*, but the *Lab10 max* constraint means that this is not possible. At best the model can select one unit of *Labor 10* and one of *Labor 20*.

The model does not select the *Labor 40* activity since the cost of the last 10 workers ($10 \times 50 = 500$) is greater than the returns from the two extra television sets they produce ($2 \times 120 = 240$). The shadow cost of *Labor 40* is \$260, indicating that the returns from this activity would have to be increased by \$260 before it would be selected. In other words, the last 10 workers would have to produce an extra $\frac{260}{120} = 2.17$ television sets (for a total of 4.17) before it would be worth employing them. The other interpretation of this shadow cost is that if the company did employ 40 workers, the company's profits would be \$260 less than the maximum possible level.

Because the model does select a unit of *Labor 30* but not one of *Labor 40*, one unit of capacity is generated into the *Lab40 max* constraint but not used. That is why there is one unit of slack in the solution for *Lab40 max*. This example shows that slack can occur for constraints with limits of zero, because a negative coefficient in the matrix is in some ways equivalent to a constraint limit with the opposite sign.

The Shadow prices of *Labor tr* and *TV tr* are straightforward, but those of the four *LabXX max* constraints are more complicated. Start with the *Lab40 max* constraint, which has a slack value of one and thus a shadow price of zero. Even if the constraint limit were increased above zero, the model would not select the *Labor 40* unit.

The shadow price of *Lab30 max* is \$100, indicating that an increase of the constraint limit of *Lab30 max* by one unit would increase profits by \$100. What does this mean? Remember that shadow costs and shadow prices are based on a single change to the matrix. Thus the shadow price for *Lab30 max* is based on a solution in which the maximum level of *Labor 30* in something other than one. For example, consider a solution with one unit of *Labor 10*, one of *Labor 20*, and two of *Labor 30*. This solution would use up 40 units of labor and generate 90 television sets. But this is not consistent with the original problem definition, which stated that if 40 workers are employed, the last 10 workers contribute a total of two television sets and the total level of output is 87 sets.

It does not make sense to talk about a solution in which there is more than one unit of *Labor 30*. That is why the *Lab30 max* constraint was included in the model in the first place. So it is not valid or meaningful to interpret this shadow price as the benefit of increasing the constraint limit.

There is, however, a more meaningful interpretation. The shadow prices also represent the effect on profit of reducing the constraint limit. (It does not matter that this would theoretically take it down from zero to a negative value initially.) When viewed in this way, the shadow price gives the contribution to profit of activities constrained by that activity. This include *Labor 30*, but also all higher level activities that depend on it (i.e., *Labor 40*, which is linked to *Labor 30* by the *Lab40 max* constraint). In the case of *Lab30 max* there are no higher level activities making a contribution to profit (*Labor 40* is not selected), so $100 is the net profit earned as a result of the last 10 workers being employed (to take the total number of employees from 20 to 30). The shadow price of *Lab20 max* ($2000) includes the returns from both the second 10 workers and the third 10 workers employed. We know from *Lab30 max* that the third 10 workers contribute $100 to company profits, so the contribution of the second 10 workers must be $1900 (= $2000 − $100).

Now consider the solution in Table 7.5. This version of the matrix (Table 7.2) differs from the previous version in that the selection of each of the labor activities is not linked to the selection of lower-level activities. The constraints on labor activities have fixed constraint limits of one unit. We saw in the previous solution that *Labor 40* would not be selected even if the constraint limit were increased. It is not necessary to make the labor activities depend on

TABLE 7.5 Optimal Solution for Example 7.1 for Version of Matrix Shown in Table 7.2

Objective function value: 8700.000000
Problem direction: max

Activity		Level	Shadow Cost
1 Hire labor	A	30.0000	0.0000
2 Labor 10	A	1.0000	0.0000
3 Labor 20	A	1.0000	0.0000
4 Labor 30	A	1.0000	0.0000
5 Labor 40	Z	0.0000	260.0000
6 Sell TVs	A	85.0000	0.0000

Constraint		Slack	Shadow Price
1 Labor tr	L	0.0000	50.0000
2 TV tr	L	0.0000	120.0000
3 Lab10 max	L	0.0000	6,700.0000
4 Lab20 max	L	0.0000	1,900.0000
5 Lab30 max	L	0.0000	100.0000
6 Lab40 max	L	1.0000	0.0000

each other as in Table 7.1. If it is economically profitable to select one of the activities, it will be selected in either of the matrix approaches. Thus the activity levels, shadow costs, and constraint slacks in Table 7.5 are the same as in Table 7.4. The only differences are in the shadow prices. Because each unit is now independent and unlinked to any other, the shadow prices now give the individual contribution to profit of each activity. That is, the shadow price of *Lab20 max* is now the profit arising from the second 10 workers, not the total profit from the second 10 plus the third 10 as it was in Table 7.4. It still does not make sense to interpret the shadow price as the effect of an increase in the constraint limit.

The matrix for Example 7.1 shown in Table 7.3 is structured quite differently from the previous two. Although the solution identified by the model is equivalent, the information presented about the solution is somewhat different (Table 7.6). The first difference is that the solution includes one unit of *Labor 30*, but this time none of *Labor 10* or *Labor 20*. In this version of the matrix, these activities are alternatives, not cumulative. *Labor 30* represents in a single activity the act of employing 30 workers. It draws 30 laborers from the *Labor tr* row and generates 85 television sets into the *TV tr* row.

As a side effect of this change, the shadow costs of the *Labor* activities are more informative than previously. They now give the increase in profit that would be necessary for that number of workers to be the optimal level. For example, if the firm employed 10 workers instead of 30, profits would be $2000 lower than they are. Employment of 20 workers would reduce profits by $100. Can you see how these figures are related to the shadow prices of *Lab20 max* and *Lab30 max*? Why is there this equality of values? It is certainly not a mere coincidence.

TABLE 7.6 Optimal Solution for Example 7.1 for Version of Matrix Shown in Table 7.3

Objective function value: 8700.000000
Problem direction: max

Activity		Level	Shadow Cost
1 Hire labor	A	30.0000	0.0000
2 Labor 10	Z	0.0000	2,000.0000
3 Labor 20	Z	0.0000	100.0000
4 Labor 30	A	1.0000	0.0000
5 Labor 40	Z	0.0000	260.0000
6 Sell TVs	A	85.0000	0.0000

Constraint		Slack	Shadow Price
1 Labor tr	L	0.0000	50.0000
2 TV tr	L	0.0000	120.0000
3 Labor unit	L	0.0000	8,700.0000

The *Labor unit* constraint in this matrix replaces the four labor constraints in the previous versions. It limits the levels of the labor activities to one unit in total. If its constraint limit were reduced by one unit, it would not be possible to employ any workers or produce any television sets, so the profit would go to zero. This is why the shadow price is equal to the maximum objective function value; the entire profit is dependent on this constraint. This information does not help very much since the level of profit is already shown by the objective function value. However, this need not worry us since *Labor unit* is not a constraint on a real physical resource, but is used as a device to ensure the correct functioning of the matrix. If we did alter its constraint limit, the matrix would not function as required, so the shadow price (which is based on changing the constraint limit) is not really relevant.

You may have noticed that the solution to Example 7.1 includes exactly 30 workers and wondered whether the solution could ever include some number of workers that was not represented by one of the activities. For example, could the model select 24 workers? This would be feasible, but is unlikely to be optimal. Unless there is another constraint preventing it, the solution will always include one of the corner points of the approximated curve. These corner points correspond to the activities of the matrix.

Suppose there was a constraint limiting the level of labor to 24 units. Table 7.7 shows the output for Example 7.1 with the addition of a simple less-than constraint called *Labor max* that limits the level of *Hire labor* to a maximum level of 24 units, resulting in production of 82 television sets. Understanding and interpreting the levels of the *Labor 20* and *Labor 30* activities is more difficult than before. Let us examine in detail the reasons for the levels shown

TABLE 7.7   Optimal Solution for Example 7.1 for Matrix Like that in Table 7.3 But with *Labor max* Constraint Imposed

Objective function value: 8640.000000
Problem direction: max

Activity		Level	Shadow Cost
1 Hire labor	A	24.0000	0.0000
2 Labor 10	Z	0.0000	1,800.0000
3 Labor 20	Z	0.6000	0.0000
4 Labor 30	A	0.4000	0.0000
5 Labor 40	Z	0.0000	360.0000
6 Sell TVs	A	82.0000	0.0000

Constraint		Slack	Shadow Price
1 Labor tr	L	0.0000	60.0000
2 TV tr	L	0.0000	120.0000
3 Labor unit	L	0.0000	8,400.0000
4 Labor max	L	0.0000	10.0000

in Table 7.7. In the following discussion, it is important to keep in mind that the *Labor unit* constraint limits the total level of the *Labor 10* to *Labor 40* activities to one unit. Also bear in mind that, in the absence of the *Labor max* constraint, the optimal level of labor is 30 units (Table 7.6).

One way of reducing the amount of labor used from 30 to 24 units would be to reduce the level of the *Labor 30* activity from one unit to 0.8 unit. Then the output would be $0.8 \times 85 = 68$, which is less than the output actually achieved in Table 7.7 by combining 0.6 unit of *Labor 20* and 0.4 unit of *Labor 30*. This is the combination of these activities that adds up to one unit ($0.6 + 0.4 = 1.0$) and uses exactly 24 units of labor. This combination gives the highest possible output of television sets from 24 workers without violating the *Labor unit* and *Labor max* constraints. Experiment yourself with different levels of *Labor 20* and *Labor 30* and see if you can find a combination that adds up to 1.0 or less, uses 24 units of labor or less, and generates as many as 82 television sets. You will find that the combination given in Table 7.7 is the only possible combination that satisfies all these criteria. Remember that to calculate the level of labor used by your combination of activities, multiply the level of each by its coefficient in the *Labor tr* row and add up the results. For example, in Table 7.7 the level of labor used is $(0.6 \times 20) + (0.4 \times 30)$, which equals 24, as indicated by the level of *Hire labor*.

Multidimensional Curves

Sometimes it is necessary to represent a curve that depends on more than one causal factor. For example, suppose that in Example 7.1 the relationship between the number of employees and the rate of television production per employee depends on the temperature in the factory. At very low temperatures, productivity is lower than at intermediate temperatures due to worker discomfort. The function describing television output is then a curved three-dimensional surface, rather than a curved line. The manager wishes to select the optimal trade-off between output, labor costs, and heating costs.

It is possible to approximate this curved surface in the LP model by (a) specifying several discrete levels of labor, as in Tables 7.1 to 7.3, (b) specifying several temperatures to consider, and (c) having an activity for each combination of temperature and labor. A simple example for two temperatures and the same four employee levels is shown in Table 7.8. We can expand this to include any number of temperatures and labor levels. For each of the activities representing the curve, there are corresponding coefficients in transfer rows for heating cost and labor as well as a coefficient to generate the appropriate number of television sets for this combination of inputs. The full set of activities is constrained by a single less-than constraint similar to the *Labor unit* constraint in Table 7.3. Each activity representing a combination of labor and heating level has a coefficient of one in this constraint, which has a constraint limit of one.

TABLE 7.8 Third Version of Matrix for Example 7.1

	Hire Labor (No.)	Labor10— Temp1 (—)	Labor20— Temp1 (—)	Labor30— Temp1 (—)	Labor40— Temp1 (—)	Labor10— Temp2 (—)	Labor20— Temp2 (—)	Labor30— Temp2 (—)	Labor40— Temp2 (—)	Sell TVs (TVs)	Pay Heating ($)	Type	Limit
Objective ($)	−50									120	−1	max	0
Labor tr (No.)	−1	10	20	30	40	10	20	30	40			≤	0
TV tr (TVs)		−60	−80	−85	−87	−61	−85	−92	−95	1		≤	0
Unit (—)		1	1	1	1	1	1	1	1			≤	1
Heating cost ($)		100	100	100	100	200	200	200	200		−1	≤	0

140

Curve Bending the "Wrong" Way

It is crucial to recognize that all the methods given previously will work for curves that bend in one direction but not in the other. For beneficial factors (e.g., returns or profits) curves can be successfully represented in LP models in situations where the objective is increased at a decreasing rate or decreased at an increasing rate (i.e., concave down or convex up). When representing detrimental factors (e.g., costs) the rule is that the factor can decrease at a decreasing rate or increase at an increasing rate (i.e., convex down or concave up). Figure 7.2 shows the direction in which it is possible for beneficial factors to bend in an LP model (concave down). Figure 7.3 shows the acceptable direction of bend for detrimental factors (convex down). If you use an LP model to represent curves that are not consistent with these figures, the problem discussed earlier relating to selection of mixtures of activities will inevitably arise.

To illustrate, Table 7.9 shows a matrix similar to Table 7.3, except that the incremental productivity of labor is increased as the size of the labor pool increases. The addition of 10 workers to the workforce increases output by progressively greater amounts: 2, 8, 15. This might occur in situations where larger numbers allowed efficiencies through specialization or teamwork, offsetting any crowding problems or physical constraints. An additional constraint, that the level of hired labor cannot exceed 25, has been added. This means that the optimal solution *should* contain a mixture of *Labor 20* and *Labor 30*.

Although the matrix looks the same as Table 7.3, a solution consistent with the specified curve cannot be obtained. Table 7.10 shows the "optimal" solution obtained from the computer package. It specifies 0.5 unit of *Labor 10* and 0.5 of *Labor 40*. The resulting level of hired labor is 25, but the output of television sets is

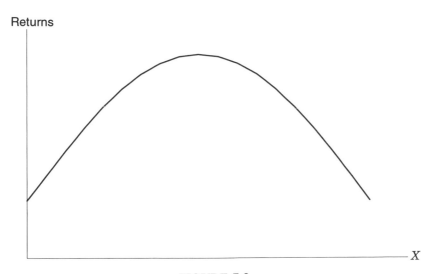

FIGURE 7.2

Costs

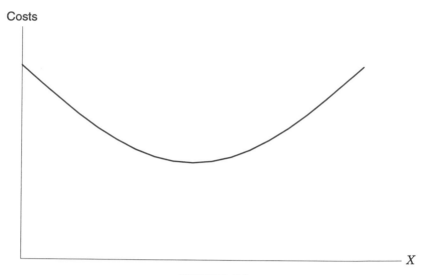

FIGURE 7.3

$$(0.5 \times 60) + (0.5 \times 85) = 72.5$$

which is greater than could be obtained from combining the correct activities, *Labor 20* and *Labor 30*:

$$(0.5 \times 62) + (0.5 \times 70) = 66$$

Note that television sets are a beneficial factor in this model and that the curve in Table 7.9 is convex down, which is inconsistent with the rule given earlier for beneficial factors.

In case you are confused about when a curve *can* be represented, here is a simple method to check a particular curve. First, set up a matrix like Table 7.3. From the activities that make up the curve, select two nonadjacent ones and two adjacent ones that lie between the chosen nonadjacent activities. For each pair of activities, calculate the cost and output for a combination of 0.5

TABLE 7.9   Matrix for Revised Version of Example 7.1 where Output Increases at an Increasing Rate

	Hire Labor (No.)	Labor 10 (−)	Labor 20 (−)	Labor 30 (−)	Labor 40 (−)	Sell TVs (TVs)	Type	Limit
Objective ($)	−50					120	max	
Labor tr (No.)	−1	10	20	30	40		≤	0
TV tr (TVs)		−60	−62	−70	−85	1	≤	0
Labor unit (−)		1	1	1	1		≤	1
Labor max (No.)	1						≤	25

TABLE 7.10 Optimal Solution for Matrix in Table 7.9

Objective function value: 7450.000000
Problem direction: max

Activity		Level	Shadow Cost
1 Hire labor	A	25.0000	0.0000
2 Labor 10	A	0.5000	0.0000
3 Labor 20	Z	0.0000	760.0000
4 Labor 30	Z	0.0000	800.0000
5 Labor 40	A	0.5000	0.0000
6 Sell TVs	A	72.5000	0.0000
Constraint		Slack	Shadow Price
1 Labor tr	L	0.0000	100.0000
2 TV tr	L	0.0000	120.0000
3 Labor unit	L	0.0000	6,200.0000
4 Labor max	L	0.0000	50.0000

unit of each activity. The approaches suggested in this section will work as long as the two adjacent activities perform better than the nonadjacent pair. They should produce the given level of output at less cost, or more output for the same cost.

Despite the limitations mentioned here, if you can master curve approximation and transfer rows, there is a vast array of real-world problems you can handle using LP. There are really no tricks or special devices in LP other than these two.

BOX 7.1 When Can Curves Be Approximated in LP?

Maximization Problem

(a) Returns concave down/convex up (increasing at a decreasing rate or decreasing at an increasing rate).

(b) Costs convex down/concave up (decreasing at a decreasing rate or increasing at an increasing rate). Since costs are represented as negative objective function coefficients in a maximization problem, a graph of the actual matrix coefficients is concave down.

Minimization Problem

(a) Returns concave down/convex up (increasing at a decreasing rate or decreasing at an increasing rate). Since returns are represented as negative objective function coefficients in a minimization problem, a graph of the actual matrix coefficients is convex down.

(b) Costs convex down/concave up (decreasing at a decreasing rate or increasing at an increasing rate).

7.2 MULTIPERIOD MODELS

Many planning problems involve selecting activity levels over several time periods. There is nothing really new in this section; multiperiod models simply use transfer rows to link one period to the next.

Example 7.2: Wool Processing

A wool processor takes raw wool, cleans it, and spins it to produce woolen thread for knitting and weaving. The processor is planning production activities for the four-month period commencing on January 1. The prices of raw wool and woolen thread change in predictable ways over time:

Month	Raw Wool Price ($/kg)	Woolen Thread Price ($/kg)
January	4.00	7.00
February	4.70	7.67
March	4.80	8.33
April	5.00	9.00

Raw wool can be stored from one month to the next at a cost of $0.1 per kilogram. Each kilogram of raw wool gives 0.75 kg of woolen thread after processing. The processing capacity of the factory is 10,000 kg of raw wool per month. Each kilogram of woolen thread costs $1.00 to produce. There are $50,000 available for purchase of raw wool at the start of the period. Costs of buying wool are borne on the first day of the month of purchase, while storage costs are paid on day one of the month when the wool is put into storage. Proceeds from sales of processed wool and costs of processing occur on the first day of the following month. Interest of one percent per month is received for unspent cash.

Develop an LP matrix to select the timing of purchases, storage, and processing that would yield maximum profit to the processor. ∎

A matrix for this problem is shown in Table 7.11. It is larger and more complex than the other matrices presented so far, so we will examine it in some detail.

The matrix consists of four submatrices, one for each month, January to April. The submatrices are linked because the activities of one period affect the transfer rows of the following period.

For each month there are four activities: one each for buying raw wool (e.g., *Buy Jan*, in kilograms of raw wool), processing wool (e.g., *Proc Jan*, in kilograms of woolen thread), storing raw wool from one month to the next

TABLE 7.11 Matrix for Example 7.2

	Buy Jan (kg)	Proc Jan (kg)	Stor Jan (kg)	Cred Jan ($)	Buy Feb (kg)	Proc Feb (kg)	Stor Feb (kg)	Cred Feb ($)	Buy Mar (kg)	Proc Mar (kg)	Stor Mar (kg)	Cred Mar ($)	Buy Apr (kg)	Proc Apr (kg)	Cred Apr ($)	Type	Limit
Objective ($)	-1													8	1.01	max	0
Jan W tr (kg)		1.33	1													$\leq$	0
Jan $ tr ($)	4		0.1	1												$\leq$	50,000
JanProcMax (kg)		1														$\leq$	7,500
Feb W tr (kg)			-1		-1	1.33	1									$\leq$	0
Feb $ tr ($)		-6		-1.01	4.7		0.1	1								$\leq$	0
FebProcMax (kg)						1										$\leq$	7,500
Mar W tr (kg)							-1		-1	1.33	1					$\leq$	0
Mar $ tr ($)						-6.67		-1.01	4.8		0.1	1				$\leq$	0
MarProcMax (kg)										1						$\leq$	7,500
Apr W tr (kg)											-1		-1	1.33		$\leq$	0
Apr $ tr ($)										-7.33		-1.01	5		1	$\leq$	0
AprProcMax (kg)														1		$\leq$	7,500

145

(e.g., *Stor Jan*, in kilograms of raw wool), and carrying over credit (unspent cash) from one month to the next (e.g., *Cred Jan*, in dollars). The exception is April, for which there is no activity to store wool since there is no submatrix for May to make use of the stored wool.

For each month there are three constraints: a transfer row for wool (e.g., *Jan W tr*, in kilograms of raw wool), a transfer row for credit (e.g., *Jan $ tr*, in dollars), and a limit on the level of processing (e.g., *JanProcMax*, in kilograms of woolen thread).

Buying raw wool generates a kilogram of raw wool into the wool transfer row for the relevant month. The other way of generating raw wool in a month is to store it from the previous month. In both cases, the coefficient is -1; either buying or storing one kilogram of wool generates one kilogram of wool available for use.

The possible uses of raw wool in a month are to process it or to store it to the next month. Storage activities are also in units of kilograms of raw wool, so they have coefficients of 1 in the appropriate wool transfer rows. Processing activities are in kilograms of *processed* wool. Since each kilogram of raw wool produces 0.75 kg of processed wool, each kilogram of processed wool requires $1\frac{1}{3}$ kilograms of raw wool. This is the coefficient of the processing activities in the wool transfer rows. According to Chapter 3, to determine the matrix coefficient for [*Jan W tr, Proc Jan*] ask, "How much of the available resource is used up by each unit of this activity?" Since each kilogram of woolen thread uses up $1\frac{1}{3}$ kilogram of raw wool, the coefficient for [*Jan W tr, Proc Jan*] is 1.3333.

The credit transfer rows have up to five coefficients. For February, March, and April, selection of wool processing in the previous month generates some income. For example, processing wool in January generates $7 in February at the cost of $1, so the coefficient of [Feb $ tr, Proc Jan] is -6. This is consistent with asking "How much of the available resource is used up by each unit of this activity?"—to which the answer is -6, since *Proc Jan* does not use up any of the cash available in February, but increases it by $6. Similarly, the coefficient for [Feb $ tr, Cred Jan] is -1.01, since each unit of *Cred Jan* increases the amount of cash available in February by $1.01, given that cash earns 1 percent interest per month.

The three ways of using up credit in a month are to buy raw wool (e.g., *Buy Feb*), to store wool (which has a small cost attached), or to carry over credit to the following month. The matrix coefficients for these activities are the positive values indicating how much of the credit is being used. For example, [*Feb $ tr, Buy Feb*] = 4.7, since wool purchased in February costs $4.70, [*Feb $ tr, Stor Feb*] = 0.1, which is the monthly storage cost, and [*Feb $ tr, Cred Feb*] = 1, since keeping a dollar until March means that it is unavailable for spending in February.

All of the transfer rows in this example are consistent with the example given in Section 6.2. They are all specified as less-than constraints, so negative coefficients represent sources of the factor and positive coefficients represent uses. In each case, the uses of wool or credit must be less than or equal to the sources. The use of these transfer rows allows the easy linking of periods, which is achieved by the activities of one period having coefficients in the transfer rows of the following period.

If needed it would be a simple matter to represent an activity in a period with influences on more than one subsequent period. All that would be necessary is for the activity to have appropriate coefficients in the transfer rows of all affected periods.

Finally, the model includes four straightforward less-than constraints limiting the level of processing in each month. Note that the units for these rows are kilograms of processed wool. It was stated in the problem definition that up to 10,000 kilograms of *raw* wool can be processed. This implies that the upper limit for *processed* wool is 7500 kilograms, so this is the constraint limit for *JanProcMax*, *FebProcMax*, and so on.

Notice that the objective function for the model has only two nonzero coefficients: those for processing wool and for carrying over credit in April. The reason that coefficients are not required for the earlier months is that credit is automatically carried forward (and accumulated) by the credit activities. The effects of earlier earnings are fully reflected in the April activities. Some earlier credit is used to buy wool and pay for processing, and this is reflected in the final objective function value.

Optimal Solution

Now consider the solution shown in Table 7.12, which is for the matrix shown in Table 7.11. We focus only on selected parts of this large solution.

The problem is to select the levels of wool purchase, wool processing, and wool storage in each month from January to April. The interpretation of activity levels in the solution is straightforward. For example, the firm should purchase a large amount of wool in January (due to its low purchase price at that time), but not process much until February (due to the low sale price in January). This requires a large amount of storage in January. Purchase of the wool uses up all available capital, so there is no available credit to carry forward from January to February. All this is revealed by the levels of the first six activities in Table 7.12.

The shadow costs also have useful interpretations. For example, the shadow cost of *Buy Feb* is $0.0795. Since the objective function is expressed as dollars at the end of April, that is the unit for this shadow cost. To convert this to dollars at the beginning of February, we need to allow for either the interest that a dollar in February earns or the value of using the dollar to purchase wool for processing. To make this allowance, divide the shadow cost by the shadow price of *Feb $ tr* (which conveniently gives the contribution that an extra dollar on February 1 would make to final profits). Thus the February 1 equivalent of $0.0795 on April 30 is $0.0795/1.0472 = $0.0759. This means that the purchase price of unprocessed wool in February would have to improve by at least

TABLE 7.12 Optimal Solution for Example 7.2

Objective function value: 78,111.984017
Problem direction: max

Activity		Level	Shadow Cost
1 Buy Jan	A	12,196.2969	0.0000
2 Proc Jan	A	36.2188	0.0000
3 Store Jan	A	12,148.1259	0.0000
4 Jan credit	Z	0.0000	0.1234
5 Buy Feb	Z	0.0000	0.0795
6 Proc Feb	A	7,500.0000	0.0000
7 Store Feb	A	2,173.1259	0.0000
8 Feb credit	Z	0.0000	0.0063
9 Buy Mar	A	10,368.4056	0.0000
10 Proc Mar	A	7,500.0000	0.0000
11 Store Mar	A	2,566.5315	0.0000
12 Mar credit	Z	0.0000	0.0105
13 Buy Apr	A	7,408.4685	0.0000
14 Proc Apr	A	7,500.0000	0.0000
15 Apr credit	A	17,932.6574	0.0000

Constraint		Slack	Shadow Price
1 Jan W tr	L	0.0000	4.7241
2 Jan $ tr	L	0.0000	1.1810
3 JanProcMax	L	7,463.7812	0.0000
4 Feb W tr	L	0.0000	4.8422
5 Feb $ tr	L	0.0000	1.0472
6 FebProcMax	L	0.0000	0.4340
7 Mar W tr	L	0.0000	4.9469
8 Mar $ tr	L	0.0000	1.0306
9 MarProcMax	L	0.0000	0.8239
10 Apr W tr	L	0.0000	5.0500
11 Apr $ tr	L	0.0000	1.0100
12 AprProcMax	L	0.0000	1.2835

$0.0759/kg (i.e., fall from $4.70/kg to $4.62) before any wool would be purchased in February. Under current price assumptions, it is cheaper to purchase the wool in January and bear the cost of storing it for a month.

There is only one constraint with any slack in the solution: the large amount of spare processing capacity in January. This is because the wool is stored and processed in February.

Interpretation of the shadow prices of this solution is complicated by the multiperiod structure of the model. When interpreting the shadow prices it is important to be mindful of the potential links of a constraint with activities in future periods, including, potentially, all future periods. To illustrate, the shadow price of *Jan W tr* (the transfer row linking sources to uses of wool in January) is $4.72, indicating that if another kilogram of wool could be obtained in January, profits would rise by this amount. This is not the cost of wool in January, but its cost in April. If an extra kilogram of wool were to become available in January, the model calculates that it could be most profitably used to reduce the amount of wool purchased in April.

This most profitable use is not indicated in the solution shown in Table 7.12, which just indicates the marginal value of an extra kilogram of wool in its best use, *whatever that may be*. The model implicitly has to calculate what that best use is, but this use is not indicated in the solution. The only reliable way to find the best use is to alter the constraint limit of the model and re-solve it. This is true not just of multiperiod models, but of all models in which there are several possible uses of a particular resource.

A second illustration is the shadow price of the *$ tr* row for each month. An extra dollar of cash obtained in April would increase returns overall by $1.01, due to the payment of a small amount of interest. An extra dollar of cash in March would be worth $1.03. This would be generated by the purchase of extra wool in March, which would be stored and processed in April. An extra dollar in January is worth $1.18 for final profits, due to the dollar being used to purchase extra wool in January. This extra wool would be used in three ways: a small amount of extra processing in January, a reduction of wool purchases in March, and a reduction of wool purchases in April. Clearly, the value of an extra dollar of finance is different in each month, depending on what the optimal use(s) of that dollar is (are) in each month. In all the examples given here, we determined what the optimal use was by increasing the relevant constraint limit by one unit and re-solving the model.

A similar principle applies to resources that have possible uses in different regions. The marginal value of extra resources becoming available depends on its region of availability, and the possible uses and costs associated with that region. This is illustrated in the next example.

7.3 MULTIREGION MODELS

A model representing a problem spanning several regions is conceptually very similar to a multiperiod model. Each region is represented as a separate sub-matrix and any links between regions are accomplished by activities for one region having coefficients in the constraints for other regions.

To illustrate, consider Example 7.3.

Example 7.3: Paper Recycling

This problem involves coordination of production and consumption in different regions.

A business has paper recycling plants in two towns: Abbot and Barnes. The supply of paper and demand for recycled paper products is different in each town, and in neither town is the capacity of the recycling plant perfectly suited to servicing that town alone. Consequently, transport of waste paper and recycled paper between the towns may be necessary.

Each year the supply of waste paper is 1000 tonnes in Abbot and 1400 tonnes in Barnes. Each tonne of waste paper can generate 0.5 tonne of recycled paper. Demand for recycled paper is 800 tonnes per year in Abbot and 500 tonnes in Barnes. The Abbot plant cannot meet local demands solely from local waste paper and the Barnes plant has excess waste paper. The business can transport either waste or recycled paper between the towns for $30 per tonne. The recycling process costs $100 per tonne of waste paper at the Abbot plant and $110 per tonne at the Barnes plant. Recycled paper sells for $500 per tonne in Abbot and $480 per tonne in Barnes.

Finally, the plant at Barnes has a limited capacity for recycling. The maximum level is 500 tonnes of waste paper per year. The plant at Abbot is large enough to handle all anticipated requirements.

Build an LP matrix to determine the profit-maximizing strategy for recycling, selling, and transporting paper.   ■

A matrix for this problem is shown in Table 7.13. There are two sets of activities and constraints: one each for Abbot and Barnes. For Abbot, the activities are *Recycle A* (recycle a tonne of waste paper in Abbot), *Sell to A* (sell a tonne of recycled paper in Abbot), *Waste A-B* (transport a tonne of waste paper from Abbot to Barnes), and *Paper A-B* (transport a tonne of recycled paper from Abbot to Barnes). There is a corresponding set of activities for Barnes, including activities for transport from Barnes to Abbot.

The constraints for Abbot are *Waste A* (the maximum number of tonnes of waste paper available in Abbot), *Paper A tr* (a transfer row for the number of tonnes of recycled paper available in Abbot), and *PaperA max* (the maximum number of tonnes of recycled paper that can be sold in Abbot). Again there is a corresponding set of constraints for Barnes, with the addition of a constraint to limit the level of recycling to 500 tonnes.

The two regions are linked by the four transport activities. It would be feasible for the waste paper from one town to be transported to the other for recycling and transported back again for sale. Given the limited recycling capacity in Barnes, this may be economically justified.

In order to see how the matrix works, examine the *Waste A* constraint. The initial availability of 1000 tonnes of waste paper can be increased by transporting paper from Barnes. That is why the *Waste B-A* activity has a coefficient of -1; it is generating paper into the *Waste A* row. The two ways of using up waste paper in Abbot are to recycle it (*Recycle A*) or to transport it to Barnes (*Waste A-B*). Both these activities are in tonnes of waste paper, so both have coefficients of 1 in the *Waste A* row. Overall the constraint says that

$$(1 \times Recycle\ A) + (1 \times Waste\ A\text{-}B) + (-1 \times Waste\ B\text{-}A) \leq 1000$$

TABLE 7.13 Matrix for Example 7.3

	Recycle A (t)	Sell to A (t)	Waste A-B (t)	Paper A-B (t)	Recycle B (t)	Sell to B (t)	Waste B-A (t)	Paper B-A (t)	Type	Limit
Objective ($)	-100	500	-30	-30	-110	480	-30	-30	max	
Waste A (t)	1		1				-1		$\leq$	1,000
Paper A tr (t)	-0.5	1		1				-1	$\leq$	0
PaperA max (t)		1							$\leq$	800
Waste B (t)					1		1		$\leq$	1,400
Paper B tr (t)				-1	-0.5	1		1	$\leq$	0
PaperB max (t)						1			$\leq$	500
RecycB max (t)					1				$\leq$	500

151

or

$$(1 \times \textit{Recycle A}) + (1 \times \textit{Waste A-B}) \leq 1000 + (1 \times \textit{Waste B-A})$$

which is stating that uses of waste paper in Abbot must not exceed the sources of waste paper in Abbot.

The *Paper A tr* row is for recycled paper in Abbot. This paper can be sold in Abbot (*Sell to A*) or transported to Barnes (*Paper A-B*). These two activities are in tonnes of recycled paper and represent using up some of the available recycled paper, so their coefficients in the *Paper A tr* row are 1 in each case. There is initially no recycled paper in Abbot. It must be generated by recycling waste paper in Abbot (*Recycle A* has a coefficient of -0.5 since each tonne of waste paper generates half a tonne of recycled paper) or by transporting recycled paper from Barnes (*Paper B-A*). The complete constraint is

$$(1 \times \textit{Sell to A}) + (1 \times \textit{Paper A-B})$$
$$+ (-0.5 \times \textit{Recycle A}) + (-1 \times \textit{Paper B-A}) \leq 0$$

or

$$(1 \times \textit{Sell to A}) + (1 \times \textit{Paper A-B})$$
$$\leq (0.5 \times \textit{Recycle A}) + (1 \times \textit{Paper B-A})$$

Again the effect of the constraint is to limit uses of recycled paper to less than or equal to the total of all sources of recycled paper.

Optimal Solution

The sites of waste generation, recycling, and final use are all potentially independent, although transport costs must be borne if they differ. The optimal solution includes some transport of waste paper from Barnes to Abbot and transport of some recycled paper back to Barnes. The solution (shown in Table 7.14) includes 900 tonnes of *Waste B-A* and 150 tonnes of *Paper A-B*.

Like the solution to Example 7.2, the interpretation of most elements of this output is straightforward. The possible exception is, again, the shadow prices. For example, consider the question of how much an extra tonne of waste paper would be worth to the company. The answer depends on which town generates the extra paper. If it is Abbot, the waste paper would be worth \$125/tonne, but in Barnes it would only yield returns of \$95/tonne. This is primarily due to the need to transport any extra waste paper to Abbot for recycling and back to Barnes again for sale (due to the *RecycB max* constraint). As has been stressed, LP factors in considerations like this when calculating the shadow price of a constraint.

On the other hand, if an extra tonne of recycled paper suddenly became

TABLE 7.14 Optimal Solution for Example 7.3

Objective function value: 315,500.000000
Problem direction: max

Activity		Level	Shadow Cost
1 Recycle A	A	1,900.0000	0.0000
2 Sell to A	A	800.0000	0.0000
3 Waste A-B	Z	0.0000	60.0000
4 Paper A-B	A	150.0000	0.0000
5 Recycle B	A	500.0000	0.0000
6 Sell to B	A	400.0000	0.0000
7 Waste B-A	A	900.0000	0.0000
8 Paper B-A	Z	0.0000	60.0000

Constraint		Slack	Shadow Price
1 Waste A	L	0.0000	125.0000
2 Paper A tr	L	0.0000	450.0000
3 PaperA max	L	0.0000	50.0000
4 Waste B	L	0.0000	95.0000
5 Paper B tr	L	0.0000	480.0000
6 PaperB max	L	100.0000	0.0000
7 RecycB max	L	0.0000	35.0000

available in Abbot, it would be worth less than paper made available in Barnes ($450 versus $480/tonne). This is because of the *PaperA max* constraint that requires that any extra paper must be sold in Barnes, wherever it is obtained. Any paper arising in Abbot would have to be transported to Barnes for sale.

In the discussion of output for Example 6.2 we saw how the costs of obtaining a resource may or may not be reflected in the shadow price of a constraint. Table 7.14 includes examples of both situations. The transfer row *Paper A tr* has a shadow price of $450, which reflects the value of extra paper if it could be obtained for free in Abbot. It would have to be transported to Barnes (at a cost of $30 per tonne) and sold for $480 per tonne. Thus, the shadow price gives the net benefit of $480 − $30 = $450. On the other hand, a loosening of the *PaperA max* constraint does allow extra paper to be sold, but not without extra recycling in Abbot or transport of recycled paper from Barnes to Abbot. This is because even if *PaperA max* is loosened, *Paper A tr* is still in force. For this reason, the shadow price of *PaperA max* includes the extra cost of obtaining the extra paper.

Putting it another way, recall that a shadow price indicates the net increase in returns after all desirable and necessary adjustments are made to the solution. For *Paper A tr* the desirable change is an increase in *Sell to B*, and the necessary change is an increase in *Paper A-B*. For *PaperA max* the desirable change is an increase in *Sell to A*, and the necessary change is an increase in the levels of *Recycle A* and/or *Paper B-A*.

7.4   INDIVISIBLE ACTIVITIES

In a standard LP model it is not possible to specify that a particular activity can take only integer (i.e., nonfractional) values. There is a technique called *integer programming* in which this *is* possible. However, many LP packages do not include a facility for integer programming. This section describes how to use standard LP to address simple problems involving integer variables.

The strength of integer programming is that it allows you to specify in advance that, although you do not know what the value of a particular variable will be, it must be an integer. Although this is not possible in LP, it *is* possible to specify in advance that the level of an activity must take a particular integer value. By generating one optimal solution for each reasonable integer value that the variable might take, you can identify the optimal solution from a comparison of the objective function values of the solutions.

The values you examine may be further apart than one unit. For example, some activities can only be undertaken in larger lumps. It may be that the level of an activity must be a multiple of 10.

Table 7.15 shows how a matrix can be adjusted to allow the approach just descibed. The matrix is based on the levels of two feeds in a ration for pigs discussed in Example 5.4. Table 7.15 is the same matrix as in Table 5.12, except it has an extra constraint on the level of wheat, *Set wheat*. This constraint can be used to set the level of wheat to any feasible level. Here the constraint is that

$$(1 \times Wheat) = 120$$

Suppose that for the price used in this example, wheat can only be purchased in multiples of 10 kg and that the pig farmer does not wish to leave any wheat uneaten. The original optimal solution in Table 5.13 included 120.7443 kg of wheat, but this is inconsistent with the new conditions just stated. Our approach is to generate two extra optimal solutions, one with the level of wheat constrained to 120 kg (as in Table 7.15), and the other with 130 kg of wheat (achieved by changing the constraint limit of *Set wheat* to 130). The two solutions have optimal objective function values of $35.39 and $36.02, re-

TABLE 7.15   Matrix for Example 5.4 with an Extra Constraint to Set Level of Wheat

	Wheat (kg)	Lupins (kg)	Type	Limit
Objective ($)	0.13	0.15	min	
Energy (MJ)	14.6	14.2	≥	3,625
Protein (g)	110	280	≥	50,000
Mass (kg)	1	1	≤	350
Set wheat (kg)	1		=	120

spectively. Since this is a minimization problem, we choose the solution with the lower objective function value: that with 120 kg of wheat. The level of the other feed (lupins) consistent with this level of wheat and with the nutritional constraints is different for the two solutions being compared. The correct value is given in the solution for 120 kg of wheat.

This systematic search approach is not always practical. If the number of integer variables is not small, it may be too slow and inconvenient. In that case, the only alternative is to obtain an integer programming package.

7.5 EXCLUDING GROUPS OF ACTIVITIES

Sometimes a modeler wishes to exclude a set of activities from a particular solution in order to find the best option that does not include them. One way of achieving this is to delete them from the matrix. However, if you are going to be frequently excluding and including activities, it may be preferable to include a constraint that limits the levels of certain variables to zero. For example, Table 7.16 shows a version of Example 6.2 that includes the less-than constraint *Exclude*. The constraint has a limit of zero, so as long as there are no negative coefficients in the row, any activity with a coefficient greater than zero cannot be included in the solution for this model. A coefficient of 1 has been incorporated in several of the activities to exclude them, but any coefficient greater than zero would be equally effective. The unit of measurement is given as '' − '' to indicate that it is irrelevant; any activity with any unit of measurement can be excluded by including any coefficient greater than zero in this row.

7.6 THE DUAL

For every LP model there exists a kind of mirror-image model called *the dual* that solves the same problem from the reverse perspective. The original version of the model is said to be *the primal*. The dual has intentionally not been emphasized in this text because novice LP users often find it more confusing than enlightening. However, it is referred to so commonly in the LP literature that it is at least worth becoming familiar with the idea. Later as you become more experienced with LP and wish to learn more about it, you can investigate it more thoroughly in other texts.

Suppose you have a maximization model with a set of less-than constraints. To create the dual of this model, transpose it, specify that the new constraints are greater-thans, and convert the objective to minimization. Each constraint of the original model becomes an activity in the dual, with the original constraint limit as its objective function value. Likewise, each activity becomes a greater-than constraint, with the objective function value as its constraint limit.

Matrices for the primal and dual versions of Example 3.1 are shown in

TABLE 7.16 Matrix for Example 6.2 with Several Activities Constrained out of the Solution

	Own Iron (t)	Local Iron (t)	Import Iron (t)	Thin Steel (t)	Thick Steel (t)	Tube Steel (t)	Type	Limit
Objective ($)	−1,000	−1,200	−1,500	2,200	2,000	1,750	max	0
Iron tr (t)	−1	−1	−1	1.20	1.21	1.25	≤	0
Own max (t)	1						≤	3,000
Local max (t)		1					≤	10,000
Output max (t)				1	1	1	≤	15,000
Exclude (−)	1	1		1	1		≤	0

TABLE 7.17 Matrix for Primal Version of Example 3.1

	Computer (tonnes)	Writing (tonnes)	Type	Limit
Objective ($)	600	1,000	max	
Labor (days)	4	6	≤	126
Wood chips (tonnes)	2	2	≤	56
Chlorine (kg)	0.2857	1.5	≤	24

TABLE 7.18 Matrix for Dual Version of Example 3.1

	Labor (days)	Wood Chips (tonnes)	Chlorine (kg)	Type	Limit ($)
Objective (−)	126	56	24	min	
Computer (tonnes)	4	2	0.2857	≥	600
Writing (tonnes)	6	2	1.5	≥	1,000

Tables 7.17 and 7.18. You can see that the columns and rows have been transposed, and that the activities of the dual represent the marginal values (the shadow prices) of the resources of the primal. The dual problem, then, is to minimize the total value of resource usage, subject to the constraints that the value of resource usage for each output must be at least as great as the output price.

The solution of the dual is shown in Table 7.19. All the numbers are the same as in the primal solution (Table 3.2), except that they appear in different places. The dual activity levels and shadow costs are the primal shadow prices and slacks, while the dual slacks and shadow prices are the primal shadow costs and activity levels. You can see from this why shadow costs and shadow prices are sometimes referred to as *dual values*.

TABLE 7.19 Optimal Solution for Dual Version of Example 3.1

Objective function value: 20,300.000000
Problem direction: min

Activity		Level	Shadow Cost
1 Labor	A	143.3333	0.0000
2 Wood chips	Z	0.0000	7.0000
3 Chlorine	A	93.3333	0.0000

Constraint		Slack	Shadow Price
1 Computer	G	0.0000	−10.5000
2 Writing	G	0.0000	−14.0000

7.7   KEY POINTS

- It is possible to closely approximate many nonlinear relationships in an LP model by the use of a series of straight line segments to represent the curve. Whether this is possible depends on the direction in which the curve bends.

- Multiperiod or multiregion models can be constructed, using transfer rows to link periods or regions.

- If the number of integer variables is small, it may be practical to solve the problem using LP. The procedure involves generating several solutions, with variables limited in advance to integer values.

- A simple and convenient device to exclude any number of variables from the optimal solution is a less-than constraint with a zero limit and no negative coefficients.

- Every LP model can be expressed in two equivalent ways: the primal and the dual.

CHAPTER 8

MORE EXAMPLES AND EXERCISES

Example 8.1: Scheduling Manufacture of Machine Components

A company has two factories that manufacture only electric generators. The generators are assembled from three components. Each factory can produce the three components, but each factory has different equipment, so components are produced at different rates. Due to an agreement with staff, one factory is able to work more hours per week. The differences between the factories are summarized below.

	Hours to Produce Each Component			Maximum Hours per Week
	Component 1	Component 2	Component 3	
Factory 1	3	2	4	40
Factory 2	3	3	3	60

The problem is to coordinate production between the two factories to produce the greatest number of generators per week given that each generator requires one of each component. Excess components of any type have no individual sale value. ∎

The difficulty in this problem is to ensure that there is one of each component available for each generator. Given the different production rates and different hours of production per week, it is difficult to identify the optimal production schedule.

In designing the matrix, an activity is needed for the production of each component at each factory, called *Comp1-2* for production of component 1 at factory 2, and so on. In addition we will have an activity that is the number of generators produced, *Generators*.

The obvious constraints are on the number of hours each factory operates each week. Call these *Hours 1* and *Hours 2*. The model also needs to be constrained to ensure that the number of units of each component produced is sufficient for the number of generators produced. We do not know in advance how many generators will be produced, so the minimum number of components must be linked to the *Generators* activity. Call these constraints on components *Comp1 min*, *Comp2 min*, and *Comp3 min*.

The completed matrix is shown in Table 8.1. The *Hours* constraints are straightforward less-than constraints, and the *Comp min* constraints are similar to the linking constraints in the two previous chapters.

Consider for now the *Comp1 min* constraint. For each generator produced, a coefficient of -1 is put into this row. This is equivalent to increasing the limit of the constraint by one unit. Since the initial value of the constraint limit is zero, its final value will be the total number of generators produced. Thus the constraint is equivalent to saying that the number of units of component 1 produced must be greater than or equal to the number of generators.

Using another suggested interpretation of this negative coefficient, we can think of it as deepening a hole that must be filled in by selection of activities with positive coefficients.

Algebraically, the constraint says that

$$(1 \times \textit{Comp 1-1}) + (1 \times \textit{Comp 1-2}) + (-1 \times \textit{Generators}) \geq 0$$

which is equivalent to

$$(1 \times \textit{Comp 1-1}) + (1 \times \textit{Comp 1-2}) \geq (1 \times \textit{Generators})$$

That is

Total production of component 1 $\geq$ Generators

A crucial thing to understand with linear programming (LP) is that *all* constraints must be satisfied at the same time. This means that the three *Comp min* constraints combine to ensure that there is at least one of each component produced for each generator. There could potentially be an excess of one of the components, but the number of generators is determined by the least plentiful component. The three constraints combine to represent the following mathematical statement:

Generators = min(Component 1, Component 2, Component 3)

The *Comp min* constraints also bear strong resemblance to transfer rows, although previously we have specified transfer rows as less-thans. This is quite

TABLE 8.1 Matrix for Example 8.1

	Comp 1-1 (No.)	Comp 1-2 (No.)	Comp 2-1 (No.)	Comp 2-2 (No.)	Comp 3-1 (No.)	Comp 3-2 (No.)	Generators (No.)	Type	Limit
Objective (No.)							1	max	
Hours 1 (h)	3	3	2		4			$\leq$	40
Hours 2 (h)		1		3		3		$\leq$	60
Comp1 min (No.)	1	1					-1	$\geq$	0
Comp2 min (No.)			1	1			-1	$\geq$	0
Comp3 min (No.)					1	1	-1	$\geq$	0

TABLE 8.2   Alternative Matrix for Example 8.1

	Comp 1-1 (No.)	Comp 1-2 (No.)	Comp 2-1 (No.)	Comp 2-2 (No.)	Comp 3-1 (No.)	Comp 3-2 (No.)	Generators (No.)	Type	Limit
Objective (No.)							1	max	
Hours 1 (h)	3		2		4			≤	40
Hours 2 (h)		3		3		3		≤	60
Comp1 min (No.)	−1	−1					1	≤	0
Comp2 min (No.)			−1	−1			1	≤	0
Comp3 min (No.)					−1	−1	1	≤	0

arbitrary; the direction of the *Comp min* constraints could be reversed without affecting the problem. Table 8.2 shows a matrix in which this has been done. The coefficients of these rows have been reversed in sign and are now consistent with the interpretations given earlier to less-than transfer rows. Negative coefficients correspond to components being generated by the factories and positive coefficients are for use of these components in the assembly of generators.

Optimal Solution

The novel feature of this problem is that its objective function is expressed in units of "generators," since the objective of the problem is to maximize the number of generators produced. It is important to understand that, whatever the units of measurement of the objective function are, the same units of measurement will apply to all shadow costs and shadow prices.

For Example 8.1, the shadow costs and shadow prices in the solution (Table 8.3) are expressed in units of generators. This can potentially pose difficulties for some of the approaches to output interpretation explained in Chapter 4. To illustrate, the shadow cost of *Comp 2-2* is 0.125 generator. One valid interpretation of this is that if a unit of *Comp 2-2* were forced into the solution, the number of generators produced would be reduced by 0.125. This would occur because of the need to give up some of the *Comp 1-2* or *Comp 3-2* activities as a result of the *Hours 2* constraint.

Another possible interpretation, consistent with our previous examples, is that the contribution of each unit of *Comp 2-2* to production of generators has to improve by at least 0.125 before the activity could be selected in the optimal solution. Literally, if the objective function coefficient of *Comp 2-2* were to be increased from zero to at least 0.125, *Comp 2-2* would come into the solution. However, there is no conceivable reason why the objective function should be increased in this way. There is also no purpose in discussing a potential change to the [*Comp2 min*, *Comp 2-2*] coefficient. The only coefficient of the *Comp 2-2* column that could conceivably change is that for [*Hours 2*, *Comp 2-2*]. Even then, it is not clear what change in this coefficient would be sufficient to bring *Comp 2-2* into the optimal solution. It certainly is not given

TABLE 8.3   Optimal Solution for Example 8.1

Objective function value: 12.5000000
Problem direction: max

Activity		Level	Shadow Cost
1 Comp 1-1	A	5.0000	0.0000
2 Comp 1-2	A	7.5000	0.0000
3 Comp 2-1	A	12.5000	0.0000
4 Comp 2-2	Z	0.0000	0.1250
5 Comp 3-1	Z	0.0000	0.1250
6 Comp 3-2	A	12.5000	0.0000
7 Generators	A	12.5000	0.0000

Constraint		Slack	Shadow Price
1 Hours 1	L	0.0000	0.1250
2 Hours 2	L	0.0000	0.1250
3 Comp1 min	G	0.0000	−0.3750
4 Comp2 min	G	0.0000	−0.2500
5 Comp3 min	G	0.0000	−0.3750

by the shadow cost, which is in generators rather than hours (the units for this coefficient). Trial and error reveals that if the [*Hours 2, Comp 2-2*] coefficient were reduced from 3 to 2 or less, *Comp 2-2* would be selected, but there is no obvious way of relating this to the shadow cost. There is no way other than trial and error (or some sophisticated logic) of obtaining the "shadow cost" equivalent of a coefficient that is not in the objective function. Clearly, the interpretation of a shadow cost as the improvement necessary to bring an activity into the solution is not useful or appropriate in this example.

The shadow prices of *Hours 1* and *Hours 2* do reveal, however, that an extension of working hours by one hour per week at either of the factories would increase output of generators by 0.125.

For *Comp1 min*, *Comp2 min*, and *Comp3 min*, the shadow prices are less meaningful. They show the reduction of generator output if the constraint limit of any of these constraints were increased by one unit. Again, however, there is no sensible reason for or meaningful interpretation of a rise in any of these constraint limits. In order to function correctly as transfer rows, they need to have zero constraint limits.

Example 8.2: A Shortest-Route Problem

A delivery firm makes a regular trip from town A to town G. Figure 8.1 shows the available roads by which the firm may travel. Distances in miles are shown for each road. Develop an LP matrix that minimizes the total distance traveled between A and G.   ■

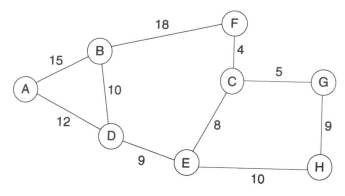

FIGURE 8.1

This is an example of a "network" problem with various "nodes" (towns in this example) and "links" (roads between the towns). The two most common network problems are to determine either the shortest route or the maximum flow. We will examine a maximum-flow problem in the next example. For a small problem like the one just stated, it is not difficult to determine the optimal route by a process of trial and error. However, where there are many possible routes, a model can be very helpful.

In Example 8.2, it is easy to identify the minimization of total distance traveled in miles as the objective. The decision variables are the roads by which the firm can travel. Each activity represents a potential component of the route from A to G, and the set of active variables represents the entire route. The objective function value for an activity is the length of the corresponding road.

The model needs constraints to ensure that (a) the route starts at A, (b) it finishes at G, and (c) the components of the route are connected. That is, if a town is going to be the beginning of one component of the route, it must be the end of another component of the route. The matrix for this problem is shown in Table 8.4.

The various activities are named according to their starting and finishing points. For example, *A-D* represents traveling from town A to town D. The objective function of this activity is 12, representing the distance between A and D. Constraint *A* represents the fact that there must be exactly one component of the route that departs from town A. It has a constraint limit of one and coefficients of one in each activity that represents a road leaving A. The constraint says that

$$(1 \times A\text{-}B) + (1 \times A\text{-}D) = 1$$

The solution will have to include either a unit of *A-B* or of *A-D*. It would be feasible to select a combination of the two activities that adds up to one, but because of the way the model is structured, this will not be optimal unless there are two routes with the same distance. Even then, because LP works by

TABLE 8.4 Matrix for Example 8.2

		A-B (−)	A-D (−)	B-D (−)	B-C (−)	D-E (−)	E-C (−)	C-E (−)	C-G (−)	E-G (−)	Type	Limit
Objective	(km)	15	12	10	22	9	8	8	5	19	min	
A	(−)	1	1								=	1
B	(−)	−1		1	1						≤	0
C	(−)				−1		−1	1	1		≤	0
D	(−)		−1	−1		1					≤	0
E	(−)					−1	1	−1		1	≤	0
G	(−)								1	1	=	1

going to the corners of the feasible region, the optimal solution will show only one of the routes.

Similarly, constraint *G* requires the selection of an activity that represents a road into G. Note that no matter which road into G is selected, there is a constraint to ensure that a road connecting to that road is also selected. For example, if the *C-G* activity is selected, the *C* constraint ensures that one of the roads leading into *C* must also be selected. If you think of constraint *C* as representing a resource (being something like "capacity to depart from C"), *C-G* uses up one unit of that resource. However, the constraint limit of *C* is zero, so there is none of this resource initially available. We need to generate some resource by selecting an activity with a negative coefficient in the row. Thus selection of either *E-C* or *B-C* is required.

The other constraints, *B*, *D*, and *E*, act similarly to ensure that no town can be left if it has not already been arrived at. These constraints closely resemble transfer rows, with arrival activities generating the potential to select activities for departure.

It would be possible to specify that these transfer rows are equals constraints. After all, you cannot arrive at a town a different number of times than you depart from it, except at the beginning and end of your journey. However, it is good practice to use less-than constraints where possible because unnecessary overuse of equals constraints sometimes causes a model to be impossible to solve (see Chapter 10).

Optimal Solution

The activity levels in Table 8.5 show a 1 for roads that are part of the shortest route and zero for others. The solution does form a continuous link between A and G.

The shadow costs, which are in miles, indicate by how much the route would be lengthened if the corresponding road had to be included in the route. This is based on the shortest possible route that does include the road. Another valid interpretation is that if a shorter road were constructed between two of the towns, the shadow cost shows how much shorter than the existing road it would have to be for it to be selected in the optimal solution.

There are no nonzero slacks in the solution.

Constraint *A* requires that the route depart from *A*, and constraint *G* requires that it arrive at *G*. The shadow prices of *A* and *G* show that if you removed either of these requirements, the route could be shortened by 12 or 22 miles, respectively. However, as with the previous example, the idea of increasing or decreasing these constraint limits is not helpful. They were set at their values for very good reasons, and any change would upset the functioning of the model.

Similarly, constraints *B*, *C*, *D*, and *E* must have constraint limits of zero in order to ensure that the number of arrivals at a town is matched by the number of departures. Any change in the constraint limit would mean that the route

TABLE 8.5   Optimal Solution for Example 8.2

Objective function value: 34.000000
Problem direction: min

Activity		Level	Shadow Cost
1 A-B	Z	0.0000	3.0000
2 A-D	A	1.0000	0.0000
3 B-D	Z	0.0000	10.0000
4 B-C	Z	0.0000	5.0000
5 D-E	A	1.0000	0.0000
6 E-C	A	1.0000	0.0000
7 C-E	Z	0.0000	16.0000
8 C-G	A	1.0000	0.0000
9 E-G	Z	0.0000	6.0000

Constraint		Slack	Shadow Price
1 A	E	0.0000	−12.0000
2 B	L	0.0000	0.0000
3 C	L	0.0000	17.0000
4 D	L	0.0000	0.0000
5 E	L	0.0000	9.0000
6 G	E	0.0000	−22.0000

would involve a different number of departures than arrivals at one of the intermediate towns. Clearly, this is a nonsensical notion.

Example 8.3: A Maximum-Flow Problem

A water supply utility has a shortage of water at a particular reservoir. It wishes to pump excess water from another source to relieve this shortage. Figure 8.2 shows the available pipes from the source (at 1) to the reservoir (at 5). Each pipe in the network has a maximum capacity in megaliters (ML) per hour, as

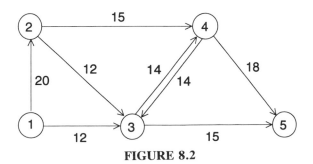

FIGURE 8.2

shown on the graph. Build a matrix to calculate the maximum rate at which water can be delivered to the reservoir via this network of pipes. ∎

This problem has major elements in common with the shortest-route model in Example 8.2. The problem is again based on a network of nodes with links of various size connecting them. In this example, the size of the link is its maximum rate of flow, not its length. The maximum rate of flow would be affected by the pipe's length but also by its diameter, its gradient, and by the power of the pump.

As before, each link of the network is an activity of the matrix. The objective function coefficient for each of these activities is zero, as the overall level of flow through the system is captured by the *Flow* activity. Since each unit of this activity represents 1 unit of water flow, it has a coefficient of 1 in the objective function.

There are two sets of constraints in this model: transfer rows to ensure that the amount of water leaving a node is no greater than the amount arriving at the node (*1 tr*, *2 tr*, etc.), and less-than constraints to ensure that the level of flow through a pipe section is no greater than its capacity (*1-2 max*, *1-3 max*, etc.). These maximum flow constraints are straightforward. The matrix is shown in Table 8.6.

The model works as follows. The *Flow* activity is the only variable that directly increases the objective function, so the model wants to select as much of it as possible. However, selecting the *Flow* activity uses up one unit of the "resource" represented by the *5 tr* activity. The initial availability of this resource is zero (constraint limit = zero), so the selection of *Flow* can only occur if the solution also includes some of the *3-5* or *4-5* activities. That is, for there to be any flow through the system, water must be delivered to node 5.

In a similar fashion, the flow of water from node 3 or 4 requires the selection of activities to deliver water to these nodes. Eventually, the requirement for water from node 1 is met by choosing *Flow*. That is, *Flow* represents the amount of water arriving at node 5 and simultaneously constrains the amount of water leaving node 1 by virtue of its effect on the *1 tr* constraint. Each megaliter of water arriving at 5 generates the capacity for a megaliter of water to leave 1. This sounds like water could go on indefinitely, arriving at 5 and being generated at 1. However, the set of less-than constraints at the bottom of the matrix ensures that this cannot happen. These constraints set the maximum level of each activity to the maximum flow rate for that pipe section.

Optimal Solution

The activity levels in Table 8.7 indicate the level of flow through various branch pipes in order to maximize total flow of water from node 1 to node 5. The levels are self-explanatory and, because they are almost all nonzero, the shadow costs are all zero. The output for activity *4-3* has something unusual about it:

TABLE 8.6 Matrix for Example 8.3

	Flow (ML)	1-2 (ML)	1-3 (ML)	2-3 (ML)	2-4 (ML)	3-4 (ML)	3-5 (ML)	4-3 (ML)	4-5 (ML)	Type	Limit
Objective (ML)	1									max	0
1 tr (ML)	-1	1	1							≤	0
2 tr (ML)		-1		1	1					≤	0
3 tr (ML)			-1	-1		1	1	-1		≤	0
4 tr (ML)					-1	-1		1	1	≤	0
5 tr (ML)	1						-1		-1	≤	0
1-2 max (ML)		1								≤	20
1-3 max (ML)			1							≤	12
2-3 max (ML)				1						≤	12
2-4 max (ML)					1					≤	15
3-4 max (ML)						1				≤	14
3-5 max (ML)							1			≤	15
4-3 max (ML)								1		≤	14
4-5 max (ML)									1	≤	18

TABLE 8.7 Optimal Solution for Example 8.3

Objective function value: 32.000000
Problem direction: max

Activity		Level	Shadow Cost
1 Flow	A	32.0000	0.0000
2 1-2	A	20.0000	0.0000
3 1-3	A	12.0000	0.0000
4 2-3	A	5.0000	0.0000
5 2-4	A	15.0000	0.0000
6 3-4	A	2.0000	0.0000
7 3-5	A	15.0000	0.0000
8 4-3	ZM	0.0000	0.0000
9 4-5	A	17.0000	0.0000

Constraint		Slack	Shadow Price
1 1 tr	L	0.0000	0.0000
2 2 tr	L	0.0000	1.0000
3 3 tr	L	0.0000	1.0000
4 4 tr	L	0.0000	1.0000
5 5 tr	L	0.0000	1.0000
6 1-2 max	L	0.0000	1.0000
7 1-3 max	L	0.0000	1.0000
8 2-3 max	L	7.0000	0.0000
9 2-4 max	L	0.0000	0.0000
10 3-4 max	L	12.0000	0.0000
11 3-5 max	L	0.0000	0.0000
12 4-3 max	L	14.0000	0.0000
13 4-5 max	L	1.0000	0.0000

zero values for both the activity level and shadow cost. This is because there are "multiple optimal solutions" for this problem. (See Chapter 10 for a detailed explanation.)

Constraints *1 tr* to *5 tr* are transfer rows that follow the now familiar pattern of having zero slacks and meaningless shadow prices. Transfer rows do not *always* have meaningless shadow prices. On the contrary, transfer rows that represent real, concrete resources usually do have a meaningful shadow price, but those included for structural or logical reasons often do not.

Some of the constraints *1-2 max* to *4-5 max* have nonzero levels of slack, indicating that the flow along these pipes is less than their capacity. Only *1-2 max* and *1-3 max* have nonzero shadow prices, indicating that these are the only two pipes for which an increase in maximum flow rate would increase the overall flow of water through the pipe network. A shadow price of 1 indicates that increasing the flow through this pipe by one unit would increase overall flow by one unit.

Example 8.4: A Transportation Problem

A company has to deliver its goods from stockpiles at two similar factories to its three warehouses that are all spatially separated from the factories. The different transport costs between factories and warehouses are shown below.

	Warehouse		
Factory	1	2	3
1	$12	$5	$12
2	$3	$20	$11

The stockpiles contain 110 units for factory 1 and 200 units for factory 2. The maximum storage capacity of the warehouses are 75, 100, and 160 units for warehouses 1, 2, and 3, respectively. Construct an LP matrix to select how many units from each factory should be transported to each warehouse in order to minimize transport costs.   ∎

This is a simpler model to construct. It does not require the use of negative coefficients, but it is included here so that the three types of transport problems can be considered together.

The objective of this model is to minimize transport costs. The activities represent transport of one good from a factory to a warehouse. Since there are two factories and three warehouses, there must be six such transport activities. Our names for these activities reflect the source and the destination of the good. For example *F1-W3* represents transport of one good from factory 1 to warehouse 3.

There is a constraint for each warehouse and for each factory. The factory constraints ensure that all goods currently held at the factories are transported to one of the warehouses. For example, *Fact1 min* is

$$(1 \times F1\text{-}W1) + (1 \times F1\text{-}W2) + (1 \times F1\text{-}W3) \geq 110$$

These activities each represent transport of a unit of the good from factory 1 to one of the warehouses, so the constraint states that their combined levels must be sufficient to move all the goods out of factory 1.

The warehouse constraints are similar except that they limit the reception of goods at each warehouse to a maximum of its storage capacity. The matrix is shown in Table 8.8.

Optimal Solution

The matrix in Table 8.8 shows that this is a straightforward model, and consequently it has standard interpretations for all parts of the solution shown in Table 8.9. The optimal (i.e., least expensive) solution is to transport 100 units

TABLE 8.8 Matrix for Example 8.4

	F1-W1 (No.)	F1-W2 (No.)	F1-W3 (No.)	F2-W1 (No.)	F2-W2 (No.)	F2-W3 (No.)	Type	Limit
Objective ($)	12	5	12	3	20	11	min	
Fact1 min (No.)	1	1	1				≥	110
Fact2 min (No.)				1	1	1	≥	200
Ware1 max (No.)	1			1			≤	75
Ware2 max (No.)		1			1		≤	100
Ware3 max (No.)			1			1	≤	160

from factory 1 to warehouse 2, 10 units from factory 1 to warehouse 3, 75 units from factory 2 to warehouse 1, and 125 units from factory 2 to warehouse 3. The shadow costs show that for a change in the optimal solution to occur, the minimum reduction in transport cost between factory and warehouse is $8 for factory 1–warehouse 1 and $16 for factory 2–warehouse 2.

The slack values indicate that the solution includes 25 units of unused storage capacity at warehouse 3.

The shadow prices show the marginal increase in cost for an increase in goods held at factories, and the reduction in costs for increased storage capacity at warehouses. For example, if there was an extra unit of product at factory 1, costs would increase by a minimum of $12. An extra unit of storage capacity at warehouse 2 would reduce costs by $7 coupled with a reduction in transport from factory 1 to warehouse 3.

TABLE 8.9 Optimal Solution for Example 8.4

Objective function value: 2220.000000
Problem direction: min

Activity		Level	Shadow Cost
1 F1-W1	Z	0.0000	8.0000
2 F1-W2	A	100.0000	0.0000
3 F1-W3	A	10.0000	0.0000
4 F2-W1	A	75.0000	0.0000
5 F2-W2	Z	0.0000	16.0000
6 F2-W3	A	125.0000	0.0000

Constraint		Slack	Shadow Price
1 Fact1 min	G	0.0000	−12.0000
2 Fact2 min	G	0.0000	−11.0000
3 Ware1 max	L	0.0000	8.0000
4 Ware2 max	L	0.0000	7.0000
5 Ware3 max	L	25.0000	0.0000

Example 8.5: Frequency of Advertising

The manager of a large shopping complex wants to find the optimal frequency of distributing advertising leaflets to consumers. The objective is to maximize the net gain in profit generated through advertising. Net profit is calculated as the total value of sales generated minus the cost of advertising. Through experience, the manager knows that the value of sales is related to advertising frequency in a nonlinear fashion. Below are some points from the relationship.

Frequency of Advertising (times per year)	Value of Sales Generated ($)
10	50,000
20	90,000
30	120,000
40	135,000
50	140,000

Each distribution of leaflets costs $2000. Construct an LP matrix to select the optimal frequency of advertising.   ■

This problem is similar in structure to the earlier nonlinear model in Example 7.1. The model will include an activity to count the frequency of advertisements (called *Frequency*) and activities to represent the nonlinear response to advertising. We need to choose how many points of the curve to include in our approximation of it. The values at five points have been given, so we will use them as the corner points of the approximated curve. Call the activities on the curve *Sales 10*, *Sales 20*, and so forth.

There are two constraints in the model: a transfer row for the level of advertising and a constraint to limit the selection of activities representing the curve to one unit. The matrix is shown in Table 8.10.

If the model selects *Sales 10*, sales worth $50,000 are generated into the objective function. However, the *Advert tr* constraint requires that the *Frequency* activity also be selected at a level of 10 and a total cost of $20,000. Thus the net profit for a frequency of 10 is $30,000.

If instead the solution includes a unit of *Sales 20*, the *Adv unit* constraint requires that the *Sales 10* activity be dropped from the solution. Returns increase to $90,000, but now 20 units of *Frequency* must be selected at a total cost of $40,000. The net profit is $50,000.

In a similar fashion, the various frequencies of advertising can be compared to determine the optimal level. For a simple problem like this, it is hardly necessary to build an LP model, but for larger problems that include a nonlinear function, this approach is very valuable.

TABLE 8.10 Matrix for Example 8.5

	Frequency (No.)	Sales 10 (−)	Sales 20 (−)	Sales 30 (−)	Sales 40 (−)	Sales 50 (−)	Type	Limit
Objective ($)	−2,000	50,000	90,000	120,000	135,000	140,000	max	
Advert tr (No.)	−1	10	20	30	40	50	≤	0
Ad unit (−)	1	1	1	1	1	1	≤	1

TABLE 8.11   Optimal Solution for Example 8.5

Objective function value: 60,000.000000
Problem direction: max

Activity		Level	Shadow Cost
1 Frequency	A	30.0000	0.0000
2 Sales 10	Z	0.0000	30,000.0000
3 Sales 20	Z	0.0000	10,000.0000
4 Sales 30	A	1.0000	0.0000
5 Sales 40	Z	0.0000	5,000.0000
6 Sales 50	Z	0.0000	20,000.0000
Constraint		Slack	Shadow Price
1 Advert tr	L	0.0000	2,000.0000
2 Ad unit	L	0.0000	60,000.0000

Optimal Solution

The solution in Table 8.11 shows that the optimal frequency of advertising is 30 times per year, and the shadow costs indicate how far the other frequencies are from being optimal.

There is no slack on either constraint. The shadow price of *Advert tr* shows the marginal benefit in dollars from an extra advertisement. The *Ad unit* constraint is included for structural reasons, and its shadow price adds no useful information to the solution.

Example 8.6: Investment Planning

An investor has $100,000 to invest over the next four years. In each year there are four possible uses of funds: shares, 3-year government bonds, 2-year fixed-term bank investment accounts, and a standard bank savings account. If invested in 3-year government bonds or 2-year fixed-term bank investment accounts, the money is not available until the end of the 3-year or 2-year period. The table below shows the rates of return available in the current year and expected rates for future years.

Annual Return on Investment (Percent)

Year in which Investment Commenced	Shares	Three-year Bond	Fixed-term Account	Savings Account
1	15	12	10	8
2	15	12	10	8
3	15	*	10	8
4	15	*	*	8

*Not an option due to requirement for all funds to be available at the end of year 4.

These rates of return are cumulative, calculated on an annual basis, and paid at the end of the investment period. In the case of shares, the return reflects any dividend and the increased market value of the shares. For the other investments, the return is an interest payment.

Due to the riskiness of shares, the investor is only willing to have at most $20,000 invested in shares at one time. At the end of the 4-year period all funds must be available in a liquid form, not locked into any long-term investment. Construct an LP matrix to select the investment strategy that will maximize the level of funds available at the end of the 4-year period. ■

The matrix is shown in Table 8.12. There is an activity for each of the investment options given in the table of the problem definition. Shares and savings are an option in each year, since they only tie up money for one year, but bonds and fixed-term accounts are not options toward the end of the 4-year period, since they would render the money unavailable at the time when it is needed: day 1 of year 5. The activities of the matrix are grouped according to the year in which the money is invested in that option.

The key constraints are the set of transfer rows for funds in each year. These transfer rows represent cash being available for investment on the first day of that investment year. Thus the activity *Share 1* uses up a dollar of funds available on year 1, day 1 and generates some funds available on year 2, day 1. These funds can then be used up by the year 2 investment activities. The amount of funds generated by *Share 1* in *$ 2 tr* reflects the expected return on shares of 15 percent. The matrix coefficient in row *$ 2 tr* is -1.15, which includes the original $1 invested plus the 15 percent return. Thus for every dollar invested in shares in year 1, there is $1.15 available for investment in year 2. This can be reinvested in shares or diverted to some other type of investment.

For bonds and fixed-term accounts, the funds are tied up for a period of more than one year. This is represented in the matrix by the fact that there are no funds generated into transfer rows except for the period when the funds become available again. For example, *Fix 1* uses up $1 in year 1, but because funds are unavailable for two years, there is no negative coefficient for [*$ tr 2, Fix 1*]. The coefficient of -1.21 for [*$ tr 3, Fix 1*] reflects two years of interest compounded and paid at the end of two years. The interest in both years is 10 percent. In year 1 this results in a payment of $0.10 per dollar, which is added to the principle. Interest in year 2 is then based on this new higher principle of $1.10, resulting in a payment of $0.11. The total interest payment is thus $0.10 + $0.11 = $0.21. The other way to calculate the coefficient of [*$ tr 3, Fix 1*] is that it equals 1.1×1.1.

There are also four constraints preventing the level of investment in shares from exceeding $20,000 in any year. These straightforward less-than constraints are called *ShareMax1*, *ShareMax2*, and so forth.

TABLE 8.12 Matrix for Example 8.6

	Share 1 ($)	Bond 1 ($)	Fix 1 ($)	Save 1 ($)	Share 2 ($)	Bond 2 ($)	Fix 2 ($)	Save 2 ($)	Share 3 ($)	Fix 3 ($)	Save 3 ($)	Share 4 ($)	Save 4 ($)	Type	Limit
Objective ($)						1.405				1.21		1.15	1.08	max	
$1 tr ($)	1	1	1	1										≤	100,000
$2 tr ($)	−1.15			−1.08	1	1	1	1						≤	0
$3 tr ($)			−1.21		−1.15			−1.08	1	1	1			≤	0
$4 tr ($)		−1.405					−1.21		−1.15		−1.08	1	1	≤	0
ShareMax1 ($)	1													≤	20,000
ShareMax2 ($)					1									≤	20,000
ShareMax3 ($)									1					≤	20,000
ShareMax4 ($)												1		≤	20,000

177

Optimal Solution

Since this model has a relatively large solution, we will not examine it in detail (see Table 8.13), although there are some aspects of it that are worth discussing. For one, it is similar to the multiperiod model in Table 7.11 in that shadow costs and shadow prices for a period reflect linked activities in future periods. For example, the shadow price of *$ 1 tr* shows that if an extra dollar can be generated in year 1, it makes a contribution of $1.51 to the objective function, which measures profit at the end of year 4. This is due to the interest earned or dividends paid in future periods. As the period approaches the end of year four, the duration over which interest or dividends can be earned diminishes, so the shadow costs decline as well.

The only slack in the model is for *ShareMax2*, indicating that a loosening of the constraint on the number of shares in period 2 would not affect returns, because of the current surplus of share capacity in that period. Shadow prices of the *ShareMax* constraints indicate the benefits of loosening these constraints on share purchases.

TABLE 8.13   Optimal Solution for Example 8.6

Objective function value: 155,503.016520
Problem direction: max

Activity		Level	Shadow Cost
1 Share 1	A	20,000.0000	0.0000
2 Bond 1	A	80,000.0000	0.0000
3 Fix 1	Z	0.0000	0.0391
4 Save 1	M	0.0000	0.0000
5 Share 2	A	17,391.3043	0.0000
6 Bond 2	A	5,608.6957	0.0000
7 Fix 2	Z	0.0000	0.0981
8 Save 2	Z	0.0000	0.0855
9 Share 3	A	20,000.0000	0.0000
0 Fix 3	Z	0.0000	0.0117
1 Save 3	Z	0.0000	0.0553
2 Share 4	A	20,000.0000	0.0000
3 Save 4	A	115,392.0000	0.0000

Constraint		Slack	Shadow Price
1 $ 1 tr	L	0.0000	1.5173
2 $ 2 tr	L	0.0000	1.4049
3 $ 3 tr	L	0.0000	1.2217
4 $ 4 tr	L	0.0000	1.0800
5 ShareMax1	L	0.0000	0.0983
6 ShareMax2	L	2,608.6957	0.0000
7 ShareMax3	L	0.0000	0.0203
8 ShareMax4	L	0.0000	0.0700

TABLE 8.14

	Make Shoes (workers)	Sell Shoes (pairs)	Type	Limit
Objective ($)	−50	8	max	
Worker max (workers)	1		≤	5
Shoe tr (shoes)	?	?	≤	?

Exercises

8.1   The matrix in Table 8.14 is incomplete; it has no coefficients in the *Shoe tr* row. What coefficients should be entered if each worker produces 36 individual shoes per day and shoes are sold in pairs?

8.2   A farmer grows three different varieties of wheat that are all sold for the same price. The yields are 1000 kg/ha for wheat 1, 1100 for wheat 2, and 975 for wheat 3. Complete the section of the matrix shown in Table 8.15. (1000 kg equals 1 tonne.)

8.3   A factory makes television sets and transformers, which are a key component of the sets. Each television set requires one transformer. Manufacture of transformers has a direct cost of $100 each, while they can be purchased for $120 each. There are two types of television set produced: type A sells for $450, while a type B set sells for $500. They have production costs, apart from the transformer, of $200 each. No more than 25 transformers can be purchased. Complete the matrix shown in Table 8.16.

TABLE 8.15

	Wheat 1 (ha)	Wheat 2 (ha)	Wheat 3 (ha)	Sell Wheat (tonne)	Type	Limit
Objective ($)	−50	−65	−60	160	max	
Land (ha)	1	1	1		≤	125
Wheat tr (kg)	?	?	?	?	≤	?

TABLE 8.16

	Make Trans. (No.)	Buy Trans. (No.)	Sell TV A (No.)	Sell TV B (No.)	Type	Limit
Objective ($)	−100	?	?	?	max	
Max buy (transformers)		1			≤	25
Trans tr (transformers)	?	?	?	?	≤	?

8.4 Build a matrix for the following problem. A firm makes three types of fencing material: wood, wire, and metal. The labor requirement for each is, respectively, 0.1, 0.15, and 0.18 person days per meter. Each week, 100 person days of labor are available. Profit per meter of fencing is $20, $25, and $35 for wood, wire, and metal fencing, respectively. The manager wants to impose the constraint that there must be at least twice as much wooden fencing as wire fencing. The objective is to maximize weekly profit.

8.5 Adjust the matrix for Exercise 8.4 so that the amount of wooden fencing is *exactly* twice as much as the amount of wire fencing.

8.6 Adjust the matrix for Exercise 8.4 so that the amount of wooden fencing is at least twice as much as the sum of the other two types of fencing: wire fencing plus metal fencing.

8.7 Suppose that in Example 8.2, the delivery firm has a package to deliver in town B, which is not on the shortest route from A to G. Add a constraint to the model to force the model to find the shortest route that includes B.

8.8 The model specified for Example 8.3 maximized flow without regard to the cost of pumping. Suppose that the benefit per unit of water reaching the reservoir at node 5 is valued at $0.50/ML, and that the cost of pumping is $0.16/ML from 1 to 2 and 4 to 5, $0.10/ML from 2 to 4 and 3 to 5, and $0.12/mL for the other pipelines. Revise the matrix so that it maximizes the total net benefit in dollars.

8.9 A company has to deliver new telephone books from several storage sites to regional depots for distribution to local residences. There are three storage sites and four local depots. The distance from each storage site to each depot is shown in Table 8.17.

Storage sites 1, 2, and 3 hold 10,000, 25,000, and 20,000 telephone books, respectively. The required numbers to be delivered to depots 1, 2, 3, and 4 are 9,000, 13,000, 18,000, and 11,000, respectively. Any books in excess of these requirements should be left at one or more of the storage sites. Suppose delivery of the books costs $0.01 per book per kilometer traveled. Build an LP matrix to calculate the least costly method for distributing telephone books from storage sites to depots.

TABLE 8.17 Distances in Kilometers between Storage Sites and Depots

Storage Site	Depot 1	Depot 2	Depot 3	Depot 4
1	15	14	20	9
2	19	11	8	16
3	6	8	2	17

TABLE 8.18

Hours of Labor Hired	Returns ($/ha)
0	200
1	320
2	350
3	360
4	365

8.10 The following problem requires you to approximate a nonlinear relationship in LP.

A fruit grower has 2 hectares of strawberries and wants to work out how many hours a week of labor should be hired for monitoring and managing the crop. If the crop is ignored completely until harvest time (10 weeks from now), the expected net return is $200 per hectare. If an hour of extra labor per hectare per week is hired, expected profit increases to $320 per hectare. Longer hours give the results shown in Table 8.18. Each extra hour of labor costs $5 (i.e., $50 for one hour per week for 10 weeks).

Construct a matrix to select how many extra hours should be hired. Use a transfer row to link the hiring and use of labor.

8.11 (A maximum flow problem.) The flow of traffic through a particular section of city streets is a problem. Most of the streets allow traffic in only one direction, but one street is two-way. The network in Figure 8.3 shows the maximum rate of traffic flow along each street. Arrows indicate the permissible rate of traffic flow along each street. Arrows indicate the permissible direction(s) of flow. The flow is measured in

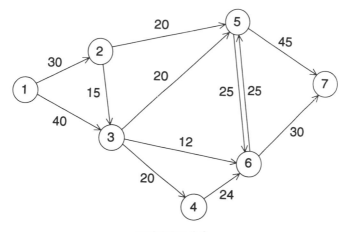

FIGURE 8.3

cars per minute. Build a matrix to calculate the maximum total rate of flow from points 1 to 7.

8.12   (A multiperiod problem.) An accountant has to plan the investment of $250,000 of the company's funds for the next three years. The possible uses are a 1-year fixed-term account, a 2-year fixed-term account, or a savings account that may be accessed at any time. The annual interest rates on these three accounts are 8 percent per year, 12 percent, and 6 percent. These rates are not expected to change over the 3-year period. Money in fixed-term accounts is not accessible until the end of the term. To allow for urgent needs, at least 25 percent of the funds must be held in a savings account at all times. Also the level of funds in a 1-year fixed-term account must always be at least 30 percent of the level in a 2-year fixed-term account. Interest is calculated on an annual basis and paid at the end of the investment period. Construct an LP matrix to select the investment strategy that will maximize the value of funds at the end of the 3-year period. Funds may be partway through a 2-year fixed-term investment at that time. In that case, their value should be calculated as their initial value plus any interest earned to that time.

8.13   (A scheduling problem.) A game manufacturer is facing very high demand for a particular board game. The game has three components: a board, a pack of cards, and a pair of dice. Manufacture of these components occurs at two factories that each operate for 40 hours per week. The rates of production of each component are different for each factory, as shown in Table 8.19.

Construct an LP matrix to determine how many of each component should be made at each factory in order to maximize the production of complete games.

8.14   A farmer can choose whether to use an area of land for pasture, the legume crop lupins, or the cereal crop wheat. Pasture can carry up to 4.5 sheep per hectare, or 5.5 sheep per hectare if supplemented with 0.1 tonnes of lupins per year per hectare. Sheep give profits of $18 per head. Grain yields are 1.2 tonne/ha for wheat (if not grown in rotation) and 1.0 tonne/ha for lupins.

Costs of sowing the crop are $35 and $38 per hectare for wheat and lupins, respectively. Lupins have the advantage of increasing subsequent wheat yields by 0.3 tonne/ha due to nitrogen fixation. Pasture also affects subsequent cereal growth. The boost is 0.3 tonne/ha cereal in a pas-

TABLE 8.19

| | Hours to Produce Each Component | | |
	Board	Card Pack	Pair of Dice
Factory 1	0.09	0.19	0.014
Factory 2	0.15	0.21	0.011

ture : pasture : wheat rotation (two years of pasture followed by one year of wheat) or 0.15 tonne/ha in a pasture : wheat rotation. Grain prices for wheat and lupins are $110 and $102, respectively. The rotations under consideration are pasture : pasture : wheat, pasture : wheat, wheat : lupins, and continuous wheat.

Construct a matrix to choose the rotation, the number of sheep, and level of grain feeding that will maximize profit for the 100-ha area. Use transfer rows and separate selling activities for each commodity sold.

The problem definitions for the following problems are given in Exercises 8.4 to 8.13. You may wish to refer to the matrices that are given in the Solutions section at the back of the book. Some of these questions can be answered directly from the solution output, but others require you to make adjustments to the original matrix and re-solve the model on a computer.

8.15   The optimal solution below is for the model developed for Exercise 8.4.

(a) By how much would the returns per meter of wire fencing have to improve before it would be optimal to include wire fencing in the firm's activities?

(b) If the returns from wire fencing increased by $7/m, by how much would the optimal level of production for wire fencing increase? By how much would the level of wood fencing decrease?

(c) How would the solution change if we specified that the level of wood fencing had to be *exactly* twice as much as the level of wire fencing? In answering this question, assume *Wire* returns $25/m again.

8.16   The optimal solution in Table 8.21 is for the model developed for Exercise 8.7. Each activity represents one load linking two of the towns. There are several activities in the solution that have zero value for both their level and their shadow cost. "Degenerate" activities, such as these are explained fully in Chapter 10.

TABLE 8.20   Optimal Solution for Exercise 8.4

Objective function value: 20,000.000000
Problem direction: max

Activity		Level	Shadow Cost
1 Wood	A	1,000.0000	0.0000
2 Wire	Z	0.0000	5.0000
3 Metal	Z	0.0000	1.0000

Constraint		Slack	Shadow Price
1 Labor	L	0.0000	200.0000
2 Wood-wire	L	1,000.0000	0.0000

TABLE 8.21 Optimal Solution for Exercise 8.7

Objective function value: 42.000000
Problem direction: min

Activity		Level	Shadow Cost
1 A-B	A	1.0000	0.0000
2 A-D	AD	0.0000	0.0000
3 B-D	Z	0.0000	5.0000
4 B-C	A	1.0000	0.0000
5 D-E	AD	0.0000	0.0000
6 E-C	AD	0.0000	0.0000
7 C-E	Z	0.0000	16.0000
8 C-G	A	1.0000	0.0000
9 E-G	Z	0.0000	6.0000

Constraint		Slack	Shadow Price
1 A	E	0.0000	−7.0000
2 B	LD	0.0000	0.0000
3 C	L	0.0000	22.0000
4 D	L	0.0000	5.0000
5 E	L	0.0000	14.0000
6 G	E	0.0000	−27.0000
7 B min	G	0.0000	−8.0000

(a) What is the shortest route that includes B?

(b) Explain the interpretation(s) of the shadow cost of the *C-E* activity.

(c) Why do none of the constraints have any slack?

(d) What does the shadow price of 5 on the *D* constraint indicate?

(e) Why does the *A* constraint have a negative shadow price? What does the magnitude of this shadow price indicate?

(f) How should we interpret the output for the *B* constraint?

(g) Suppose that a new road between *B* and *D* is built. Suppose further that it is shorter by 3 km than the old road. How does the shortest route change?

(h) Suppose that the road from B through F to C is being repaired, necessitating the use of a side road, which lengthens the trip from B to C by 6 km. How does the optimal route change while these repairs are in progress?

8.17 The optimal solution in Table 8.22 is for the model developed for Exercise 8.8.

(a) The difference between this model (Exercise 8.8) and the model for Example 8.3 is the objective function. In Example 8.3, the objective is to maximize flow, while in Exercise 8.8 it is to maximize profit. Why does this change result in different solutions? (Compare this solution with that in Table 8.7).

TABLE 8.22   Optimal Solution for Exercise 8.8

Objective function value: 4.920000
Problem direction: max

Activity		Level	Shadow Cost
1 Flow	A	30.0000	0.0000
2 1-2	A	18.0000	0.0000
3 1-3	A	12.0000	0.0000
4 2-3	A	3.0000	0.0000
5 2-4	A	15.0000	0.0000
6 3-4	Z	0.0000	0.0600
7 3-5	A	15.0000	0.0000
8 4-3	Z	0.0000	0.1800
9 4-5	A	15.0000	0.0000

Constraint		Slack	Shadow Price
1 1 tr	LD	0.0000	0.0000
2 2 tr	L	0.0000	0.1600
3 3 tr	L	0.0000	0.2800
4 4 tr	L	0.0000	0.3400
5 5 tr	L	0.0000	0.5000
6 1-2 max	L	2.0000	0.0000
7 1-3 max	L	0.0000	0.1600
8 2-3 max	L	9.0000	0.0000
9 2-4 max	L	0.0000	0.0800
10 3-4 max	L	14.0000	0.0000
11 3-5 max	L	0.0000	0.1200
12 4-3 max	L	14.0000	0.0000
13 4-5 max	L	3.0000	0.0000

(b) What do the levels of the activities *1-2*, *1-3*, and so on, represent?

(c) Given that the aim is to maximize profit, why do several of the pipes have unused capacity? (See the slacks in the solution in Table 8.22.)

(d) Suppose that there is a proposal to increase the capacities of the *2-3* and *3-5* pipes to 18 megaliters per hour. Should either or both of these pipes be upgraded? Are there any pipes that should be given a higher priority for upgrading. What would be the gross benefits of replacing the *2-3* and *3-5* pipes?

(e) Can you interpret the shadow prices of the transfer rows?

(f) Can you interpret the shadow prices of the "*max*" rows?

8.18 The optimal solution in Table 8.23 is for the model developed for Exercise 8.9.

(a) At present all the telephone books from storage site 1 are delivered to depot 4? What changes would be required for it to be optimal to deliver some of the books from site 1 to depot 1?

TABLE 8.23 Optimal Solution for Exercise 8.9

Objective function value: 3810.000000
Problem direction: min

Activity		Level	Shadow Cost
1 S1-D1	Z	0.00	0.1000
2 S1-D2	Z	0.00	0.1000
3 S1-D3	Z	0.00	0.1900
4 S1-D4	A	10,000.00	0.0000
5 S2-D1	Z	0.00	0.0700
6 S2-D2	Z	13,000.00	0.0000
7 S2-D3	A	7,000.00	0.0000
8 S2-D4	A	1,000.00	0.0000
9 S3-D1	A	9,000.00	0.0000
10 S3-D2	Z	0.00	0.0300
11 S3-D3	A	11,000.00	0.0000
12 S3-D4	Z	0.00	0.0700

Constraint		Slack	Shadow price
1 Site1 max	L	0.0000	0.0700
2 Site2 max	L	4,000.0000	0.0000
3 Site3 max	L	0.0000	0.0600
4 Depot1 min	G	0.0000	−0.1200
5 Depot2 min	G	0.0000	−0.1100
6 Depot3 min	G	0.0000	−0.0800
7 Depot4 min	G	0.0000	−0.1600

(b) Suppose that by linking with another delivery service, the cost of delivery from site 1 to depot 1 could be reduced to $0.04 per book. How would the optimal solution change?

(c) Explain the shadow price of *Site1 max*.

(d) Explain the shadow price of *Depot1 min*.

(e) What does the slack on *Site2 max* mean?

8.19 The optimal solution in Table 8.24 is for the model developed for Exercise 8.10.

(a) Explain the levels of *Labor 1* and *Hire labor*.

(b) Explain the shadow costs of the labor activities.

(c) Explain the shadow price of the *Labor tr* row.

(d) If one unit of free labor became available, how would the optimal solution change?

8.20 The optimal solution in Table 8.25 is for the model developed for Exercise 8.13.

(a) How many sets are produced?

(b) How many work hours at each factory are spent producing the sets?

TABLE 8.24 Optimal Solution for Exercise 8.10

Objective function value: 540.000000
Problem direction: max

Activity		Level	Shadow Cost
1 Labor 0	Z	0.00	70.0000
2 Labor 1	Z	2.00	0.0000
3 Labor 2	Z	0.00	20.0000
4 Labor 3	A	0.00	60.0000
5 Labor 4	Z	0.00	105.0000
6 Hire labor	Z	2.00	0.0000

Constraint		Slack	Shadow Price
1 Labor tr	L	0.0000	50.0000
2 Land	L	0.0000	270.0000

TABLE 8.25 Optimal Solution for Exercise 8.13

Objective function value: 262.768928
Problem direction: max

Activity		Level	Shadow Cost
1 Board 1	Λ	262.7689	0.0000
2 Board 2	A	0.0000	0.1577
3 Cards 1	A	86.0568	0.0000
4 Cards 2	Z	176.7121	0.0000
5 Dice 1	Z	0.0000	0.0140
6 Dice 2	A	262.7689	0.0000
7 Full sets	A	262.7689	0.0000

Constraint		Slack	Shadow Price
1 Hours 1	L	0.0000	3.4488
2 Hours 2	L	0.0000	3.1204
3 Board min	G	0.0000	−0.3104
4 Cards min	G	0.0000	−0.6553
5 Dice min	G	0.0000	−0.0343

(c) How many hours at each factory are spent producing cards?

(d) Why do *Hours 1* and *Hours 2* have different shadow prices? If extra hours could be worked at only one of the factories, which would you choose it to be?

(e) Can you interpret the shadow prices of *Board min*, *Cards min* and *Dice min*?

CHAPTER 9

INTERPRETING RANGE ANALYSIS OUTPUT

In Chapters 4 to 8 we have looked at basic linear programming (LP) output and found that a lot more information is provided than just the optimal level of each activity. There is also information about how far suboptimal activities are from being selected, how much of each constraint is "unused," and how marginal changes in resource levels (i.e., constraint limits) affect the objective function. All this information is calculated automatically in the process of finding the optimal solution.

Most LP packages can provide even more information about the optimal solution. The extra output is called *range analysis*, or sometimes *sensitivity analysis*. Because the term sensitivity analysis is often used in a different way (see Chapter 12) we will use range analysis to describe this extra LP output.

Range analysis tells you how much the objective function values or constraint limits would have to change before the optimal selection of activities would change. However, range analysis for objective values differs slightly from that for constraint limits, and some care is needed in interpreting each.

Range analysis is often neglected or even completely ignored in texts on LP. This is surprising since in real-world LP applications, range analysis can be useful. Nevertheless, it is true that it is not essential to understand range analysis to make good use of LP. If you wish to skip this chapter or postpone your study of it, your capacity to apply LP will not suffer greatly.

The example used for illustration in the following discussion is the iron and steel processing model from Example 6.2. (See Table 6.6 for the matrix.) Example 6.2 is very simple, but is quite suitable for the purposes of this explanation. Table 9.1 shows the complete output for this model, including range analysis. The format and headings used for range analysis output vary greatly between computer packages, but the information they present is fun-

TABLE 9.1   Optimal Solution for Example 6.2 for Version of Matrix Shown in Table 6.6

Objective function value: 10,500,000.000000
Problem direction: max

Activity		Level	Shadow Cost	Lower Objective	Original Objective	Upper Objective
1 Own iron	A	3,000.00	0.00	−1,500.00	−1,000.00	infinity
2 Local iron	A	10,000.00	0.00	−1,500.00	−1,200.00	infinity
3 Import iron	A	5,000.00	0.00	−1,833.33	−1,500.00	−1,200.00
4 Thin steel	A	15,000.00	0.00	1,985.00	2,200.00	infinity
5 Thick steel	Z	0.00	215.00	−infinity	2,000.00	2,215.00
6 Tube steel	Z	0.00	525.00	−infinity	1,750.00	2,275.00

Constraint		Slack	Shadow Price	Lower Limit	Original Limit	Upper Limit
1 Iron tr	L	0.00	1,500.00	−infinity	0.00	5,000.00
2 Own max	L	0.00	500.00	0.00	3,000.00	8,000.00
3 Local max	L	0.00	300.00	0.00	10,000.00	15,000.00
4 Output max	L	0.00	400.00	10,833.33	15,000.00	infinity

damentally the same as that shown in Table 9.1. There is a section of range analysis for activities and a section for constraints.

9.1 RANGE ANALYSIS FOR ACTIVITIES

The range analysis for activities is presented in two new columns labeled Lower objective and Upper objective. These indicate the range within which the objective function value for each activity can be changed without affecting the composition of the optimal solution. The current objective function value is shown in the column labeled Original objective to allow easy comparison. The original objective value can never be lower than the value in the Lower objective column or higher than the Upper objective value.

The objective function value for *Thick steel* is $2000 per tonne (t). The upper objective value for *Thick steel* is $2215/t. This means that if the price of thick steel were to exceed $2215/t, the activity levels shown in Table 9.1 would no longer be optimal. There is nothing in the range-analysis output to indicate precisely how the solution would change, but with a bit of thought, it is usually possible to work out the main features of the change. In this example, *Thick steel* is currently not selected (the value in the Level column is zero), but if the price exceeded $2215/t, the optimal level of thick steel would increase. Accompanying this increase would be a decrease in the optimal level of *Thin steel*. To find out exactly what the changes would be, you normally need to change the coefficient and re-solve the problem.

The lower objective value for *Thick steel* is −infinity, meaning that no matter how much worse the profitability of thick steel becomes, the optimal selection of activities will not change. Remember that *Thick steel* is not selected in the optimal strategy, so its level cannot get any lower, and making it even less profitable is not going to bring it into the optimal solution at a higher level. In a maximization problem, the lower objective value for a zero-leveled activity is always negative infinity (unless the activity is "degenerate"—see the next chapter). On the other hand, if your objective is minimization, activities with zero levels will have upper objective values of positive infinity. (*Explanation:* They are already too expensive to be selected, so making them more expensive will not change anything.)

As well as the levels of activities, if an objective function value strays outside the range given in the range analysis, there will also be a change in the *optimal basis* (or *basis* for short). The basis is, more or less, the set of activities that the model has selected to include in the optimal solution at levels greater than zero, together with constraints that have slack greater than zero. We will refine this definition later, but for now it is adequate.

The range-analysis output defines the points at which the basis changes, so that one activity or constraint enters the optimal solution and another activity or constraint leaves it. As far as membership of the basis goes, it does not matter what the activity level or constraint slack is, as long as it is not zero. (Again degeneracy is an exception here.) The basis is a useful concept because it simplifies the explanation of the range-analysis output for constraint limits. It also helps in understanding the mathematical approach used to solve LP (which we do not examine).

Before leaving thick steel, there is one more point to cover: the relationship between shadow costs and range analysis. The shadow cost for *Thick steel* is \$215/t. Using the first interpretation of shadow costs in Chapter 4, this \$215 is the amount by which the objective value of *Thick steel* has to improve before the activity would be selected as part of this optimal solution. This is perfectly consistent with the upper objective value of \$2215, \$215 more than the original objective value of \$2000. The objective of this problem is maximization, so a \$215 "improvement" means a \$215 increase. This is why the shadow cost relates to the *upper* objective value. On the other hand, in a minimization problem an "improvement" in the objective is a reduction (e.g., a reduction in costs) so the shadow cost is the difference between the lower objective value and the original objective function value.

Note that these interpretations only apply to nonactive (zero-leveled) activities. Activities selected at a nonzero level always have a shadow cost of zero (see Section 4.3), so you cannot tell how far the activity is from being dropped out of the optimal solution. Thus, although range analysis tells you nothing you do not already know about zero-leveled activities, it does provide useful information about activities that *are* in the current solution. The information is of a similar nature to a shadow cost except that it is more detailed, since it includes both upper and lower objective function values.

Import iron is an interesting example of an activity with a level greater than zero in Table 9.1. Its objective range of $-\$1833.33$ to $-\$1200$ has the interpretation you would expect from our previous discussion: at objective values below (more negative than) -1833.33, or greater than (less negative than) -1200.00, the optimal solution changes from that shown in Table 9.1. In any realistic problem, range analysis for nonzero activities gives information that is not otherwise obvious.

Finally, it is important to understand that activity range analysis applies only to individual changes in an objective value. If more than one price or cost varies, or another coefficient in the matrix varies at the same time, the range-analysis results may not hold.

9.2 RANGE ANALYSIS FOR CONSTRAINTS

The range analysis for constraints is somewhat similar to that for activities. The current constraint limit is shown in the column labeled Original limit to allow easy comparison. The original constraint limit can never be lower than the value in the Lower limit column or higher than the Upper limit value.

If we are changing the objective function value of an activity, as long as it remains within the range given in range-analysis output, the levels of all activities do not change. The range analysis for constraints differs slightly in that if a constraint limit is changed within the range shown, there may be changes in the levels of some activities. For example, the original constraint limit on *Local max* shown in Table 9.1 is 10,000 (which is within the range 0.0 to 15,000.0 in Table 9.1). If we reduce the constraint limit to 9000, the solution changes as shown in Table 9.2.

The new solution includes a different level of *Local iron*, down from 10,000 to 9000, while the level of *Import iron* is up from 5000 to 6000 tonnes. What does remain the same is the basis: the set of activity levels and constraint slacks with nonzero values. If we change the constraint limit for *Local max* to any value within the range 0.0 to 15,000.0, the solution will always contain some *Own iron*, *Local iron*, *Import iron*, and *Thin steel* but no *Thick steel* or *Tube steel*.

Apart from the basis, the shadow costs, shadow prices, and all output for the activity range analysis remains unchanged when a constraint limit is changed within its allowable range. However, activity levels, constraint slacks, and constraint range analysis can change.

Conversely, the range analysis for activities indicates the range within which changes in value of the objective function coefficient will not affect activity levels, constraint slacks, and constraint range analysis. However, even within the indicated range, changes in the objective function value can affect shadow costs, shadow prices, and the activity range analysis.

Thus range analysis for constraints is mainly useful for indicating the range within which shadow costs and shadow prices do not change. This makes it, perhaps, a little less useful than range analysis for activities.

The same warnings about range analysis only being accurate for a single

TABLE 9.2   Optimal Solution for Example 6.2 with Constraint Limit for *Local max* Reduced to 9000

Objective function value: 10,200,000.000000
Problem direction: max

Activity		Level	Shadow Cost	Lower Objective	Original Objective	Upper Objective
1 Own iron	A	3,000.00	0.00	−1,500.000	−1,000.00	infinity
2 Local iron	A	9,000.00	0.00	−1,500.000	−1,200.00	infinity
3 Import iron	A	6,000.00	0.00	−1,833.333	−1,500.00	−1,200.000
4 Thin steel	A	15,000.00	0.00	1,985.000	2,200.00	infinity
5 Thick steel	Z	0.00	215.00	−infinity	2,000.00	2,215.000
6 Tube steel	Z	0.00	525.00	−infinity	1,750.00	2,275.000

Constraint		Slack	Shadow Price	Lower Limit	Original Limit	Upper Limit
1 Iron tr	L	0.00	1,500.00	−infinity	0.00	6,000.00
2 Own max	L	0.00	500.00	0.00	3,000.00	9,000.00
3 Local max	L	0.00	300.00	0.00	9,000.00	15,000.00
4 Output max	L	0.00	400.00	10,000.00	15,000.00	infinity

change at a time apply to both activities and constraints. If you change one constraint limit to the extent that the basis changes, the range analysis for other constraints is liable to change.

9.3   THE EFFECT OF DIFFERENT UNITS

In Section 4.6 we looked at what the effect of using different units of measurement is on the interpretation of basic output. This section covers the related effect of units on range analysis.

Table 6.6 shows the matrix for the iron/steel problem we have been working with. Table 9.3 shows the same matrix, but with two of the activities and one of the constraints rescaled (i.e., measured in different units): *Own iron* in tens of tonnes, *Thick steel* in tenths of a tonne, and *Iron tr* in kilograms. The full solution to this rescaled problem is shown in Table 9.4.

Recall from Section 4.6 that when activities are scaled (e.g., the coefficients for *Thick steel* are multiplied by 0.1), the shadow cost is adjusted by the same factor. In this example, the shadow cost of *Thick steel* is now $21.5 per 0.1 tonne instead of $215 per tonne, but these are equivalent. The same scaling factor also applies to the activity range-analysis output. Therefore the values for *Thick steel* are decreased tenfold; the Upper objective value is now $221.50 compared with $2215.00 in Table 9.1. Remember that range analysis behaves the same as the shadow costs rather than the levels (which are divided by the

TABLE 9.3 Matrix for Example 6.2: Some Activities and Constraints Rescaled

	Own Iron (10 t)	Local Iron (t)	Import Iron (t)	Thin Steel (t)	Thick Steel (t/10)	Tube Steel (t)	Type	Limit
Objective ($)	−10,000	−1,200	−1,500	2,200	200	1,750	max	0
Iron tr (kg)	−10,000	−1,000	−1,000	1,200	121	1,250	≤	
Own max (t)	10						≤	3,000
Local max (t)		1					≤	10,000
Output max (t)				1	0.1	1	≤	15,000

TABLE 9.4   Optimal Solution for Example 6.2 for Version of Matrix Shown in Table 9.3

Objective function value: 10,500,000.000000
Problem direction: max

Activity		Level	Shadow Cost	Lower Objective	Original Objective	Upper Objective
1 Own iron	A	300.00	0.00	−15,000.00	−10,000.00	infinity
2 Local iron	A	1,000.00	0.00	−1,500.00	−1,200.00	infinity
3 Import iron	A	5,000.00	0.00	−1,833.33	−1,500.00	−1,200.00
4 Thin steel	A	15,000.00	0.00	1,985.00	2,200.00	infinity
5 Thick steel	Z	0.00	21.50	−infinity	200.00	221.50
6 Tube steel	Z	0.00	525.00	−infinity	1,750.00	2,275.00

Constraint		Slack	Shadow Price	Lower Limit	Original Limit	Upper Limit
1 Iron tr	L	0.00	1.50	−infinity	0.00	5,000,000.00
2 Own max	L	0.00	500.00	0.00	3,000.00	8,000.00
3 Local max	L	0.00	300.00	0.00	10,000.00	15,000.00
4 Output max	L	0.00	400.00	10,833.33	15,000.00	infinity

scaling factor, not multiplied) because both range analysis and shadow costs are concerned with the objective function rather than activity levels.

Similarly, range analysis for constraints behaves the same as constraint slacks since both are concerned with constraint limits. This time the effect is to multiply the values by the same factor used to scale the row's coefficients. So where the upper limit for *Iron tr* was 5000 (Table 9.1), after iron is measured in kilograms and the coefficients of the row have been multiplied by 1000, the upper limit has become 5,000,000 (Table 9.4). This is 5,000,000 thousandths of a tonne, which is the same as 5000 tonnes, the value in Table 9.1. It is obviously essential to be aware of the units of measurement used when interpreting range-analysis output.

9.4   KEY POINTS

- Activity range analysis gives the range within which objective function values can be changed without altering activity levels and slack values in the optimal solution. Shadow costs and shadow prices do, however, change.

- Constraint range analysis gives the range within which constraint limits can be changed without altering the basis (i.e., the set of activities with

---

BOX 9.1 Effects on Output of Changing Units of Measurement

Activities

A larger unit of measurement (e.g., tonnes instead of kilograms, miles instead of yards) will

(a) Decrease the numeric magnitude of the activity level.
(b) Increase the numeric magnitude of the shadow cost.
(c) Increase the numeric magnitude of the range analysis.

Constraints

A larger unit of measurement (e.g., tonnes instead of kilograms, miles instead of yards) will

(a) Decrease the numeric magnitude of the constraint slack.
(b) Increase the numeric magnitude of the shadow price.
(c) Decrease the numeric magnitude of the range analysis.

In all cases the magnitude of the effect on output values is the same as the magnitude of the change in units of measurement. For example, if the units of an activity are multiplied by a number X (i.e., the coefficients in the relevant column of the matrix are multiplied by X), the range analysis of the activity is multiplied by X. If the units of a constraint are multiplied by a number Y (i.e., the coefficients in the relevant row of the matrix are multiplied by $1/Y$), its range analysis is multiplied by $1/Y$.

---

positive values, or constraints with positive slacks in the solution), the shadow costs or the shadow prices. The activity levels and constraint slacks do change.

- If a column is scaled (multiplied) by a number X, its upper and lower objective values in the range analysis are multiplied by X.
- If a constraint is scaled (multiplied) by a number Y, its upper and lower limits in the range analysis are multiplied by Y.

Exercises

The problem definitions for these problems are given at the end of Chapter 8. You may wish to refer to the matrices that are given in the Solutions section at the back of the book.

TABLE 9.5 Optimal Solution for Exercise 8.4

Objective function value: 20,000.000000
Problem direction: max

Activity		Level	Shadow Cost	Lower Objective	Original Objective	Upper Objective
1 Wood	A	1,000.00	0.00	19.44	20.00	infinity
2 Wire	Z	0.00	5.00	−infinity	25.00	30.00
3 Metal	Z	0.00	1.00	−infinity	35.00	36.00

Constraint		Slack	Shadow Price	Lower Limit	Original Limit	Upper Limit
1 Labor	L	0.00	200.00	0.00	100.00	infinity
2 Wood-wire	L	1,000.00	0.00	−1,000.00	0.00	infinity

9.1 This optimal solution (Table 9.5) is for the model developed for Exercise 8.4.

(a) If the returns per meter of wood fencing fell to $19.00, would the optimal level of wood fencing be altered?

(b) Explain the relationship between the shadow cost of *Wire* and the range analysis for *Wire*.

(c) Explain the relationship between the shadow cost of *Wood* and the range analysis for *Wood*.

(d) The upper limit for the *Wood-wire* constraint is infinity. What does this mean?

(e) The *Labor* constraint is binding, but it has an upper limit of infinity. Explain why.

9.2 This optimal solution (Table 9.6) is for the model developed for Exercise 8.8.

(a) There are three occurrences of "infinity" in the upper limits for activities. What do they signify?

(b) What does the lower limit of 0.0 for *2-4 max* mean?

(c) Most of the range analysis results for activities are negative. Apart from cases of infinity, the only positive results are for *Flow*. Why does *Flow* have positive upper and lower objective values while the other activities have negatives?

(d) Suppose there is a plan to replace the pump that links nodes 1 and 2. The new pump will have the same capacity as the old pump (20 ML/h), but will be more economical, costing $0.12/ML pumped. Would the optimal pumping strategy change if this pump was replaced?

(e) If the pump described in part (d) was replaced as proposed, would there by any change in the net benefit in dollars per hour? If so, how much? (Ignore the cost of replacing the pump.)

TABLE 9.6   Optimal Solution for Exercise 8.8

Objective function value: 4.920000
Problem direction: max

Activity		Level	Shadow Cost	Lower Objective	Original Objective	Upper Objective
1 Flow	A	30.00	0.00	0.42	0.50	0.56
2 1-2	A	18.00	0.00	−0.24	−0.16	−0.10
3 1-3	A	12.00	0.00	−0.28	−0.12	infinity
4 2-3	A	3.00	0.00	−0.24	−0.12	−0.06
5 2-4	A	15.00	0.00	−0.18	−0.10	infinity
6 3-4	Z	0.00	0.06	−infinity	−0.12	−0.06
7 3-5	A	15.00	0.00	−0.22	−0.10	infinity
8 4-3	Z	0.00	0.18	−infinity	−0.12	0.06
9 4-5	A	15.00	0.00	−0.24	−0.16	−0.10

Constraint		Slack	Shadow Price	Lower Limit	Original Limit	Upper Limit
1 1 tr	L	0.00	0.00	−0.00	0.00	infinity
2 2 tr	L	0.00	0.16	−0.00	0.00	18.00
3 3 tr	L	0.00	0.28	−0.00	0.00	3.00
4 4 tr	L	0.00	0.34	−0.00	0.00	3.00
5 5 tr	L	0.00	0.50	−0.00	0.00	infinity
6 1-2 max	L	2.00	0.00	18.00	20.00	infinity
7 1-3 max	L	0.00	0.16	10.00	12.00	15.00
8 2-3 max	L	9.00	0.00	3.00	12.00	infinity
9 2-4 max	L	0.00	0.08	0.00	15.00	17.00
10 3-4 max	L	14.00	0.00	0.00	14.00	infinity
11 3-5 max	L	0.00	0.12	12.00	15.00	17.00
12 4-3 max	L	14.00	0.00	0.00	14.00	infinity
13 4-5 max	L	3.00	0.00	15.00	18.00	infinity

(f) Suppose that as well as replacing the pump for nodes 1 to 2, as in part (d), the company is also considering replacing the pump linking nodes 4 and 5. Again there would be no change in the flow rate per hour and again the cost of pumping would fall to $0.12/ML. Would the optimal pumping strategy change if both these pumps were replaced?

(g) If both pumps were replaced as proposed in part (f), would there be any change in the net benefit in dollars per hour? If so, how much? (Ignore the cost of replacing the pumps.)

(h) The pump supply company suggests to the water utility that they should consider a different approach: the pumps should be replaced with models that cost the same per megaliter pumped as the old pumps, but that are able to pump 25 ML/h. Would this be a good suggestion for the pipelines from 1 to 2 and/or from 4 to 5?

TABLE 9.7   Optimal Solution for Exercise 8.9

Objective function value: 3810.000000
Problem direction: min

Activity		Level	Shadow Cost	Lower Objective	Original Objective	Upper Objective
1 S1-D1	Z	0.00	0.10	0.05	0.15	infinity
2 S1-D2	Z	0.00	0.10	0.04	0.14	infinity
3 S1-D3	Z	0.00	0.19	0.01	0.20	infinity
4 S1-D4	A	10,000.00	0.00	−infinity	0.09	0.16
5 S2-D1	Z	0.00	0.07	0.12	0.19	infinity
6 S2-D2	Z	13,000.00	0.00	0.00	0.11	0.14
7 S2-D3	A	7,000.00	0.00	0.05	0.08	0.15
8 S2-D4	A	1,000.00	0.00	0.09	0.16	0.23
9 S3-D1	A	9,000.00	0.00	−0.06	0.06	0.13
10 S3-D2	Z	0.00	0.03	0.05	0.08	infinity
11 S3-D3	A	11,000.00	0.00	−0.05	0.02	0.05
12 S3-D4	Z	0.00	0.07	0.10	0.17	infinity

Constraint		Slack	Shadow Price	Lower Limit	Original Limit	Upper Limit
1 Site1 max	L	0.00	0.07	6,000.0	10,000.0	11,000.0
2 Site2 max	L	4,000.00	0.00	21,000.0	25,000.0	infinity
3 Site3 max	L	0.00	0.06	16,000.0	20,000.0	27,000.0
4 Depot1 min	G	0.00	−0.12	2,000.0	9,000.0	13,000.0
5 Depot2 min	G	0.00	−0.11	0.0	13,000.0	17,000.0
6 Depot3 min	G	0.00	−0.08	11,000.0	18,000.0	22,000.0
7 Depot4 min	G	0.00	−0.16	10,000.0	11,000.0	15,000.0

9.3   This optimal solution (Table 9.7) is for the model developed for Exercise 8.9.

    (a) What interpretation would you give to the lower objective value of 0.05 for *S1-D3*?

    (b) What interpretation would you give to the lower objective of −0.06 for *S3-D1*?

    (c) Why does *S1-D4* have a lower objective value of −infinity?

    (d) Suppose the required level of books at depot 2 increases from 13,000 to 15,000. Would the optimal basis change?

    (e) Given your answer to part (d), would the optimal level of any activities change?

    (f) If your answer to part (e) is yes, what would the changes be?

9.4   This optimal solution (Table 9.8) is for the model developed for Exercise 8.10.

    (a) If the cost of hired labor increased to $6/h, how would the optimal activity levels change?

TABLE 9.8   Optimal Solution for Exercise 8.10

Objective function value: 540.000000
Problem direction: max

Activity		Level	Shadow Cost	Lower Objective	Original Objective	Upper Objective
1 Labor 0	Z	0.00	70.00	$-$infinity	200.00	270.00
2 Labor 1	A	2.00	0.00	300.00	320.00	infinity
3 Labor 2	Z	0.00	20.00	$-$infinity	350.00	370.00
4 Labor 3	A	0.00	60.00	$-$infinity	360.00	420.00
5 Labor 4	Z	0.00	105.00	$-$infinity	365.00	470.00
6 Hire labor	A	2.00	0.00	$-$120.00	$-$50.00	$-$30.00

Constraint		Slack	Shadow Price	Lower Limit	Original Limit	Upper Limit
1 Labor tr	L	0.00	50.00	$-$infinity	0.00	2.00
2 Land	L	0.00	270.00	0.00	2.00	infinity

(b) If the cost of hired labor decreased to \$2.90/h, how would the optimal activity levels change?

(c) Interpret the upper objective value of *Labor 3*.

(d) Interpret the range-analysis output for the *Land* constraint.

CHAPTER 10

SOME COMPLICATIONS

In linear programming (LP) modeling things do not always go smoothly. There are several problems that can arise during solution of the problem on a computer, and some that relate to interpretation of output. If you have been doing the exercises at the ends of some of the previous chapters, you have probably already encountered some of the complications described in this chapter. The aim here and in the next chapter is to help you to recognize the problem (which is normally easy), to identify its specific causes in your model (which is often difficult), and to know what to do about it (which can be anything from obvious to impossible).

10.1 NO FEASIBLE SOLUTION

If an LP package gives an error message that the model being processed has no feasible solution, it means that it is not possible to find any combination of activities that simultaneously satisfies *all* the constraints. If a model has no feasible solution it is usually because the modeler has made a mistake, either in the structure of the model or when entering one of the model coefficients into the computer, but it can mean that the problem as defined has no solution.

Table 10.1 shows an example of a model with no feasible solution (sometimes referred to as an *infeasible model*). The matrix specifies that a mix of feeds must include at least 1300 MJ of energy but must not exceed 100-kg mass. This combination of requirements is impossible with the range of feeds included in the matrix. Either the energy content of the feed will have to be less than 1300, or the mass of feed will have to exceed 100 kg. The problem is illustrated in Figure 10.1. The energy constraint can only be met with com-

TABLE 10.1 An Infeasible Model

		Wheat (kg)	Oats (kg)	Type	Limit
Objective	($)	0.155	0.125	min	
Energy	(MJ)	11.52	10.26	≥	1,300
Intake	(kg)	1	1	≤	100

binations of wheat and oats on or above the line labeled Energy, while the intake constraint limits feed levels to combinations on or below the Intake line. Clearly, it is not possible to satisfy both constraints at the same time.

In general, an LP package will not identify all of the conflicting constraints. Given this problem to solve, an LP computer package would respond that there is no feasible solution and indicate which of the constraints was violated at the time the infeasibility was discovered. It will not indicate that the *Energy* constraint is incompatible with the *Intake* constraint; it will just say either that the energy constraint is violated or that the intake constraint is violated. Which of the incompatible constraints is signaled as being violated is more or less random. This inability of the LP package to be very specific about the causes of the infeasibility is a result of the way LP problems are solved.

In such a small problem, it does not matter much that you are not given information about both constraints, but in a model with many constraints it does matter. In a large problem with many constraints, it can be quite difficult to identify the constraint(s) that conflict with the constraint given in the error message. If the infeasibility arises from an error by the modeler (which is quite likely), there is no guarantee that the constraint given in the error message will

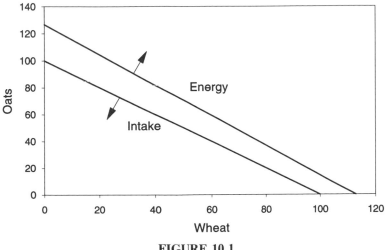

FIGURE 10.1

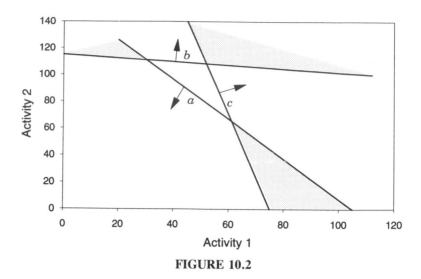

FIGURE 10.2

be the one that contains the error. The constraint indicated may just be the one that conflicts as a result of your error.

It may even be that a set of constraints that appears compatible when constraints are compared in pairs is infeasible when all the constraints are considered at once. Figure 10.2 shows a simple example of this. It is easy to identify combinations of *Activity 1* and *Activity 2* that satisfy constraints *a* and *b* (anywhere in the top left corner of the graph). Similarly, it is possible to satisfy both *b* and *c* or both *a* and *c*. However, there is no combination of *Activity 1* and *Activity 2* that will simultaneously meet all three constraints. The computer package asked to solve this model would say that *one* of these constraints could not be satisfied. But of course the problem is really the combination of all three constraints.

Unfortunately, there is no easy way of determining why an infeasibility arises or even which constraints are involved. You generally have to do some detective work to trace the problem. In the next chapter, we look in detail at strategies for diagnosing the cause of infeasibility.

10.2 UNBOUNDEDNESS

An unbounded problem is one in which a favorable activity appears to the computer to be available in unlimited quantities. For example, if you were modeling a footwear factory, you might accidentally include an option to make a particular type of shoe without representing the resources that would be required to make it. In this case, the computer package would calculate that an infinite amount of money could be made by making an infinite number of

TABLE 10.2 A Simple Unbounded Problem

	Activity 1 (kg)	Activity 2 (kg)	Type	Limit
Objective ($)	10	5	max	
Constraint 1 (kg)	1		≤	9
Constraint 2 (kg)	0.43		≥	2

these particular shoes; it would give a message saying that the problem was unbounded. LP requires that all relevant details be spelled out clearly, even if the detail is something as apparently obvious as the fact that making shoes requires some inputs of labor, leather, and so on.

Note that whereas infeasibility was something associated with constraints, unboundedness is an attribute of activities. The simplest unbounded activity is one with a favorable coefficient in the objective row but no coefficients in any of the other rows (e.g., Table 10.2). A "favorable" coefficient is positive if the objective is maximization or negative in a minimization problem. Fortunately, a simple unbounded activity like that in Table 10.2 is usually easy to recognize and easy to fix.

Figure 10.3 shows a graphical representation of this model. The level of *Activity 2* can be increased indefinitely without violating either of the two constraints, which affect only *Activity 1*. Notice that the feasible region is not a "closed" space. It extends indefinitely up the page. A graph of an unbounded solution will always be "open" in this way.

Although problems with an unbounded solution always have a feasible region that is not closed, not all problems with an open feasible region are

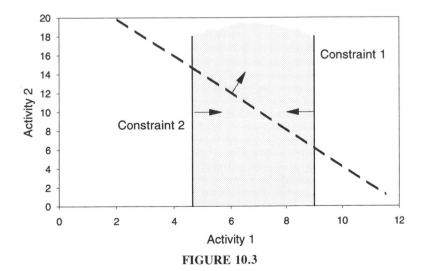

FIGURE 10.3

unbounded. It depends on whether the direction in which the region is open is consistent with the direction of the objective function.

In other words, even if it is feasible to select an unlimited amount of *Activity 2*, the solution is not unbounded unless *Activity 2* contributes in a favorable way to the objective function. If the objective for the problem was to *minimize* the objective function instead of to maximize it there would be a feasible optimal solution to the problem. The reason why the open feasible region is not a problem in this case is that although it is feasible to select an unlimited amount of *Activity 2*, it is not optimal to select any of it. The LP package will not select any of an undesirable activity unless forced to do so by a constraint. *Activity 2* is undesirable in this example because it has an objective function coefficient greater than zero and the objective is to minimize the value of the objective function.

Slightly more troublesome than this simple example are activities that cause other activities to be unbounded. An example of this is shown in Table 10.3. If the model did not include *Activity 2*, *Activity 1* would not be unbounded; Constraint 1 would limit the level of *Activity 1* to 9 units. However, *Activity 2* has a negative coefficient in Constraint 1. Remember from Chapter 6 that this is like having a positive coefficient in the Limit column, only the constraint limit can effectively be increased by selecting more of *Activity 2*. Each extra unit of *Activity 2* costs $4 but allows selection of an extra unit of *Activity 1*, which gives returns of $10. There is nothing to stop the model from increasing *Activity 2* indefinitely and in the process, increasing *Activity 1* with a net benefit of $6 per unit. Thus the problem is unbounded.

This problem is illustrated in Figure 10.4. The problem does not have a closed feasible region, and the direction in which it is open is consistent with an increase in the objective function.

It is also possible for a minimization problem to have an unbounded solution. This would occur if an activity that can feasibly be selected at an unlimited level has a negative objective function coefficient, since the more units of this activity that are selected, the lower (and hence the better) will be the objective function.

Finally, note that, as was the case with infeasible combinations of constraints, when unboundedness is due to a combination of activities, the computer program generally attributes the problem to just one activity, and you have to do some further investigation to find the cause of the problem. Suggested strategies for this are given in the next chapter.

TABLE 10.3   A More Subtle Unbounded Problem

	Activity 1 (kg)	Activity 2 (kg)	Type	Limit
Objective ($)	10	−4	max	
Constraint 1 (kg)	1	−1	≤	9
Constraint 2 (kg)	0.43		≥	2

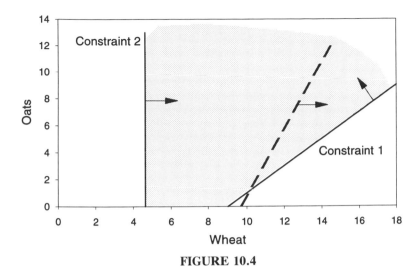

FIGURE 10.4

10.3 MULTIPLE OPTIMAL SOLUTIONS

Some LP problems have more than one optimal solution. Such a situation is not at all bad. It means there is a degree of flexibility open to the decision maker, who can take account of other preferences or prejudices in deciding what to do without suffering any loss in terms of the main objective, whether that be profit maximization, cost minimization, or anything else.

Let us start this explanation of multiple optimal solutions with a new problem. This problem relates to the decision of a commercial flower grower who has to decide which of three varieties of flowers to grow. The matrix and solution are shown in Tables 10.4 and 10.5, respectively.

As it stands, this problem has a single optimal solution. Profit is maximized with 60 ha of *Variety 1* and 40 ha of *Variety 2*. The shadow cost of *Variety 3* is $5, which means *Variety 3* is $5 away from being included in the optimal solution. If the profit from *Variety 3* increased by more than $5/ha, it would be selected. But what if it increased by exactly $5.00? Then the best solution including *Variety 3* would be exactly as profitable as the best solution without it. In other words, there would be more than one optimal solution.

TABLE 10.4 Matrix for Commercial Flower-Grower Problem

	Variety 1 (ha)	Variety 2 (ha)	Variety 3 (ha)	Type	Limit
Objective ($)	130	150	120	max	
Land (ha)	1	1	1	≤	100
Labor (h)	0.4	1	0.25	≤	64
Capital ($)	85	110	80	≤	10,000

TABLE 10.5 Optimal Solution for Matrix in Table 10.4

Objective function value: 13,800.000000
Problem direction: max

Activity		Level	Shadow Cost
1 Variety 1	A	60.00	0.00
2 Variety 2	A	40.00	0.00
3 Variety 3	Z	0.00	5.00
Constraint		Slack	Shadow Price
1 Land	L	0.00	116.67
2 Labor	L	0.00	33.33
3 Capital	L	500.00	0.00

Even if there are multiple optimal solutions, LP computer packages print only one of them. Within that solution, the fact that there are other equally profitable solutions is indicated. Table 10.6 shows one of the optimal solutions when the objective function coefficient for *Variety 3* is increased by $5.00 to $125/ha. It is just the same as Table 10.5 except that the shadow cost of *Variety 3* has been reduced to zero. *Variety 3* now has zero values for both level and shadow cost. Remember that selected activities have a level greater than zero and a shadow cost of zero, while nonselected activities have a zero level and nonzero shadow price. The fact that *Variety 3* has zero values for both indicates that *Variety 3* is on the border between being selected and not selected. The slightest improvement in profits from *Variety 3* would see it clearly in the optimal solution and any decline would put it clearly out.

LP computer packages include an additional indicator for a multiple solution

TABLE 10.6 One of Multiple Optimal Solutions for the Modified Flower-Grower Problem

Objective function value: 13,800.000000
Problem direction: max

Activity		Level	Shadow Cost
1 Variety 1	A	60.00	0.00
2 Variety 2	A	40.00	0.00
3 Variety 3	ZM	0.00	0.00
Constraint		Slack	Shadow Price
1 Land	L	0.00	116.67
2 Labor	L	0.00	33.33
3 Capital	L	500.00	0.00

since the double zero values are not an unambiguous sign of multiple solutions. They also occur when there is degeneracy, which is discussed in the next section. In Table 10.6 there is an M next to *Variety 3* to indicate that there are multiple solutions.

Remember that only one of the alternative optimal solutions is printed in the computer output. The output in Table 10.6 happens to be the one that came out when the problem was solved. However, you may want to see the other, equally good, solution that includes *Variety 3* at a nonzero level. One way of accomplishing this is to improve the objective function value of the relevant activity (the one with zero level and shadow cost) by a very small amount and then to re-solve the problem. Table 10.7 shows the result of adding 0.000001 to the objective value for *Variety 3*. Most of the area that was previously allocated to *Variety 1* is now *Variety 3* and the rest is reallocated to *Variety 2*.

Table 10.7 shows that the constraint slacks also change. The LP package sees the level of slack of a constraint as being similar to the level of an activity, so if there are multiple optimal sets of activity levels, there are also probably multiple optimal sets of slacks. In some cases, multiple optimal solutions will not be indicated by an activity with zero level/zero shadow cost, but instead by a constraint with zero slack and zero shadow price.

Multiple solutions have a graphical interpretation. They can only occur when every point along one of the constraint boundaries is equally profitable. This happens when a binding constraint is parallel to the objective function line. To illustrate, Figure 10.5 shows a graph of the model from Example 2.1, which was about selecting the optimal combination of women's and men's shoes to produce. The optimal solution for this problem is shown in Table 10.8.

The range analysis for *Men's* indicates that if its objective function coefficient was reduced to below 27.00, the optimal solution would change. But what if the coefficient was reduced to exactly 27.00? Figure 10.6 shows this

TABLE 10.7 Another of the Multiple Optimal Solutions for the Modified Flower-Grower Problem

Objective function value: 13,800.000000
Problem direction: max

Activity		Level	Shadow Cost
1 Variety 1	ZM	0.00	0.00
2 Variety 2	A	52.00	0.00
3 Variety 3	A	48.00	0.00
Constraint		Slack	Shadow Price
1 Land	L	0.00	116.67
2 Labor	L	0.00	33.33
3 Capital	L	440.00	0.00

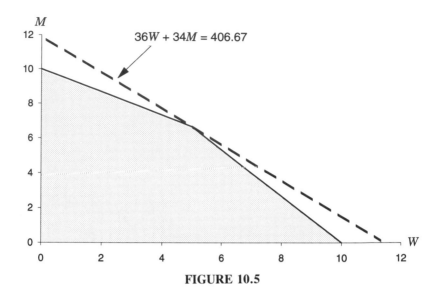

FIGURE 10.5

scenario. The line representing the highest possible objective function is now parallel to the *Labor* constraint. This means that all points along the feasible segment of *Labor* are now equally profitable. This includes *all* points between (5, 6.67) and (10, 0).

Check that these points do have the same level of profit. The objective function to be maximized is $(36 \times L) + (27 \times M)$. For the point (10, 0) the value of this function is $360 + 0 = 360$. For the point (5, 6.67) the function equals $180 + 180 = 360$. In addition it can be shown that any point on the line segment between these endpoints also has a profit of $360. For example, the point (7.5, 3.33) lies on this segment and it has a profit of $270 + 90 = 360$.

TABLE 10.8 Optimal Solution for Example 2.1

Objective function value: 406.666667
Problem direction: max

Activity		Level	Shadow Cost	Lower Objective	Original Objective	Upper Objective
1 Women's	A	5.00	0.00	22.67	36.00	45.33
2 Men's	A	6.67	0.00	27.00	34.00	54.00

Constraint		Slack	Shadow Price	Lower Limit	Original Limit	Upper Limit
1 Labor	L	0.00	6.67	30.00	40.00	60.00
2 Leather	L	0.00	46.67	2.00	3.00	4.00

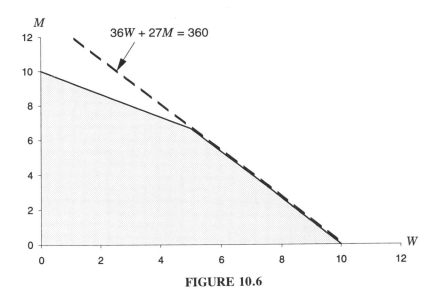

FIGURE 10.6

The two optimal solutions corresponding to the endpoints of this line segment are shown in Tables 10.9 and 10.10. In Table 10.9, the existence of multiple optimal solutions is indicated in this solution by the M in the *Men's* results. Table 10.10 was generated by increasing the objective function coefficient of *Men's* fractionally to 27.0001. In Table 10.10, there is an M marker for the *Leather* constraint, and in addition the existence of alternative optimal solutions is indicated by the range-analysis output for activities. The upper objective value for *Women's* and the lower objective value for *Men's* indicate that any change at all in favor of *Women's* or against *Men's* will swing the solution back to that shown in Table 10.9.

TABLE 10.9   Optimal Solution for Example 2.1 with the Objective Function Coefficient of *Men's* Reduced to 27.00

Objective function value: 360.000000
Problem direction: max

Activity		Level	Shadow Cost	Lower Objective	Original Objective	Upper Objective
1 Women's	A	10.00	0.00	36.00	36.00	infinity
2 Men's	ZM	0.00	0.00	−infinity	27.00	27.00

Constraint		Slack	Shadow Price	Lower Limit	Original Limit	Upper Limit
1 Labor	L	0.00	9.00	0.00	40.00	60.00
2 Leather	L	1.00	0.00	2.00	3.00	infinity

TABLE 10.10 Optimal Solution for Example 2.1 with the Objective Function Coefficient of *Men's* Set to 27.0001

Objective function value: 360.000667
Problem direction: max

Activity		Level	Shadow Cost	Lower Objective	Original Objective	Upper Objective
1 Women's	A	5.00	0.00	18.0001	36.00	36.0001
2 Men's	A	6.67	0.00	27.00	27.0001	54.00

Constraint		Slack	Shadow Price	Lower Limit	Original Limit	Upper Limit
1 Labor	L	0.00	9.00	30.00	40.00	60.00
2 Leather	LM	0.00	0.00	2.00	3.00	4.00

If desirable, it would also be possible to have the LP package generate an optimal solution intermediate between Table 10.9 and 10.10. The way to achieve this is to add a constraint limiting the level of one of the variables to an intermediate value. For example, Table 10.11 shows the solution for a model in which the level of *Women's* is constrained to exactly 7.50.

Notice the results for *Fix Women's*, which represents the constraint

$$1 \times Women's = 7.5$$

The shadow price is zero, indicating that marginal changes in the constraint limit would have no effect on the objective function value. This makes sense, since any change in the level of *Women's* would be accompanied by a change

TABLE 10.11 Optimal Solution for Example 2.1 with the Objective Function Coefficient of *Men's* Reduced to 27 and *Women's* Constrained to 7.5

Objective function value: 360.000000
Problem direction: max

Activity		Level	Shadow Cost	Lower Objective	Original Objective	Upper Objective
1 Women's	A	7.50	0.00	−infinity	36.00	infinity
2 Men's	A	3.33	0.00	0.00	27.00	infinity

Constraint		Slack	Shadow Price	Lower Limit	Original Limit	Upper Limit
1 Labor	L	0.00	9.00	30.00	40.00	45.00
2 Leather	L	0.50	0.00	2.50	3.00	infinity
3 Fix Women's	EM	0.00	0.00	5.00	7.50	10.00

in *Men's* such that the new solution was another point along the line segment of equal profitability.

In conclusion, multiple optimal solutions should not be viewed as a problem, but as allowing some flexibility of strategy at no cost.

10.4 DEGENERATE SOLUTIONS

A degenerate solution is one where there is more than one valid set of shadow costs and shadow prices. It is similar in some ways to a case of multiple optimal solutions, but it occurs in the shadow costs and shadow prices rather than the activity levels and constraint slacks.*

Degeneracy occurs when there is more than one constraint limiting an activity level (or constraint slack) to zero level. This allows the activity to be ''selected'' as part of the optimal solution, but at zero level. Although this sounds illogical, it is useful to distinguish between the activities that are not selected and those that are selected at zero level. Degeneracy is not usually a serious problem, but it can be a nuisance if the set of shadow costs and shadow prices printed by the LP package is not the one of interest.

A degenerate solution is indicated in the solution output by an activity at zero level with zero shadow cost or by a constraint with zero slack and zero shadow price. Because this is indistinguishable from a case of multiple optimal solutions, the output from LP packages includes an indication of whether such an activity or constraint results from degeneracy or a multiple solution. The difference between the two is that in a degenerate solution, the activity is selected as part of the optimal basis, although at zero level, whereas in a multiple solution, the activity is not selected but has a zero shadow cost. (A similar distinction applies to constraints with zero slack/zero shadow price.)

In a case of multiple optimal solutions, a zero shadow cost indicates that the activity is close to entering the solution in the sense that a small change in its objective function coefficient can cause it to enter the optimal basis. When there is degeneracy, a zero shadow cost does not have this interpretation. The activity may actually be far too unprofitable to enter the solution at any value greater than zero, but it can still enter the basis at a level of zero. On the other hand, the degenerate activity *is* close to entering the basis in the sense that a small change in the *constraint limit of the redundant constraint* can cause it to be selected at a nonzero level (assuming no other constraint prevents this).

The result of degeneracy is that it is impossible to tell from shadow costs or the range analysis how much the objective function coefficient of the degenerate activity needs to improve for it to be selected as a real part of the plan. As far as the LP package is concerned, the activity already *is* part of the optimal solution, so it has a shadow cost of zero.

---

*In fact a model with a degenerate solution has a dual with multiple optimal solutions.

TABLE 10.12   Matrix for Modified Example 2.1 with the Objective Function Coefficient of *Men's* Set to 72 and an Extra Constraint on Glue

	Women's (pairs)	Men's (pairs)	Type	Limit
Objective ($)	36	72	max	
Labor (hours)	4	3	≤	40
Leather (square m)	0.2	0.3	≤	3
Glue (mL)	0.5	2	≤	22

To illustrate the issue, consider another modified version of Example 2.1 (production of women's and men's shoes). The matrix is shown in Table 10.12. This matrix has a higher objective function value for *Men's* than the original version, and an additional constraint on *Glue*. Availability of a particular special glue is limited to 22 mL per week. Women's and men's shoes require 0.5 and 2.0 mL of this glue per pair.

This model is illustrated in Figure 10.7, and the optimal solution is given in Table 10.13. The optimal solution is to produce 10 pairs of men's shoes. There is slack of 2.0 on the *Glue* constraint.

If the constraint limit on *Glue* were to be reduced slightly, the level of slack on *Glue* would fall. If we reduced the limit on *Glue* to 20.0, there would be no slack left. (This is indicated by the Lower Limit of *Glue* in Table 10.13.) Figure 10.8 illustrates the model, and Table 10.14 shows the output for this case. The shadow costs and shadow prices have not changed from Table 10.13, but the *Glue* constraint is now indicated as being degenerate by inclusion of a

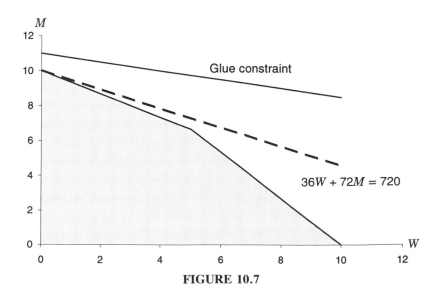

FIGURE 10.7

TABLE 10.13 Optimal Solution for Modified Example 2.1 (See Table 10.12)

Objective function value: 720.000000
Problem direction: max

Activity		Level	Shadow Cost	Lower Objective	Original Objective	Upper Objective
1 Women's	Z	0.00	12.00	−infinity	36.00	48.00
2 Men's	A	10.00	0.00	54.00	72.00	infinity

Constraint		Slack	Shadow Price	Lower Limit	Original Limit	Upper Limit
1 Labor	L	10.00	0.00	30.00	40.00	infinity
2 Leather	L	0.00	240.00	0.00	3.00	3.30
3 Glue	L	2.00	0.00	20.00	22.00	infinity

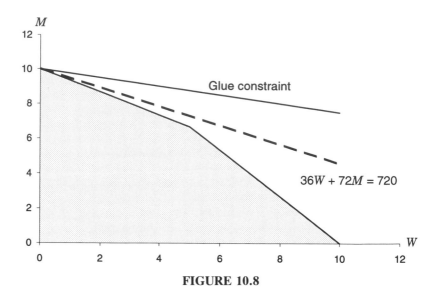

FIGURE 10.8

D in the output. This means that there is another set of shadow costs and shadow prices that is valid for this set of activity levels and constraint slacks.

If we wish to see this other set, we can reduce the constraint limit by a small amount and re-solve the model. The resulting solution is shown in Table 10.15. It has the same activity levels and constraint slacks as Table 10.14, but the shadow cost of *Women's* has fallen to zero and the shadow price of *Glue* has increased to 14.4. Now the *Women's* activity is shown as being degenerate, meaning that it is active but at the zero level. If the constraint limit of *Glue* were to be reduced further, the level of *Women's* would rise, while the level

TABLE 10.14   Optimal Solution for Modified Example 2.1 with *Glue* Constraint Limit Set to 20.00

Objective function value: 720.000000
Problem direction: max

Activity		Level	Shadow Cost	Lower Objective	Original Objective	Upper Objectiv
1 Women's	Z	0.00	12.00	−infinity	36.00	48.00
2 Men's	A	10.00	0.00	54.00	72.00	infinity

Constraint		Slack	Shadow Price	Lower Limit	Original Limit	Upper Limit
1 Labor	L	10.00	0.00	30.00	40.00	infinity
2 Leather	L	0.00	240.00	0.00	3.00	3.00
3 Glue	LD	0.00	0.00	20.00	20.00	infinity

TABLE 10.15   Optimal Solution for Modified Example 2.1 with *Glue* Constraint Limit Set to 19.99999999

Objective function value: 720.000000
Problem direction: max

Activity		Level	Shadow Cost	Lower Objective	Original Objective	Upper Objective
1 Women's	AD	0.00	0.00	18.00	36.00	48.00
2 Men's	A	10.00	0.00	54.00	72.00	144.00

Constraint		Slack	Shadow Price	Lower Limit	Original Limit	Upper Limit
1 Labor	L	10.00	0.00	30.00	40.00	infinity
2 Leather	L	0.00	144.00	3.00	3.00	3.38
3 Glue	L	0.00	14.40	15.83	20.00	20.00

of *Men's* and the slack on *Labor* would fall. However, the shadow costs and shadow prices would stay as in Table 10.15. This is shown in Table 10.16, which is for a constraint limit of 19 on *Glue*. This model is illustrated in Figure 10.9.

You may have noticed that the difference between the two sets of shadow costs and shadow prices relevant to Figure 10.8 (in Tables 10.14 and 10.15) is that they are relevant to different directions of change of the constraint limit of *Glue*. This difference in direction occurs whenever a solution is degenerate. As illustration, Table 10.14 applies to increases in the constraint limit while Table 10.15 applies to decreases.

TABLE 10.16   Optimal Solution for Modified Example 2.1 with *Glue* Constraint Limit Set to 19.00

Objective function value: 691.200000
Problem direction: max

Activity		Level	Shadow Cost	Lower Objective	Original Objective	Upper Objective
1 Women's	A	3.00	0.00	30.00	36.00	40.00
2 Men's	A	8.00	0.00	54.00	60.00	72.00

Constraint		Slack	Shadow Price	Lower Limit	Original Limit	Upper Limit
1 Labor	L	4.00	0.00	36.00	40.00	infinity
2 Leather	L	0.00	120.00	2.85	3.00	3.08
3 Glue	L	0.00	12.00	18.33	19.00	20.00

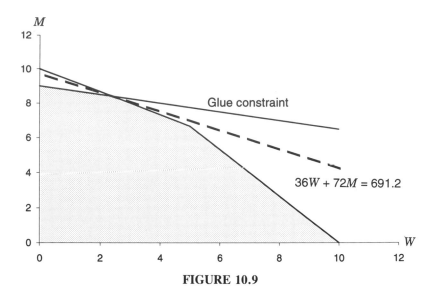

FIGURE 10.9

Normally, one is more interested in one of the sets of shadow costs and shadow prices than the other. If the printed set is not the one of interest, you can obtain the other set by altering the relevant constraint limit slightly, as illustrated earlier. Notice that this technique reflects the similarities between degeneracy and multiple optimal solutions; that is, the approach for identifying an alternative optimal solution is to make a tiny alteration in the objective function coefficient of a relevant activity.

Degeneracy and Transfer Rows

A potential disadvantage of using transfer rows in an LP matrix is that they can increase the occurrence of degeneracy in the optimal solution. This commonly happens when:

(a) The optimal level of a particular activity is zero.
(b) The activity, if selected, uses some of a resource represented in a particular transfer row (which we assume is a less-than constraint).
(c) Even if the transfer row were to be deleted from the model, the optimal level of the activity would still be zero.
(d) The transfer row has a constraint limit of zero, and none of the resource it represents is generated into the row (i.e., no activities with negative coefficients in the row have optimal levels greater than zero).

In this case, the redundant transfer row or the activity may be degenerate in the optimal solution. If the LP package prints the solution where an activity is degenerate and you want to know how much you would need to increase the objective function of the activity before it would be selected at a level greater than zero, you can obtain the desired shadow cost information by increasing the constraint limit of the transfer row by a very small amount so that it is not binding. For more on degeneracy and interpretation of shadow prices, see Rubin and Wagner (1990).

BOX 10.1   Degeneracy and Multiple Optimal Solutions:
Similarities and Differences

(a) Both can result in activities with zero levels and zero shadow costs or in constraints with zero slacks and zero shadow prices.

(b) In both cases, the solution is on the verge of changing. For multiple optimal solutions the trigger would be a change in the objective function, while for degeneracy the trigger would be a change in a constraint limit.

(c) In a case of multiple optimal solutions, a zero level/zero shadow cost activity *is not active*. In degeneracy, such an activity *is active* but at zero level.

(d) In a solution with multiple optimal solutions, there are alternative valid sets of activity levels and constraint slacks. In a degenerate solution there are alternative valid sets of shadow costs and shadow prices.

10.5 ROUNDING ERRORS

LP problems are mathematically difficult to solve, even on a computer. This is partly due to the nature of the *simplex algorithm:* the series of rules and steps used during the solution process. The algorithm proceeds by "iterations" in which every cell of the matrix is multiplied or divided or added to. For a moderately large problem, a great many iterations (often hundreds or even thousands) might be needed to find the solution. Computers do not do arithmetic operations with perfect accuracy, even though they do their calculations to many decimal places. They have to round off the answer to some number of decimal places and every time they do so, a tiny degree of accuracy is lost. For most matrices this is no problem, but occasionally the rounding errors accumulate and compound each other, resulting in the LP computer package reaching a solution that is not optimal and may not even be feasible. When this occurs, it is usually easy to tell because the selected solution is so ridiculous.

There is no way of telling in advance whether any particular matrix will cause problems with rounding errors, but the probability of failure is increased if the matrix includes coefficients of vastly different magnitudes. If this is the case, there is the possibility of a large number being divided by a very small number, resulting in an enormous number. Also, if small and large numbers are added, the result may be indistinguishable from the original large number.

When rounding errors become a problem, it is necessary to scale the matrix so that the largest coefficient is not too different in size from the smallest. (Note that when talking about large and small numbers in this context, you should ignore whether they are positive or negative). Scaling was discussed in Sections 4.6 and 9.3 on the importance of units. Basically scaling involves multiplying all the coefficients in a row or column by some factor. Some packages have an automatic scaling option built in, while others require you to do the scaling before entering the coefficients into the computer.

There are no hard and fast rules about which factors should be used for scaling, but the smaller the range of coefficients, the lower the risk of errors. To keep output interpretation simple, try to keep things measured in units that make sense to you. For example, if the largest coefficient in a column is 20,000 and the activity is measured in grams, you could reduce the coefficient to 20 by measuring the activity in kilograms. If you manage to remove the very large and very small coefficients from your matrix, but the LP package still has problems with rounding errors, there are two strategies worth trying:

(a) Alter the structure of the matrix in some way, such as adding or removing a transfer row.

(b) Use a different computer package if one is available.

10.6 KEY POINTS

- If a model has no feasible solution, it means that it is not possible to find any combination of activities that simultaneously satisfies *all* the constraints.

- A model with no feasible solution normally results from a mistake by the modeler, either in the structure of the model or in entering one of the model coefficients into the computer.

- A model with no feasible solution results from two or more constraints being in conflict.

- LP packages identify only one of the conflicting constraints. If the infeasibility is the result of an error, the constraint identified by the LP package will not necessarily be the one that includes the error.

- It is possible to have a set of three or more constraints that appear not to be in conflict when examined in pairs, but that are infeasible when all are considered simultaneously.

- An unbounded problem is one where the computer sees a favorable activity as being available in unlimited quantities.

- Whereas ''no feasible solution'' is a problem associated with constraints, unboundedness is a problem of activities.

- Problems with an unbounded solution always have a feasible region that is not closed.

- Not all problems with an open feasible region are unbounded, depending on the direction of the objective function.

- When unboundedness is due to a combination of activities, the computer program generally attributes the problem to just one activity.

- Multiple optimal solutions occur when a binding constraint is parallel to the objective function line.

- Where a problem has multiple optimal solutions, the solution printed by the LP package includes an activity that has a zero level and zero shadow cost, or a constraint with zero slack and zero shadow price. This activity or constraint is close to entering the optimal solution in the sense that a small change in an objective function coefficient of the model causes it to enter the optimal basis.

- A degenerate solution occurs when there is more than one valid set of shadow costs and shadow prices. It can arise when there is more than one constraint limiting an activity to zero level.

- Where a problem has a degenerate optimal solution, the solution printed by the LP package includes an activity that has a zero level and zero shadow cost, or a constraint with zero slack and zero shadow price. This activity or constraint is close to entering the optimal solution in the sense that a small change in a constraint limit of the model causes it to enter the optimal basis.

- If an activity has a zero value for both its level and its shadow cost, or a constraint has a zero slack and zero shadow price, the solution is either degenerate or one of multiple optimal solutions.

- In the case of multiple optimal solutions, the zero/zero activity or constraint *is not* active. It is not part of the optimal basis, but there is an equally good basis that does include it.

- In the case of a degenerate solution, the zero/zero activity or constraint *is* active; that is, it is part of the optimal basis.

- Degeneracy is like multiple optimal solutions for shadow costs and shadow prices rather than for activity levels and slacks.

- The LP package can be made to display the alternative optimal solution by slightly altering the appropriate objective function coefficient (multiple optimal solutions) or constraint limit (degeneracy).

- Occasionally in the process of solving a model, rounding errors accumulate to the point where the optimal solution cannot be found. In this case, scaling the matrix may be necessary.

Exercises

Determine whether the LP problems presented in Exercises 10.1 to 10.6 have any of the first four problems described in this chapter: no feasible solution, unboundedness, multiple optimal solutions, or degeneracy. You should initially use either your own logic or the graphical approach of Chapter 2. Check your answers by entering the models into your LP computer package and attempting to solve them.

10.1   Maximize

$$P = 5X + 4Y$$

Subject to

$$3X + 4Y \le 6$$
$$5X + 2Y \le 10$$
$$X \ge 0; \quad Y \ge 0$$

10.2   Minimize

$$P = 25X + 15Y$$

Subject to

$$2X + 2Y \ge 40$$
$$10X + 2Y \ge 50$$
$$X + 3Y \le 15$$
$$X \ge 0; \quad Y \ge 0$$

10.3   Maximize

$$P = X + Y$$

Subject to

$$3X - 2Y \le 10$$
$$3Y \ge 20$$
$$X \le 3$$
$$X \ge 0; \quad Y \ge 0$$

10.4 Minimize

$$P = 5X + 6Y$$

Subject to

$$X + Y \geq 11$$
$$8X + 2Y \geq 80$$
$$Y \geq 40$$
$$X \geq 0; \quad Y \geq 0$$

10.5 Maximize

$$P = 25X + 37.5Y$$

Subject to

$$5X + 4Y \leq 600$$
$$2X + 3Y \leq 300$$
$$X \leq 100$$
$$Y \leq 100$$
$$X \geq 0; \quad Y \geq 0$$

10.6 As for Exercise 10.5 but with the objective function revised to

Maximize

$$P = 25X - 20Y$$

CHAPTER 11

DEBUGGING YOUR MODEL

Once a model has been constructed, there are two broad ways in which it may be in error: (a) the matrix may be inconsistent with the problem definition (e.g., due to a coefficient being placed in the wrong cell), or (b) the problem definition may be incorrect or inappropriate in some way. Checking for the first type of error is often referred to as *verification*, while the second type is called *validation*. In practice, when you suspect a problem, it is often difficult to tell whether it is due to a verification problem or a validation problem. For this reason it is preferable to call them both *bugs*, and the process of trying to solve them, *debugging*.

Bugs are an unavoidable aspect of linear programming (LP) modeling. The prevention and diagnosis of bugs in LP models is often neglected, but is crucial to the success of modeling projects. While some of the material in this chapter is particularly relevant to large models, which would probably only be developed by a more experienced modeler, it is equally germane to beginners.

Finding a bug and understanding an unexpected result (whether or not it is due to a bug) are very closely related activities. This chapter outlines different types of bugs and practical strategies for dealing with each. Adopting procedures for prevention of bugs is essential, especially for large models. Section 11.5 describes bug-prevention strategies that have been successful for real-world LP models.

Validation of LP and other types of models has been discussed by a number of authors (e.g., Gass, 1983; McCarl, 1984), but verification has generally been given a cursory treatment by these authors. For example, McCarl's (1984) "procedure for model validation" includes the following: "If the model has failed, discover why. . . . Repair the model and go to step 2" (p. 161). It can be extremely difficult and time-consuming to obey these simple instructions.

11.1 GUIDING PRINCIPLES FOR DEBUGGING

There are two broad areas about which we can identify some general principles of debugging: diagnosing suspected bugs and preventing bugs. The principles are as follows:

1. *Prevention is better than cure.* This is an old but apt adage that applies as much in debugging LP models as anywhere. We discuss prevention of bugs at some length later.

2. *An unexpected model result is caused by a bug unless you can convince yourself otherwise.* This implies a conservative approach to interpreting model results. It means that you do not accept a plausible explanation for a result without examining and testing the alternative explanation that the result is at least partly due to a bug. It is easy to invent a more or less convincing explanation for almost any result in a complex model. Such explanations should not be accepted uncritically. On the other hand, you cannot prove there is no bug. There are parallels here with the dominant paradigm for science in which it is possible to disprove a hypothesis, but not to prove it (Magee, 1973). It comes down to the modeler taking ''reasonable'' care, a matter of subjective judgment.

3. *Maintaining a bug-free (or at least low-bug) model requires discipline.* Most importantly, you need discipline to pursue every unexpected result or suspicious looking matrix coefficient to the point where you are convinced that it is or is not due to a bug. It is easy to move on to the far more interesting task of doing further model runs. Discipline is also required to keep model documentation up to date. This leads to the next principle.

4. *A well-documented model is easier to debug and maintain.* This is possibly the most obvious but also the most frequently ignored of these principles. You should keep clear and up-to-date records of all data and assumptions of the model.

5 *Knowledge of the model is essential for debugging.* Knowledge of the model's assumptions and structure is essential for uncovering some bugs. Further, detailed knowledge of the real-world system being modeled is also useful, particularly for recognizing model solutions that reveal of a bug.

6. *In a well-maintained model the number of bugs in a matrix decreases over time as they are discovered and fixed, but not to zero.* After a long period of model use and maintenance, any remaining bugs are unlikely to be serious, or at least to conflict with the expectations of those who use the model. Such bugs can remain undetected for a long time. For example, we recently found 15 wrong coefficients in an intensively maintained and widely used LP model. The model, with approximately 400 activities and 200 constraints, is not especially large as LP matrices go, yet it took several years to find these bugs.

Long-standing bugs like these will generally only be discovered if the model is used in a new and innovative way, model input or output is examined in different ways, or a new person joins the modeling team. The 15 bugs just mentioned were discovered when a new format for output was created. However, these new approaches to model use rapidly dissipate their capacity for revealing bugs as they too become routine.

7. *The number of bugs in a matrix increases rapidly with the size of the matrix.* For example, suppose there is a one in 10,000 chance of any coefficient chosen at random (including zeros) being wrong. If you have a small 100×100 matrix, the expected number of bugs in coefficients is 1, the probability of no bugs is 0.37, and the probability of five or more coefficients being wrong is 0.0037. Table 11.1 shows how these probabilities change as matrix size increases.

The probability of there being at least one bug in the matrix increases to over 99 percent for a matrix with 50,000 coefficients. Even more worrying, the probability of there being five or more errors in the matrix is almost 20 percent for a 30,000-coefficient matrix, which would not be considered particularly large.

The probabilities in Table 11.1 are based on the assumption that the probability of an error is independent of the size of a matrix. In reality, the probability may increase with matrix size due to the fact that it is more difficult to examine larger matrices and more difficult to recognize a bug. Table 11.2 is similar to Table 11.1 except that it is based on the assumption that the probability of an error in a randomly chosen coefficient is proportional to the matrix size (0.0001 for a 10,000-coefficient matrix, 0.0002 for 20,000, etc.).

This assumption has a big effect on the probabilities. A 30,000-coefficient matrix now has a 94 percent chance of containing five or more errors and a 41 percent chance of 10 or more errors.

These probabilities are based on simple assumptions and should be viewed as illustrative only. However, they do highlight the great risk of bugs in large matrices, especially when you consider that the matrix sizes used here are not large. Matrices with millions of coefficients are in active use.

With modern software and hardware, human ability to maintain and debug models is the only factor limiting their size and complexity. This ability does

TABLE 11.1   Probabilities of Errors in Coefficients If the Probability of an Error in a Randomly Chosen Coefficient Is 0.0001

Matrix Size (rows × cols)	E(N)	Probability ($N = 0$)	Probability ($N \geq 5$)	Probability ($N \geq 10$)
10,000	1	0.37	0.0037	*
20,000	2	0.14	0.053	*
30,000	3	0.050	0.18	0.0011
40,000	4	0.018	0.37	0.0080
50,000	5	0.0067	0.56	0.030

*$p < 0.001$.
Note: N = number of errors; E(N) = expected number of errors.

TABLE 11.2 Probabilities of Errors in Coefficients If the Probability of an Error in a Randomly Chosen Coefficient Is Proportional to Matrix Size

Matrix Size (rows × cols)	E(N)	Probability (N = 0)	Probability (N ≥ 5)	Probability (N ≥ 10)
10,000	1	0.37	0.0037	*
20,000	4	0.018	0.37	0.0081
30,000	9	*	0.94	0.41
40,000	16	*	0.9996	0.96
50,000	25	*	0.9999	0.9998

*$p < 0.001$.
Note: N = number of errors; $E(N)$ = expected number of errors.

pose real limits that need to be recognized and respected. There is a matrix size beyond which no amount of human resources can ensure the correctness of the matrix. Because of the repetitiveness of some models, it is difficult to say how big is too big. For example, the MIDAS farm model (Kingwell and Pannell, 1987) has little repetition. With allocation of adequate resources (0.3 to 0.5 person years per year) and adherence to the sorts of bug-prevention strategies suggested below, its 400-by-300 matrix can be maintained with only occasional errors. The MUDAS model (Kingwell et al., 1992) is much bigger (1500 by 1300), but it is also more repetitive. I believe that a matrix of this size is right at the limit of what can realistically be maintained in a usable and fairly error-free state.

A number of LP models have been developed with tens of thousands of columns. There is little or no prospect of satisfactorily debugging such a model, so any results from them must be viewed with suspicion.

8. *Maintaining a large LP model in a fairly bug-free state requires a large commitment of human resources.* Rarely are sufficient resources provided for this purpose, so it is likely that many large LP models in active use contain important bugs.

9. *Bugs you thought you had fixed can easily come back to haunt you.* Anyone who has been responsible for debugging a large model over a long period of time will be well acquainted with this principle. The bug-prevention strategies presented later should minimize this problem.

10. *When you are actively searching for one bug, you are quite likely to discover other, unsuspected bugs.* The act of searching for a bug requires a higher degree of mental acuity. It may also require you to critically examine aspects of the model that have previously been neglected. Both of these factors can lead to the modeler stumbling onto previously unsuspected bugs.

11. *Good hardware and software can make debugging much less of an onerous task.* Debugging often involves making numerous changes to the model and conducting several model runs. Obviously, using the fastest available hardware minimizes the response time for tests of hypotheses.

Software can probably make an even bigger difference in finding bugs. Here are some software tools that can be very valuable during debugging.

- A program that allows you to view and edit the model in matrix format.
- A task-switching or multitasking operating environment. Often when debugging it is necessary to swap quickly between several different programs (e.g., a matrix editor, a spreadsheet, a text editor). Multitasking or task-switching makes this much easier.
- A spreadsheet package. The uses an LP modeler can make of a spreadsheet include identification of differences between similar matrices and identification of all differences between two solutions. This is in addition to using spreadsheet templates to calculate model coefficients from basic assumptions and to provide a user-friendly tabular interface for data entry. Recent releases of major commercial spreadsheet packages even have LP and nonlinear programming components built in.
- A program that undertakes intelligent comparisons of text files. This is a very quick way of identifying minor differences between two matrix data files.

11.2 SYMPTOMS OF BUGS

The more serious bugs are usually detected through one of the following symptoms appearing in the model solution:

- An unlikely model solution.
- No feasible solution.
- An unbounded solution.

The majority of these symptoms is observed during the model development and testing phase, but they can also occur when the model is changed for a particular analysis. The change may introduce a new bug or it may allow an existing bug to express itself.

Infeasible or unbounded solutions are clearly indicated in the output from the computer package, but identification of unlikely solutions requires a degree of subjective judgment. An unlikely solution can be blatantly obvious or very subtle. In general an unlikely solution is one where one of the elements is outside its expected range. The suspect element may be the level of an activity, the shadow cost of an activity, the level of slack for a constraint, or the shadow price for a constraint. Examples of various types of unlikely solution include:

- An activity is selected at a level judged to be too high.
- An activity that you expected to be included in the solution at nonzero level is not included.

- An activity that you did not expect to be included in the solution at nonzero level is included.
- The shadow price of a constraint is very different from its expected range.
- The shadow cost of an activity is very different from its expected range. A constraint that you considered should be binding in the solution has a nonzero slack value.
- You have two similar copies of a model you believe should give the same basic solution but do not.

Later in this chapter we suggest some strategies for determining what type of bug, if any, is causing these symptoms.

The symptoms just listed all relate to problems with the model solution. However, many bugs are too subtle or minor to have a detectable effect on the solution. It may be that a bug affects the levels of several activities, but that the resulting levels are plausible, even though they are incorrect. Alternatively, the model user may have no prior expectation about which of a range of activities will be included in the optimal solution. In this situation a mistyped coefficient could dramatically alter the optimal solution without arousing suspicion.

There are two ways of dealing with these more subtle bugs. One is to detect them through careful examination of the model's coefficients, checking their consistency with the underlying assumptions of the model. The potential for tedium in this task is great, especially in large models. The other way is to prevent them occurring in the first place, as we discuss later.

11.3 TYPES OF BUGS

Once a symptom has been detected, the next step is diagnosis of the cause. An important element of the diagnosis is an awareness of the full range of possible causes of the observed symptom. Box 11.1 shows one way of categorizing the range of possible diagnoses.

11.4 STRATEGIES FOR DEBUGGING

Here we are concerned with symptoms that occur in a model solution, not with bugs that are initially detected through checking model inputs. There is no foolproof strategy that will lead you directly to the diagnosis of a bug, and it is difficult to generalize about the best strategy. However, a methodical approach is bound to be more productive than a random search. A useful analogy can be drawn between debugging and scientific research. The practice of science and efficient debugging involve similar elements.

BOX 11.1   Possible Diagnoses of a Suspected Bug

1. The model is not consistent with the underlying assumptions.
   1.1 A coefficient is incorrect.
      1.1.1 A coefficient has been mistyped.
      1.1.2 A coefficient has been given the wrong sign.
      1.1.3 Inconsistent units of measurement have been used when deciding on the value for a coefficient.
      1.1.4 A coefficient has been miscalculated.
      1.1.5 A coefficient has been omitted from the matrix.
      1.1.6 A coefficient has been placed in the wrong place in a matrix.
   1.2 A constraint is incorrect.
      1.2.1 A constraint is operating in the wrong direction (e.g., as a greater-than when it should be a less-than).
      1.2.2 A needed constraint is omitted.
      1.2.3 A constraint is ill-conceived (e.g., coefficients omitted or in the wrong activities).
      1.2.4 The model is overconstrained; an extra, unnecessary constraint has been included.
   1.3 An activity is incorrect.
      1.3.1 An activity is ill-conceived (e.g., coefficients omitted or placed in the wrong constraints).
      1.3.2 A needed activity is omitted.
2. The model is consistent with the underlying assumptions.
   2.1 The underlying assumptions are consistent with the real world.
      2.1.1 The unexpected result is a new insight about the real world.
      2.1.2 The model result is correct but is being misinterpreted (e.g., the level of an activity may be interpreted using incorrect units of measurement).
      2.1.3 There is a bug in the software used to solve the model.
      2.1.4 Bad or inadequate control instructions were given to the software used to solve the model (e.g., instruct program to maximize the objective function when it should be minimized).
      2.1.5 The model is badly scaled, resulting in an accumulation of rounding errors when the model is solved.
   2.2 The underlying assumptions are not consistent with the real world. The model may need new constraints or activities or changes in the values of some coefficients.

- First there is the requirement that the scientist (or modeler) immerses herself or himself in the problem. This involves detailed study of the general field of research (or of the model and its assumptions).
- The second element is identification of a range of possible explanations for the problem being addressed.
- Third, specific hypotheses are formulated and tested in experiments.
- Fourth, if the process is successful, information from the experiments is integrated with information about the general field to provide an understanding of the problem.
- Finally, the new understanding may allow improved management of the system being studied (or correction of the bug).

Debugging is also similar to science in that it is a human, creative process (Koestler, 1964), not a cold, calculating, and linear process as it is sometimes portrayed. Both debugging and science involve essential elements of inspired guesswork, hunches, and sudden flashes of insight that cut through the mist. Neither process will proceed neatly and linearly through the stages just described. There will be overlap between stages and possibly feedback of information to an earlier stage.

Let us now examine these elements of the debugging process in more detail. Suppose a model solution causes you to suspect the existence of a bug but you have not yet identified it.

The first stage (immersion in the problem) will be already partially complete since, presumably, the person doing the debugging is thoroughly familiar with the model. The other element of this phase is to become familiar with the behavior of the bug. Extra model runs may be needed to reveal circumstances in which the bug does and does not occur.

In general terms, the second phase (identification of a range of possible explanations) simply requires familiarity with Box 11.1. However, it is sometimes possible to narrow down the range of reasonable diagnoses. Table 11.3 shows a checklist of how the range of possible diagnoses can be narrowed for particular symptoms apparent in the model solution. Where the table indicates that a diagnosis can be ruled out, it means it can be ruled out as the cause of the symptom indicated. It does not necessarily mean that the problem is completely absent from the matrix. Some diagnoses cannot be ruled out altogether but are quite unlikely to cause the indicated symptom.

Notice that most diagnoses indicated in Table 11.3 fall under heading 2, where the model is consistent with the underlying assumptions. It is usually impossible to rule out the converse diagnosis (that the model is not consistent with the underlying assumptions) without exhaustively checking the matrix structure and contents.

Techniques for Testing Hypotheses

The third element of the debugging process previously listed is to formulate and test hypotheses. There are many techniques for looking at a model's inputs

TABLE 11.3   Diagnoses from Box 11.2 that Can Be Ruled Out as the Cause of Particular Symptoms or Are Unlikely To Be the Cause

Symptom	Ruled-out Diagnoses[a]	Unlikely Diagnoses
No feasible solution	2.1,[b] 2.2, 1.2.2	2.1.3, 2.1.4
Unbounded solution	2.1,[b] 2.2, 1.2.4	2.1.3
The solution includes elements that are not possible in the real-world system being modeled	2.1.1	
The solution algorithm includes an automatic facility for scaling a matrix and this is switched on		2.1.5

[a]Ruling out a diagnosis at one level rules out all diagnoses at a lower level. For example, if 2.3 is ruled out, then so are 2.3.1. and 2.3.2.

[b]Although unlikely if a reputable package is used, diagnoses 2.1.3 and 2.1.4 should not be completely ruled out. Sometimes adjustments to the "feasibility tolerance" used will cure the problem of no feasible solution in a model that is actually feasible.

and/or outputs or of manipulating and comparing model solutions that can help to test for particular problems. These techniques vary in their usefulness for dealing with different symptoms, but many are useful for several types of symptom. First we examine the various techniques categorized according to the diagnoses in Box 11.1. This is followed by a suggested order for applying the different techniques, depending on the symptoms observed.

Diagnosis 1: The model is not consistent with the underlying assumptions. Testing for an error in the matrix coefficients is conceptually quite simple. It requires that you examine coefficients in the appropriate region to ensure that they are consistent with the underlying assumptions of the model. In practice the problem is deciding which coefficients to examine. Several of the techniques suggested here are designed to help narrow the focus of your search for bugs. Searching for a bug generally starts with use of a technique to identify a suspicious section of the matrix. Greenberg (1993c) calls this first stage *isolation* of the cause.

For now, suppose that you have narrowed the hunt to a section of the matrix: a row or column or small block of coefficients. At this stage there is no alternative to a visual examination of all coefficients in the suspect region. You can use a text editor to look at data in the format used by the computer algorithm, but it is probably more productive to examine the data in situ in the matrix. This provides additional visual cues (presuming that the model has been thoughtfully and consistently constructed) that can make a difference in recognizing a problem. A matrix editor like GULP (Pannell, 1988) is invaluable for this purpose as it allows you to see coefficients in context without having to print out the matrix. Clearly, the person undertaking the examination needs to be thoroughly familiar with LP and the model's assumptions so that he or she can recognize an incorrect coefficient. The person also needs to be aware of all the ways in which a coefficient, constraint, or activity can be in error, as listed in Box 11.1, and check thoroughly for each. Identification of an error must, in the end, involve an examination of this type. Greenberg (1993c) calls this stage the search for an "explanation," Isolation is usually necessary before reaching an explanation. Once the problem has been fully diagnosed, selection of a treatment to correct the problem is usually straightforward. Consider now the possible methods for isolating a problem.

- Often the symptom observed in the model solution provides valuable clues. If the problem area is not obvious, examine the solution for logical inconsistencies in the relative levels of different activities, unrealistic shadow costs of nonbasic activities, or unrealistic shadow prices of binding constraints. If this leads you to question a particular section of the matrix, proceed to a detailed examination of the coefficients in that section.

- Conduct model runs to determine circumstances where the bug* does and does not occur. Does it always have an impact on the solution or does it only express itself when some parameters take particular values? For example, if a bug occurs in a coefficient of activity A that causes the selection of unrealistic levels of activity B, the bug will only be apparent when activity A is included in the optimal solution. A series of runs in which a key parameter is varied over a wide range is a good way of examining the behavior of the bug. Try to use information about its behavior to determine which constraints and which activities are the root of the problem.

- If you suspect that a bug occurs in a particular activity but are unable to identify the specific problem, a potentially useful technique is to compare the solutions of two very similar models: one with the activity constrained to zero level and the other with the activity constrained to a low level (e.g., one unit). Then calculate the difference between the solutions in the level of each activity and the degree of slack for each constraint. This reveals all the direct and indirect impacts of the activity on other activities and constraints, sometimes including a linkage between the suspect activity and another activity or constraint that should not be occurring, which leads you to examine the matrix for unintended links.

  Undertaking such a comparison can be a very tedious operation without some computerization. A custom-written program in a high-level programming language is one approach. For those without the skills to write such a program, an alternative is to use a spreadsheet package. Import the two solutions into adjacent areas of the spreadsheet so that the numerical values in the solution are stored in cells as individual numbers (rather than strings of text). Then create a column of formulas that calculate the differences between the two solutions.

---

*In general, reference to a "bug" in this section should be interpreted as a "hypothesized bug."

- If you have a recent previous version of the model in which the unexpected result does not occur, conduct a comprehensive comparison of the data for the two versions. This may reveal a bug that has been introduced. It is possible that the bug was present in the previous version without manifesting itself in the model solution. In that case, the bug will not be revealed directly by the comparison of data. However, the comparison will at least show which coefficients have changed, allowing you to search for the change that has caused the bug to show up. Such information can give clues to the location of the actual bug.

  If the data are stored in a text file, a spreadsheet approach, similar to that just described, can greatly ease comparison of input data files.

- Another technique is to delete sections of the matrix (groups of rows or columns) and see if the problematic result still occurs. You need to be quite careful about which parts to delete, as it is easy to introduce new problems by removing a crucial constraint or activity. The safest approach is to limit such deletions to discrete and fairly self-contained sections of the model. For example, if a model includes several different regions, it will probably be possible to delete one of the regions without disturbing the functionality of the other regions. Greenberg (1993c) presented several isolation techniques for diagnosing infeasible models. These are outlined later in this chapter.

Tests of hypotheses that do not involve bugs in the matrix tend to be quite specific to particular diagnoses.

Diagnosis 2.1.1: The unexpected result is a new insight about the real world. Testing a hypothesis that an unexpected result is correct and that the model is free of bugs is, unfortunately, impossible. McCarl (1984) states that ''models can never be validated, only invalidated. . . . The outcome of a model validation process is either a model that has been proved invalid or a model about which one has an increased degree of confidence.'' (p. 157)

Although this is strictly true, it is possible to indirectly test the validity of a particular result. Suppose that you have searched thoroughly for a bug without finding one but are unable to convince yourself that a particular unexpected result is valid. Even if you do have a plausible explanation, some results clash so strongly with prior expectations that any attempt to publicize them without very convincing supporting arguments will threaten your credibility. One approach is to try reproducing the result using a different modeling approach or a much simpler LP model. If you can independently reproduce the result, you can be more confident that the result is correct, and you may also find that elusive convincing explanation of the result.

Apart from this, one is limited to validation through absence of invalidation. If you do have a plausible explanation, conduct additional model runs to attempt to falsify it. This can be done by preventing the mechanism for your plausible explanation from operating. For example, suppose you have two similar models, but there is an unexpected difference in the level of activity A between the two solutions. You hypothesize that this is due to changes in the level of activity B. Try constraining the level of activity B to be the same in both models. If the difference in activity A then disappears, this lends support to your hypothesis about the mechanism.

Diagnosis 2.1.2: The model result is correct but is being misinterpreted. This is a matter of careful checking. For example, if the level of an activity seems wrong, refer to your documentation and check that the coefficients for that activity are consistent with the unit of measurement you are using to interpret the result.

You should also check that the software reports that the solution you are questioning is optimal. It may be that the activity levels are so strange because the solution is infeasible or unbounded.

Diagnosis 2.1.3: There is a bug in the software used to solve the model. Implementing an accurate and reliable computer package for mathematical programming is notoriously difficult. Even the most highly respected packages are not immune from bugs. For example, Tice and Kletke (1984) reported a serious bug in a version of MPSX, a powerful and widely used package for mainframe computers.

After a period of experience with your model you may become confident that your software is in fact correctly finding optimal solutions. However, in the development phase you should not rule out the possibility of errors associated with an algorithm.

Diagnosis 2.1.4: Bad or inadequate control instructions were given to the software. Occasionally, you can resolve puzzling model solutions by correctly informing the algorithm that the objective is maximization or minimization.

Some LP computer packages allow you to adjust the "tolerances" used to test whether a given solution is feasible or optimal. A feasibility tolerance is a small number (e.g., 1×10^{-8}) that gives the maximum sum of infeasibilities for all constraints before the basis is considered to be feasible. If the package is reporting that it cannot find any feasible solution, but you are unable to find any problem with the model's structure or coefficients, adjustments to the feasibility tolerance may solve the problem. For example, try relaxing the tolerance to 1×10^{-6}. The documentation for your algorithm may give guidance about which values to try.

The optimality tolerance is the minimum improvement to the objective function that an activity must make before it will be brought into the basis. If the computer package appears to be getting stuck in a loop so that it never reaches the optimal solution, adjustments to the optimality tolerance may solve the problem.

Diagnosis 2.1.5: The model is badly scaled. A badly scaled matrix is one in which there is a big difference in the magnitudes of coefficients used. A badly scaled matrix has a greater chance of failing to solve because of the accumulation of rounding errors that occur in every mathematical operation on real numbers in a computer. Such rounding errors are exacerbated by poor scaling. Symptoms of accumulated rounding errors can include an unbounded solution, an infeasible solution, or an apparently optimal solution that is actually not consistent with the constraints of the model.

There is no hard and fast rule about how bad scaling can be before serious rounding errors occur. Many packages include warning messages based on a rule of thumb regarding the ratio between the largest and smallest coefficients in the matrix.

If you feel you need to change scaling, it is simply a matter of using different units of measurement for some rows and/or columns. Converting the units of measurement entails multiplying all the coefficients in a row or column by the same value. This can be done for as many rows or columns as necessary to ensure that coefficients are not too different. It is wise to use scaling multipliers that do not make the interpretation of output too difficult.

Diagnosis 2.2: The underlying assumptions are not consistent with the real world. Sometimes you will come to believe that the model is correct within itself, but that it is failing to capture some aspect of the real world. Typically, you may feel the need for new constraints or for distinguishing between similar but slightly different activities or constraints. This requires interaction with someone with a good knowledge of the real-world problem being modeled. Such interaction should be viewed as part of the ongoing process of model development (e.g., Morrison, 1987). Your expert may volunteer suggestions of changes that are needed. Thorough and up-to-date documentation can facilitate your interaction with outside experts.

Matching Hypotheses to Symptoms

Having surveyed the available techniques and tools, let us now consider how one should approach particular symptoms. In what order should hypotheses be tested and these techniques applied? The suggestions that follow certainly do not cover the full range of symptoms. Also they cannot be applied in an unthinking "cookbook" manner; successful debugging requires careful thought, creativity, and inspiration.

There are two considerations when deciding on the order in which hypotheses should be tested: the relative likelihood of alternative hypotheses and the ease with which they can be tested. Commonly there are several hypotheses that could explain the symptom equally well and that are about equally likely to be true. However, the difficulty of testing different hypotheses can vary widely, so in the absence of any reason to suspect a particular type of bug, ease of testing should be the main criterion used in the first instance.

No Feasible Solution: For infeasible and unbounded solutions, one part of the diagnosis problem requires no effort: there clearly *is* something wrong with your matrix. You also are given a clue about where to start looking: there is an indication that one or more constraints is infeasible, or one of the activities is listed as unbounded. Unfortunately, the clue rarely leads to easy identification of the problem's cause. This applies particularly to infeasible models, where the cause of the problem may lie in a constraint that is not reported as being infeasible.

Start by observing which rows are infeasible in the program output. If there are not too many infeasible rows, carefully check their coefficients. Coefficients being entered with the wrong sign (i.e., positive when they should be negative) or in the wrong place are possible causes of infeasibility.

If these coefficients are correct, check that all constraints are operating in the correct direction. Do you have any less-than constraints that should actually be greater-than constraints?

Next see if there are any equals constraints in the model that can be relaxed to less-than or greater-than constraints. Some modelers overuse equals constraints, and this can easily lead to unnecessary infeasibilities.

After exhausting these simple approaches you must resort to more time-consuming techniques. Greenberg (1993c) outlined several techniques that can help to isolate an infeasibility. One is based on a theorem by Dantzig (1963) that says that if an LP is infeasible, there is an infeasible one-constraint LP formed by adding up the constraints, weighted by their shadow costs in the infeasible solution. The one-constraint LP potentially has the same number of activities as the original, although some coefficients are likely to be zero. The coefficient for an activity in the one-constraint model is calculated by multiplying each coefficient of the activity by its corresponding shadow price in the infeasible solution and adding up the results. Greenberg (1993c, p. 124) observed that "This has great appeal for diagnosis formation because, on the surface, it seems that explaining a one-constraint infeasibility is easy, at least compare to the original LP."

The most useful information from this technique is which activities have nonzero coefficients in the aggregated constraint, not necessarily the numerical values of their coefficients. If the number of nonzero coefficients in the aggregated constraint is low, identifying the cause of the infeasibility may be straightforward. On the other hand, there may be *no* nonzero coefficients, which provides no new information, or a very large number of them, which does not help to clarify the issue.

A second technique is to find a smaller subset of the matrix that is still infeasible. Ideally, you seek the "irreducible infeasible subsystem" that is no longer infeasible if *any* of its constraints are dropped (Greenberg, 1993c). This method was first suggested by Debrosse and Westerberg (1973). Also, Chinneck and Dravnieks (1991) have developed several different methods for identifying the irreducible infeasible subsystem. One of their methods proceeds as follows. Start by removing all constraints with zero-shadow prices in the infeasible solution. Then remove activities that have no coefficients in any of the remaining constraints. The resulting model is still infeasible but it may be further reducible. To test this, drop another constraint at random (and any further activities with no coefficients). If the model is still infeasible, leave that constraint out and proceed to drop another constraint at random. When the model becomes feasible, add back in the constraint that made the difference (and any activities you dropped with the constraint). Keep this constraint in the model, but drop each of the remaining constraints one at a time. If dropping a constraint does not make the model feasible, leave it out. After testing all of the remaining constraints, the resulting subsystem is irreducibly infeasible.

Like the one-constraint approach, while this can isolate the infeasibility, it does not necessarily provide an easy explanation of its cause. Nevertheless, it is now possible to search for that explanation in what is almost certainly a much smaller model than the original.

Another way to reduce the model that may be useful in some circumstances is to add ''artificial activities'' or ''artificial variables'' to the model. For each less-than constraint, add an activity with a coefficient of -1 in the row and zero coefficients in every other row except the objective function. For each greater-than, add a similar activity with a coefficient of 1 in the row. For each equals constraint, add two artifical activities, one of each type. Include an unfavorable coefficient in the objective function of each artificial activity, such as 1000 in a minimization problem or -1000 in a maximization problem. These artificial activities will not be selected unless they have to be, but they allow the package to find a feasible solution when it would otherwise be impossible. Observe which artificial activities are selected at nonzero levels and delete them. Attempt to solve the model again. Delete any new nonzero artificial activities. Repeat this until the model becomes infeasible again. At this point, the constraints with deleted artificial activities contain the cause of the infeasibility. The resulting infeasible subsystem is not necessarily irreducible, but the technique is simple to apply and does not use the shadow prices from the infeasible solution, which are not provided by some LP packages. If desired, one of Chinneck and Dravnieks' (1991) techniques (such as the one just described) can be applied to the subsystem to achieve irreducibility.

Note that this approach could cause the model to become unbounded. This will occur if the objective function coefficient of one of the artificial activities is not sufficiently unfavorable to counteract a benefit that it allows to be generated elsewhere in the matrix. To avoid this, use very large unfavorable objective function coefficients in the artificial activities.

The third technique outlined by Greenberg (1993c) is ''successive bounding.'' This is not described in detail here because it is only a practical option if your LP software has the capacity to conduct it automatically. The advantage of successive bounding is that, when it does work, is provides not just an isolation, but an explanation of the cause of the infeasibility.

If you have been unable to find the cause of an infeasibility and suspect that there is actually nothing wrong with the matrix, try adjusting the feasibility tolerance in your computer package. Alternatively, some packages allow you to save details of the basis for later use. Instruct your package to save the basis that is nearest to being feasible. Then instruct it to solve again, starting from this basis. The different accumulation of rounding errors may allow the package to correctly identify that the model is feasible. This suggestion applies to relatively large models. If that does not work, test for a failure of the LP software by making substantial changes to key objective function coefficients and trying to solve the model. If it does correctly solve, then the original model is not infeasible, since changing only objective function coefficients cannot affect the feasibility of a model. In this case, you may be able to find the optimal solution for the original model by solving it starting from the optimal basis for this revised model.

If you have tried all these techniques and are still unable to obtain an optimal solution, it may be that your model correctly represents the problem but the problem has no feasible solution.

Unbounded Solution: Start by checking that the direction of optimization (maximization or minimization) used by your computer package is consistent with your model.

Second, identify the unbounded column from the program output. The problem is that there is nothing preventing this activity from being selected at an infinite level (see Chapter 10). Thus you should work through all constraints of the model and check whether one of them should be affecting the activity but is not. Possible reasons for the problem include:

- Coefficients with the wrong sign.
- Constraints operating in the wrong direction.
- Coefficients missing or in the wrong place.

Alternatively it may be that a constraint has been omitted from the model.

Computer packages do not always correctly identify which activity is unbounded. One way to find out is to add a series of constraints that limit the maximum level of each activity to a large number (say 10,000). Like the artificial activities approach for infeasibilities, this allows you to obtain an optimal solution (of sorts) and to identify from it which activities are selected at levels equal to the large upper limit you specified. If your LP package has the capacity to specify "bounds" on activities, you can use these instead of adding new constraints.

Solution Conflicts with Expectations: It is common to be surprised by a result obtained from a large LP model. Such a surprise should be met with skepticism and followed by a careful search for causes. It may be efficient for the search to proceed by the following steps, which are in order of increasing difficulty:

(a) Check your interpretation of the output.
(b) Check for errors in the instructions you gave the computer and for obvious errors made by the computer algorithm.

(c) Check for bugs in the model.

(d) Check hypothetical explanations of why the result may be correct.

Checking interpretation of output includes checking that the solution is reported to be optimal, not infeasible or unbounded. Is it really a surprising result, or have you misread it? In particular, check that the units of measurement you are using in your interpretation are consistent with the matrix.

Technical problems to check for include the direction in which the model was optimized and other problems with the control instructions given to the program. Bugs with the computer package you are using may leave obvious clues (e.g., a mix of positive and negative shadow costs of activities). If you suspect that the solution is not truly optimal, check that the tolerances being used by your algorithm are consistent with any instructions given in program documentation. If in doubt, try changing these tolerances within the range 10^{-4} to 10^{-9}.

If you have not identified the problem by this stage, there is no alternative to searching for bugs in the matrix. In practice you are likely to investigate alternative hypotheses in the other suggested by the particular symptoms observed. However, the following suggested order in which to test hypotheses may be useful in cases where the modeler is uncertain how to proceed.

If the problem appears to be in a particular activity or constraint, examine it for obvious errors in coefficients: typing errors, coefficients with the wrong sign, coefficients missing or in the wrong place, inconsistent units of measurement, or an error of calculation. If appropriate, check that constraints are operating in the correct direction.

Unexpected solutions are often associated with one or more activities being selected at levels outside the reasonable range. (For convenience let us call these *target activities*.) If you do not initially find any problem with the coefficients or constraints of the model, add a new constraint that forces the target activity to be selected at a level that corresponds to your prior expectations. It may be that there is some error that is forcing a high or low level of the activity. This will be revealed either by an infeasible solution or by the behavior of the constrained model.

If the modified model is infeasible, it means that the original model contains a "forcing substructure" (Greenberg, 1994). This is where an activity is forced to take a particular value by the model's constraints, rather than as a result of its impact on the objective function. The constraint used in Section 7.5 to exclude certain activities is an example of a forcing substructure. If an activity is forced to its lower bound of zero in every feasible solution, it is said to be *nonviable* (Chinneck, 1992), and if this is not intentional, it probably indicates a bug. An activity's level may be determined by a forcing substructure even if the level varies in different model solutions. Forcing substructures are not necessarily bugs, but even if they are not, detecting and explaining them is valuable in understanding the model's results. One method of searching for forcing substructures is to use the successive bounding technique to identify redundant constraints on individual activities (Greenberg, 1994). For example, if an activity must have a positive value in every feasible solution, its non-negativity constraint is redundant. Greenberg (1994) argued that "seeking re-dundancies reveals forced levels that deepen our understanding of a solution by separating that which is forced by implication and that which is determined by economic trade-off." (p. 125)

If the unusual activity level is not due to a forcing substructure, it could be that the activity has a larger or smaller impact on the objective function than you expect. To test this, use the technique described earlier in this chapter for comparing two solutions in which the level of an activity is constrained to differ by a small amount (say, one unit). First constrain the activity to a low level (e.g., zero) and then to a slightly higher level. The difference in objective function values can easily be calculated, but it is also possible to determine which factors are contributing to the difference. Do this by (a) calculating the difference between the two solutions in the level of each activity and (b) mul-tiplying each difference by the objective function value for that activity. The sum of these values gives you the net difference in the objective function value. You may find unexpected indirect effects on the objective function that explain the unusual result.

A possible reason for the high or low level of the target activity is a problem with an alternative activity that competes with it for resources. Check for activities that compete with your target activity and examine them for bugs. If the level of the target activity seems too low, search for bugs that bias the model toward high levels of the alternative activity.

It is still possible to suspect a bug even if all activity levels conform to your prior expectations. Inappropriate values for shadow prices, shadow costs, or constraint slacks may be symptomatic of a bug that will affect activity levels if the model is altered (e.g., in sensitivity analysis; see Chapter 12).

A very high shadow price can be investigated by comparing two solutions in which the constraint limit (right-hand-side term) is varied by a small amount (say, one unit). Calculate all differences in activity levels. Unexpected large differences may indicate a bug. A very large shadow cost for an activity is fundamentally the same situation as an activity being selected at a lower level than expected. Investigate it using the strategy described earlier for unusual activity levels. A large constraint slack may indicate (a) an error in the right-hand-side term for that constraint, (b) a low or missing positive coefficient or an erroneous negative coefficient in an activity (for less-than constraints), or (c) low availability or high usage of a resource represented in another constraint.

Diagnosis of an unusual model result is sometimes particularly elusive. In these cases adopt the techniques described earlier for locating the bug (or other explanation) within the matrix: conduct model runs to determine situations where the bug does and does not occur; if possible delete sections of the matrix and see if the problem still occurs. A deletion that cures the symptoms of a bug may indicate that the bug occurs in the deleted section.

If no bug has been found by now, it may be that there is no error in the matrix coefficients or solving algorithm. Instead the problem may be a failure to correctly represent the system being modeled. Some aspect of the system may have been incorrectly excluded from the model or included in it in a way that fails to accurately represent it. Alternatively, you may need to look for hypotheses that explain why the result is, in fact, correct. If possible, conduct tests to attempt to refute these hypotheses.

Finally, when a model is first constructed, it is advisable to conduct runs to reveal bugs hidden in the matrix. One strategy, suggested by McCarl and Apland (1986), is to restrict the values of all activities (using constraints or bounds) to a set of values observed in the real world. Then try to solve the model to check whether the real-world solution is feasible within your model. If the solution is not feasible, you need to find out why and correct the problem. If the model does correctly solve, still check for unusual activity levels or constraint slacks.

If a lack of data means that you cannot constrain every activity in the model to a real-world value, it can be valuable to constraint subsections of the model for which you do have information about levels. Check for feasibility and for any unusual side effects.

Another useful approach is to run a wide-ranging sensitivity analysis (Chapter 12), varying key parameters through plausible (or even implausible) values and observing how the model behaves. Errors in the model are often revealed most starkly when it includes unusual or unlikely combinations of parameter values.

11.5 STRATEGIES FOR PREVENTING BUGS

Debugging is difficult, frustrating, and time-consuming. The discovery of a bug after a set of model results has been publicized is potentially damaging to the credibility of the model and its developers. Many bugs go undetected for a very long time, some forever. For these reasons, prevention of bugs is crucial to the success of a modeling project. Key elements of bug prevention are discipline and care, but there is also a range of relatively simple strategies that can contribute to the prevention of bugs. The following are useful elements of an overall bug-prevention strategy.

- During model development and construction, proceed in small steps. Thoroughly test and debug the model before adding the next component or the next level of complexity. This is one of the most important and effective strategies.
- For a particular LP package, if you have a choice between entering the data with a text editor or with a matrix editor, use the matrix editor. This will dramatically reduce the risk of typing errors and save considerable time. Also you are more likely to spot existing errors if you are working with a matrix format than in awkward formats like ''MPS,'' which is used by a number of major packages. Use of a text editor to change MPS data should be limited to small and simple changes.

- Use a "macro" to automate repeated key strokes when entering or editing a model. Some programs (e.g., all spreadsheets) have a macro facility built in, or it can be obtained in a separate package. Macros not only save time but also reduce the likelihood of errors being introduced.

- For models with an intended long life, develop a computerized system for data entry. One useful approach is to create spreadsheet templates that allow users to view and change model assumptions without needing to be familiar with the model matrix. A simple example is given by Pannell and Falconer (1987), and a full system of such spreadsheets for a large model is described by Pannell and Bathgate (1991). These spreadsheets allow users to view parameters in a format and with units of measurement to which they can relate easily. The spreadsheets perform arithmetic operations on the parameters to calculate the required matrix coefficients. Of course there is a risk that the formulas entered in the spreadsheet contain errors, but at least these errors only need to be detected and corrected once. Without such a system, coefficients must be calculated by hand and are prone to error every time they are changed.

    The GAMS system (GAMS, 1988) provides an alternative approach to data entry that also may contribute to bug prevention. Data are presented to the package in tables and algebraic inequalities rather than in the usual matrix format. Data changes are made using a text editor to alter the main data file, which provides some of the advantages of the spreadsheet approach just described.

- Occasionally print out part or all of the matrix showing numbers. Some computer packages include the facility to print out very compact summaries of the matrix using symbols to represent coefficients of different magnitudes. While this can be very convenient and useful for checking the consistency of a model's structure, it can also mask errors that would be obvious from an examination of the complete matrix.

- Have one person with ultimate responsibility for changes to the model and for ensuring that it is up to date and free of bugs. Personal responsibility is very important. There is a research institution at which a major model was generating implausible solutions, but because of a lack of individual responsibility, the problems went undiagnosed and unresolved. This general problem is compounded by the lack of recognition among administrators of the resource requirements and importance of model maintenance and debugging. There is often little incentive for individuals to assume this role; they can earn more recognition and higher rewards in other activities.

- Have only one master copy of the matrix to which changes can be made. (Of course keep backups of this copy.) Failure to do this is the usual cause of bugs that return after you thought you had fixed them.

- Have a meaningful and consistent system for naming model data files according to the model version.

- Have a meaningful and consistent system for naming rows and columns. Make sure that a legend is included in the model documentation and that the documentation is readily available.

- Use intuitively obvious units for rows and constraints. Do not worry about scaling unless you have to. Record units of measurement within the legend of row and column names.

- The structure of the matrix (i.e., order of rows and columns) can be important. Group related rows and columns together and be consistent about the order used so that the visual pattern of coefficients can help highlight a coefficient out of place or with the wrong sign.

- Have a good system for reporting bugs or problems or suggested changes to the person responsible for the model. One approach is to distribute "bug report sheets" with appropriate headings and questions to all model users.

- Have a system for recording all changes to a model. Keep a file or log book showing the date, the reason for and the substance of each change, and the revised name of the new version produced. Also record the sources of information used to make the change.

- If you use a system for summarizing and condensing output, be sure to examine a complete model solution occasionally. The reason for this is the same as for the summarized (symbolic) matrix printout.

- Ask someone who is unfamiliar with the model to go over the entire matrix in detail, checking calculations and questioning the logic of matrix structure. The aim is for them to become convinced that they understand the reasoning behind and derivation of every coefficient. This should occur whenever a new person is employed to work on an existing model. As well as giving them a thorough knowledge of the model, such detailed attention can detect even quite subtle bugs. It is also helpful to have as many people as possible examine the assumptions and logic of the model, even if each person only covers a small subsection of the model.

11.6 CONCLUDING COMMENTS

How many bugs are too many? We would hope to keep searching for bugs for as long as the cost of finding an extra bug does not exceed the expected benefit of finding it. With large models the cost of debugging is high, but presumably the value of the information is also high, otherwise resources would not have been put into the model. It comes down to a difficult judgment about the probability of bugs, the importance of the information, the size of the model, and personal reputation. On the other hand, fear of potential (but unknown) bugs should not prevent use of the model. All reasonable care is care enough.

Keeping a large model up to date and bug-free is a difficult, thankless, underrecognized task. No large LP modeling project should be contemplated without providing an adequate budget for debugging and maintenance. Given the rapid increase in probability of bugs in large models, "adequate" probably means more than is usually allocated.

11.7 KEY POINTS

- The term *debugging* encompasses those functions sometimes referred to as verification and validation.
- Bugs are unavoidable, especially for large models.
- An unexpected model result is due to a bug, unless you can convince yourself otherwise.
- The number of bugs in a matrix increases rapidly with the size of the matrix.
- The more serious bugs are usually detected when one of the following symptoms appears in the model solution: an unlikely model solution, no feasible solution, an unbounded solution.
- There is no foolproof strategy to help you find the diagnosis of a bug, and it is difficult to generalize about the best strategy. However, a methodical approach is bound to be more productive than a random search.
- If a solution conflicts with your expectations, it may be efficient to proceed by the following steps, which are in order of increasing difficulty:
  - (a) Check your interpretation of the output.
  - (b) Check for errors in computer commands used and for obvious errors made by the computer algorithm.
  - (c) Check for bugs in the model.
  - (d) Check hypothetical explanations of why the result may be correct.
- There are many strategies that can help prevent bugs.

CHAPTER 12

SENSITIVITY ANALYSIS

The purpose of using a linear-programming (LP) model is usually to help a decision maker make a better decision. In previous chapters, the focus has been on the use of LP to find the optimal solution to a problem. While this is of some value, in real-world applications of LP, a model used *only* to identify a single optimal solution would be greatly underutilized and, probably, quite ineffective. A decision maker needs to

- Understand how the optimal solution changes in different situations.
- Know how far parameters can change before the optimal solution changes.
- Understand subtleties of the system and any interactions between variables.
- Be convinced that the model is a credible and reliable source of information before acting on its recommendations.

These needs and others can only be met by *sensitivity analysis*, which is broadly defined here as the investigation of "the responsiveness of conclusions to changes or errors in parameter values and assumptions" (Baird, 1989, p. 358). Fiacco (1983, p. 3) emphasized the importance of sensitivity analysis: "A method for conducting [sensitivity analysis] is a well-established requirement of any scientific discipline. A sensitivity and stability analysis should be an integral part of any solution methodology. The status of a solution cannot be understood without such information."

In this chapter we consider several approaches to sensitivity analysis using LP models. In most cases they involve comparison of the results from an initial "base" model with results from models with altered parameters. The base model contains standard or best-bet parameter values, while the other models explore plausible changes in the parameters.

This is one of the most important chapters of the book. It is about the general approach that modelers should take when applying their models. The underlying principle is that in almost all situations, it is much more effective and more valuable to inform and enlighten the decision maker than to try to provide a simple prescription.*

The next section is a brief outline of the wide range of uses and benefits of sensitivity analysis. This is followed by sections on various approaches to conducting sensitivity analyses, communicating their results, and drawing conclusions from them. Some of the information included in LP solutions is useful in sensitivity analysis (shadow costs, shadow prices, range analysis). Indeed this information is sometimes referred to as sensitivity analysis. As you will see, however, there are many other useful methods of analysis.

12.1 USES OF SENSITIVITY ANALYSIS

Most of what has been written about sensitivity analysis has taken a very narrow view about what it is and what it can be useful for. In fact there is a very wide range of uses to which sensitivity analysis is put. An incomplete list is given in Box 12.1. The uses are grouped into four main categories which are discussed further below.

Decision Making or Development of Recommendations for Decision Makers

In all models, parameters are more or less uncertain. We are likely to be unsure of their current values and to be even more uncertain about their future values. This applies to things like prices, costs, productivity, and technology. Uncertainty is one of the primary reasons why sensitivity analysis is helpful in making decisions or recommendations. If parameters are uncertain, we can use sensitivity analysis to give us information like

(a) How robust the optimal solution is in the face of different parameter values (use 1.1 from Box 12.1).
(b) Under what circumstances the optimal solution would change (uses 1.2, 1.3, 1.5).
(c) How the optimal solution changes in different circumstances (use 3.1).
(d) How much worse off we would be if we ignored the changed circum-

---

*The exceptions are very simple models or models where the constraints and coefficients are known with some certainty (e.g., in determining least-cost feed rations for livestock).

BOX 12.1 Uses of Sensitivity Analysis

1. Decision making or development of recommendations for decision makers
   1.1 Testing the robustness of an optimal solution.
   1.2 Identifying critical values, thresholds, or break-even values where the optimal strategy changes.
   1.3 Identifying sensitive or important variables.
   1.4 Investigating suboptimal solutions.
   1.5 Developing flexible recommendations that depend on circumstances.
   1.6 Comparing the values of simple and complex decision strategies.
   1.7 Assessing the ''riskiness'' of a strategy or scenario.
2. Communication
   2.1 Making recommendations more credible, understandable, compelling, or persuasive.
   2.2 Allowing decision makers to select assumptions.
   2.3 Conveying lack of committment to any single strategy.
3. Increased understanding or quantification of the system
   3.1 Estimating relationships between input and output variables.
   3.2 Understanding relationships between input and output variables.
   3.3 Developing hypotheses for testing
4. Model development
   4.1 Testing the model for validity or accuracy.
   4.2 Searching for errors in the model.
   4.3 Simplifying the model.
   4.4 Calibrating the model.
   4.5 Coping with poor or missing data.
   4.6 Prioritizing acquisition of information.

---

stances and stayed with the original optimal strategy or some other strategy (uses 1.4, 1.6).

This information is extremely valuable in making a decision or recommendation. If we find that the optimal strategy is robust (insensitive to changes in parameters), this gives us confidence in implementing or recommending it. On the other hand, if we find that it is not robust, sensitivity analysis tells us how important it is to make the changes to management suggested by the changing optimal solution. Perhaps the base solution is only slightly suboptimal in the plausible range of circumstances; it is therefore reasonable to adopt it anyway.

Even if the levels of variables in the optimal solution are changed dramatically by a higher or lower parameter value, we should examine the difference in objective function value between these solutions and the base solution. If the objective function is barely affected by these changes in management, a decision maker may be willing to bear the small cost of not altering the strategy for the sake of simplicity.

If the base solution is not always acceptable, there may be another strategy that is not optimal in the original model but that performs well across the relevant range of circumstances. If there is no such single strategy, we can identify different strategies for different circumstances. We can clearly identify the circumstances (the sets of parameter values) in which the strategy should be changed.

Even if we are not uncertain about parameter values, we may be certain that they will change in particular ways in different times or places. In a similar way to that outlined earlier, sensitivity analysis can be used to test whether a simple decision strategy is adequate or whether a complex conditional strategy is worth the trouble.

Use 1.7 is to assess the ''riskiness' of a strategy or scenario. It is not always possible to adjust your strategy to suit the given circumstances. Sometimes the final circumstances are unknown at the time when you commit yourself to a strategy (e.g., a manufacturer has to make decisions about levels of production well before the goods reach the market, so actual prices may vary from those expected at the time of the decisions). In these circumstances it may be valuable to estimate the range of final income levels caused by different circumstances. Two strategies that have similar objective function values for the base-case assumptions may have very different risks of very bad outcomes. In the manufacturing example, a strategy including high levels of production of a new product may appear desirable on the basis of best-bet levels of market demand, but if the product is not successful in the market, the company stands to lose a lot of money. A strategy based on a well-established product may appear slightly less profitable in the base model, but demand for it can be predicted with more confidence. By observing the range of objective function values for the two strategies in different circumstances, the extent of the difference in riskiness can be estimated and subjectively factored into the decision. It is also possible to explicitly represent the trade-off between risk and benefit within the model, as outlined in the next chapter.

Communication

There are at least three ways in which sensitivity analysis can improve the communication of results from a model. First, recommendations can be made more compelling if they are backed with results from sensitivity analyses. The mere act of presenting results from alternative strategies demonstrates that you have considered a range of options. It conveys a sense of rigor, thoroughness, and objectivity missing from a single solution no matter how detailed or sophisticated your model is. It may also help the decision maker to understand the reasons why your recommended strategy is the best, which further enhances your persuasiveness.

Second, if the decision makers disagree with an assumption or parameter value you have used, they are likely to place a very low value on your results. By conducting sensitivity analysis you are able to show them how the optimal solution is affected by the differences in assumptions and how these differences affect the performance of the base strategy. It allows you to completely avoid the task of recommending a strategy. You adopt the role of providing the decision maker with information to support their decision rather than the role of making a recommendation.

Third, in some cases sensitivity analysis is helpful in conveying the tentative nature of a plan (Alexander, 1989). This may be important when a model is used to provide information for public planning, especially if the planning process involves consultation with people without a technical background, or people who may be suspicious of the process.

> Often, to lay persons, a single plan, even when presented for the first time for information, input and discussion, conveys a deceptive sense of commitment to the course of action shown in the plan. The premature impression of commitment is avoided when a plan includes several alternatives and uses sensitivity analysis in their evaluation.   (Alexander, 1989, p. 324)

In this way, sensitivity analysis keeps people from thinking that it is too late for them to have a meaningful input to the plan.

Increased Understanding or Quantification of the System

Sensitivity analysis allows you to quantify the relationships between parameter values and the outputs of the model (activity levels, objective function value, etc.). If parameters are varied in combination, it is possible to quantify multidimensional response surfaces relating inputs to outputs. As suggested earlier, these surfaces may provide useful input to the making of decisions or recommendations.

Furthermore, the process of sensitivity analysis often allows the analyst to develop a deeper understanding of the reasons why inputs affect outputs in the way they do. Without sensitivity analysis, it is easy for a large model to become a "black box," so that if results are at all counterintuitive, it is the model that will be doubted, rather than the intuition.

In complex models, sensitivity analysis may not lead directly to improved understanding of the system, but it is still likely to allow you to develop hypotheses about it. These hypotheses can then be tested in various ways, such as by further modeling or real-world experiments.

Model Development

It was suggested in Chapter 11 that a useful method for revealing bugs in a model is to run wide-ranging sensitivity analysis and observe model behavior, looking for anomalies or inconsistencies. In this application of sensitivity analysis, it is not necessary to use only realistic parameter values. Often unrealistically high or low values reveal bugs that otherwise remain undetected. The bugs revealed may be either errors in the construction of the matrix, or errors in the definition or quantification of the problem.

Sensitivity analysis may be used to investigate the scope for model simplification. Reiman and Weiss (1989) note that "if a parameter is very insensitive, it is likely that the model is needlessly complex" (p. 830). While this does not necessarily mean that you *should* simplify the model (e.g., complexity may be useful in making the model more flexible, or more credible to decision makers), it does indicate the potential for simplification if that is desired.

Another potential use of sensitivity analysis is to calibrate a model: to select parameter values so that the model behaves in a certain way (e.g., Canova, 1995). You might follow this approach when good empirical information about the values of model outputs and some model inputs is available, but the values of some other model inputs are unknown. Indeed, in some circumstances, calibration may be the only feasible way of obtaining realistic parameter values (Jorgenson, 1984).

In this way, sensitivity analysis helps you cope with a lack of empirical data for estimating parameter values. It can also do this by allowing you to test whether the parameters for which you lack data are important to the decision. If the optimal decision is insensitive to changes in the parameters, you may be content to live with the available estimates despite their poor quality or subjective nature. On the other hand, if the solution is highly sensitive to the magnitudes of parameters, experiments may be needed to produce more accurate parameter values (Lomas and Eppel, 1992). Sensitivity analysis helps to estimate the benefits of acquiring better information about parameters, and together with information about the costs of collecting different types of information, this can be used to prioritize the parameters for which information collection is being considered.

So the needs of the decision maker, the imperfections of all models, and the uncertainties of the real world create the need for more information than can be obtained from a single optimal solution. Thus, the primary use of LP is to put issues into perspective, rather than to provide an exact, complete prescription. Its greatest value is in improving the understanding of a management problem and determining how important or trivial a particular issue is. Sensitivity analysis is invaluable in this process, as well as in the model-development phase.

12.2 APPROACHES TO SENSITIVITY ANALYSIS

In principle, sensitivity analysis is a simple idea: you change the model and observe its behavior. In practice, there are many different ways you can go about changing and observing the model.

What to Vary

One might choose to vary any or all of the following.

(a) The contribution of an activity to the objective.
(b) The objective (e.g., minimize risk of failure instead of maximizing profit).
(c) A constraint limit.
(d) The number of constraints (e.g., add or remove a constraint designed to express personal preferences of the decision maker for or against a particular activity).
(e) Technical parameters (coefficients).

Option (a) is at least partly addressed automatically in the optimal solution's shadow costs and activity range analysis. However, you may wish to consider wider ranges of objective function values than represented by these outputs, or you may wish to vary more than one objective function value at a time. You may also wish to know how the activity levels change when the solution changes, and this is not indicated in the standard output. Similarly, shadow prices and constraint range analysis provide a limited sensitivity analysis for option (c), but for similar reasons this is usually not sufficient either. For options (b), (d), and (e) the standard computer output provides no information at all, so you need to generate the information yourself, probably by altering the model and re-solving it.

The usual approach is to vary the value of a numerical parameter through several levels. In other cases there is uncertainty about a situation with only two possible outcomes: either a certain situation will occur or it will not. Examples include:

- What if the government legislates to ban a particular technology for environmental reasons?
- In a shortest route problem, what if a new freeway were built between two major centers?
- What if a new input or ingredient with unique properties becomes available?

Often this type of question requires some structural changes to the model to add or delete activities or constraints or to fix the levels of particular variables. Once these changes are made, output from the revised model can be compared to the original solution, or the revised model can be used in a sensitivity analysis of uncertain parameters to investigate wider implications of the change.

What to Observe

Whichever items you choose to vary, there are numerous aspects of a model output to look at:

(a) The value of the objective function.

(b) The value of the objective function for suboptimal strategies (e.g., strategies that are optimal for other scenarios, or particular strategies suggested by the decision maker).

(c) The difference in objective function values between two strategies (e.g., between the optimal strategy and a particular strategy suggested by the decision maker).

(d) The values of decision variables.

(e) The values of shadow costs, constraint slacks, or shadow prices.

It is uncommon to focus on shadow costs, constraint slacks, or shadow prices during sensitivity analyses since these are themselves forms of sensitivity analysis.

Experimental Design

The experimental design is the combinations of parameters that will be varied and the levels at which they will be set. The modeler must decide whether to vary parameters one at a time, leaving all others at standard or base values, or whether to examine combinations of changes. An important issue in this decision is the relative likelihood of combinations of changes. If two parameters tend to be positively correlated (e.g., the prices of two similar outputs), the possibility that they will both take on relatively high values at the same time is worth considering. Conversely, if two parameters are negatively correlated, you should examine high values of one in combination with low values of the other. If there is no systematic relationship between parameters, it may be reasonable to ignore the low risk that they will both differ substantially from their base values at the same time, especially if they are not expected to vary widely.

In selecting the parameter levels to use in the sensitivity analysis, a common and normally adequate approach is to specify values in advance, usually with equal-sized intervals between the levels (e.g., Nordblom et al., 1994). The levels selected for each parameter should encompass the range of possible outcomes for that variable, or at least the "reasonably likely" range. Here "reasonably likely" is an arbitrary choice of the modeler, but one possible approach is to select maximum and minimum levels where there is a 10 percent probability that an actual value will be outside the selected range.

If combinations of changes to two or more parameters are being analyzed, a common approach is to use a "complete factorial" experimental design, in which the model is solved for all possible combinations of the parameters. While this provides a wealth of information, if there are a number of parameters to analyze, the number of model solutions that must be obtained can be enormous. To conduct a complete factorial sensitivity analysis for eight parameters each with five levels would require 390,625 solutions. If these take one minute each to process, the task would take nine months, after which the volume of output created would be too large to be used effectively. In practice one must compromise by reducing the number of variables and/or the number of levels included in the complete factorial. Preliminary sensitivity analyses on individual parameters are helpful in deciding which are the most important parameters for inclusion in a complete factorial experiment.

Alternatively, one may reduce the number of model solutions required by adopting an incomplete design with only a subset of the possible combinations included. Possibilities include central composite designs (e.g., Hall and Menz, 1985), Taguchi methods (e.g., Clemson et al., 1995), or some system of random sampling or "Monte Carlo" analysis (e.g. Uyeno, 1992).

The Monte Carlo approach involves random generation of sets of parameter values based on a joint probability distribution provided by the user. The parameters can be drawn from either discrete or continuous probability distributions. Clemson et al. (1995) argued that this approach is inefficient and inappropriate for sensitivity analysis since "an inordinate number of trials may be required to ensure a reasonably thorough exploration of the total sample space." (p. 33)

A more efficient approach is to use a "stratified" sampling method, such as Latin hypercube sampling (Clemson et al., 1995). The modeler divides the probability distribution of each parameter into intervals of equal probability. For a single parameter with a two-level sensitivity analysis, the two intervals would be the parts of the distribution above and below the median. The parameter value representing an interval is chosen at random from within the interval (or perhaps set at the conditional expected value of the parameter within the interval; Harrison and Vinod, 1992). Once a full set of representative parameter values has been defined, the user selects a random sample of parameter sets from the full set. The way parameter sets have been defined to have equal probability facilitates this process of random selection. The approach allows the full range of possible parameter combinations to be considered without the need for prohibitively large numbers of model solutions. The approach can accommodate multiple intervals and multiple parameters. Although in its standard form it assumes that the parameters are independent of each other, the method can be adapted to include dependent sampling that allows for the correlation between parameters (e.g., Harrison and Vinod, 1992). Commercial software that can be "added-in" to the major spreadsheet packages now simplifies the application of Monte Carlo approaches, including Latin hypercube sampling.

Another approach available in some LP packages is called *parametric programming*, which can be used to vary a single objective function coefficient or constraint limit. Within a specified range for the parameter, parametric programming generates a solution for every value of the parameter at which the optimal basis changes. It has the advantage that the process is automated and that *every* optimal basis is identified within the specified range for the parameter. On the other hand, it is only possible to vary objective function coefficients or constraint limits. In any realistic model, there are important coefficients that you will wish to vary within the body of the matrix.

One final way of dealing with uncertain parameters is to explicitly represent them in the model as random variables with specific probability distributions. In such a "stochastic programming" model, the optimal solution is a best-bet strategy that accounts for the different possible values the variables might take. Stochastic programming fits within our definition of sensitivity analysis, but because it is a somewhat specialized set of techniques, it is described separately in the next chapter.

12.3 ANALYSIS AND COMMUNICATION OF SENSITIVITY-ANALYSIS RESULTS

So much information can be generated in sensitivity analysis that there is a risk of the volume of data obscuring the important issues (Eschenbach and McKeague, 1989). For this reason, the modeler must analyze and/or display the results in a way that summarizes the information and allows decision makers to identify the key issues. The following subsections cover various possible methods for analyzing the results of a sensitivity analysis, ranging from very simple to very complex. For many of the methods of analysis, we suggest possible layouts for graphs and tables. There are many other possible layouts that may be more suitable than these for particular purposes. A number of examples are drawn from my research in agricultural economics. The suggested methods are relevant to any discipline that uses LP models.

Summaries of Activity Levels or Objective Function Values: One Dimension

The simplest approach to the analysis of sensitivity analysis results is to present summaries of activity levels or objective function values for different parameter values. It may be unnecessary to conduct any further analysis of the results.

A simple example of such a summary is presented in Figure 12.1. This example (like several that follow) is from MIDAS (Morrison et al., 1986; Kingwell and Pannell, 1987), an LP model that selects optimal combinations of farming enterprises for representative farms in a region of Western Australia. The figure shows how the optimal area of wheat varies as a number of parameters are varied on either side of their standard values. Each of the parameters in this example is varied up or down by 25 and 50 percent. The commonly used format in Figure 12.1 allows results from several parameters to be presented on a single graph. This allows easy comparison of the relative impacts of these parameters when varied over the same range. In this example, you can see that for a given percentage change in each of these three parameters, wheat yields have the biggest impact on the optimal area of wheat. Eschenbach and McKeague (1989) refer to this type of graph as a "spider diagram," for obvious reasons.

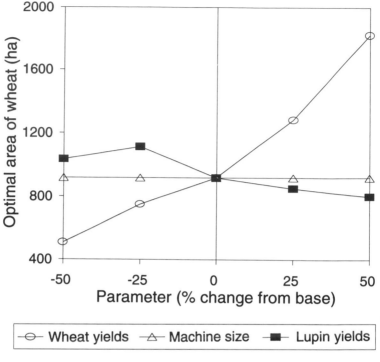

FIGURE 12.1

A problem with this layout is that the changes are the same in percentage terms for each parameter. In practice, realistic percentage changes may vary widely between parameters. Figure 12.2 shows a layout suggested by Eschenbach and McKeague (1989) that overcomes this problem by limiting the length of the lines to parameter values considered reasonable by the decision maker. This allows the decision maker to more easily gauge the sensitivity of results to parameter changes within reasonable ranges. It also communicates information about the size of those reasonable ranges. This figure confirms that wheat yields are the most important of these three parameters in determining optimal wheat area. Indeed, the relative sensitivity to wheat yields is even greater in Figure 12.2 than in Figure 12.1, due to it having the widest reasonable range of the three parameters.

Spider diagrams like these can also be constructed with the objective function value rather than an activity level as the dependent variable, allowing the decision maker to assess the sensitivity of the objective function value to parameter changes. For example, if the objective is to maximize profit, this type of diagram reveals whether any parameter changes would result in a negative profit.

A potential problem with the use of percentage changes in spider diagrams

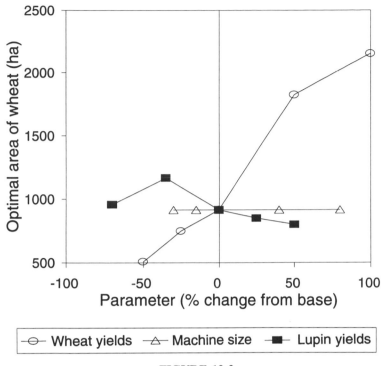

FIGURE 12.2

is that if the parameter is small (e.g., variation is centered around zero), percentage changes may be large relative to those for other variables. In fact if
the initial parameter value is zero, percentage changes to the parameter are not
defined. For these parameters, use an absolute change.

Spider diagrams are usually only practical for displaying the levels of a
single activity. Where there are several important variables to display, one
normally needs to limit results to changes in a single parameter. Figure 12.3
is an example from MIDAS showing production of wheat grain, lupin grain,
pea grain, and wool as functions of wheat price. Because of the different scales
of production, wool is shown on the right-hand axis. This graph reveals that
the main effect of increasing wheat prices is to increase wheat production at
the expense of wool. There are also smaller changes in the production of lupin
grain and pea grain.

A different way of summarizing the same model results is to show the
allocation of a particular input or resource to the different possible outputs. The
way these allocations vary can be effectively displayed by stacking the lines or
bars, as shown in Figure 12.4. This figure shows the allocation of land to
production of each of the four products, with the allocations mirroring the
trends in Figure 12.3.

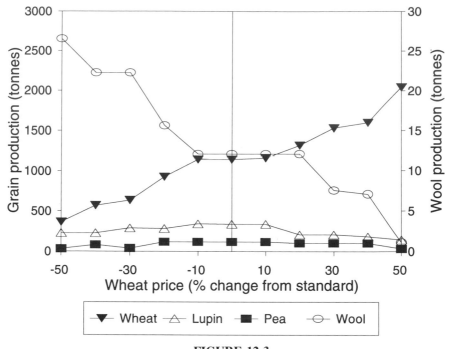

FIGURE 12.3

Summaries of Activity Levels or Objective Function Values: Higher Dimensions

In Figures 12.1 and 12.2, because we held constant all but one parameter for each line on the graph, it was possible to display results for several parameters on the same graph. If we wish to display the results of changing parameters simultaneously, it is difficult to handle more than two parameters in a graph without it becoming complex and difficult to follow. Figures 12.5 and 12.6 show examples of methods for displaying results from sensitivity analyses on two parameters. These figures show the impacts of changing wheat price and wool price on the optimal area of wheat selected by MIDAS.

For more than two parameters, you could have a series of graphs or use a table. Well-structured tables are probably the better option. Another approach is to develop an interactive database of model results, allowing decision makers to select the parameter values and displaying the corresponding optimal solution. This type of database acts as a simplified (and much quicker) version of the full model. We have had some success using this approach with the MIDAS model.

A final possible approach to the analysis of multidimensional sensitivity analysis is to use statistical-regression techniques to fit a smooth surface to the results. This approach provides an equation that approximates the functional relationship between the parameter values and the dependent variable (e.g., the activity level or objective function value). Such an equation will be smoother

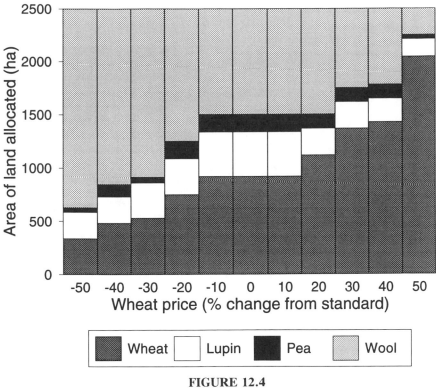

FIGURE 12.4

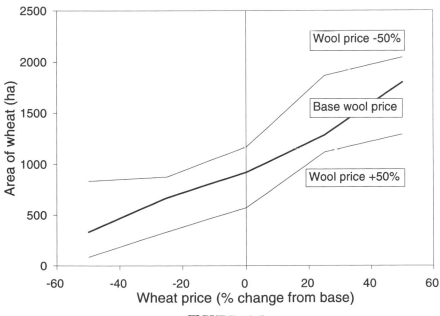

FIGURE 12.5

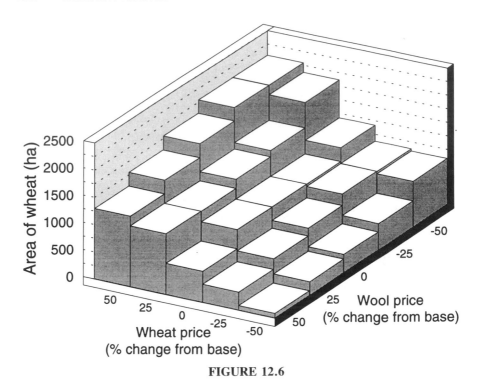

FIGURE 12.6

than the step functions typically produced by LP models, and this may be useful for producing graphs or for conducting some of the analyses outlined below.

Slopes and Elasticities

The rate of change (the slope) of an activity level or of the objective function with respect to changes in a parameter is an even briefer summary of the issue than the graphs shown so far. The shadow prices provided with standard LP output represent the slope of the objective function with respect to changes in constraint limits. However, for slopes of activity levels or for changes in parameters other than constraint limits, it is necessary to conduct further model solutions to estimate the slopes.

One issue in calculating slopes is the way LPs produce step functions, making it difficult to calculate meaningful slopes. The use of statistical regression to fit a smooth surface to the results, as suggested earlier, overcomes this problem.

Another issue is the need to compare slopes for different parameters. The units of measure of different parameters are not necessarily comparable, so neither are absolute slopes with respect to changes in different parameters. One can often overcome this problem by calculating "elasticities," which are measures of the percentage change in a dependent variable (e.g., an activity level) divided by the percentage change in an independent variable (e.g., a parameter):

$$e = \frac{(y_2 - y_1)/y_1}{(x_2 - x_1)/x_1}$$

or

$$e = \frac{dy}{dx} \times \frac{x}{y}$$

Comparing the elasticities of an activity level with respect to different parameters provides a good indication of which parameters the activity is most sensitive to. Table 12.1 is an example of such a comparison for MIDAS. The elasticities have been calculated assuming base values for parameters other than the one in question. Results have been smoothed using regression and elasticities calculated from the fitted smooth curves.

Sensitivity Indices

A *sensitivity index* is a number that gives information about the relative sensitivity of results to different parameters of the model. The elasticities just described are examples; the higher the elasticity, the higher the sensitivity of results to changes in that parameter. Hamby (1994) has outlined 14 possible sensitivity indices for cases where only a single output variable is to be evaluated, including the ''importance index,'' the ''relative deviation'' index, the ''partial rank correlation coefficient,'' the Smirnov test, the Cramer-von Mises test, and a number of others. These are not outlined in detail here because many of them are complex and time-consuming to calculate. Furthermore, Hamby (1995) conducted a detailed comparison of the performance of each of the indices relative of a composite index based on ten of them. None of the complex indices tested performed as well a simple index proposed by Hoffman and Gardner (1983):

$$SI = (D_{max} - D_{min})/D_{max}$$

TABLE 12.1 Elasticities of Optimal Wheat Area with Respect to Changes in Various Parameters

Parameter	Elasticity of Optimal Wheat Area
Wheat price	1.5
Wheat yield	1.4
Wool price	−0.5
Lupin price	−0.3
Machinery size	0.0

where D_{max} is the output result when the parameter in question is set at its maximum value and D_{min} is the result for the minimum parameter value.

Alexander (1989) suggested a number of complex indices for use in situations where the modeler wishes to assess the sensitivity of several output variables simultaneously. For example, for cases where the result of interest is a ranking of several variables, Alexander provides an index that indicates the sensitivity of the ranking to changes in a parameter.

Break-Even Values

Consider the question, If parameter X were to change from its current value, by how much would it have to change in order for the optimal solution to change in a particular way? This addresses the issue of uncertainty about parameter values in a way that is often particularly helpful to decision makers. Here are some specific examples of this type of question:

- By how much would the penalties for pollution have to increase before it would be worthwhile for a firm to adopt new, low-pollution technology?
- A company is considering a new production system for a factory. Given that the operating costs of the new system are higher, by how much would the output of the factory have to increase to break even from the change?
- An agricultural scientist is planning to breed a new variety of wheat with a higher yield. If the new variety has a higher cost of production due to increased requirements for fertilizer, by how much would the yield of the new variety have to be increased in order to be at least as profitable as the current variety?
- A company has the capacity to manufacture six different products. At present one of them is not being produced because its profitability is too low. If prices and costs remain unchanged, by how much would the efficiency of production of this product have to improve before it would be worthwhile for the company to include it in its portfolio of products?

In some cases, this type of question can be answered by range-analysis output, but it is often necessary to solve the model for various levels of the uncertain parameter and determine the break-even level. This approach helps assess whether the critical value of the variable falls within the range of values considered reasonable for the variable. If it does not, the decision maker can be advised, for the purposes of planning, to disregard the possibility of the variable taking a different value. If the critical value is in the realistic range, this information can be used to justify collection of additional information to help predict the actual value of the parameter.

Table 12.2 shows an example from MIDAS. In the standard version of this model, the optimal use of land of a particular type (soil type 1) is to grow pasture for grazing sheep. We wish to know the circumstances in which crop-

TABLE 12.2   Break-Even Changes in Parameter Values for Crops To Be as Profitable as Pasture Production on Soil Type 1

Parameter	Break-even Parameter Change (%)
Wheat price	+50
Wheat yield on soil type 1	+40
Wool price	−80
Pasture yield on soil type 1	−70
Lupin price	+130
Lupin yield on soil type 1	+120

ping would be as good or better than pasture. The table shows break-even percentage changes in various parameters, changes needed for the profitability of growing crops on soil type 1 to equal that for pasture. By judging whether parameter changes of at least this magnitude are ever likely to occur, we can judge whether crops are ever likely to be recommended on this soil type.

The next example is from Syria (Nordblom et al., 1994). A group of scientists conducting research on medic, a valuable type of pasture plant, wanted to know how the profitability of growing wheat and medic in rotation compares with current crops grown by farmers in a particular region. An LP model showed the medic–wheat rotation was not as profitable as traditional farm practices (given current yields). This led to a sensitivity analysis addressing the question, How much more productive would medic pasture and/or wheat have to be for the medic–wheat rotation to be as profitable as the best traditional rotation? Table 12.3 shows some results for a particular scenario. Three different levels of medic production and four wheat yields were examined. The traditional rotation gives annual farm profits of 243,000 Syrian Lira. Combinations of medic production and wheat yield that are at least this profitable are marked in the table. This analysis provided the scientists with a set of targets that they must meet if their research is to benefit Syrian farmers.

TABLE 12.3   Whole-farm Income ('000 Syrian Lira) for Medic–Wheat Rotation

Medic Offtake (Percent of Base Case)	Wheat Yield Following Medic (Percent of Base Case)			
	100	115	130	145
100	184	216	249[a]	281[a]
150	214	248[a]	282[a]	315[a]
200	244[a]	277[a]	311[a]	345[a]

[a]Medic–wheat rotation as profitable as best traditional rotation.

Ranges

Range analysis (Chapter 9) is similar to the break-even approach just outlined in that it indicates allowable parameter changes before there is a change in activity/slack levels (activity range analysis) or before there is a change in the basis (constraint range analysis). This is rather limited because the change that occurs outside the indicated range may not be the change that interests you, and because there is no standard facility for range analysis of coefficients other than those in the objective function and constraint limits. For both these reasons, range analysis could not be used for the previous example on medic pasture (Table 12.3). Nevertheless, the idea of presenting results of a sensitivity analysis in a format similar to range analysis may be useful in some circumstances. By altering parameters and re-solving the model, one can construct range-analysis output for any matrix coefficient, using any criterion to define the range and, if desired, making parallel changes to related parameters.

Comparing Constrained and Unconstrained Solutions

The approaches we have discussed so far are based on assessing the sensitivity of the model to changes in parameters. A different approach is to add constraints to the model so that it is forced to adopt other interesting strategies. It is often valuable to know how other strategies perform relative to the optimum. Figure 12.7 shows an example, where the MIDAS model has been constrained to plant

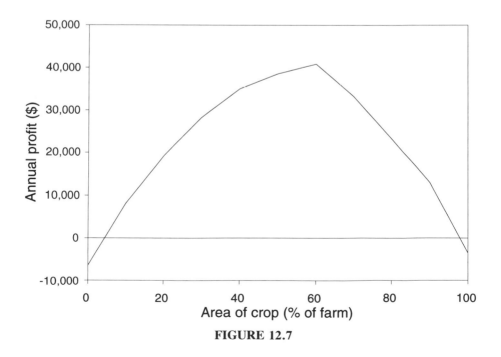

FIGURE 12.7

crops on various percentages of the farm area. Such a graph is valuable if the decision maker wishes to consider other strategies that achieve objectives other than that represented in the model. Figure 12.7 shows how much profit must be sacrificed if the farmer wishes to deviate from the optimal 60 percent growing area.

A useful way of indicating the flexibility available to the decision maker is to report the set of strategies with objective function values within a certain distance of the optimum. For example, any crop area between 40 and 70 percent of the farm is within $5000 of the maximum profit.

It is sometimes useful to constrain the model to exclude an option in order to calculate the total contribution of this option to the objective, and to identify the best strategy that does not include it. Table 12.4 is summary of the MIDAS solutions that include and exclude the option of growing lupins on the farm. You can see that the inclusion of lupins increases profits by around 66 percent.

To gain more information on the impact of excluding an option, one can conduct further sensitivity analyses, either changing parameters or investigating particular types of strategies. Figure 12.8 shows the impact of excluding lupins on the relationship between crop area and profit (as in Figure 12.7). This shows that without the lupin option, the reduction in profit is most pronounced for very high areas of crop.

Figure 12.9 shows an example of combining approaches: comparing constrained and unconstrained models, *and* varying model parameters. The graph shows the impact of various parameter changes on the increase in profit resulting from including lupins on the farm. The question is, Do lupins always make a large contribution to total profit, or might they be less important in some circumstances? The graph shows that the total contribution of lupins is very sensitive to the price of lupins, but relatively insensitive to the prices of wheat and wool.

TABLE 12.4 Profit and Optimal Rotations with and without Lupins

	Lupins	
	Included	Excluded
Whole-farm profit ($)	40,870	24,553
Rotation selected[a]		
Soil type 1	PPPP	PPPP
Soil type 2	CL	PPPC
Soil type 3	CCL	CCCC
Soil type 4	CCL	CCCC
Soil type 5	CCF	CCF
Soil type 6	PPPP	PPPP
Soil type 7	CCF	CCF

[a]C = cereal crop; P = pasture; L = lupins; F = field peas.

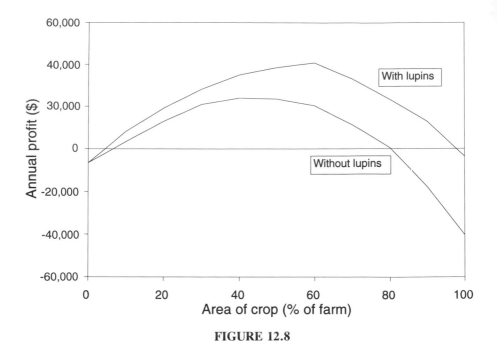

FIGURE 12.8

Using Probabilities

A common characteristic of the methods of analysis just presented is that they do not require the modeler to explicitly specify probabilities of different situations. Sensitivity analysis can be extremely effective and useful even without taking this extra step to a more formal and complex analysis of results. In excluding probabilities from your analysis, you are relying on the decision maker to give appropriate weight to each scenario. On the other hand, an analysis using probabilities may be unnecessarily difficult and time-consuming to conduct, and is likely to be more difficult to explain to the decision maker. One of the attractions of sensitivity analysis is its potential simplicity, and an analysis that is not understood is unlikely to be believed. Depending on the importance of the issue and the attitudes and knowledge of the decision maker, the best approach to sensitivity analysis might not involve formal and explicit use of probabilities. Even if you do intend to conduct such a sensitivity analysis, a simpler preliminary analysis may be useful in planning your final analysis.

If you do wish to formally represent the probabilities of different outcomes, there are many approaches to choose from. One set of approaches involves the representation of probabilities of alternative outcomes within the LP matrix. These are described in detail in the next chapter. The other set of approaches, which is described here, requires further calculations after the LP model has been solved for the range of potential circumstances.

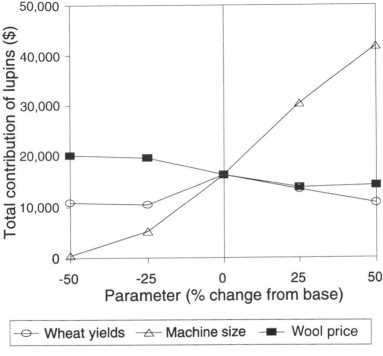

FIGURE 12.9

The extra information requirements to properly represent probabilities are: (a) which parameters are to be represented as random variables with probabilities, and (b) what is the "joint probability distribution" for all these parameters. Item (b) describes the probabilities of all possible combinations of parameter values. Note that identifying a probability distribution for each parameter individually does not necessarily provide you with enough information to form the joint probability distribution. You also need to know how the parameters are related to each other. Do parameters A and B tend to be both high or both low at the same time (positive covariance), do they tend to move in opposite directions (negative convariance), or are they completely uncorrelated (zero covariance). Only in the case of zero covariance can you form the joint probability distribution solely from the probability distributions of individual parameters. This is done by multiplying the probabilities of each of the parameters taking their respective values.

To illustrate, suppose that wheat and wool prices are the only important random variables in the MIDAS model. We saw the results of a sensitivity analysis for this case in Figures 12.5 and 12.6. Suppose that we have estimated the joint probability distribution for wheat and wool prices as shown in Table 12.5. In reality, it is possible to observe prices other than those given in the

TABLE 12.5   Joint Probability Distribution of Wheat and Wool Prices

Wool Price (Percent of Base Case)	Wheat Price (Percent of Base Case)				
	50	75	100	125	150
50	0.01	0.02	0.04	0.02	0.01
75	0.02	0.04	0.08	0.04	0.02
100	0.04	0.08	0.16	0.08	0.04
125	0.02	0.04	0.08	0.04	0.02
150	0.01	0.02	0.04	0.02	0.01

table, but we have chosen to use this "discrete" distribution to approximate the true distribution, which is probably almost smooth or "continuous."*

We can use this distribution in various ways, including:

(a) Calculating the probability distribution of some variable from a corresponding set of 25 solutions.
(b) Calculating the "expected value" (i.e., the weighted average) of some variable from a corresponding set of 25 solutions.
(c) Calculating the probability of some particular event or circumstance.

Figure 12.10 is an example of use (a), where the probability distribution of profit has been calculated for the set of solutions underlying Figure 12.6. Care is needed in interpreting this distribution. It is not the probability distribution of profit for a particular strategy, as the strategy changes in different scenarios (as shown in Figure 12.6). Rather it is the probability distribution of profit for decision makers who use the recommendations of MIDAS to adjust their strategy. To calculate the probability distribution of profit for a particular strategy you must constrain the model to that strategy and solve it for each combination of parameter values.

To illustrate use (b), the expected value of the distribution shown in Figure 12.10 is $48,300, which is obtained by multiplying the probability of each circumstance by its corresponding profit value and summing the results. The result is somewhat higher than the profit for the base case ($40,900), revealing the potential for bias if one relies on a single optimal solution.

Examples of use (c) include:

---

*One version of the Monte Carlo approach, described earlier, involves random selection of parameter values from defined probability distributions. If sufficient solutions are generated, the probability distributions resulting from this approach are smoother than using discrete approximations. The disadvantage of Monte Carlo is that is may require a larger number of model solutions for the sample distribution to converge on the true distribution.

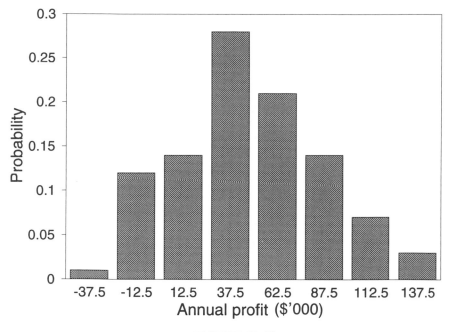

FIGURE 12.10

- The probability that the best available strategy will generate a profit of at least $25,000 at .73.
- The probability that the best strategy will include at lease 1000 ha of wheat is .34;
- The probability that a fixed strategy of sowing 40 percent of the farm area to crops will be within $5000 of the optimum for any given circumstance is .33. This example requires you to compare two probability distributions of profit (two sets of 25 model solutions). One is from the set of optimal strategies, and the other is from a model constrained to a particular strategy of 40 percent cropping.
- The probability that a fixed strategy of sowing 40 percent of the farm area to crops will be better than the optimal strategy for the base case (60 percent crop) is .27. This example also requires you to compare two probability distributions of profit: for the model constrained to 40 percent crops and 60 percent crops.

This leads to another example of use (b): the expected value of the profit difference between 40 and 60 percent cropy area is $10,300 in favor of 60 percent. A useful concept here is the ''confidence interval.'' For example, the 80 percent confidence interval for the profit difference between 40 and 60

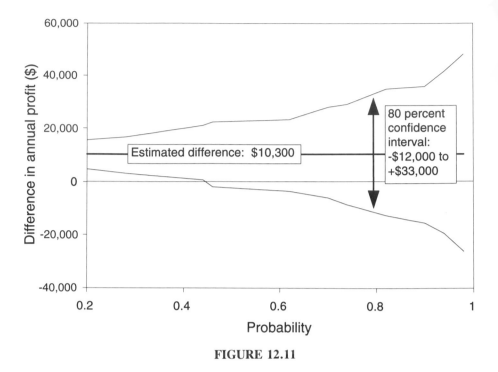

FIGURE 12.11

percent crop growth is $-\$12,000$ to $+\$33,000$, meaning that there is an 80 percent probability that the difference will lie within this range. You can plot the confidence interval for different levels of confidence (Harrison and Vinod, 1992), as shown in Figure 12.11. These suggested approaches to the use of probabilities in analysis and presentation of sensitivity analysis certainly do not cover all possibilities; see Eschenbach and Gimpel (1990) for further suggestions.

To conclude this section, note that care is needed when interpreting the results of applying probabilities to the results of a sensitivity analysis from an LP model. In particular, be cautious when applying probabilities to results where the strategy is allowed to vary in different scenarios. In this situation, one is assuming that the strategy *can* be adjusted, implying that the parameter values can be predicted before decisions have to be finalized. This is frequently not the case. If probabilities are applied to results for a fixed strategy evaluated in different scenarios, this problem does not arise.

Another potential problem arises where the model includes nonlinear relationships (including linear approximations of curvilinear relationships, as in Chapter 7) and one of the parameters of this relationship is uncertain. In this case, the expected value of the objective function will be correctly calculated if probabilities are applied inside the model (as in Chapter 13), but possibly not if they are applied outside the model (as in this chapter).

12.4 AN OVERALL STRATEGY FOR SENSITIVITY ANALYSIS

The techniques just outlined are a powerful set of tools for assisting a decision maker. However, you need to avoid conducting sensitivity analysis in an aimless or mechanical fashion. Adjust your approach to suit the decision problem and draw conclusions as you proceed, conducting further model runs to test ideas or answer questions that arise. In a thorough sensitivity analysis, you might use a number of the approaches suggested in the previous section.

Within these broad guidelines, there are numerous overall strategies for sensitivity analysis that you might adopt. Here is one systematic and comprehensive suggestion that is likely to be effective in cases where the analysis is used to help make a decision or recommendation about the optimal strategy.

1. Select the parameters to be varied. Identify a reasonable range for each parameter (e.g., maximum and minimum values, or 90 percent confidence interval). Also identify other possible discrete scenarios requiring changes to the model structure or formulation (e.g., changes in the objective to be optimized, inclusion of additional constraints).

2. Conduct sensitivity analyses for each parameter individually, using three or five equally spaced parameter values. Conduct sensitivity analysis for each discrete scenario individually.

3. Identify parameters and discrete scenarios to which the key decision variables are relatively unresponsive.

4. Exclude unresponsive parameters from further analysis. For the remaining parameters, consider whether they are likely to have high-positive high-negative, or low correlation with each other. If you intend to use probability distributions for random sampling of scenarios or to summarize results, estimate the distribution for each parameter and, for cases of high correlation, estimate the joint probability distributions. Possibly also estimate probabilities for the discrete scenarios selected in step 1.

5. Design and conduct a modeling experiment that allows appropriately for combinations of parameter changes, paying particular attention to the cases of high correlation between parameters. You might use Latin hypercube sampling or, if the number of combinations is manageable, a complete factorial design. Repeat this for each of the discrete scenarios individually, or if practical, for all combinations of the discrete scenarios.

6. Summarize results. Report the responsiveness of the optimal practice (i.e., levels of key activities) to parameter changes using spider diagrams or elasticities. Calculate break-even parameter values for particular circumstances of interest. To avoid an overload of graphs and tables, demonstrate that certain parameters have little impact on the important decision variables, and then excluding these parameters from subsequent graphs and tables. This approach allows the decision maker to focus on important parameters and relationships.

7. On the basis of results so far, identify a tentative best-bet strategy and several others of interest. The other strategies might be chosen because they contribute to objectives other than that represented in the model, or because they are of personal interest to the decision maker. French (1992) suggested that we focus on "adjacent potentially optimal" alternative solutions, meaning strategies that are close to the base-case optimum, and that would become optimal if parameters changed sufficiently. You need not limit yourself to such a narrow set of strategies, although you should be mindful of the number of solutions required in the next step.

8. Repeat the experiment (step 5) with the model constrained to each of the strategies (from step 7). Summarize these results. Identify scenarios (if any) where each strategy is optimal. Calculate the cost of each strategy relative to the best-bet one. Possibly repeat this with another strategy as the best bet. At this stage you may wish to use probability distributions to make probabilistic statements about the results.

9. Attempt to draw conclusions. It can be helpful to focus your thinking by trying to couch your conclusions in terms similar to one of the following examples. These are mutually exclusive alternative conclusions. Try to identify which is most appropriate for your decision problem.

    (a) The optimal strategy is X is almost any plausible scenario, so X is a safe best-bet strategy.

    (b) In some scenarios the optimal strategy is X, while in other scenarios, the optimal strategy is Y. If you can predict or identify the scenario, it is important to do the right strategy in the right scenario.

    (c) In some scenarios the optimal strategy is X, while in other scenarios, the optimal strategy is Y. However, the cost of doing the wrong strategy is very low, so it is not very important to worry about doing the right strategy in the right scenario.

    (d) In some scenarios the optimal strategy is X, while in other scenarios, the optimal strategy is Y. The cost of doing the wrong strategy when you should be doing Y is low, but the cost of doing the wrong strategy when you should be doing X is high, so if you cannot predict or identify the scenario, X is a safe best-bet strategy.

These conclusions correspond to the following recommendations: (a) do X; (b) do either X or Y depending on specific circumstances; (c) do either X or Y, whichever you like; (d) if in doubt, do X.

In addition there is a converse set of conclusions one can draw, about which strategies are never likely to be optimal: (e) never do Z; (f) if certain circumstances do not do Z; (g) if in doubt, do not do Z. As well as identifying which of the categories (a) to (d) the problem falls into, check whether it is possible to specify any strategies like Z in categories (e) to (g).

A less comprehensive but still systematic and useful procedure would include only steps 1, 2, 3, 6, and 9. An intermediate approach would include all steps except 7 and 8.

12.5 CONCLUDING COMMENTS

There is clearly much more to LP use than finding a single optimal solution. That solution should be viewed as the starting point for a wide-ranging set of sensitivity analyses to improve your knowledge and understanding of the system's behavior. The shadow prices, shadow costs, and range analysis provided with an LP solution are not adequate to develop this knowledge and understanding.

Even without undertaking the relatively complex procedures that explicitly involve probabilities in the sampling of scenarios or interpretation of results, sensitivity analysis is a powerful and illuminating methodology. The simple approach to sensitivity analysis is easy to do, easy to understand, and easy to communicate. As a decision aid it is often adequate even though not perfect. Given its ease and transparency, the simple approach may even be the best for the purpose of practical decision making.

12.6 KEY POINTS

- Except where the model's structure and coefficients are known with some certainty, a single optimal solution from an LP model is usually an inadequate basis for decision making. Decision makers are better off if the modeler generates solutions for plausible values of key parameters and for important discrete scenarios.

- Sensitivity analysis allows the decision maker to identify and focus on those aspects of the decision problem that are most important in determining the optimal decision.

- A sensitivity analysis might involve some or all of the following steps: (1) select parameters and discrete scenarios; (2) conduct individual sensitivity analyses for these parameters and scenarios; (3) identify parameters and scenarios to which the model is unresponsive; (4) estimate joint probabilities for responsive parameters and scenarios; (5) conduct a modeling experiment for combinations of parameter changes and scenarios; (6) summarize initial results; (7) select a best-bet strategy plus several others; (8) repeat the modeling experiment with the model constrained to each of these strategies; (9) draw conclusions.

- For most of these steps, there is a range of approaches that might be used.

CHAPTER 13

REPRESENTING RISK AND UNCERTAINTY

The definitions of "risk" and "uncertainty" sometimes differ,* but they both mean that some parameters have probability distributions rather than fixed values. For the purposes of decision modeling, they are usually treated as being equivalent. This is true for the linear programming (LP) techniques in this chapter, so the two terms will be used interchangeably.

In Chapter 12 we covered approaches that are useful for investigating the impacts of uncertainty about a parameter. They all involved varying the parameter, solving the model several times, and examining the combined outputs. In this chapter you will learn how to include uncertainty within a single model solution. The model will be *stochastic* (i.e., one that represents risky outcomes) rather than *deterministic* (i.e., fixed and known with certainty). The methods presented in this chapter are often referred to collectively as *risk programming* or *stochastic programming*.

13.1 REPRESENTING PROBABILITIES OF DIFFERENT OUTCOMES

To illustrate the various methods, we return to the paper milling example. Here is the problem definition, modified to include uncertainty.

---

*According to definitions, *risk* means that a parameter has a probability distribution and we know what it is, while *uncertainty* means that we don't know what the probability distribution is. To make a decision when faced with uncertainty, we must make a subjective estimate of the probability distribution. By these definitions, most practical decisions are made under uncertainty.

Example 13.1: Paper Milling with Price Uncertainty

The manager of a paper mill wants to plan daily production. Two types of paper are produced: computer paper and writing paper. The mill employs 126 workers. Each tonne of computer paper produced requires four days of labor, whereas production of writing paper is more labor intensive, requiring six days of labor per tonne. Each tonne of paper (of either type) requires two tonnes of wood chips, and there are 56 tonnes of wood chips available each day. The mill is situated on a river that provides water for the production process. In order to make the paper white, the mill uses chlorine-based bleaches. This process causes contamination of the water that is discharged back into the river with traces of the extremely toxic chemical, dioxin. To avoid pollution of the river the government has imposed strict environmental regulations on the mill; no more than 24 kg of chlorine residues per day may be discharged. Each tonne of writing paper produced results in the discharge of 1.5 kg of chlorine. Computer paper does not have to be as white, and so is much cleaner to produce, with only $\frac{2}{7}$ kg of chlorine residue per tonne. Net profits per tonne for writing paper are uncertain at this stage due to instability in its market price. The manager judges that there are three possible outcomes: net profit equals $500 (with probability .25), $1000 (with probability .5), or $1500 (with probability .25). Decisions must be made before the actual price is known. The price of computer paper is fixed at $600, due to a contract. Construct a matrix to select the levels of writing paper and computer paper that maximize the expected value* of profits for the mill subject to the constraints of mill capacity, wood chip availability, and chlorine pollution limits. ∎

Note that the uncertain parameter, the price of writing paper, has a "discrete probability distribution"; it can only take on certain specified values, each of which has a given probability of occurring. In reality this is an approximation. The actual price might fall between or outside the prices given in the problem definition. However, discrete approximations are usually accurate enough when analyzing practical risky decisions. We rarely know what the probability distribution is with sufficient accuracy to be able to say that a particular continuous (i.e., smooth) distribution is a more accurate representation of reality than a similar discrete (lumpy) distribution. You can make the approximation more accurate by including more levels, each with their own probabilities attached. However, the techniques presented in this chapter cannot be used to represent a continuous probability distribution exactly.

Example 13.1 has two important characteristics: (a) the only uncertainty is about objective function coefficients (in this case, only one of them: the profit for writing paper), and (b) decisions must be finalized before any further in-

---

*The term *expected value* is used here in the statistical sense. It means the "weighted average" or "mean" value.

formation about the actual value of the uncertain parameter is obtained. When both these conditions exist, there is actually no need to represent risk in the matrix in order to correctly select the optimal levels of activities. If we use the expected values of the objective function coefficients in a deterministic model, like the one in Table 3.1, we obtain the correct solution to the risky problem (Schrage, 1991).

On the other hand, you may wish to use the model to calculate the probability distribution of the objective function value (profit, in this example). This can be achieved by using a transfer row to measure profit for each "state of nature." A state of nature is one possible set of observations of the uncertain parameters. In Example 13.1 there are three states of nature, one for each possible price. In a model with two independent uncertain parameters, each with three possible levels, the model might include nine states of nature.

A matrix for Example 13.1 is shown in Table 13.1. The *Labor, Wood chips*, and *Chlorine* constraints are identical to the earlier model in Table 3.1. The three states of nature are referred to as A, B, and C, and each has a transfer row for profit (e.g., *$ tr A*) and an accounting column that links the transfer row to the objective function (e.g., *Profit A*). *Computer* generates the same profit regardless of the state of nature, so it generates the same profit into each of the transfer rows. *Writing*, however, has a different parameter in each row, reflecting its value in each state of nature. The level of profit being transferred into the objective function for each state of nature needs to be weighted by the probability of that state of nature. Thus the *Profit A* activity has an objective function coefficient of 0.25, since each dollar of profit in state-of-nature A contributes only $0.25 to the expected value of profit. Note that the objective function values in this model are not probabilities, but dollar values that have been multiplied by probabilities.

The solution for this model is shown in Table 13.2. As you would expect, the original activities and constraints have identical solution values as before (see Table 3.2). The new activities show the profit levels for the different states of nature. These are all conditional profit values: if state A occurred, the profit

TABLE 13.1 Matrix for Example 13.1

	Computer (tonnes)	Writing (tonnes)	Profit A ($)	Profit B ($)	Profit C ($)	Type	Li
Objective ($)			0.25	0.5	0.25	max	1
Labor (days)	4	6				≤	1
Wood chips (tonnes)	2	2				≤	
Chlorine (kg)	0.2857	1.5				≤	
$ tr A ($)	−600	−500	1			≤	
$ tr B ($)	−600	−1,000		1		≤	
$ tr C ($)	−600	−1,500			1	≤	

TABLE 13.2   Optimal Solution for Example 13.1

Objective function value: 20,300.000000
Problem direction: max

Activity		Level	Shadow Cost
1 Computer	A	10.5000	0.0000
2 Writing	A	14.0000	0.0000
3 Profit A	A	13,000.0000	0.0000
4 Profit B	A	20,300.0000	0.0000
5 Profit C	A	27,300.0000	0.0000

Constraint		Slack	Shadow Price
1 Labor	L	0.0000	143.3333
2 Wood chips	L	7.0000	0.0000
3 Chlorine	L	0.0000	93.3333
4 $ tr A	L	0.0000	0.2500
5 $ tr B	L	0.0000	0.5000
6 $ tr C	L	0.0000	0.2500

would be $13,300. However, as we saw, their contribution to the objective function is reduced to reflect the probability of each state of nature.

The matrix in Table 13.1 is an extremely simple version of what is called *discrete stochastic programming* (DSP). This model is based on an assumption that you cannot predict the actual price of writing paper before deciding on activity levels. Your decisions must be based on your knowledge of the probability distribution. If you are able to discover the price before making a decision, the model structure is different, as shown in the next section.

The matrix is also based on an assumption that the objective of the decision maker is to maximize the expected value of profit. The decision maker may actually wish to weight poor outcomes more heavily than good outcomes when selecting activity levels. This is also possible, as you will see in Section 13.3.

13.2 SELECTING FLEXIBLE STRATEGIES

Consider a slight modification to Example 13.1.

Example 13.2: Paper Milling with Price Known before Decision Made

Suppose that the decision maker is able to learn the actual price for writing paper before deciding on the activity levels. Construct a matrix to calculate the optimal activity levels for each state of nature in order to maximize the expected value of profit. ∎

TABLE 13.3 Matrix for Example 13.2

	Computer A (tonnes)	Writing A (tonnes)	Profit A ($)	Computer B (tonnes)	Writing B (tonnes)	Profit B ($)	Computer C (tonnes)	Writing C (tonnes)	Profit C ($)	Type	Limit
Objective ($)			0.25			0.5			0.25	max	
Labor A (days)	4	6								≤	126
Wood chips A (tonnes)	2	2								≤	56
Chlorine A (kg)	0.2857	1.5								≤	24
$ tr A ($)	−600	−500	1							≤	0
Labor B (days)				4	6					≤	126
Wood chips B (tonnes)				2	2					≤	56
Chlorine B (kg)				0.2857	1.5					≤	24
$ tr B ($)				−600	−1,000	1				≤	0
Labor C (days)							4	6		≤	126
Wood chips C (tonnes)							2	2		≤	56
Chlorine C (kg)							0.2857	1.5		≤	24
$ tr C ($)							−600	−1,500	1	≤	0

This time we need separate activities for computer paper and writing paper for each state of nature, to allow for the possibility that their optimal levels may vary in different circumstances. We also need a set of the resource constraints for each state of nature. This is because activity levels can vary between states of nature, and we must be sure that the constraints are satisfied in every state. Thus we reproduce something very similar to the entire original matrix (Table 3.1) for each state of nature. The matrix is shown in Table 13.3, with the solution in Table 13.4.

In this example, representing the uncertainty does make a difference compared with the original model. It reveals that if you are able to predict the low price for writing paper, you should adjust the strategy to include 28.5 tonnes of computer paper and no writing paper. For average or high prices, the optimal strategy is the same as in the original example (Table 13.2).

The improvement in the expected value of profit (i.e., the objective function) from Table 13.2 to 13.4 is the "expected value of perfect information." To the decision maker it is the value of being able to perfectly predict and respond

TABLE 13.4 Optimal Solution for Example 13.2

Objective function value: 21,175.000000
Problem direction: max

Activity		Level	Shadow Cost
1 Computer A	A	28.0000	0.0000
2 Writing A	Z	0.0000	25.0000
3 Profit A	A	16,800.0000	0.0000
4 Computer B	A	10.5000	0.0000
5 Writing B	A	14.0000	0.0000
6 Profit B	A	20,300.0000	0.0000
7 Computer C	A	10.5000	0.0000
8 Writing C	A	14.0000	0.0000
9 Profit C	A	27,300.0000	0.0000

Constraint		Slack	Shadow Price
1 Labor A	L	14.0000	0.0000
2 Wood chips A	L	0.0000	75.0000
3 Chlorine A	L	16.0000	0.0000
4 $ tr A	L	0.0000	0.2500
5 Labor B	L	0.0000	71.6667
6 Wood chips B	L	7.0000	0.0000
7 Chlorine B	L	0.0000	46.6667
8 $ tr B	L	0.0000	0.5000
9 Labor C	L	0.0000	27.5000
10 Wood chips C	L	7.0000	0.0000
11 Chlorine C	L	0.0000	140.0000
12 $ tr C	L	0.0000	0.2500

to the price of writing paper. It is also possible to represent partial or imperfect information in a similar model (see Exercise 13.3).

Notice in Table 13.3 the consistent way columns and rows for each state of nature are grouped together. This practice is highly recommended, as it makes it easier to understand the matrix. Another recommended practice is to group together the inflexible activities (i.e., those whose levels must be fixed in advance). In this chapter, these are always placed at the left of the matrix.

Example 13.3: Paper Milling with Uncertainty about Chlorine Level

Suppose that instead of price, one of the technical coefficients is uncertain: the output of chlorine by writing paper. Due to random variations in the production process, the output of chlorine per tonne of writing paper may take on the following values: 2.0 (with probability .3), 1.5 (with probability .4), 1.0 (with probability .3). This represents the probability distribution of the coefficient for [*Chlorine, Writing*]. Construct a matrix to calculate the activity levels that maximize the expected value of profit.   ∎

The problem definition does not specify whether we are allowed to adjust the strategy in response to the different values of [*Chlorine, Writing*]. Suppose initially that we are not; we do not know how much chlorine has been released until after the paper has been produced. Suppose that even if the chlorine production is above average, the strategy selected must not produce more than 24 kg of chlorine. In this case, we do not need a stochastic model. We should simply include the *worst* possible chlorine output level in the deterministic model and solve it. The inclusion of additional constraints for other states of nature would be pointless because they can never affect the solution. Any strategy that satisfies the chlorine constraint in the worst case would also satisfy the chlorine constraint in every other case.

Suppose instead that we still cannot predict chlorine output in advance, but that we can choose a strategy that violates the chlorine constraint in some cases, at the cost of having to pay a fine of $150 for every kilogram of chlorine in excess of 24. Table 13.5 shows a matrix for this example. It must be possible in the model to select a different penalty level for each state of nature, so the model includes a separate *Excess* activity for each state.

Finally, instead of accepting a penalty, suppose that the chlorine output can be determined in advance, allowing the strategy to be adjusted. We then need separate activities for computer paper and writing paper for each state of nature. It is not sufficient to include multiple activities for writing paper but only a single activity for computer paper, since any adjustment in the level of writing paper necessarily means that the level of computer paper must also be adjusted to ensure that the constraints are met. We thus need to determine optimal levels for each type of paper for each state of nature. The matrix, shown in Table 13.6, is very similar to Table 13.3 for flexible strategies given a variable price.

TABLE 13.5 Matrix for Example 13.3 If Chlorine Output Is Not Predictable and a Penalty Is Charged on Excessive Chlorine

	Computer (tonnes)	Writing (tonnes)	Excess A (kg)	Profit A ($)	Excess B (kg)	Profit B ($)	Excess C (kg)	Profit C ($)	Type	Limit
Objective ($)				0.3		0.4		0.3	max	
Labor (days)	4	6							≤	126
Wood chips (tonnes)	2	2							≤	56
Chlorine A (kg)	0.2857	2	−1						≤	24
$ tr A ($)	−600	−1,000	150	1					≤	0
Chlorine B (kg)	0.2857	1.5			−1				≤	24
$ tr B ($)	−600	−1,000			150	1			≤	0
Chlorine C (kg)	0.2857	1					−1		≤	24
$ tr C ($)	−600	−1,000					150	1	≤	0

TABLE 13.6 Matrix for Example 13.3 If Paper Levels Can Be Adjusted to Suit Chlorine Level

	Computer A (tonnes)	Writing A (tonnes)	Profit A ($)	Computer B (tonnes)	Writing B (tonnes)	Profit B ($)	Computer C (tonnes)	Writing C (tonnes)	Profit C ($)	Type	Limit
Objective ($)			0.3			0.4			0.3	max	
Labor A (days)	4	6								$\leq$	126
Wood chips A (tonnes)	2	2								$\leq$	56
Chlorine A (kg)	0.2857	2								$\leq$	24
$ tr A ($)	−600	−1,000	1							$\leq$	0
Labor B (days)				4	6					$\leq$	126
Wood chips B (tonnes)				2	2					$\leq$	56
Chlorine B (kg)				0.2857	1.5					$\leq$	24
$ tr B ($)				−600	−1,000	1				$\leq$	0
Labor C (days)							4	6		$\leq$	126
Wood chips C (tonnes)							2	2		$\leq$	56
Chlorine C (kg)							0.2857	1		$\leq$	24
$ tr C ($)							−600	−1,000	1	$\leq$	0

TABLE 13.7   Optimal Solution for Matrix in Table 13.6

Objective function value: 20,376.363636
Problem direction: max

Activity		Level	Shadow Cost
1 Computer A	A	17.1818	0.0000
2 Writing A	A	9.5455	0.0000
3 Profit A	A	19.854.5455	0.0000
4 Computer B	A	10.5000	0.0000
5 Writing B	A	14.0000	0.0000
6 Profit B	A	20,300.0000	0.0000
7 Computer C	Z	0.0000	20.0000
8 Writing C	A	21.0000	0.0000
9 Profit C	A	21,000.0000	0.0000

Constraint		Slack	Shadow Price
1 Labor A	L	0.0000	43.6364
2 Wood chips A	L	2.5455	0.0000
3 Chlorine A	L	0.0000	19.0909
4 $ tr A	L	0.0000	0.3000
5 Labor B	L	0.0000	57.3333
6 Wood chips B	L	7.0000	0.0000
7 Chlorine B	L	0.0000	37.3333
8 $ tr B	L	0.0000	0.4000
9 Labor C	L	0.0000	50.0000
10 Wood chips C	L	14.0000	0.0000
11 Chlorine C	L	3.0000	0.0000
12 $ tr C	L	0.0000	0.3000

The difference is that in Table 13.6 price is constant between the submatrices representing states of nature, while [*Chlorine, Writing*] varies. The solution is shown in Table 13.7. In this example, the optimal paper levels are quite different in each state of nature.

13.3   WEIGHTING BAD OUTCOMES MORE HIGHLY THAN GOOD OUTCOMES

Studies have shown that most people prefer certainty to uncertainty and are willing to accept a lower expected value of benefits (e.g., lower profits) in return for a reduction in uncertainty about the outcome of a strategy. The term *risk aversion* is used to describe this negative attitude to risk. The commonness of risk aversion among people is one of the reasons modeling of risk is given so much attention.

People who are risk averse wish to give a greater weighting to bad outcomes than to good outcomes when choosing a strategy. A technique developed recently means that it is now, for the first time, possible to represent risk aversion fairly accurately in an LP model. There have long been available methods for approximating the effects of risk aversion in an LP model, including chance constrained programming (Kirby, 1970), MOTAD (Hazell, 1971), and target MOTAD (Tauer, 1983). See Boisvert and McCarl (1990) and Hardaker et al. (1991) for useful reviews of these and other techniques. However, the new group of techniques, known as DEMP (Lambert and McCarl, 1985) and Utility Efficient Programming (UEP) (Patten et al., 1988), is superior to these in that it involves a lower level of approximation and is more consistent with the accepted methodology for decision analysis (Hardaker et al., 1991). Practical applications of the new technique include studies by Kingwell (1994) and Torkamani (1994).

Example 13.4: Paper Milling with Price Uncertainty and Risk Aversion

This example is exactly the same as Example 13.1 except that the decision maker is risk averse. Represent this risk aversion by giving half the weight to dollars earned in excess of $20,000 compared to dollars earned below $20,000. The objective function is to measure the "utility" of the decision maker—meaning the psychological value of the profit—not the level of profit. For the first $20,000 earned, each dollar contributes a full unit of utility (one "util") to the objective function. For profit above $20,000, each dollar contributes only 0.50 unit of utility to the objective function. This is not to say that the extra income is not earned, but that it is not worth as much psychologically to the decision maker. (It has lower "marginal utility.") Construct a matrix to calculate the optimal activity levels in order to maximize the expected value of utility. ∎

A matrix for this example is shown in Table 13.8. Like Table 13.1 it includes *Computer* and *Writing* activities and *Labor*, *Wood chips*, *Chlorine*, and the three *$ tr* constraints. However, each of the three profit activities has been replaced by two utility activities, one for profit below $20,000 and one for profit above $20,000 (up to $60,000). What we are measuring with these activities is the psychological value (or utility) of different levels of profit. This psychological value is measured in imaginary units called *utils* rather than dollars. The model calculates the level of profit for each state of nature in the *$ tr* rows and then translates this profit into a number of utils in the objective function via the *Utility* activities. The relationship between the number of utils and the number of dollars is not linear, but has a corner at $20,000. For this reason we use the method for nonlinear relationships (Chapter 7) to represent the relationship in the model. That is why the matrix includes the three extra *Unit* constraints. As in previous models of this chapter, the objective function

TABLE 13.8 Matrix for Example 13.4

	Computer (tonnes)	Writing (tonnes)	Utility A-1 (Utils)	Utility A-2 (Utils)	Utility B-1 (Utils)	Utility B-2 (Utils)	Utility C-1 (Utils)	Utility C-2 (Utils)	Type	Limit
Objective (utils)			5,000	10,000	10,000	20,000	5,000	10,000	max	
Labor (days)	4	6							$\leq$	126
Wood chips (tonnes)	2	2							$\leq$	56
Chlorine (kg)	0.2857	1.5							$\leq$	24
\$ tr A (\$)	−600	−500	20,000	60,000					$\leq$	0
Unit A (−)			1	1					$\leq$	1
\$ tr B (\$)	−600	−1,000			20,000	60,000			$\leq$	0
Unit B (−)					1	1			$\leq$	1
\$ tr C (\$)	−600	−1,500					20,000	60,000	$\leq$	0
Unit C (−)							1	1	$\leq$	1

coefficients are weighted by their probabilities. For example, the coefficient for *Utility A-2* is calculated as .25 times the utility value of $60,000 profit, 40,000 utils (20,000 utils for the first $20,000 plus 20,000 utils for the next $40,000).

The optimal solution is shown in Table 13.9. Compared to Table 13.2 it includes less of the risky writing paper and more of the safe computer paper. You can calculate that the levels of profit for the three states of nature are $14,500, $20,000, and $25,500, compared with $13,300, $20,300, and $27,300 in the profit-maximizing version. Thus the risk-averse person prefers a strategy with a lower expected value of profit ($20,000 versus $20,300) in order to narrow the distribution of possible outcomes. Statistically, the probability distribution of profit for the risk-averse solution has a lower "variance."

Although we used a two-segment utility function for this model, one would expect the utility function to be smooth, becoming steadily flatter at higher profit levels. This can be approximated more accurately by including more segments in the utility function (i.e., more utility activities in the matrix).

Utility functions can take many forms. One convenient and commonly used function is

$$U = a + b \times [1 - \exp(-R \times \pi)]$$

TABLE 13.9   Optimal Solution for Example 13.4

Objective function value: 19,312.500000
Problem direction: max

Activity		Level	Shadow Cost
1 Computer	A	15.0000	0.0000
2 Writing	A	11.0000	0.0000
3 Utils A-1	A	0.7250	0.0000
4 Utils A-2	Z	0.0000	5000.0000
5 Utils B-1	A	1.0000	0.0000
6 Utils B-2	ZM	0.0000	0.0000
7 Utils C-1	A	0.8625	0.0000
8 Utils C-2	A	0.1375	0.0000

Constraint		Slack	Shadow Price
1 Labor	L	0.0000	93.7500
2 Wood chips	L	4.0000	0.0000
3 Chlorine	L	3.2143	0.0000
4 $ tr A	L	0.0000	0.2500
5 Unit A	L	0.2750	0.0000
6 $ tr B	L	0.0000	0.2500
7 Unit B	L	0.0000	5000.0000
8 $ tr C	L	0.0000	0.1250
9 Unit C	L	0.0000	2500.0000

where U is utility, R is the coefficient of risk aversion, π is profit, and a and b are parameters. Higher values of R correspond to higher risk aversion. The value of R varies widely between different people, depending on their wealth and personal attitudes. A realistic range of R for people in developed countries is probably between 1.0×10^{-7} and 1.0×10^{-4}. For people with very low wealth, R may be higher. The optimal solution is not affected by the values of a and b used, provided b is greater than zero. In practice it is useful to choose values for a and b such that the resulting utilities are not extremely small, which can be a problem for high levels of risk aversion. A safe approach is to choose a and b such that utilities are close to one.

For further background on the utility-based approach to decision making that underlies this model structure, see Raiffa (1968), Anderson et al. (1977), Gregory (1988), Gordon et al. (1990), Goodwin and Wright (1991), or one of the many other available texts on decision theory or decision analysis.

13.4 OTHER ISSUES

The simple models presented in this chapter each have only a single uncertain parameter. However, it is straightforward to represent multiple uncertain variables, by including states of nature for each possible combination of parameters (other than those with zero probability). For example, a model with three uncertain variables each with three possible values would have up to 27 states of nature.

The single-period models presented in this chapter can be extended to encompass multiple periods if desired. However, a potential problem in this case is the "curse of dimensionality," which refers to the way the model can become impractically large in multiperiod models that include risk. For example, if the preceding model with 27 states of nature is to be solved over two periods, there are 729 possible states of nature for the whole model. Depending on the nature of the problem, you may need to reproduce the set of constraints 729 times within the matrix. For problems with more than two periods, the matrix may be too large to solve on the available software, requiring some compromises and simplifications, such as reducing the number of constraints per period, the number of periods, or the number of states of nature modeled.

The methods presented here do not necessarily replace the need for the sensitivity-analysis techniques of Chapter 12. In many circumstances sensitivity analysis is still a useful approach for a model that includes risk explicitly. For example, if you use the UEP method presented in Section 13.3, you might conduct sensitivity analysis on the utility function used (the weightings given to good and bad outcomes). Alternatively, you may limit your explicit representation of risk to those parameters that you are unable to predict prior to making decisions. In this case, you could use sensitivity analysis to determine optimal solutions for different values of parameters whose values will become known in time to adjust the strategy. As a third example, you may have good information about the variance of a parameter, but not about its expected value. You could conduct sensitivity analysis looking at changes in the mean while holding the variance constant.

13.5 KEY POINTS

- The most practical methods of representing risk in LP models use discrete probability distributions. Variables with continuous probability distributions must be represented approximately using these methods.
- If the level of an activity must be decided before the state of nature is known, use a single column for the activity. This single column may have coefficients in the constraints for each state of nature.
- If the state of nature is known before deciding on the level of an activity, so that the strategy may be adjusted to suit the state of nature, represent the activity using a different column for each state of nature. Each of these columns probably only affects the constraints for its particular state of nature.
- It is possible to represent "risk aversion" in the objective, meaning that bad outcomes are given a higher weighting than good outcomes.

Exercises

13.1 Suppose that instead of price, one of the constraint limits of Example 3.1 (the availability of labor) is uncertain. Due to illnesses, the number of workers available may assume the following values: 126 (with probability .5), 125 (with probability .3), 124 (with probability .2). This represents the probability distribution of the constraint limit for *Labor*. Construct a matrix to calculate the activity levels that maximize the expected value of profit.

13.2 Adjust Example 3.1 so that both labor availability and chlorine output per tonne of writing paper are uncertain (but prices are certain). The joint probability distribution for these variables is given in Table 13.10. Values within the body of the table are probabilities. Construct a matrix to calculate the activity levels which maximize the expected value of profit.

TABLE 13.10

Chlorine Output (kg/tonne)	Labor Availability (days)	
	124	126
2.0	0.17	0.33
1.0	0.21	0.29

13.3 Adjust Example 13.2 so that prices are uncertain and imperfectly pre-dictable. The manager is able to forecast that the price will be either high or low. If the forecast is for a high price, there is a .67 probability that the actual price will be $1500 and a .33 probability that the actual price will be $1000. If the forecast is for a low price, the probabilities are .5 for $1000 and .5 for $500. There are thus four possible states of nature: high/$1500, high/$1000, low/$1000 and low/$500. However, you only need to allow for two alternative sets of activity levels for *Computer* and *Writing* because there are only two possible forecast val-ues. Allowing for this partial predictability, construct a matrix to cal-culate the activity levels that maximize the expected value of profit. In the long run, the manager expects to predict high prices one-third of the time and low prices the other two-thirds. Weight the objective function values to allow for these probabilities, so that the objective function measures the long-run expected value of profit.

13.4 Adjust Example 13.4 to allow for an additional segment in the utility function. Suppose that for profits above $25,000, the weighting given to an extra dollar is 0.25 times the weighting given to profits below $20,000. The weight for profits between $20,000 and $25,000 remains at 0.5. Construct a matrix to calculate the optimal activity levels in order to maximize the expected value of utility.

CHAPTER 14

FURTHER PRACTICAL ISSUES

There are many facets to the successful use of a linear programming (LP) model. In previous chapters we have covered matrix construction for various types of model, interpretation of the various elements of output, potential problems in the matrix or its output, and techniques for debugging and sensitivity analysis. This chapter is a brief look at some further practical issues that arise in the use of LP to address real-world problems. It includes a review of the strengths and weaknesses of LP as a decision-aiding technique. This discussion presumes that you, as the modeler, are working within an institution (e.g., a business or government department) where others are making decisions based in part on your model results and where other experts within the institution have information and experience that is valuable in developing and applying your model.

14.1 HAVING AN IMPACT

Communication and Credibility

Frequent communication to the client group will enhance the impact of your model. Involve relevant people throughout each phase of a modeling project: design, construction, testing, and use. Only then will your target audience have the knowledge of what you have done and the confidence in your approach and assumptions to be prepared to act on the results. The most important form of communication for achieving this credibility is face-to-face meetings and discussions.

Another important form of communication is model documentation. Thorough and up-to-date documentation is valuable for several purposes: informing your audience about the model, generating discussion and constructive criticism of the model's assumptions, demonstrating your competence and thoroughness, recording your achievements and activities, as well as the more obvious task of keeping a record of the details of the model. Maintain open access to your assumptions and a responsive attitude to any comments and criticisms received.

Publishing model results for a wider audience can also be beneficial in achieving more local goals. Such publications may take many forms: professional journal articles, magazine or newspaper articles, a book, and so on. If allowed by your institution, publications about your model serve to increase your credibility, to record your activities, to increase your audience, and provide an impetus for you to formally review your model and its findings. The process of publishing also opens up the model to a wider range of critical comments, which can only improve it in the long run.

Dealing with Criticisms

Always be prepared to respond to criticisms and suggestions. Even if you do not agree with some suggestions for change, it can be helpful from a public relations viewpoint to investigate their impact within the model with a sensitivity analysis. If you do adopt a suggestion, let the suggester know that you have done so and what impact it had. If you do not, let the suggester know why.

Not all criticism you receive will be helpful or even well intentioned. In some cases, criticisms can be disarmed by showing that changing the model to overcome the criticism has no significant impact on the model solution. Unconstructive criticisms come most commonly from people whose preconceptions or vested interests have been threatened by a model result, or from people who have had no direct involvement with the model.

Consider the question of how we obtain data for the model. In some cases we have sufficient data from previous experiences or from published information to make a good estimate of a parameter (or possibly of its probability distribution). Often, however, we only have good data for some of the parameters. For the others, we must use whatever information is available to help us make informed guesses about them. Ideally, the decision maker should be closely involved in this process. Sometimes, decision makers are uneasy about using subjectively estimated (''soft'') data in the model. You might try to counter these concerns by arguing that a model based on subjective data is better than no model at all. This is true for the following reasons:

(a) If the model is abandoned or ignored because of lack of ''hard'' data to estimate parameters, decisions will still be made subjectively.

(b) By making assumptions explicit, as you must do to build the model, you may enable different people to recognize the reasons for their dif-

fering views about the optimal strategy. The consequences and importance of different assumptions can be tested consistently and rigorously.

(c) Even if current parameters are not well known, by having the model
structure in place you are able to test which parameter estimates most
need to be improved (i.e., which parameters make the biggest difference
to the optimal solution).

14.2   STRENGTHS OF LINEAR PROGRAMMING

Flexibility and Wide Applicability

We have already seen how wide a range of topics can be addressed using LP.
Areas of actual use include manufacturing, finance, transport, storage, oil refining, blending, agriculture, forestry, engineering, economics, and personnel
management.

Even within these broad areas, there are many different potential roles and
modes of use for LP, including:

- Direct support for planners and decision makers. This is the role most
commonly emphasized in texts.

- Evaluation of priorities for applied research and development. This is
especially relevant given the diminishing availability of research funds.
A formal evaluation of research priorities not only allows more valuable
research to be targeted, but by demonstrating the likely value of the proposed research, it can increase the probability of obtaining funding for
the research.

- Provision of data and knowledge for public dissemination. LP models that
provide an economic dimension to what is otherwise technical or biological information can be especially valuable for increasing the value and
acceptance of that information.

- Provision of information to policy makers in government institutions. LP
has been widely used for this purpose in agriculture and natural resource
management.

- Direct control of an industrial or manufacturing process (without human
intervention). This is relatively rare, but does occur, for example, in some
systems for blending ingredients.

- Education. This includes not only education about LP as a technique, but
also education that uses LP models to illustrate and enliven other topics.

- Training of staff about the elements, structure, and management of a
particular system important to the organization.

- Integration and coordination of effort in an area. An LP model can be a
useful tool for bringing together the efforts of many people of different
professions and/or different disciplines. The process of building the model

requires the contributing participants to consider their area of responsibility within a broader perspective and to develop an appreciation of how they fit in with other areas of the organization.

- A database of quantitative information. An LP model provides a concise summary of the structure and elements of a system, and the coefficients estimated and collated in the process of building the model can often prove useful for a range of other unforeseen purposes.
- An aid to thinking and hypothesizing. A model can be a useful stimulus for intuition and a means of testing ideas.

It is worth noting that for at least the last five of these uses, much of the benefit of the model does not necessarily arise from its accuracy in representing the real world, but rather from the process of building and using the model. It has even been argued that a "bad" model can still have major benefits of these types (Hodges, 1991).

Ability to Represent Technical and Biological Relationships within a Management Framework

An LP model allows the modelers to put technical and biological information into an economic context and to quantify the economic, technical, and biological trade-offs in the system. Often a lot of information is collected about a system, but managers may not know how to integrate it into a system to allow them to make better management decisions. An LP model fills this need very well for many systems.

A Global Perspective on a Problem

Some management problems consist of component problems that have links and interactions between them. To adequately address these problems, managers need a tool that can simultaneously represent all the components and their linkages. The global perspective of an LP model used in this way also gets around the common difficulty of allocating costs between components of the system where inputs have benefits in more than one component. Within a global model, there is no need to make any allocation of costs between linked variables. All costs are assessed simultaneously without any need to say exactly which of the costs were the cause of particular benefits.

Optimization

A primary benefit of an LP model is the unexpected insights it reveals by virtue of its objective analysis of the options. Unlike humans, an LP model is free to consider all strategies without preconceptions or prejudices. This is particularly valuable in situations where the accepted wisdom on an issue is no longer applicable or where the complexity of an issue makes it very difficult to identify the true optimal solution. The other advantage of LP stemming from its optimization approach is the greater amount of information generated about values of resource and the relative performance of alternative activities.

Highlighting Data Deficiencies and Allowing Prioritization of Them

The process of developing an LP model has the effect of focusing attention on the least known aspects of the system. Furthermore, once an initial version has been completed, the model itself can contribute greatly to considerations about which of the unknown information is likely to make the greatest difference to profit and the selection of activities.

Bringing Different Groups of People Together

LP can play an important role in bringing together people of different disciplines, departments, and responsibilities. This coordinating and integrating role is usually not the primary reason for building a model and not the focus of the modelers involved, but it is often one of the major benefits that result.

Determining the Relative Importance of Issues

For models with poorly known parameters, the aim of modeling should be to help discern issues and strategies that are of different broad levels of importance: trivial, significant, or crucial. The ability of LP to contribute in this area is a major strength, given the fragmented and undisciplined thinking that otherwise often occurs.

Improved Understanding of the Management System

LP is valuable for developing an understanding of the subtleties and interactions of a complex management system. This role of educating managers about their own system is often a major benefit of building a model. Sometimes enlightenment is a painful and unwanted process, but overall the benefits of LP in this area are large, possibly having a greater long-term impact than the benefits from directly implementing the results of an LP model.

Linear versus Nonlinear Programming

Nonlinear programming (NLP) packages have dramatically improved in power and usability in recent years. Now, for small- to medium-sized models it is practical to use NLP rather than LP if a suitable package is available. Nevertheless, LP is far from dead as a technique because:

- LP is a useful stepping stone to NLP.
- LP is better able to solve very large models that are often built for practical problems.

- NLP is sometimes sensitive to the activity levels specified as "starting values" in an NLP run. Different starting values can result in a different "optimal" solution.
- LP packages are more widely available.

14.3 WEAKNESSES OF LINEAR PROGRAMMING

In practical terms, the issues that most texts list as the weaknesses or limitations of LP are usually of little or no significance. These issues were presented in Chapter 1 as being inherent in the assumptions of LP: divisibility of variables, linearity of Constraints, additivity, and non-negativity of activities. Dent et al. (1986, p. 196) observed that "the limitations imposed by the assumptions of linear programming are more perceived than real; given sufficient time and ingenuity it is possible to achieve a high degree of realism in representing a complex farm business."

Often the supposed limitations of LP are repeated too glibly and too un-questioningly. Some texts also mistakenly state that certainty of data is an assumption of LP. Nevertheless, there are some weaknesses in the use of LP to address practical problems. In general, the important limitations relate to the institutional environment in which the model is used and the people who use it.

Need for Skills and Knowledge

The skills and knowledge necessary to apply LP are attainable by most people. It is not a techique that requires outstanding aptitude or intellect. Nevertheless, a competent LP modeler does need to master a substantial amount of infor-mation and a range of skills, including human relations. This limits the extent to which an organization can implement an LP model even if it is recognized that such a model would be helpful for a particular problem. People with the required skills are in high demand and accordingly may be expensive. Hirshfeld (1990) argued that model-building skills are and will remain the factor most limiting the application of LP to real-world problems.

High Information Requirements

Often there is a severe lack of good-quality information for use in determining the parameters of a model. Thus, it may seem that a meaningful LP model cannot be built in a particular circumstance. However, using a modeling tech-nique with lower information requirements merely sidesteps the problem by producing lower quality information.

Rarely is the lack of information so profound that even subjective estimates of parameters cannot be made. As noted earlier, a model based on such esti-mates can be very valuable.

Danger of Misuse

Uninformed managers may be inclined to read too much into an individual model result. If the model is not based on very well-quantified and measured parameters, such an event could lead to dangerous and costly decisions being made on the basis of inadequate information. It is worth stressing again that the primary benefit of an LP model is not in providing a prescription for action but in improving understanding of the management issues and determining in broad terms the relative importance of different issues when deciding on a strategy. If managers understand this, they are unlikely to badly misuse model results.

Maintenance and Use of a Model Is Very Resource Hungry

Chapter 11 stressed that a large LP model requires an ongoing commitment of resources to maintain its credibility and usefulness. For example, a detailed model of around 400 columns and 300 constraints may require up to 0.5 person year per year for updating, debugging, reviewing data, improving model structure, and documenting (as well as normal usage to address current problems).

Success Depends on Support from the Hierarchy

The impact of an LP model in an institution is dependent on support from key people within the organization. As well as providing inputs of their expertise, managers need to encourage other key people to contribute fully. They also need to look for opportunities to use the model and encourage others to do so. An enlightened manager with a good modeler will involve the modeler in the thinking and planning processes of the organization. Without support of this kind, even good models can fall far short of their potential in generating benefits for the institution.

14.4 CONCLUDING COMMENTS

LP as a practical technique is coming of age. In 1990, Hirshfeld predicted that by the year 2000, the number of people applying mathematical programming in their work will have increased two to four times. If he is correct, this is by far the greatest absolute rate of increase in the number of LP users since it was first developed. This book is partly an attempt to cater to the many new nonspecialist LP users who do not need or want to know about the intricacies of the mathematics used to solve an LP model. Even without the mathematics, there is much to learn before you should make practical use of the technique. We hope with this book to have eased the learning process somewhat, allowing LP to be even more widely used.

APPENDIX: SOLUTIONS TO EXERCISES

Note that there is no single correct matrix for any problem. There are always several different approaches, all of which will give the same answer. The matrices presented here are suggestions that consider where in the text each exercise was set. For example, no negative coefficients are used in matrices for exercises from Chapter 5.

Chapter 2

2.1

X	Y	Objective Function Value
0.4286	1.4286	7.857143
0	1.75	7
1	0	5
0	0	0

2.2

X	Y	Objective Function Value
0	25	450
20	0	440
3.3333	16.6667	373.3333

2.3

X	Y	Objective Function Value
25	0	550
15	5	420
10	10	400
12	12	480

2.4

X	Y	Objective Function Value
0	5	5
3	0	3
3	0.5	3.5
0	0	0

2.5

X	Y	Objective Function Value
12	8	108
2.8571	17.1429	117.142857
0	40	240

2.6 Yes. New optimal solution: $X = 2.8571$, $Y = 17.1429$, objective function $= 122.857143$.

2.7 No. The optimal solution remains: $X = 2.8571$, $Y = 17.1429$, but the objective function increases to 174.285714

2.8

X	Y	Objective Function Value
100	25	5250
85.7143	42.8571	4714.285714
0	100	1000
100	0	5000
0	0	0

Chapter 5

5.1

	Sedans (vehicles)	Wagons (vehicles)	Type	Limit
Objective ($)	1,800	1,500	max	
Thru-put (−)	1.3333	1	≤	120.00
Tires (vehicles)	1	1	≤	110.00
Min sedan (vehicles)	1		≥	33.00
Min wagon (vehicles)		1	≥	20.00

5.2

	Radio (ads)	TV (ads)	Type	Limit
Objective ($)	20	150	max	
Budget ($)	100	700	≤	4,200
Radio max (ads)	1		≤	30
TV contract (ads)		1	≥	2

5.3

	Wheat (ha)	Barley (ha)	Oats (ha)	Lupins (ha)	M ewes (head)	X ewes (head)	Wethers (head)	Type	Limit
Objective ($)	120	105	100	118	21	18	12	max	
Labor (h/week)	0.02	0.02	0.02	0.025	0.005	0.005	0.002	≤	50
Land (ha)	1	1	1	1	0.4	0.4	0.25	≤	3,000
Finance ($)	40	35	35	42	3	3	2	≤	30,000
Cereal max (ha)	1	1	1					≤	2,000
Wheat mix (ha)	1							≤	1,500
Lupin max (ha)				1				≤	1,500
Ewe min (ewes)					1	1		≥	500

5.4

	Maths (h)	History (h)	Literature (h)	Type	Limit
Objective ($)	1	1	1	min	
Math min (marks)	1			$\geq$	30
Hist min (marks)		2		$\geq$	20
Litr min (marks)			0.5	$\geq$	5
Total min (marks)	1	2	0.5	$\geq$	70
Math max (marks)	1			$\leq$	60
Hist max (marks)		2		$\leq$	70
Litr max (marks)			0.5	$\leq$	55

The last three constraints are included as a precaution to prevent the mark for any one subject exceeding 100. Although they are slack in the solution to this model, they might be needed if the minimum required marks of some subjects are reduced.

5.5

	8 A.M. (No.)	10 A.M. (No.)	12 noon (No.)	2 P.M. (No.)	8 A.M. PT (No.)	10 A.M. PT (No.)	12 noon PT (No.)	2 P.M. PT (No.)	4 P.M. PT (No.)	Type	Limit
Objective (No.)	1	1	1	1	0.67	0.67	0.67	0.67	0.67	min	
8 A.M.-10 A.M. (No.)	1				1					≥	9
10 A.M.-12 noon (No.)	1	1			1	1				≥	7
12 noon-2 P.M. (No.)	1	1	1			1	1			≥	14
2 P.M.-4 P.M. (No.)	1	1	1	1			1	1		≥	8
4 P.M.-6 P.M. (No.)		1	1	1				1	1	≥	12
6 P.M.-8 P.M. (No.)			1	1					1	≥	4
PT eq (No.)					1	1	1	1	1	=	3

5.6

	Lupins (kg)	Oats (kg)	Hay (kg)	Wheat (kg)	Rock Phos (kg)	Type	Limit
Objective ($)	0.14	0.125	0.08	0.155	0.13	min	
MEnergy (MJ)	11.9	10.3	7.8	11.5		≥	14,740
CProtein (g)	219	54	85.5	58.5		≥	105,500
Phosphate (g)	2.88	3.06	2.16	2.61	150	≥	5,350
Hay max (kg)			1			≤	250
Intake (kg)	1	1	1	1	1	≤	1,700

5.7 (a) No effect. The constraint would be slack.

(b) Profit would increase by $1500, the shadow price of *Thru-put*.

(c) Nothing. There is slack on the *Tires* constraint.

(d) The contract on sedans.

(e) For every unit reduction in sedans, profit would increase by $200 (the shadow price of *Min sedan*).

(f) *Thru-put* is a less-than constraint. Increasing its constraint limit would have a positive impact on profit. *Min sedan* is a greater-than constraint. Increasing its constraint limit would have a negative impact on profit.

5.8 (a) 900, the value of the objective function.

(b) If the level of sales generated per radio advertisement were to increase by more than 1.43, radio advertising would be part of the optimal solution. Alternatively, if the company included radio advertising given its current productivity, the ads would reduce sales by 1.43 per radio advertisement (relative to the optimal solution).

(c) 0.2143, the shadow price of *Budget*.

(d) Reduce costs by $7 (from $100 to $93) per radio advertisement. This is determined by changing the coefficient in the matrix and re-solving the model on a trial-and-error basis.

5.9 (a) $4.62 per hectare, the shadow cost of *Barley*.

(b) $9.62 per hectare, the shadow cost of *Oats*.

(c) No.

(d) 39.2 hours (50 minus the slack on *Labor*).

(e) Yes. Extra land would generate $36.92 per hectare in returns (the shadow price of *Land*), allowing a net benefit of $6.92.

(f) The solution contains 6923 ewes, which is 6423 in excess of the minimum specified in *Ewe min*.

5.10 (a) 57.5 hours, the objective function value.

(b) 0.5 hour, the shadow price of *Math min*. This is valid because 1 hour studying mathematics is worth one mark.

(c) If the required mark for literature were to increase, each extra mark would require 1.5 extra hours of study. Alternatively, if the student studied more than 10 hours for literature, each extra hour of study would increase the total required study time by 0.75 hour (1 literature mark = 0.5 hour study).

(d) The amount by which each mark falls short of 100 percent.

(e) 0.5 hour, the shadow price of *Total min*.

(f) If the student obtains the minimum mark for each subject, the combined total is not sufficient. Extra study can most profitably be spent on history since the rate of marks per hour of study is highest.

5.11 (a) All three should be scheduled to start work at 4 P.M.

(b) 1, three times the shadow price on *PT eq*. Also can be determined by altering the constraint limit on *PT eq* and re-solving.

(c) To replace the part-time inspector no longer available at 4 P.M., an extra full-time inspector must be scheduled on at 2 P.M.

(d) A less-than; its shadow price is positive.

(e) 10 A.M. to 12 noon (2 idle), 2 P.M. to 4 P.M. (1 idle), 6 P.M. to 8 P.M. (3 idle). Indicated by the constraint slacks.

(f) An increase of one in the requirement for inspectors in this period would worsen the objective function by one unit.

5.12 (a) $171.96, the objective function value.

(b) 11.43 kg, the level of *Rock phos*.

(c) No. Wheat is already not part of the least expensive ration. Making it even more expensive will not change that.

(d) Yes. The fall of $0.02 is more than the shadow cost of *Wheat*.

(e) Each extra megajoule of energy would increase the total cost by $0.0116, the shadow price of *MEnergy*.

(f) Zero. There is slack on the *CProtein* constraint.

(g) Yes. The shadow price on *Hay max* is $0.012, indicating that it would be worth paying up to $0.092/kg for extra hay ($0.092 = $0.08 + $0.012).

Chapter 8

8.1 [*Shoe tr, Make shoes*] = −36; [*Shoe tr, Sell shoes*] = 2; [*Shoe tr, Limit*] = 0.

8.2 [*Wheat tr, Wheat 1*] = −1000; [*Wheat tr, Wheat 2*] = −1100; [*Wheat tr, Wheat 3*] = −975; [*Wheat tr, Sell wheat*] = 1000; [*Wheat tr, Limit*] = 0.

8.3 [*Objective, Buy trans*] = −120; [*Objective, Sell TV A*] = 250; [*Objective, Sell TV B*] = 300; [*Trans tr, Make trans*] = −1; [*Trans tr, Buy trans*] = −1; [*Trans tr, Sell TV A*] = 1; [*Trans tr, Sell TV B*] = 1; [*Trans tr, Limit*] = 0.

8.4

	Wood (m)	Wire (m)	Metal (m)	Type	Limit
Objective ($)	20	25	35	max	
Labor (days)	0.1	0.15	0.18	≤	100
Wood-wire (−)	−1	2		≤	0

8.5 Convert *Wood-wire* to an equals constraint.

8.6 **Only *Wood-wire* Constraint Shown**

	Wood (m)	Wire (m)	Metal (m)	Type	Limit
Wood-wire (−)	−1	2	2	≤	0

| Objective | A-B | A-D | B-D | B-C | D-E | E-C | C-E | C-G | E-G | Type | Limit |
	(km)	(-)	(-)	(-)	(-)	(-)	(-)	(-)	(-)	(-)	
Objective (km)	15	12	10	22	9	8	8	5	19	min	
A	1	1								=	1
B	-1		1	1						≤	0
C		-1		-1		-1	1	1		≤	0
D		-1	-1		1					≤	0
E					-1	1	-1		1	≤	0
G								1	1	=	1
B min	1									≥	1

| | Flow | 1-2 | 1-3 | 2-3 | 2-4 | 3-4 | 3-5 | 4-3 | 4-5 | Type | Limit |
	(ML)	(ML)	(ML)	(ML)	(ML)	(ML)	(ML)	(ML)	(ML)		
Objective (ML)	0.5	-0.16	-0.12	-0.12	-0.1	-0.12	-0.1	-0.12	-0.16	max	0
1 tr (ML)	-1	1	1							≤	0
2 tr (ML)		-1		1	1					≤	0
3 tr (ML)			-1	-1		1	1	-1		≤	0
4 tr (ML)					-1	-1		1	1	≤	0
5 tr (ML)	1						-1		-1	≤	0
1-2 max (ML)		1								≤	20
1-3 max (ML)			1							≤	12
2-3 max (ML)				1						≤	12
2-4 max (ML)					1					≤	15
3-4 max (ML)						1				≤	14
3-5 max (ML)							1			≤	15
4-3 max (ML)								1		≤	14
4-5 max (ML)									1	≤	18

8.9

	S1-D1 (Book)	S1-D2 (Book)	S1-D3 (Book)	S1-D4 (Book)	S2-D1 (Book)	S2-D2 (Book)	S2-D3 (Book)	S2-D4 (Book)	S3-D1 (Book)	S3-D2 (Book)	S3-D3 (Book)	S3-D4 (Book)	Type	Limit
Objective ($)	0.15	0.14	0.2	0.09	0.19	0.11	0.08	0.16	0.06	0.08	0.02	0.17	min	
Site1 max (Book)	1	1	1	1									≤	10,000
Site2 max (Book)					1	1	1	1					≤	25,000
Site3 max (Book)									1	1	1	1	≤	20,000
Depot1 min (Book)	1				1				1				≥	9,000
Depot2 min (Book)		1				1				1			≥	13,000
Depot3 min (Book)			1				1				1		≥	18,000
Depot4 min (Book)				1				1				1	≥	11,000

8.10

	Labor 0 (ML)	Labor 1 (ML)	Labor 2 (ML)	Labor 3 (ML)	Labor 4 (ML)	Hire Labor (ML)	Type	Limit
Objective (ML)	200	320	350	360	365	−50	max	
Labor tr (ML)	1	1	2	3	4	−1	≤	0
Land (ML)	1	1	1	1	1		≤	2

8.11

	Flow (car)	1-2 (car)	1-3 (car)	2-3 (car)	2-5 (car)	3-4 (car)	3-5 (car)	3-6 (car)	4-6 (car)	5-6 (car)	5-7 (car)	6-5 (car)	6-7 (car)	Type	Limit
Objective (car)	1													max	
1 tr (car)	−1	1	1											≤	0
2 tr (car)		−1		1	1									≤	0
3 tr (car)			−1	−1		1	1	1						≤	0
4 tr (car)						−1			1					≤	0
5 tr (car)					−1		−1			1	1	−1		≤	0
6 tr (car)								−1	−1	−1		1	1	≤	0
7 tr (car)	1										−1		−1	≤	0
1-2 max (car)		1												≤	30
1-3 max (car)			1											≤	40
2-3 max (car)				1										≤	15
2-5 max (car)					1									≤	20
3-4 max (car)						1								≤	20
3-5 max (car)							1							≤	20
3-6 max (car)								1						≤	12
4-6 max (car)									1					≤	24
5-6 max (car)										1				≤	25
5-7 max (car)											1			≤	45
6-5 max (car)												1		≤	25
6-7 max (car)													1	≤	30

8.12

	1yr fix 1 ($)	2yr fix 1 ($)	Savings 1 ($)	1yr fix 2 ($)	2yr fix 2 ($)	Savings 2 ($)	1yr fix 3 ($)	2yr fix 3 ($)	Savings 3 ($)	Type	Limit
Objective ($)					1.2544		1.08	1.12	1.06	max	
Yr 1 $ tr ($)	1	1	1							≤	250,000
Yr 2 $ tr ($)	−1.08		−1.06	1	1	1				≤	0
Yr 3 $ tr ($)		−1.2544		−1.08		−1.06	1	1		≤	0
Sav min 1 ($)	1	1	−3							≤	0
Sav min 2 ($)		1		1	1	−3				≤	0
Sav min 3 ($)					1		1	1	−3	≤	0
1fix min 1 ($)	−1	0.3								≤	0
1fix min 2 ($)		0.3		−1	0.3					≤	0
1fix min 3 ($)					0.3		−1	0.3		≤	0

305

8.13

	Board 1 (No.)	Board 2 (No.)	Cards 1 (No.)	Cards 2 (No.)	Dice 1 (No.)	Dice 2 (No.)	Full Sets (set)	Type	Limit
Objective (set)							1	max	
Hours 1 (h)	0.09		0.19		0.014			≤	40
Hours 2 (h)		0.15		0.21		0.011		≤	40
Board min (No.)	1	1					−1	≥	0
Cards min (No.)			1	1			−1	≥	0
Dice min (No.)					1	1	−1	≥	0

8.14

	PPW (3 ha)	PPW + Lu (3 ha)	PW (2 ha)	PW + Lu (2 ha)	WL (2 ha)	W (ha)	Sell Wheat (t)	Sell Lupin (t)	Sheep (No.)	Type	Limit
Objective ($)	−35	−35	−35	−35	−73	−35	110	102	18	max	100
Land (ha)	3	3	2	2	2	1				≤	100
Wheat tr (T)	−1.5	−1.5	−1.35	−1.35	−1.5	−1.2	1			≤	0
Lupin tr (T)	0.2			0.1	−1			1		≤	0
Sheep tr (no)	−9	−11	−4.5	−5.5					1	≤	0

8.15 (a) $5.00, the shadow cost of *Wire*.
(b) *Wire* level increased to 285.7 m. *Wood* level reduced to 571.5 m. This is found by altering the matrix and re-solving it.
(c) Optimal levels: *Wood*, 0; *Wire*, 0; *Metal*, 555.56. This is determined by altering the matrix and re-solving it.

8.16 (a) A-B-C-G
(b) The shortest route that includes *C-E* is 16 km longer than the optimal route. An alternative explanation might be "If the road from C to E could be shortened by 16 km, the shortest route would include *C-E*." However, this explanation is invalid because the road from C to E is only 8 km long and because any change in *C-E* would almost certainly affect *E-C*, with unpredictable effects. Shadow prices relate to only a single activity, but in the real world, both activities would change.
(c) *A* and *G* have no slack because they are equals constraints. *B*, *C*, *D*, and *E* have no slack because that would imply that the route involved arriving at one of these intermediate nodes but not leaving it. *B min* has no slack because it is a greater-than constraint that lengthens the route; slack on this constraint would imply that the route was being lengthened more than necessary.
(d) If the constraint limit of *D* was increased by one unit, the shortest route would be reduced by 5 km. However, this makes no sense since it implies that it would be possible to depart from D without needing to arrive there. The shadow price has no realistic interpretation.
(e) *A* is acting as a greater-than constraint. Without it, the shortest route would be 7 km shorter.
(f) *B* is not binding, but it has a slack of zero.
(g) Not at all. The shadow cost of *B-D* is 5.
(h) The optimal route would be A-B-D-E-C-G. This is determined by increasing the objective function value of *B-C* by 6 and re-solving the model.

8.17 (a) The objective of maximizing flow regardless of economic considerations results in a level of flow that is greater than that which maximizes profit. In Table 8.7, the model includes a level of 2 for *3-4*, which is absent in the profit-oriented model.
(b) The amount of water flow along a pipe in megaliters per hour.
(c) The flow of water along a route is limited by the pipe with the lowest flow capacity. Also, in the case of pipe *3-4*, the economic benefits of running the pipe are less than the costs, even though it would increase total flow.
(d) *2-3* should not be upgraded. It already has unused capacity. Pipe *3-5* should be upgraded as long as the cost of doing so is less than the gain of $0.28 per hour (the gross benefit). *1-3* may have a

higher priority, as it has a gross benefit of $0.78 per hour. These benefits are calculated by altering and re-solving the model.

(e) Each shadow price for a transfer row gives the benefit in dollars of an extra megaliter per hour becoming available at the node. This is not realistic, as it does not account for the need to pump the water to the node.

(f) Each shadow price for a "max" row gives the marginal gross benefit of increasing the pipe capacity.

8.18 (a) Cost of delivery from site 1 to depot 1 less than $0.05 per book.

(b) Optimal levels: *S1-D1*, 7000; *S1-D4*, 3000; *S2-D2*, 13,000; *S2-D4*, 8000; *S3-D1*, 2000; *S3-D3*, 18,000. Determined by altering the re-solving the model.

(c) Each unit increase in the availability of books at site 1 decreases the minimum cost by $0.07.

(d) Each unit increase in the requirement for books at depot 1 increases the minimum cost by $0.12.

(e) There are 4000 spare books at site 2 after all requirements at the depots have been met.

8.19 (a) *Labor 1* is in hectares. It indicates that the area of land for which one hour of labor is hired is 2 ha. *Hire labor* is in hours. A total of 2 hours of labor is hired.

(b) The shadow costs of *Labor 0*, *Labor 2*, *Labor 3*, and *Labor 4* indicate how much less profitable per hectare it would be to hire the corresponding level of labor rather than one hour per hectare.

(c) If the constraint limit of *Labor tr* were increased by one (representing a costless increase in labor availability by one hour), profit would increase by $50 due to a lower requirement for hiring labor.

(d) The level of *Hire labor* would decrease by one unit.

8.20 (a) Approximately 263, the level of *Full sets*.

(b) 40 at each factory. This is indicated by the slacks of zero for *Hours 1* and *Hours 2*.

(c) Factory 1: 0.19 hours per pack of cards (from the matrix) × 86.0568 (the level of *Cards 1*) = 16.35 hours. Factory 2: 0.21 hours per pack of cards (from the matrix) × 176.7121 (the level of *Cards 2*) = 37.11 hours.

(d) Because the productivity of the workers is different at the two factories (see the different coefficients for each factory in the matrix). Labor has a higher marginal value at factory 1, so it would be the preferred site for extra workers.

(e) If it were possible to obtain extra units of the individual components from another source, the absolute value of the shadow prices indicate the maximum prices it be worth paying to obtain them at the margin.

Chapter 9

9.1 (a) Yes.

(b) The shadow cost indicates that if the objective function value of *Wire* increased by more than $5, it would be included in the solution. The range analysis shows that if the objective function value increased from $25 to more than $30, it would alter the solution. These are equivalent.

(c) The shadow cost of zero for *Wood* indicates only that it is active in the solution, whereas the range analysis indicates how far the objective function value can vary without changing the solution.

(d) The constraint limit of *Wood-wire* can be increased indefinitely without affecting the optimal solution. This is because it is a less-than constraint that already has slack in the optimal solution.

(e) No matter how much additional labor is obtained, the optimal basis will remain unchanged: it will include *Wood* but not *Wire* or *Metal*. The labor constraint will continue to be binding, as it will be used to produce wood fencing.

9.2 (a) No matter how much less expensive it becomes to transport water along these pipes, the optimal strategy would not change. This is true even if the cost becomes negative.

(b) For any reduction in the capacity of the *2-4* pipe down to zero, the optimal basis would not change. The shadow price indicates that each unit reduction in flow capacity of the 2-4 pipe would reduce profits by $0.08.

(c) The *Flow* activity has a positive objective function value, reflecting the gross benefit per unit of flow. The range analysis is for variations in this positive return. The other activities have negative objective function coefficients reflecting the cost of pumping. Their range analysis results are for variations in these costs, or negative benefits.

(d) No.

(e) Yes. $0.72

(f) Yes.

(g) Yes. $1.36

(h) No. There is slack on both constraints, *1-2 max* and *4-5 max*.

9.3 (a) If the cost of delivering telephone books from site 1 to depot 3 fell to below $0.05 per book, the optimal strategy would change to include *S1-D3*.

(b) For the solution to change to include more than 9000 of *S3-D1*, the cost of delivery from site 3 to depot 1 would have to become negative.

(c) Because *S1-D4* is already selected at the highest possible level given the constraint limit of *Site max*.

(d) No.

(e)   Yes.

(f)   *S2-D2* increases to 15,000.

9.4 (a)   Optimal activity levels would not change, although the objective function would decrease.

(b)   The level of hired labor would increase to a total of 4 and *Labor 2* would replace *Labor 1* in the solution.

(c)   If the net return from hiring 3 hours of labor per hectare increased to more than $420, *Labor 3* would enter the solution. Note, however, that the returns for *Labor 4* would probably also need to be adjusted, and may potentially become preferred to *Labor 3*.

(d)   For any positive area of land, the optimal basis would be unchanged.

Chapter 10

10.1 Degeneracy

10.2 No feasible solution

10.3 Unboundedness

10.4 Degeneracy

10.5 Multiple optimal solutions and degeneracy

10.6 Multiple optimal solutions

Chapter 13

13.1

	Computer A (tonnes)	Writing A (tonnes)	Profit A ($)	Computer B (tonnes)	Writing B (tonnes)	Profit B ($)	Computer C (tonnes)	Writing C (tonnes)	Profit C ($)	Type	Limit
Objective ($)			0.5			0.3			0.2	max	
Labor A (days)	4	6								≤	126
Wood chips A (tonnes)	2	2								≤	56
Chlorine A (kg)	0.2857	1.5								≤	24
$ tr A ($)	−600	−1,000	1							≤	0
Labor B (days)				4	6					≤	125
Wood chips B (tonnes)				2	2					≤	56
Chloine B (kg)				0.2857	1.5					≤	24
$ tr B ($)				−600	−1,000	1				≤	0
Labor C (days)							4	6		≤	124
Wood chips C (tonnes)							2	2		≤	56
Chlorine C (kg)							0.2857	1.5		≤	24
$ tr C ($)							−600	−1,000	1	≤	0

13.2

	Computer AA (tonnes)	Writing AA (tonnes)	Profit AA ($)	Computer AB (tonnes)	Writing AB (tonnes)	Profit AB ($)	Computer BA (tonnes)	Writing BA (tonnes)	Profit BA ($)	Computer BB (tonnes)	Writing BB (tonnes)	Profit BB ($)	Type	Limit
Objective ($)			0.17			0.33			0.21			0.29	max	
Labor AA (days)	4	6											≤	124
Wood chips AA (tonnes)	2	2											≤	56
Chlorine AA (kg)	0.2857	2											≤	24
$ tr AA ($)	−600	−1,000	1										≤	0
Labor AB (days)				4	6								≤	126
Wood chips AB (tonnes)				2	2								≤	56
Chlorine AB (kg)				0.2857	2								≤	24
$ tr AB ($)				−600	−1,000	1							≤	0
Labor BA (days)							4	6					≤	124
Wood chips BA (tonnes)							2	2					≤	56
Chlorine BA (kg)							0.2857	1					≤	24
$ tr BA ($)							−600	−1,000	1				≤	0
Labor BB (days)										4	6		≤	126
Wood chips BB (tonnes)										2	2		≤	56
Chlorine BB (kg)										0.2857	1		≤	24
$ tr BB ($)										−600	−1,000	1	≤	0

13.3

	Computer High (tonnes)	Writing High (tonnes)	Profit H1 ($)	Profit H2 ($)	Computer Low (tonnes)	Writing Low (tonnes)	Profit L1 ($)	Profit L2 ($)	Type	Limit
Objective ($)			0.222	0.111			0.333	0.333	max	
Labor Hi (days)	4	6							≤	126
Wood chips Hi (tonnes)	2	2							≤	56
Chlorine Hi (kg)	0.2857	1.5							≤	24
$ tr H1 ($)	−600	−1,500	1						≤	0
$ tr H2 ($)	−600	−1,000		1					≤	0
Labor Lo (days)					4	6			≤	126
Wood chips Lo (tonnes)					2	2			≤	56
Chlorine Lo (kg)					0.2857	1.5			≤	24
$ tr L1 ($)					−600	−1,000	1		≤	0
$ tr L2 ($)					−600	−500		1	≤	0

313

13.4

	Computer (tonnes)	Writing (tonnes)	Utility A-1 (Utils)	Utility A-2 (Utils)	Utility A-3 (Utils)	Utility B-1 (Utils)	Utility B-2 (Utils)	Utility B-3 (Utils)	Utility C-1 (Utils)	Utility C-2 (Utils)	Utility C-3 (Utils)	Type	Limit
Objective ($)			5,000	5,625	8,625	10,000	11,250	17,250	5,000	5,625	8,625	max	
Labor (days)	4	6										$\leq$	126
Wood chips (tonnes)	2	2										$\leq$	56
Chlorine (kg)	0.2857	1.5										$\leq$	24
$ tr A ($)	−600	−500	20,000	25,000	73,000							$\leq$	0
Unit A (−)			1	1	1							$\leq$	1
$ tr B ($)	−600	−1,000				20,000	25,000	73,000				$\leq$	0
Unit B (−)						1	1	1				$\leq$	1
$ tr C ($)	−600	−1,500							20,000	25,000	73,000	$\leq$	0
Unit C (−)									1	1	1	$\leq$	1

GLOSSARY

Accounting activity An activity included in the matrix for the purpose of counting the level of a particular factor.

Active An activity that has a level greater than zero in the optimal solution is active. An activity that is not active is always at zero level. However, where there is degeneracy, it is possible for an activity to be active at zero level.

Activity A decision variable whose optimal level is to be determined. Represented as a column in an LP matrix.

Additivity An assumption inherent in LP that the effects of any two variables on the objective value or the level of resource use can be added together to obtain the combined effect.

Aim Maximization or minimization.

Algebraic Using algebra to represent a mathematical relationship. For example $3A + 4B \geq 10$.

Algorithm A sequence of mathematical steps used to solve a particular type of problem. The simplex algorithm is used for LP.

Artificial activities Activities that do not represent real decision variables, but that are added to a matrix to help it solve or to help diagnose an infeasibility problem.

Artificial variables See **Artificial activities.**

Basic activities Selected activities. Those activities that are part of the current optimal solution (i.e., the basis). Usually a basic activity has a value greater than zero, but in cases of degeneracy it has a zero value.

Basic constraints   Selected constraints. Those constraints that have slack in the current optimal solution. Usually a basic constraint has a slack value greater than zero, but in cases of degeneracy it has a zero value.

Basis   Used as a shorthand for **optimal basis.** A set that includes all activities that are part of the optimal solution and all constraints that are slack. Also has a similar meaning in solutions that are not optimal.

Binding   Limiting. A binding or limiting constraint has no slack, and any change in the constraint limit would have an immediate and direct impact on the optimal solution.

Bound   A special sort of constraint acting on an individual activity. Not available in all LP packages. More efficient than a standard constraint, but does not produce shadow price in output.

Break-even analysis   A series of model runs to determine by how much a parameter or group of parameters needs to change before the optimal solution will change in a particular way.

Bug   An error or suspected error in the matrix.

Cell   A single element of the LP matrix. The intersection of a row and a column. A cell contains a numeric coefficient that may be zero, positive, or negative, but must be represented as a decimal number with a finite number of decimal places.

Coefficient   Parameter. A number in the matrix. There are coefficients in the objective function row, in the constraint limit column, and in the main body of the matrix. A coefficient may be zero, positive, or negative, but must be represented as a decimal number with a finite number of decimal places.

Column   An activity or decision variable.

Constraint   A limit on the selection of activities. Can be stated as an algebraic equality or inequality. Represented as a row in an LP matrix.

Constraint limit   The value for each constraint that must be at least met, exactly met, or not exceeded.

Concave down   A curve or shape that goes up and then down (e.g., lower case letter n, Greek character Λ, the side view of a bell). Means the same as **convex up.**

Concave up   A curve or shape that goes down and then up (e.g., letter U, letter V, the side view of a cup). Means the same as **convex down.**

Convex down   A curve or shape that goes down and then up (e.g., letter U, letter V, the side view of a cup). Means the same as **concave up.**

Convex up   A curve of shape that goes up and then down (e.g., lower case letter n, Greek character Λ, the side view of a bell). Means the same as **concave down.**

Debugging   The process of testing and changing a model to remove any errors.

Decision variable   A factor whose optimal level must be determined. Also referred to as **activities** or **columns.**

Degenerate activity A redundant constraint allows an activity to be selected as part of the optimal solution, but at zero level. The degenerate activity is part of the basis, but its optimal value is zero.

Degenerate constraint A redundant constraint can result in a constraint being selected to have slack in the optimal solution but the level of slack is zero. The degenerate constraint is part of the basis, but its level of slack is zero.

Degenerate solution A solution that includes a degenerate activity or a degenerate constraint.

Deterministic model A model that represents all parameters as fixed values, not as probability distributions.

Diagnosis An explanation of the cause of a bug.

Discrete A finite, countable number of outcomes or levels of a parameter. Different to a ''continuous'' probability distribution in which the variable can take on any of an infinite number of values (e.g., a normal distribution). (Discrete probability distribution or discrete number of outcomes).

Discrete stochastic programming A method for representing risk and uncertainty in LP models. Uses discrete probability distributions for risky variables.

Divisible Can be divided

Dual price Term used in some texts for **shadow price.**

Equals A constraint that sets a value of some factor that must be exactly met.

Equation An algebraic statement that the level of some factor must be exactly equal to some value.

Expected value The mean or weighted average of a probability distribution.

Factor Resource, input, or output that is the subject of a constraint.

Feasible All constraints of the model are satisfied.

Feasible region The set of activity combinations that satisfy all the model's constraints.

Feasible set The set of solutions that meets all constraints of the model.

Feasible solution A solution in which all constraints are met.

Forcing substructure A subset of constraints of an LP model that predetermine the level of an activity. The level of the activity is unaffected by its objective function value.

Function A mathematical relationship saying how the value of one variable is calculated from the values of other variables.

Greater-than In LP this is short for ''greater than or equal to.'' It is impossible to represent a strictly greater-than constraint because all activities are perfectly divisible. A greater-than constraint sets a minimum value for some factor.

Implicit cost Term used in some texts for **shadow cost.**

Inequality In the context of LP, an inequality is an algebraic statement that the level of some factor must be (a) greater-than or equal to or (b) less-than or equal to some value.

Infeasible At least one constraint of the model is violated.

Infeasible constraint A constraint that is violated.

Infeasible solution A solution that includes an infeasible constraint.

Integer A whole number with no decimal figures; that is, no fractional part.

Integer programming A version of LP in which it is possible to specify that some activities can only take on integer values.

Irreducible infeasible subsystem The smallest subset of constraints from an infeasible model that remains infeasible. If *any* of the constraints of the irreducible infeasible subsystem are dropped, the model becomes feasible.

Isolation In debugging, identification of a section of the matrix in which the problem occurs. Isolation is usually needed before an explanation can be made.

Iteration In the simplex method, the optimal solution is identified by a cyclical step-by-step process of testing various combinations of the activities. An iteration refers to one cycle of this process.

Less-than In LP this is short for "less than or equal to." It is impossible to represent a strictly less-than constraint because all activities are perfectly divisible. A less-than constraint sets a maximum value for some factor.

Level The number of units of an activity in the optimal solution.

Limit Constraint limit or right-hand-side term.

Limiting Binding. A binding or limiting constraint has no slack, and any change in the constraint limit would have an immediate and direct impact on the optimal solution.

Linear Capable of being represented by a straight line. Of constant slope. Not curved.

Linear programming A mathematical technique for selecting the levels of decision variables which maximize or minimize an objective while satisfying a set of linear constraints.

Loosen Make a constraint less binding. Increase the constraint limit of a less-than constraint or decrease the constraint limit of a greater-than constraint.

Lower limit The "Lower limit" and "Upper limit" indicate the range within which constraint limits can be changed without altering the "basis" (i.e., the set of activities having positive values and constraints having positive slacks in the optimal solution), the shadow costs, or the shadow prices. The activity levels and constraint slacks do, however, change.

Lower objective The "Lower objective" and "Upper objective" indicate the range within which the objective function value for each activity can be changed without affecting activity levels and slack values in the optimal solution. Shadow costs and shadow prices do, however, change.

Marginal change A small change, usually to an objective function coefficient or a constraint limit. Shadow costs and shadow prices apply to marginal changes.

Marginal cost Term used in some texts for **shadow cost.**

Marginal value Term used in some texts for **shadow price.**

Mathematical programming A class of mathematical techniques including LP, nonlinear programming, and integer programming.

Matrix A table of numbers. An LP matrix has a particular structure. (Plural: matrices.)

Maximize Find the highest possible (or feasible) value.

Meet If a constraint is met, it means that it is satisfied or feasible. The level of the factor is consistent with the constraint.

Minimize Find the lowest possible (or feasible) value.

Model A simplified representation of a system. In LP the model is captured by the LP matrix.

MPS A format for storing the coefficients of an LP matrix on disk. Includes row names, column names, constraint types, and coefficient values in a precise but inefficient structure.

Multiple optimal solutions A set of solutions that each give the best feasible value of the objective function.

Negative coefficient A number in the LP matrix that is less than zero.

Nonlinear Curved. Not straight.

Nonlinear programming A technique for solving problems in which one or more constraints or the objective function is nonlinear.

Non-negativity constraints The implicit, and often unstated, constraints included in every LP model that the value of each activity in the optimal solution must be greater than or equal to zero.

Objective The aim of the model. The criterion used to select between alternative feasible solutions.

Objective function An equation that calculates the level of the factor being minimized or maximized.

Objective function coefficient The coefficient in the objective function row for an individual column of the matrix.

Objective function value Same as **objective function coefficient.** Sometimes used to refer to the total value of the objective function.

Objective function line A line representing the objective function in a graphical LP solution.

Opportunity cost The returns from other potential activities that must be foregone in order to undertake the activity in question. Some texts use the term in the way we have defined a shadow cost, but this is not consistent with the usual usage of the term in economics.

Optimum   Maximum or minimum, depending on the objective. The solution that provides the best possible value of the objective function.

Optimal basis   A set that includes all activities that are part of the optimal solution and all constraints that are slack.

Optimal solution   The activity levels, shadow costs, constraint slacks, and shadow prices associated with the highest or lowest feasible value of the objective function.

Optimize   Find the feasible solution that, of all the feasible solutions, has the highest or lowest (depending on the objective) value of the objective function.

Output   A table showing the optimal solution for an LP model.

Parameter   Coefficient. A numeric value in the matrix. A parameter may be zero, positive, or negative, but must be represented as a decimal number with a finite number of decimal places.

Parametric programming   A version of LP in which the value of a constraint limit or objective function coefficient is altered over a range. A new optimal solution is printed each time the optimal basis changes. Similar to an automated version of **sensitivity analysis,** except that in parametric programming changes are limited to a single parameter at a time.

Quadratic   An equation in which the highest powered term is a square, e.g., $Y = a + bX + cX^2$.

Range analysis   Output showing (1) ranges within which objective values can be changed without changing the optimal basis, and (2) ranges within which constraint limits can be changed without changing the basis. Sometimes referred to as **sensitivity analysis.**

Reduced cost   Term used in some texts for **shadow cost.**

Relax   Increase the constraint limit of a less-than constraint, or decrease the limit for a greater-than.

Restraint   **A constraint.**

Revised simplex method   A version of the simplex method that is more reliable for large LP models.

Right-hand-side term   The lower limit, upper limit, or exact limit of a constraint.

Risk aversion   An attitude that greater weight should be put on bad outcomes than on good outcomes. A risk-averse decision maker would be willing to sacrifice some of the expected value of a benefit to reduce uncertainty about the size of the benefit.

Risk programming   A group of techniques for explicitly representing risk and uncertainty in LP or nonlinear programming models. Also called **stochastic programming.**

Row   A constraint.

Run   A model solution or series of solutions generated by a computer package.

Satisfied Said of a constraint that is feasible. The level of the factor is consistent with the constraint.

Scale Measure a row or column in a different unit. The coefficients of the row or column are multiplied or divided by a factor.

Selected activities Basic activities. Activities that are part of the current optimal solution (i.e., the basis). Usually a selected activity has a value greater than zero, but in cases of degeneracy it has a zero value.

Selected constraints Basic constraints. Constraints that have slack in the current optimal solution. Usually a selected constraint has a slack value greater than zero, but in cases of degeneracy it has a zero value.

Sensitivity analysis A series of solutions investigating the impact of changing coefficients of the model or its structure. (In some other texts or computer packages, **range analysis** or **shadow costs/shadow prices.**)

Shadow cost Increase in objective value required for an activity to enter the optimal solution. Cost of forcing selection of an activity.

Shadow price Change in the objective function from a one unit change in the limit of a constraint. (Note that the term is used in some texts for **shadow cost**).

Simplex method A mathematical technique used to solve LP models on a computer.

Slack Amount by which constraint limit is exceeded or undershot in the optimal solution.

Solution See **Optimal solution.**

Solve Find the optimal solution.

Spreadsheet A type of software package consisting of a table of cells that can contain numbers or formulas. Useful for several purposes in LP modeling.

Stability analysis Sensitivity analysis.

State of nature One set of observations for a set of random variables. In a stochastic programming model, each state of nature corresponds to a particular set of values for the uncertain parameters.

Stochastic programming A group of techniques for explicitly representing risk and uncertainty in LP or nonlinear programming models. Also called **risk programming.**

Subjective The result of an educated guess. Estimated. Not based on precise measurement.

Successive bounding A facility available in some LP software that, in some cases, detects infeasibility.

Tangent A line that only touches the boundary of a region. It does not cross any point of the interior of the region.

Tighten Make a constraint more binding. Decrease the constraint limit of a less-than constraint or increase the constraint limit of a greater-than constraint.

Transfer row   A constraint linking two activities by use of negative coefficients.

Type   The direction of a constraint (greater than, less than, or equal to).

Unbounded   A model is unbounded if it includes a favorable activity that can be selected without limit. There is no constraint preventing an infinite number of units of the activity.

Units   Units of measurement. The scale used to measure activities or constraints (e.g., kilograms, dollars, days).

Upper limit   The "Lower limit" and "Upper limit" indicate the range within which constraint limits can be changed without altering the "basis" (i.e., the set of activities having positive values and constraints having positive slacks in the optimal solution), the shadow costs, or the shadow prices. The activity levels and constraint slacks do, however, change.

Upper objective   The "Lower objective" and "Upper objective" indicate the range within which the objective function value for each activity can be changed without affecting activity levels and slack values in the optimal solution. Shadow costs and shadow prices do, however, change.

Utility   Pleasure or satisfaction felt by a person. In a person who is "risk averse," the utility gained from extra income diminishes with increasing income.

Utility efficient programming   A version of discrete stochastic programming that can represent risk aversion.

Utils   Imaginary units used to measure utility.

Validation   The process of checking whether the problem definition is inconsistent with the real world.

Variable   An activity. A column of a matrix.

Verification   The process of checking whether the matrix is inconsistent with the problem definition.

Violated   Not satisfied. The level of the factor is inconsistent with the constraint limit.

Whole number   A number with no fractional part (e.g., 33 or 1, but not 5.67).

REFERENCES

Alexander, E. R. (1989). Sensitivity analysis in complex decision models, *Journal of the American Planning Association* 55: 323–333.

Anderson, J. R., Dillon, J. L., and Hardaker, J. B. (1977). *Agricultural Decision Analysis*, Iowa State University Press, Ames.

Baird, B. F. (1989). *Managerial Decisions Under Uncertainty, An Introduction to the Analysis of Decision Making*, Wiley, New York.

Beare, G. C. (1987). Linear programming in air defence modelling, *Journal of the Operational Research Society* 38: 899–905.

Boisvert, R. N., and McCarl, B. (1990). *Agricultural Risk Modeling Using Mathematical Programming*, Bulletin No. 356, Southern Cooperative Series, Department of Agricultural Economics, Cornell University, Ithaca, New York.

Canova, F. (1995). Sensitivity analysis and model evaluation in simulated dynamic general equilibrium economies, *International Economic Review* 36: 477–501.

Chinneck, J. W. (1992). Viability analysis: A formulation aid for all classes of network models, *Naval Research Logistics* 39: 531–543.

Chinneck, J. W., and Dravnieks, E. W. (1991). Locating minimal infeasible constraint sets in linear programs, *ORSA Journal on Computing* 3: 157–168.

Clemson, B., Tang, Y., Pyne, J., and Unal, R. (1995). Efficient methods for sensitivity analysis, *System Dynamics Review* 11: 31–49.

Dantzig, G. B. (1963). *Linear Programming and Extensions*, Princeton University Press, Princeton, N.J.

Debrosse, C. J., and Westerberg, A. W. (1973). A feasible-point algorithm for structured design systems in chemical engineering, *American Institute of Chemical Engineering Journal* 19: 251–258.

Dent, J. B., Harrison, S. R., and Woodford, K. B. (1986). *Farm Planning with Linear Programming: Concept and Practice*, Butterworths, Sydney.

Dorfman, R., Samuelson, P., and Solow, R. (1958). *Linear Programming and Economic Analysis.* McGraw-Hill Kogakusha, Tokyo.

Duloy, J. H., and Norton, R. D. (1975). Prices and incomes in linear programming models, *American Journal of Agricultural Economics* 57: 591–600.

Eschenbach, T. G., and McKeague, L. S. (1989). Exposition on using graphs for sensitivity analysis, *The Engineering Economist* 34: 315–333.

Eschenbach, T. G., and Gimpel, R. J. (1990). Stochastic sensitivity analysis, *The Engineering Economist* 35: 305–321.

Fabozzi, F. J., and Daddio, R. (1977). A linear programming salary evaluation model for high school personnel, *Operational Research Quarterly*, 28: 401–413.

Fiacco, A. V. (1983). *Introduction to Sensitivity and Stability Analysis in Nonlinear Programming*, Academic Press, New York.

French, S. (1992). Mathematical programming approaches to sensitivity calculations in decision analysis, *Journal of the Operational Research Society* 43: 813–819.

GAMS (1988). *GAMS*, The Scientific Press, Redwood City, Calif.

Gass, S. I. (1983). Decision-aiding models—Validation, assessment and related issues, *Operations Research* 31: 603–631.

Glen, J. (1980). A mathematical programming approach to beef feedlot optimization, *Management Science* 26: 524–535.

Goodwin, P., and Wright, G. (1991). *Decision Analysis for Management Judgement*, Wiley, Chichester, England.

Gordon, G., Pressman, I., and Cohn, S. (1990). *Quantitative Decision Making for Business*, 3rd ed., Prentice Hall, Englewood Cliffs, N.J.

Gosselin, K., and Truchon, M. (1986). Allocation of classrooms by linear programming, *Journal of the Operational Research Society* 37: 561–569.

Greenberg, H. J. (1993a). How to analyze the results of linear programs—Part 1: Preliminaries, *Interfaces* 23(4): 56–67.

Greenberg, H. J. (1993b). How to analyze the results of linear programs—Part 2: Price interpretation, *Interfaces* 23(5): 97–114.

Greenberg, H. J. (1993c). How to analyze the results of linear programs—Part 3: Infeasibility diagnosis, *Interfaces* 23(6): 120–139.

Greenberg, H. J. (1994). How to analyze the results of linear programs—Part 4: Forcing substructures, *Interfaces* 24(1): 121–130.

Gregory, G. (1988). *Decision Analysis*, Pitman, London.

Hall, N., and Menz, K. (1985). Product supply elasticities for the Australian broadacre industries estimated with a programming model, *Review of Marketing and Agricultural Economics* 53: 6–13.

Hamby, D. M. (1994). A review of techniques for parameter sensitivity analysis of environmental models, *Environmental Monitoring and Assessment* 32: 135–154.

Hardaker, J. B., Pandey, S., and Patten, L. H. (1991). Farm planning under uncertainty: A review of alternative programming models, *Review of Marketing and Agricultural Economics* 59: 9–22.

Harrison, G. W., and Vinod, H. D. (1992). The sensitivity analysis of applied general equilibrium models: Completely randomised factorial sampling designs, *The Review of Economics and Statistics* 74: 357–362.

Hazell, P. B. R. (1971). A linear alternative to quadratic and semivariance programming for farm planning under uncertainty, *American Journal of Agricultural Economics* 53: 53–62.

Hipel, K. W. (ed.) (1992). *Multiple Objective Decision Making in Water Resources*, American Water Resources Association, Bethesda, Md.

Hirshfeld, D. S. (1990). Some thoughts on math programming practice in the '90s, *Interfaces* 20(4): 158–165.

Hodges, J. S. (1991). Six (or so) things you can do with a bad model, *Operations Research* 39: 355–365.

Hoffman, F. O. and Gardner, R. H. (1983). Evaluation of uncertainties in environmental radiological assessment models, In *Radiological Assessments: A Textbook on Environmental Dose Assessment*, J. E. Till and H. R. Meyer (eds.), US Nuclear Regulatory Commission, Washington, D.C., Report No. NUREG/CR-3332, pp. 11.1–11.55.

Hwang, C. L., and Masud, A. S. M. (1979). *Multiple Objective Decision Making, Methods and Applications: A State-of-the-Art Survey*, Springer-Verlag, Berlin.

Jorgenson, D. W. (1984). Econometric methods for applied general equilibrium analysis. In *Applied General Equilibrium Analysis*, H. E. Scarf and J. B. Shoven (eds.), Cambridge University Press, Cambridge, pp. 139–203.

Kent, B., Bare, B., Field, R., and Bradley, G. (1991). Natural resource land management planning using large-scale linear programs: The USDA Forest Service experience with FORPLAN, *Operations Research* 39: 13–27.

Kingwell, R. S. (1994). Risk attitude and dryland farm management, *Agricultural Systems* 45: 191–202.

Kingwell, R. S., and Pannell, D. J.(eds.) (1987). *MIDAS, A Bioeconomic Model of a Dryland Farm System*, Pudoc, Wageningen, The Netherlands.

Kingwell, R. S., Morrison, D. A., and Bathgate, A. D. (1992). The effect of climatic risk on dryland farm management, *Agricultural Systems* 39: 153–175.

Kirby, M. J. L. (1970). The current state of chance-constrained programming. In *Proceedings of the Princeton Symposium on Mathematical Programming*, H. W. Kuhn (ed.), Princeton University Press, Princeton, N.J.

Koestler, A. (1964). *The Act of Creation*, Hutchinson, London.

Lambert, D. K., and McCarl, B. A. (1985). Risk modelling using direct solution of non-linear approximations of the utility function, *American Journal of Agricultural Economics* 67: 846–852.

Lomas, K. J., and Eppel, H. (1992). Sensitivity analysis techniques for building thermal simulation programs, *Energy and Buildings* 19: 21–44.

Loucks, D. P., Revelle, C. S., and Lynn, W. R. (1967). Linear programming models for water pollution control, *Management Science* 14: B166–B181.

Magee, B. (1973). *Popper*, Fontana/Collins, London.

Manne, A. (1956). *Scheduling of Petroleum Refining Operations*, Harvard Economic Studies, 48, Harvard University Press, Cambridge.

McCarl, B. A. (1984). Model validation: An overview with some emphasis on risk models, *Review of Marketing and Agricultural Economics* 52(3): 153–173.

McCarl, B. A., and Apland, J. (1986). Validation of linear programming models, *Southern Journal of Agricultural Economics* 1986: 155–164.

Meier, P., and Mubayi, V. (1983). Modelling energy-economic interactions in developing countries: A linear programming approach, *European Journal of Operational Research* 13: 41–59.

Morrison, D. A. (1987). Background to the development of MIDAS. In *MIDAS, A Bioeconomic Model of a Dryland Farm System*, R. S. Kingwell and D. J. Pannell (eds.), Pudoc, Wageningen, The Netherlands, 5–14.

Morrison, D. A., Kingwell, R. S., Pannell, D. J., and Ewing M. A. (1986). A mathematical programming model of a crop-livestock farm system, *Agricultural Systems* 20: 243–268.

Nordblom, T., Pannell, D. J., Christiansen, S., Nersoyan, N., and Bahhady, F. (1994). From weed to wealth? Prospects for medic pastures in Mediterranean farming systems of northwest Syria. *Agricultural Economics* 11: 29–42.

Pannell, D. J. (1988). An integrated package for linear programming. *Review of Marketing and Agricultural Economics* 56: 234–235.

Pannell, D. J., and Falconer, D. A. (1987). Solution, interpretation and revision of MIDAS. In *MIDAS, A Bioeconomic Model of a Dryland Farm System*, R. S. Kingwell and D. J. Pannell (eds.), Pudoc, Wageningen, The Netherlands, 55–63.

Pannell, D. J., and Bathgate, A. (1991). *MIDAS, Model of an Integrated Dryland Agricultural System, Manual and Documentation for the Eastern Wheatbelt Model Version EWM91-4*, Miscellaneous Publication 28/91, Department of Agriculture, Perth, Western Australian.

Patten, L. H., Hardaker, J. B., and Pannell, D. J. (1988). Utility efficient programming for whole-farm planning, *Australian Journal of Agricultural Economics* 32: 88–97.

Raiffa, H. (1968). *Decision Analysis*, Addison-Wesley, Reading, Mass.

Reiman, M. I., and Weiss, A. (1989). Sensitivity analysis for simulations via likelihood ratios, *Operations Research* 37: 830–844.

Romero, C., and Rehman, T. (1984). Goal programming and multiple criteria decision-making in farm planning: An expository analysis, *Journal of Agricultural Economics* 35: 177–190.

Romero, C., and Rehman, T. (1989). *Multiple Criteria Analysis for Agricultural Decisions*, Elsevier, Amsterdam.

Rubin, D. S., and Wagner, H. M. (1990). Shadow prices: Tips and traps for managers and instructors, *Interfaces* 20(4): 150–157.

Schrage, L. (1991). *LINDO, An Optimization Modeling System*, 4th ed., Scientific Press, San Francisco.

Spath, H., Gutgesell, W., and Grun, G. (1975). Short term liquidity management in a large concern using linear programming. In *Studies in Linear Programming*, H. M. Salkin and J. Saha (eds.), North-Holland, Amsterdam.

Tauer, L. (1983). Target MOTAD, *American Journal of Agricultural Economics* 65: 606–610.

Thomas, J. (1971). Linear programming models for production-advertising decisions. Management Science 17: B474–B484.

Tice, T. F., and Kletke, M. G. (1984). Reliability of linear programming software: An experience with the IBM Mathematical Programming System series, *American Journal of Agricultural Economics* 66: 104–107.

Torkamani, J. (1994). *A Study of Economic Efficiency in Iranian Agriculture: The Case of Farmers in Ramjerd District*, Ph.D. Thesis, Department of Agricultural and Resource Economics, University of New England, NSW, Australia.

Uyeno, D. (1992). Monte Carlo simulation on microcomputers, *Simulation* 58: 418–423.

Vandeputte, J. M., and Baker, C. B. (1970). Specifying the allocation of income among taxes, consumption, and savings in linear programming models, *American Journal of Agricultural Economics* 52: 521–527.

ABOUT THE SOFTWARE

The diskette that accompanies this book includes the GULP (General User-friendly Linear Programming) software created by the author. GULP is a spreadsheet-style data editor that includes a full range of editing functions that can be selected from menus. The program allows you to print output and then return to the editor to change results in the data matrix.

The GULP program uses less than 200 KB hard drive space. For maximum computation of 200 activities and 200 rows, you will need to have about 512 KB RAM available. The included documentation file, MANUAL.TXT, can be viewed on screen through a text editor or printed out. For your convenience, there are also two word processing files included, each containing the documentation in slightly different format. MANUAL.DOC is for Letter paper (8.5″ × 11″), while MANUALA4.DOC is for A4 paper (210 mm × 297 mm).

INSTALLING THE DISKETTE FILES

The GULP files can be installed to your hard drive by using the install program on the diskette or by manually copying the files from the GULP directory. To use the install program:

1. Assuming you will be using the drive A as the floppy drive for your diskette, at the A: > prompt type INSTALL. You may also type A:INSTALL at the C: > prompt.
2. Follow the instructions displayed by the installation program. The default choice for the installation directory is GULP and the default drive is C.

When the files have been installed, exit from the install program and move to the program directory to start running the program.

To install the files manually:

1. Create a GULP directory on your hard drive.
2. Copy the files from the GULP directory on the diskette to the new GULP directory on your hard drive.

TECHNICAL SUPPORT

If your diskette has a problem, you may obtain a new diskette by calling the Wiley technical support number at 212-850-6194.

INDEX